Muzzleloading for Deer and Turkey

Dave Ehrig

STACKPOLE
BOOKS

Published by
STACKPOLE BOOKS
5067 Ritter Road
Mechanicsburg, PA 17055
www.stackpolebooks.com

Printed in the USA

10 9 8 7 6 5 4 3 2 1

First edition

Cover design by Caroline Stover

All photographs by the author except on the following pages:
18 (top), 42, 45, 49, 79, 80, 102, 189, 296, 324, 331, 365, 374 (bottom), 384, 396, 424,
*   425: Bettina Fox Ehrig*
51, 86, 121, 220, 224, 279: Thompson/Center
264: Gary Visgaitis/ The Morning Call (Allentown, Pennsylvania)

Illustrations on pages 4 and 5 taken from The American Muzzle Loading Gunsmith's
Parts Manual, Second Edition *by Frederick Shilling. Used with permission*

Illustrations on pages 97 and 106 taken from the 1899 Winchester catalog

All other illustrations by Caroline Stover

Library of Congress Cataloging-in-Publication Data

Ehrig, Dave.
  Muzzleloading for deer and turkey / Dave Ehrig.—1st ed.
     p. cm.
  Includes bibliographical references.
  ISBN-13: 978-0-8117-0137-2
  ISBN-10: 0-8117-0137-9
  1. Deer hunting. 2. Turkey hunting. 3. Muzzleloader hunting. I. Title.

SK301.E47 2005
799.2'13—dc22

2005016941

To Bettina Fox Ehrig,
whose support made this book possible

CONTENTS

ACKNOWLEDGMENTS

I would like to thank the following people:

Dr. Samuel Gladding, whose guidance and patience helped fan the flames of a passion for hunting with muzzleloaders.

George Dech, who taught me to carve away anything on a piece of wood that didn't look like a longrifle. He was the first to teach me that a Henry gun was not a lever-action repeating rifle.

Chuck Dixon, whose enthusiasm for building Pennsylvania longrifles still inspires many to pursue this noble art.

Rich Hujsa, whose keen marksman's eye and love of the hunt translate into a passion for deer and turkey muzzleloader hunting.

Skip Hamaker and Dave Motto, who selflessly gave of their time and talents in Harrisburg so that the three of us, along with Pete Duncan, could define the regulations and spirit of the flintlock hunt in Pennsylvania.

The old muzzleloading gang at the Whitetail Camp: Bill Nester, Bob Rothenberger, Mark Flisak, Mike Watson, Matt Ehrig, Joe Tognoli, and Gary Younger. More than 30 years of hunting whitetails with flintlocks has been the fodder for many a good story, some of which ended up in print.

Kermit Henning and Dennis Scharadin, my outdoor writer hunting buddies. The quest for outdoor adventure beyond our borders began with you, and the memories we made throughout North America gave this longhunter stories to share.

All the Pennsylvania outdoor writers who have shared their time and talents with me. Tom and Betty Lou Fegely, Jim Fitser, Doyle Dietz, Bob Mitchell, and Christian Berg, to name just a few, were instrumental, providing help and encouragement.

All those who have worked endless hours for the Pennsylvania Game Commission. They brought back the deer and turkey populations from the brink of extinction at the beginning of the twentieth century, ensured the continued abundance of wild game and places to hunt well into the twenty-first, and helped establish two special muzzleloading seasons, including the unique Pennsylvania flintlock-only deer season.

The Pennsylvania Federation of Muzzleloaders, Inc., and the National Muzzle Loading Rifle Association and its president, Jim Fulmer. Without their educational programs, safety standards, promotion, and black powder competitions at local, state, and national championships, the noble sport of muzzleloading would fade into history.

The National Rifle Association and all its members for their unending efforts to support the Second Amendment.

Finally, my wife, Bettina Fox Ehrig. For 36 years, this muzzleloading longhunter has wandered the north woods, the open prairie, the snow-laden spruce forests, and the mysterious southern swamps looking for adventure. And in all of my meanderings, she has been there to inspire me, edit my work, take care of the horse farm, raise Matthew and Elizabeth, and teach other young minds how to read, write, and utilize math. No man reaches his full potential without the unending support of the one he married.

Thank you, Tina.

CHAPTER ONE

An Introduction to Muzzleloading

There is both a magic and a mystique associated with muzzle-loading arms. From the primitive Pennsylvania flintlock long-rifle to the Rocky Mountain man's Hawken percussion to today's high-tech, in-line muzzleloader, each firearm has its following. This chapter introduces the different types of muzzleloading rifles and the nuances that attract hunters to each. Information about the components of each system is presented in layperson's language, and solid how-to information is offered. The goal is to help the reader pursue the enjoyment of this new, old-fashioned shooting sport.

The History of Muzzleloaders

Muzzleloaders are guns that must be loaded from the top, or muzzle, of the barrel. Because brass cartridges cannot be loaded quickly into the rear, or breech, of the barrel, hunting with a muzzleloading gun can be a handicap. Without the ability to shoot multiple shots before reloading, the muzzleloading hunter owes his or her success to a single shot—a properly loaded powder, patch, and ball, steadily aimed and confidently fired. But it is precisely this one-shot handicap that has motivated 46 of the 50 states to offer special deer seasons for muzzleloaders. Hunters who choose to take up the sport of muzzleloading will find themselves immersed in more than hunting. They will inherit a sense of history, nostalgia, folk art, and pride that has fueled this sport for more than three centuries.

Successful muzzleloading depends upon a properly loaded gun, steadily aimed and confidently fired.

Flintlock longrifles are the oldest type of muzzleloader still used in hunting. Rifles carrying a full stock, from the heel to the muzzle, were very common during the eighteenth century. Names like "Kentucky rifle" and "Pennsylvania longrifle" are synonymous with colonial minutemen and the Appalachian longhunters. Daniel Boone's "Ol' Tick Licker" and Davy Crockett's "Betsy" personified the lock, stock, and barrel of this era. Curly maple stocks, browned octagonal barrels, and fiery flintlocks demonstrated their utility, while the brass patchboxes, relief-carved buttstocks, and silver inlays were expressions of frontier art. These were the accurate-shooting "widow-makers" of the Revolutionary War, and they extended the influence of the buckskin-clad riflemen up and down the country and westward across the Appalachian Mountains. Longrifles, noted for their accuracy, were normally built with calibers in the .40 to .50 range. Today, most black powder shoots and rendezvous east of the Mississippi bear witness to the wide popularity of this style of muzzleloader.

The Kentucky rifle and Pennsylvania longrifle were indispensable to colonial minutemen and Appalachian longhunters.

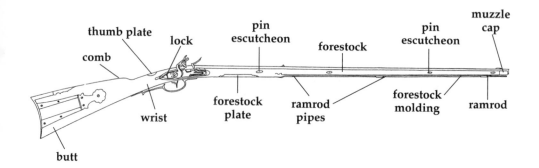

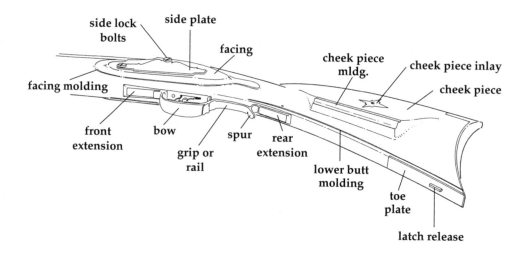

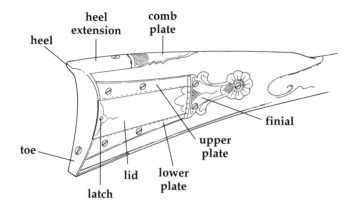

Longrifle nomenclature

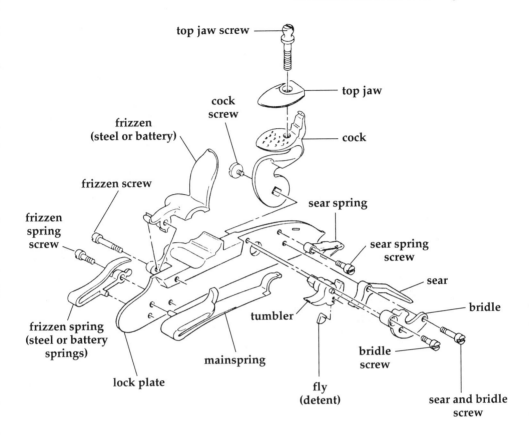

Flintlock nomenclature; archaic or optional terms are in parentheses

In 1710 and again in 1730, two great waves of German immigrants moved into the huge valleys between the Delaware and Susquehanna Rivers. Many were indentured servants to English masters; others sold most of their worldly goods just to achieve safe passage. But there was one tool they considered a necessity and carried with them across the Atlantic: the flintlock gun of Europe, the smoothbore musket. Flintlock in ignition, smooth of bore so as to shoot buckshot or roundballs, it was a utilitarian piece used for securing feathered and furred food for the table and hides for clothing, shoes, and harnesses.

Frontier tools such as axes and saws, as well as flintlocks, were used daily. Repairs were frequent, and farmers were always look-

The flintock guns of Europe, along with the trade guns of North America, were primarily smoothbores.

ing for ways to make their lives easier. Hunters quickly noticed that the German Jaeger (hunter) rifle and the longer-barreled Swiss mountain rifle shot with greater accuracy and hit with more authority than the old smoothbore musket. The German, Scots-Irish, and French Huguenot immigrants who later became known as the Pennsylvania Dutch sought out local gunsmiths and demanded improvements. Martin Meylin, a Swiss gunsmith in the Pequea Valley of southern Lancaster County, provided a new type of rifle. Foremost among the frontiersmen's desires was a rifle that was capable of hitting a deer-sized target at 100 yards. Jaegers could do that, but their loading procedure of swaging larger-caliber, oversized lead roundballs down the barrel was slow, expensive, and bothersome. From such humble beginnings, a new rifle emerged.

The evolution of the Pennsylvania longrifle commenced in several frontier-farm communities, probably because of the availability of water-powered iron forges. At the Catelin Forge, near

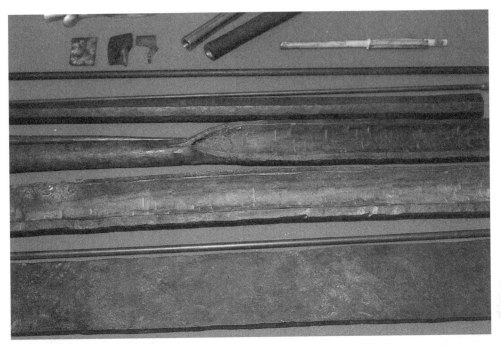

Colonial muzzleloader barrels were formed from flat strips of iron that were heated and pounded into the shape of a smoothbore tube.

Lancaster (Old Hickory Town) on the Pequea Creek, pig iron billets were heated and hammered in the strips known as "gun scallops." Another barrel-making center was in Berks County's Schmutz Deich, or Greasy Valley, along the Wyomissing Creek. The Little Lehigh Creek in Lehigh County provided energy for several forges to supply iron for early gunsmiths in the Allentown-Bethlehem area, as well as in Christian Springs to the north, near Bath.

William Henry I of Lancaster, Pennsylvania, opened his gun factory in 1750. Because of his knowledge of metallurgy and his ability to produce large numbers of rifles under contract, he became the armorer for the Braddock Campaign of 1755 and the Forbes Expedition of 1758—two efforts by the British to remove the French from Fort Duquesne, later known as Fort Pitt (Pittsburgh, Pennsylvania). Aside from being a highly regarded gunsmith, Henry was also credited with the invention of the screw auger and a model of the first steam-propelled boat, a fact admitted by both Robert Fulton and John Fitch.

As Henry's fame grew, so did his status as a politician. He became the treasurer of Lancaster County and later a member of the Continental Congress. It should also be noted that Henry discovered an exceptionally talented young sign painter and provided him with room and board and materials and encouraged him to pursue a fine arts career. That artist, Benjamin West, painted a portrait of Henry and his wife Ann that now hangs in the Philadelphia Museum of Art.

Henry, a member of the Moravian Church, sent his son William Jr. to Lititz, a Moravian settlement, to study under gunsmith Andrew Albright. Later, William Jr. continued his craft in Christian Springs, another church settlement in Northampton County. By 1780, William Jr. was serving the Nazareth community as an architect, carpenter, and gunsmith. Because of the noise of testing guns, William Jr. moved his operations from the center of town and purchased land on the banks of the Bushkill Creek, an area known as Jacobsburg. By 1793, production had begun at the Henry Gun Works, although the barrels were still marked "Nazareth." This custom continued even after the Nazareth gun shop was closed in 1798.

William Jr. had three sons, one of whom, John Joseph, established a gun business in Philadelphia in 1807. John Joseph had gun parts shipped from his father's Jacobsburg factory to the American Rifle Manufactory in Philadelphia. In 1810, John Joseph was joined by his brother, William III, and they returned home to establish the gun factory known as the Boulton Gun Works. This was located about a half mile downstream from Henry's Forge.

The War of 1812 saw Henry guns in action. The most famous person of that period to use Henry arms was Captain Oliver Hazard Perry, who won the Battle of Lake Erie with two Henry pistols tucked in his belt.

The construction of the Boulton Gun Works marked the beginning of the golden years of firearms manufacturing by the Henrys. It was under the management of John Joseph that the gun works began one of its most successful phases—gun production for the Indian fur trade. In 1826, the Boulton Gun Works became the predominant supplier of small arms to the largest American business enterprise of the early nineteenth century, John Jacob Astor's

By 1793, the Henry Gun Works in Boulton, Pennsylvania, had begun production, despite the fact that gun barrels were still being marked "Nazareth."

American Fur Company. The Henry firearm became one of the most desirable weapons of the western frontier due to its durability, accuracy, and relatively low cost. These guns cost the fur company about $7 each but were traded to the Indians for about $14 worth of furs. Records from 1829 show that the factory produced about 600 of these "Northwest" guns.

What all these pre-Revolution gunsmiths shared in common was the ability to bore smaller-calibered, long barrels with slow-twist rifling. The longer barrels generated greater velocities for the slow-burning black powder, about 10 feet per second for each inch beyond the normal 26-inch barrel. It had the added benefit of a longer sighting plane for the open iron sights. Both of these American improvements led to increased accuracy, as did the invention of the greased, patched roundball. Pennsylvania rifles soon became legendary for their accuracy.

Original pre–Revolutionary War Pennsylvania rifles were utilitarian tools. But the demand for rifles during and after the war caused a huge competition among gunsmiths. One of the first purely American improvements to the flintlock rifle was the replacement of the wooden patchbox lid with a hinged brass patchbox. More than a secure compartment for storing ramrod jags, patches, lubricant, prayer scripts (in case the farmer died in the forest during one of his winter hunting-trapping forays), and a silver bullet (the only thing that could kill a witch), these new two- and four-piece patchboxes carried folk art designs with daisy, horse, eagle, star, and heart motifs.

The Golden Age of Pennsylvania longrifles evolved from about 1776 to 1825. Gunsmiths were trained as apprentices by masters in the Lancaster, Allentown-Bethlehem, Womelsdorf-Reading, Lebanon, Dauphin, York, Littlestown, Emmitsburg, and Chambersburg schools of longrifle styles. Using the same hand tools, native hardwoods, and wrought iron, these gunsmiths competed with one another to develop highly artistic locks, stocks, and barrels. Whereas most of the early longrifles carried simple incised carvings, Golden Age longrifles exhibited intricate, raised relief carvings on the forearm, on the lock and tang, and under the cheekpiece. Engraved lock plates, brass thimbles, trigger guards, barrels, and particularly the patchboxes exemplified the typical American rifle. Precious metals such as gold, silver, and even platinum were inlaid into the barrels, as well as into the intricate relief carvings.

A typical Pennsylvania rifle weighed from 7 to 9 pounds, with an overall length of a symmetrical 55 inches from muzzle to butt plate. Supposedly, its .45-caliber ball could kill man or beast at 300 yards or "bark" a squirrel from the tallest tree. Known later as the "Kentucky" rifle because of the feats performed by Daniel Boone and other woodsmen in winning the land beyond the mountains, this superb weapon was the handiwork of several generations of Pennsylvania gunsmiths. Among the better known, in addition to Meylin and numerous members of the Henry family, were Henry Albright, Daniel Boyer, Matthew and Peter Roesser, Thomas Butler, Jacob Decherd, Peter and Henry Leman, Philip Lefevre, Henry Dreppard, and several Pannabeckers.

Renowned wildlife artist Ned Smith's *Pennsylvania Game News* cover of December 1974 depicted a Golden Age Pennsylvania longrifle. Perhaps this rifle struck Smith as an "ideal" type of flintlock

One of the first purely American improvements to the flintlock rifle was a hinged brass patchbox that replaced the wooden patchbox lid.

Golden Age longrifles of the late flintlock period exhibited intricate, raised relief carvings under the cheekpiece and on the forearm, lock, and tang.

rifle. He wrote, "A splendid example of the Pennsylvania gun maker's art which I sketched from the collection of Joe Kindig, Jr., of York, can be seen in the cover painting on this issue. It was built in the early 1800s by David Cooley, who is thought to have worked in Adams County. The drawing shows this rifle to be a slender 58^1/$_2$ inches in overall length with a 41 caliber octagon barrel 41^3/$_4$ inches long. The inlays, including a brass patchbox and a silver cheekpiece oval, are beautifully engraved. The richly figured maple stock is embellished with scroll and boasts cross-hatched carving typical of that era."

Two years later, at the height of the U.S. bicentennial celebration, Smith expressed his feelings about this native folk art in the July 1976 *Game News* in a piece titled "Notes on the Evolution of the Pennsylvania Longrifle." He wrote, "For generations it's been known as the 'Kentucky Rifle.' The reference is to that wild country beyond the Alleghenies where it proved its worth. But it's really the 'Pennsylvania Rifle,' often called the 'Pennsylvania Long Rifle,' for Pennsylvania is where it originated and, with very few exceptions, that's where it was made. I guess it shouldn't matter, but it does. After all, that old flintlock not only was the first truly American firearm, but it also played an important role in shaping a wilderness into what is now the United States of America. And that's something we Pennsylvanians shouldn't shrug off."

The Pennsylvania longrifle never really left the hearts and minds of artisans, gunsmiths, collectors, hunters, and those who cherish this early American legacy. Smith never forgot, Pennsylvanians never forgot, and today, all Americans are remembering and thrilling to the sight of the Pennsylvania flintlock longrifle, considered one of the finest works of folk art to come out of colonial America. But its history did not end in the eighteenth century. Contemporary artisans studied the works of the old master gunsmiths and faithfully re-created works of art that rival the originals. Hunters have kept the faith by establishing deer seasons that honor the contributions of their forefathers.

In the 1970s, manufacturers and retailers such as Thompson/Center (T/C) Arms, Dixie Gun Works, Navy Arms, and many others supplied a growing market with replica arms sporting both flintlocks and percussion locks. Each corner of the country had its

Howard Oesterling takes aim with the commemorative Ned Smith flintlock rifle.

The Pennsylvania flintlock longrifle is celebrated as one of the finest works of folk art ever to have been produced in colonial America.

Plains rifles, which are collectively misidentified as Hawkens, had stock profiles similar to longrifles. Since they lack most of the forestock, they were lighter and easier to handle on horseback. These "half-stocks" are popular deer-hunting rifles today.

Plains rifles like these late S. Hawken percussions were manufactured in St. Louis for the fur trade on the western plains and in the Rocky Mountains.

Close-up of a Hawken percussion

own period of history to celebrate, represented by famous hunters and daunting battles. Stock profiles, barrel lengths, and types of sighting systems reflected these regionalisms well into the 1980s.

For example, those who watched the movie *Jeremiah Johnson* flocked to his famous .50-caliber Hawken gun. The profiles of these half-stock, or plains, rifles are similar to that of the longrifle. However, instead of a full heel-to-muzzle wooden stock, the half-stock ramrods are supported by a rail slung under the barrel, and the stock begins forward of the entry thimble for the ramrod. Plains rifles are generally recognizable by their metal nosecaps. They were a product of the gunsmiths located along the Mississippi River, such as the St. Louis Hawken brothers, Sam and Jake. Their half-stocked rifle, found in both flintlock and percussion ignition, was made with a heavier barrel to support the rough handling of horse scabbards and the larger bore size of .50 to .60 calibers. Plains rifle barrels needed to control the powerful loads of powder that were demanded by huge elk and dangerous grizzly. These guns were designed to shoot game animals at longer distances than those guns found east of the Mississippi, and they became famous in the hands of the western mountain men during the Rocky Mountain fur trade era in the first half of the nineteenth century.

Less well known to deer hunters, but having a greater impact on the history of westward expansion, was the Indian trade gun of the western plains. These smoothbores were the most important tool of both Indians and trapper-traders from 1751 (oldest known Northwest trade gun) to 1905 (last manufactured Hudson Bay Company trade gun). The Museum of the Fur Trade in Chadron, Nebraska, has the world's largest and most complete collection of Indian trade guns. Products of manufacturers such as Tryon of Philadelphia, Henry of Boulton, Leman of Lancaster, and Hawkens of St. Louis, are displayed, along with trade gun muskets from England and Belgium, buffalo guns, the famous Sharps, and the modern repeating Winchesters. Each gun has a personal story to tell, such as Shawnee chief Tecumseh's Northwest gun. These guns usually carried a .58-caliber smoothbore barrel and a large trigger guard so that the Indian could enter two fingers rather than the usual one; they accurately shot a half-ounce ball of lead for big

Less well known to deer hunters, but more influential in the history of westward expansion, is the Indian trade gun.

game or an ounce of shot for turkey. These 28-gauge smoothbores may seem a bit light by today's 10-gauge standard, but historically, they got the job done.

The modern in-line muzzleloader is a product of rifle builders of the late twentieth century. The stock profile takes elements of the standard Monte Carlo and straight carbine lines found on modern centerfire rifles. Synthetic stocks, scopes, stainless steel barrels, and modern jacketed bullets are all differences found in these guns. "In-line" refers to the location of the percussion cap. An ignition tube, called the nipple, is located in the center of the breech plug, allowing a somewhat sealed and faster ignition than the externally mounted ignition on the flintlock and external percussion systems. Another benefit of the in-line action is the availability of a familiar rifle-type safety, which prevents movement of the firing pin. These contemporary muzzleloaders are not replicas from the past; they offer the conveniences and upgrades of a modern firearm.

The in-line percussion muzzleloader is the product of late-twentieth-century rifle builders.

The in-line's stock profile takes elements of the standard Monte Carlo along with the straight carbine lines found on modern centerfire rifles.

Types of Muzzeloaders: An Overview

Shooting a muzzleloader is different from using any other type of shooting system. First and foremost, these front-loading charcoal burners make a whole lot of smoke, not to mention a different kind of sound, each time you squeeze the trigger. Muzzleloaders, regardless of whether they are rifles, shotguns, or pistols, shoot with lower velocities and are handicapped by the technology from which they were born. But the sense of history and nostalgia that is intrinsic in each gun is exactly why they are so much fun to shoot. You will get much closer to a muzzleloader than to any other gun, simply because you have to in order to load the powder, patch, and ball, not to mention the prime. You will need to slow down, take 100 or more years off the calendar, and learn to relax as you align those old iron sights—and then smile at your patience as you drill the target through that haze of white smoke.

What is the best muzzleloader? This is a difficult and personal decision that each shooter must make. The answer lies in another question: What do you expect from the gun? If it is going to be a fun piece used for plinking cans and generating noise on the Fourth of July, just about any old muzzleloading gun will work. But most shooters have a hidden agenda. It is their secret desire to hunt the majestic elk or stealthy whitetail or to challenge the big black bear and make meat the old-fashioned way with a flintlock or percussion black powder rifle. Others hope to set a new world record using an ancient muzzleloading system. You need to find the tool that fits the job. Regardless of whether you make the easy transition from a bolt-action centerfire rifle to a bolt-action in-line percussion muzzleloader or choose the ultimate in primitive shooting, the flintlock, the muzzleloader offers something for everyone. Only the individual hunter can answer the question of how much handicap he or she is willing to accept.

Most "pilgrims" (the affectionate name given to novice muzzleloading shooters by the grizzled old veterans of black powder rendezvous matches) opt for a rifle for a first gun, and this is a wise choice. Rifles, by their very nature, are intended to shoot accurately—a useful asset in hunting and competitive shooting. So let's examine the most common styles of rifles to get a feel for the sport.

A typical flintlock

The most primitive and challenging of the muzzleloading systems is the flintlock. Ignition rates of 0.05 to 0.07 second are mighty slow compared with the 0.005-second rate for a modern bolt action. This can cause some hunters to flinch or move off target. Even the act of drawing sparks from flint and steel makes hunting in foul weather difficult. Furthermore, the external priming powder draws moisture and can be slow to burn, if it burns at all. Dedication to details and persistence in the face of adversity keynote this challenging system. But in spite of its handicaps, Pennsylvania's 180,000-plus muzzleloading hunters enjoy an impressive 1:6 success ratio.

Loading black powder from a scrimshawed powder horn and inserting a soft lead roundball into a greased patch and down the bore with a short starter are part of the magic of loading and shooting the venerable flintlock. But new materials and techniques are catching up with the flintlock rifle. Pyrodex pellets, once reserved for percussion rifle shooters because of Pyrodex's high 740-degree ignition temperature (its black powder base, which ignites at 480

The historic ritual of loading and shooting a flintlock includes loading black powder from an engraved powder horn, inserting a soft lead roundball into a greased patch, and then ramrodding everything down the bore.

Pyrodex pellets have changed the way deer hunters load gun powder. Their premeasured convenience was developed for in-line rifle shooters, not reenactors.

The lead roundball is well suited to slower velocities. Its legendary accuracy under 100 yards has been responsible for three centuries of whitetail harvests. Richard Hujsa took this big eight-point buck with a .54-caliber flintlock longrifle. The gun is a beautiful and accurate reproduction of an original from Christian Springs, Pennsylvania.

degrees Fahrenheit, was too low in the breech to feel the ignition heat of the burning priming powder), can now be used in certain rifles. Thompson/Center's Firestorm elevates the pellets with a coned breech that aligns the black powder base with the vent. This allows a swirl of heat from the priming pan to evenly ignite the pellets and consume one to three of them. Using three pellets (150 grains) allows for velocities above the 2,000 feet per second barrier that has traditionally handicapped muzzleloading ballistics.

Experience has shown that pellet users must be very careful when loading both the propellant and the bullet. It is easy to crush the pellet when the ramrod is tamped too hard, and if this happens, the integrity of the black powder base is lost. Ignition becomes haphazard, if the powder ignites at all.

Muskets, like these from Harpers Ferry, became deadly-accurate long-distance rifles with the advent of bullets like the minié ball. The Civil War marked the end of the roundball's popularity.

The problem with velocities above the 2,000 feet per second plateau is that they destabilize the traditional roundball, which is well suited to slower velocities. Its legendary accuracy under 100 yards has harvested whitetails for three centuries. Muzzle velocities between 1,400 and 1,800 feet per second and slow rates of rifling between 1:48 and 1:72 (one revolution in 48 to 72 inches) were ideal for the soft orb of lead. When accelerated beyond this rate, the ball takes on a "knuckleball" or unpredictable trajectory, making it worthless to hunters.

Enter a new flintlock bullet: the hollow-pointed, jacketed (or copper solid), sabotted undercaliber bullet. Unfortunately for older roundball barrels, the rifling rate of twist is too slow to stabilize this elongated slug. Ideal rifling for these sabotted rounds is 1:32 to 1:20, and this is found in the newer styles of flintlocks. To understand how and why these bullets need to be different, hunters need to back up to the round ball of lead.

Lead is the heaviest mass that can be shot out of a rifle, other than the radioactive elements. Its superdensity allows it to carry more foot-pounds of energy to a game animal than any other element. Originally, an undersized roundball compressed a cloth patch into the grooves of the rifling to achieve the proper rotation of the rifling and the maximum amount of speed. Roundballs normally mushroom back to double their diameter, releasing all their energy inside the game animal. But roundballs do not carry their energy effectively past the 100-yard mark, so the slug was invented.

The first slugs were actually two roundballs patched together. This load was quite accurate and effective out to 50 yards. Later, the patched Pickett ball became an effective slug prototype used in the Civil War to stop charging calvary horses. In time, the hollow-skirted minié-type bullets became standard for muzzleloaders. Accurate, hard-hitting, and relatively fast to load, they were standard issue for military muskets. They are still a good choice for big game when shot through rifles with faster twist.

Maxi-Balls, Maxi-Hunters, Great Plains bullets, and other types of lead slugs are desirable bullets for big game, if they are properly stabilized with appropriate rifling and not given too much speed. As lead slugs approach the 2,000 feet per second plateau, they begin to strip off lead. Besides making the bullet inaccurate, this adds lead to the shoulders of the rifling grooves.

Copper-jacketing a lead slug solved the lead-stripping problem. Bullet velocities could rise beyond the plateau with impunity. But a new problem arose. The bullets wouldn't mushroom back as well as the all-lead roundball. Serration in the nose of the jacket, hollow-pointing, and even the addition of plastic ballistic tips were necessary to duplicate the performance of the lower-velocity round.

Large-diameter, bore-sized slugs are too heavy to accelerate past the plateau. To increase velocity sufficiently, plastic sabots were introduced. Now, a .50-caliber flintlock can use a .44-caliber pistol bullet, drive it past the 2,000 feet per second plateau with three Pyrodex pellets (150 grains), and shoot it accurately if a fast rate of twist is employed in the barrel.

Although the flintlock and the bullet have the potential to accurately and lethally take deer at extended ranges (up to 200 yards),

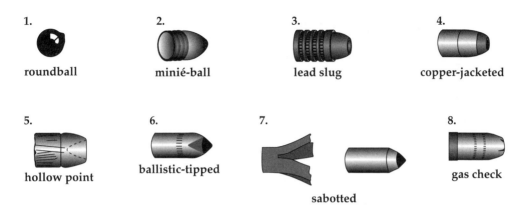

Evolution of the muzzleloading bullet

ethics demand that the sighting system be of sufficient accuracy. Now the handicap is the hunter's visual acuity. Eye disorders, fatigue, weather conditions, and the ravages of time all factor into the equation for accurate shooting.

Manufacturers of twenty-first-century flintlocks are replacing the iron sights with fiber-optics. These light-gathering sights show up as brilliant dots of red, green, and yellow in the front and rear sights. Sight pictures become clearer in morning and evening under poor lighting conditions. And although not exactly a primitive set of sights that one would want on a longrifle, they are legal.

Peep or aperture sights have long been a standard for accurate shooting. But a significant number of muzzleloaders are adding vernier tang peep sights or large aperture sights (like the popular ghost rings) to the breech area of their barrels. Unfortunately, Pennsylvania does not consider peeps to be primitive sights for its flintlock season.

Can you scope a flintlock? Probably not. Can you scope a side-hammer percussion? Maybe. On the one hand, it might seem fitting that a polycarbonate-stocked, fluted stainless steel, in-line ignition, pellet-propelled, plastic-sabotted, hollow-pointed copper solid bullet shooting rig like the modern in-line muzzleloaders should be aimed in the most precise way. That would be with an optically enhanced, light-emitting diode reticule scope. Seriously, how else could you drop a deer at 200 yards? On the other hand,

Scopes seem out of place on primitive flintlocks and percussions. Moreover, optics aren't necessary for deer hunting in hardwood forests, as you're generally shooting at distances under 50 yards.

this ancient sport was never really envisioned to compete with modern centerfire rifles.

There are approximately three million muzzleloading deer hunters in the United States. According to manufacturers' sales records, approximately 95 percent of new sales are for percussion-system muzzleloaders. This reflects the game laws in the states that allow a special muzzleloader season, most of which have accepted the easier of the two ignition systems.

Percussion rifles are handicapped by their slower ignition and single-shot systems when compared with modern centerfire repeating rifles. But they are faster and more sure to fire than flintlock rifles are. The heart of the system is the percussion cap. A copper cap is internally coated with a pressure-sensitive chemical. Placed over the nipple—the tube extension that directs ignition gases into the breech—a cap will fire in 0.02 second. This is two to

According to manufacturer's sales records, 95 percent of new muzzleloading gun sales are for percussions and in-lines. This reflects the regulations in 45 of the 46 states that sponsor muzzleloading deer seasons.

four times faster than flint and steel, obviously a real advantage when it comes to shooting accurately.

Old-style or primitive percussion rifles vent their burning cap gases into the side of the breech. This is more than adequate when hunters use bulk black powder or Pyrodex powder trains. The standard #11 percussion cap throws a 3,200-degree flame into a material that ignites at a temperature between 480 and 740 degrees (black powder and Pyrodex, respectively). But most in-line percussion rifles use pellets—Pyrodex, Triple Seven, or Clean Shot pellets. Even though the base of a Pyrodex pellet is coated with black powder, it sometimes does not ignite properly.

If you examine the anatomy of a Pyrodex pellet, you will notice that it is nearly .50 caliber in bore size. This is purposeful, because the pellet's hollow core must be aligned with that of the pellets directly above it in order for the progression of exploding gases to

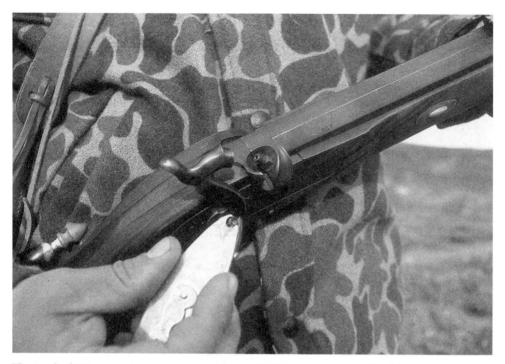

The standard #11 percussion cap generates a flame of 3,200 degrees Fahrenheit. This is more than enough to hit the 480-degree and 740-degree ignition temperatures for black powder and Pyrodex/Triple Seven powder, respectively.

ignite the pellets on top. The pellets won't fit into smaller-caliber rifles, and they won't ignite properly when unaligned in the breech of larger-bore rifles and shotguns. Therefore, only .50 calibers could use them in the past. To counter this ignition problem, manufacturers have offered several solutions. In fact, help came from a Civil War idea: make a bigger cap that explodes with a greater volume of gas—the #2 musket cap. Though not exactly a new idea, it did cause a great number of hunters to rethink their external-hammer percussion rifles. Pellets are here to stay; they are more convenient than bulk powder, and the minor inconvenience to find a hotter cap doesn't seem to upset many people.

Before you throw away your old #11 cap system, however, take heart. CCI is now offering #11 magnum caps with a significantly hotter flame than those previously available. These smaller cousins of the musket cap have just as much potential to light the fire of the propellant in the breech.

Traditions Muzzle Loaders provides the primitive percussion hunter with an alternative. The Thunder Magnum vents the gases of the hammered percussion cap directly into the base of the breech area, allowing for a more even ignition of the pellet. This too is a modification that was applied to early percussion rifles in the pre–Civil War days. Is anything really new?

Yes: locks, stocks, and barrels are revolutionary (pardon the pun). Fluted stainless steel barrels have rifling rates that were unheard of in colonial days. Synthetic stocks reduce the gun's weight and never expand or shrink in bad weather. And coil spring locks provide increased speed. These are all new ideas that have improved the gun, but the most dramatic shift in muzzleloader technology started about a decade ago with the in-line ignition percussion system.

Advertising can create a mystique that opens new markets, but performance is the key to sustaining that market. The in-line mystique created in the early 1990s caused an enormous stir among modern rifle shooters, who flocked to the gun that looked like a scoped centerfire and even approximated its ballistics. But it was the performance of the in-line muzzleloader that put it here to stay.

An in-line muzzleloader is a type of percussion rifle that uses an extremely short fire channel, from the nipple to the breech, and a centerline firing pin to crush the percussion cap. In total, its inside-the-receiver ignition system cuts the delay of the igniting propellant from 0.05 second to under 0.01 second—five times as fast as a well-tuned flintlock.

In-line systems not only fire faster; they also look and shoot differently from the traditional externally ignited percussions and flintlocks. Manufacturers have pushed the performance envelope from under 100 yards to over 200 yards. To deliver lethal accuracy and energy to a deer two football fields away, in-lines have been designed with 1:28 to 1:32 rifling. Forget the roundballs; the only way they will shoot accurately in this fast-twist rifled bore of lands and grooves is to slow down the patched ball velocity. This makes them a poor choice for lethality as well as accuracy. This faster rate of twist will only stabilize the new plastic sabots.

Sabotted, copper (jacketed or solid) pistol bullets allow large-bore .54- and .50-caliber bores to shoot .44-caliber bullets. This

Plastic sabots, copper jackets, copper solids, ballistic tips, all-lead bullets, and hollow-points comprise just some of the many types of modern muzzleloading bullet choices. To make them effective, though, the muzzleloader's rifling must produce the right amount of spin to stabilize the bullet's flight.

permits faster velocities and better sectional density and ballistic coefficients than the traditional patched roundball. These New Age muzzleloading projectiles can be accelerated past 2,000 feet per second (in fact, Knight Rifles is about to market a .45 that shoots a .40-caliber sabotted bullet at 2,400 feet per second) and can accurately carry their lethal energies to whitetails at 200 yards—if you can hit them.

To achieve optimal accuracy with an in-line percussion muzzle-loader, think optics—in a word, scopes. In-lines are mostly stocked in centerfire-type, straight, or Monte Carlo styles. This elevates the cheek and eyes of the shooter into a higher-than-normal head position. With this elevation, scopes are the best choice among sights, and traditional iron sights may be uncomfortable for the shooter.

Although many popular centerfire rifle scopes are marketed for muzzleloading guns, don't buy one until you find out the "eye relief" for each. You need to look for an eye relief distance of about $4^{1}/_{2}$ inches, because of recoil and for ease of loading the internal nipple with a percussion cap. Shorter eye relief may work, but it will be difficult to use.

Will new materials and techniques replace the venerable longrifle and its powder, patch, and ball? Hardly. The sport of deer hunting with a muzzleloader hasn't survived this long because it is a more effective way to harvest whitetails. On the contrary, it survives because it is an anachronism. Hunters are handicapped by their equipment, fulfilled by that challenge, and sustained by the knowledge that they are carrying on the traditions of their ancestors. They feel a rekindling of the spirit of wild America and its natural resources by making meat the old-fashioned way.

Within all of us burns a hunter's fire. It warms our soul as we share memories of bygone days, it sparks our imagination as we plan the next hunt, and it kindles a spirit that grows into an intense desire to share the wild woods with God's creatures. It is also the reason that many of us choose to hunt the old-fashioned way—with black powder.

Muzzeloading Features and Equipment

Hunting with a muzzleloader is a fun-filled blast from the past. It has also become a national obsession. This section explores the equipment used in hunting with a muzzleloader.

A small herd of deer wandered out of the tall grass of the marsh onto the higher ground of the cornfield. The sun had already lost its warmth as it dipped low in the red sky. A storm was imminent, and the herd's need to feed was predictable. Scouting had revealed their routine, and I had quit work early to drive the half hour necessary to intercept them before the sky let loose the predicted rain.

The lead deer, the largest of the four shadowy figures in the corner of the field, suddenly snapped its ears to attention. Eyes combed the treeline for the target that had created the unnatural *click*, which to the deer meant "alarm." A thin, brown-haired hoof stamped concern about the exposed situation. The herd responded with tensed torsos and high tails.

Boooom! roared the .54 caliber. White smoke drifted from the tight canopy of green leaves in the treeline and out across the bay.

Four deer scattered back to the security of the rushes, one more awkward than the rest. There was no need for a quick second shot. The targeted deer never escaped from the cornfield. The hunt was over, the memory made, and the family would be fed with meat attained the old-fashioned way, with a muzzleloader.

Similar hunts have probably been repeated by millions of other hunters in the 46 states with special muzzleloader deer seasons. In the eighteenth and nineteenth centuries, hunting for food was a matter of survival, but 200 years later, hunting has quickly been accepted as a form of recreation. Today, the special muzzleloading seasons are woven tightly into the outdoor fabric of our hunting heritage and serve as an important method of population control among the ever-expanding suburban deer herds.

Hunters are re-creating that which their ancestors may have engaged in: a challenging single-shot hunt with flint and steel sparks, or the spanking fire of a hammered percussion cap. Meanwhile, inventive entrepreneurs have "improved" the shortcomings of this historic equipment by changing the lock, stock, and barrel. Only 5 percent of new rifle sales are attributed to flintlock ignition. In-line percussion systems have captured the lion's share of muzzleloading rifle sales, yet seasoned veterans still have doubts about all the "new and improved" equipment.

Some hunters would argue that any single-shot rifle has the same telling effect on deer. Regardless of what the muzzleloader is loaded with (black powder, replica powders, or even smokeless powders), how it is ignited (flint, percussion cap, or shotgun primer), or even how it is aimed (open sights, aperture sights, optical sights), the muzzleloader is lethal in the hands of a practiced rifleman. Yet these are exactly the three components of muzzleloading that have caused more than a little concern among hunters and state wildlife managers.

During the rebirth of muzzleloading in the 1970s, gunpowder consisted of various grades of black powder. This simple mixture of hardwood charcoal (carbon fuel), saltpeter (potassium nitrate oxidizer), and sulfur (propelling gas) produced relatively low pressures for propelling lead through soft iron barrels. Although muzzle velocities were clocked at well under 2,000 feet per second, this

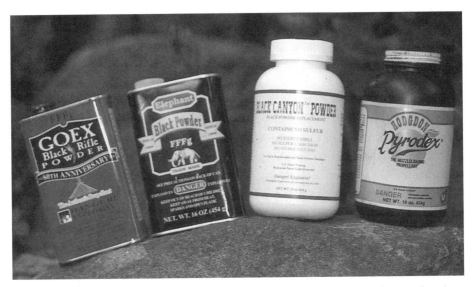

Regardless of whether a muzzleloading gun is loaded with black powder or replica powders, it only becomes a safe and lethally accurate firearm when matched to the correct rifle-bullet or shotgun-shot combination. Practice and attention to detail are vitally important.

was more than adequate. Lethal terminal ballistics were measured at over 500 foot-pounds of energy, while the soft lead of the round-ball expanded to more than twice its diameter. This "primitive load" drove an expanding hydrostatic shock wave of about 11 inches in diameter to the opposite side of the deer's rib cage. In many cases, there was no exit wound because all the energy was expended inside the animal. Not enough energy was left to push the flattened nose of the quarter-sized bullet out of the hide. But there was plenty of energy for dropping the deer, which can happen in less than 20 seconds when the deer is struck in the heart-lung-liver vital zone or immediately when the deer is struck in the brain–spinal cord zone.

In the 1960s, aircraft hijackings and urban terrorists caused the Kennedy administration to control all class A explosives; this included black powder. All but one of the domestic producers of black powder got out of the business. Even DuPont, the last of the old gunpowder and explosives manufacturers, eventually sold out. For 20 years, GOEX, which bought the old Moosic, Pennsylvania, black powder plant, produced the only legal black powder available. Hunters had a choice of Fg, FFg, FFFg, or FFFFg black powder for their flintlocks or percussion muzzleloaders. There were no substitutes. There was no debate about which propellant was best.

Today's muzzleloading hunter has a far different marketplace and a choice of basic black powder from several different manufacturers, as well as a whole group of replica powders. Elephant brand black powder was the first nondomestic manufacturer to market black powder in United States since the late 1960s. This product had been manufactured in Pernambuco, Brazil, for more than a century, but sadly, it will be available only until inventories run out. The plant was destroyed by a flood and is not scheduled for reconstruction. Schuetzen black powder, manufactured in Germany and imported by Petro-Explo of Arlington, Texas (the same company that brought Elephant to our shores), is quickly taking Elephant's place.

Now Swiss Supreme black powder has been added to the list. It is manufactured in Switzerland (also imported by Petro-Explo) and is the first noticeably different black powder. Shooters report an increased velocity, roughly 15 to 20 percent greater than with the same volume of other manufacturers' black powder.

Replica powders that could be substituted for black powder became part of the muzzleloading hunt in the late 1970s. Advertised as cleaner burning and safer to store, they quickly became a familiar item on the shelves of sporting goods stores. Pyrodex, manufactured by Hodgdon Powder Company of Shawnee Mission, Kansas, was the first of the replica powders. Created as a substitute for black powder that would offer the benefit of less fouling, it targeted the percussion cap ignition. Loaded in its P (pistol), RS or Select (rifle and shotgun), or COG (cartridge) grade, Hodgdon's propellant was safe for all types of muzzleloading guns. The downfall of Pyrodex was its ignition temperature. It was too high to be ignited consistently by the temperatures produced in the flashpan of a flintlock rifle.

Another choice of replica propellant was Clear Shot powder, manufactured by GOEX. This stuff was different from both black powder and Pyrodex. It didn't smell the same or foul the same, but it had safe breech pressures and ignition temperatures that could be used in percussion rifles. Although some cans remain on shelves, Clear Shot hasn't been produced since 2001.

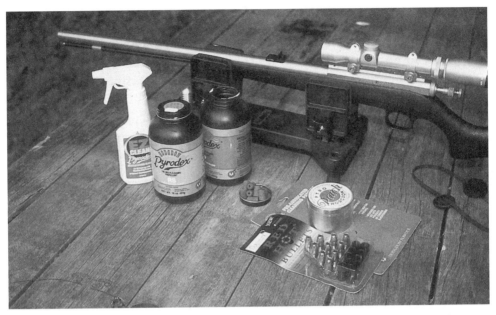

Pyrodex, now in bulk or pellet form, was the first of the replica alternatives to black powder.

Shortly after the introduction of Clear Shot, Hodgdon began to market Triple Seven replica powder. Like Swiss Supreme black powder, Triple Seven gave hunters more bang for their buck. Loaded 15 percent less by volume than Pyrodex or black powder, it produced better velocities and was far less fouling than anything else. Advertised as cleaning up with water, it seemed to be the answer to modern muzzleloaders' quest for the ultimate powder. But it still had the higher ignition temperature of its Pyrodex predecessor, which precluded its use in flintlock and some sidehammer percussions.

Flintlocks produce sparks, or minute bits of iron scraped loose from the frizzen during friction with the edge of the sharpened flint or agate rock. At temperatures near the melting point of iron, spark ignition of priming powder in the pan is not a problem. Black powder ignites at a relatively low 480 degrees Fahrenheit. Even inside the bore, the flash of heat from the exploding priming powder is enough to ignite the main charge. This is not the case with Pyrodex. Pyrodex and Triple Seven require a 740-degree ignition temperature in their bulk form. Normal percussion caps from Remington, CCI, and others provide 3,024-degree flames in a #11 cap and work very well. These caps powered external and internal percussion rifles quite well for the last quarter century. So why did in-line rifles need enhanced ignition?

Pellets of Pyrodex and Triple Seven propellant changed the muzzleloading sport in a dramatic way. No longer were powder horns and powder measurers necessary for bulk powder. They still loaded down the muzzle, but their complex chemical nature required more heat. The Pyrodex pellet, loaded in either a 50-grain or 30-grain configuration, was designed for .50-caliber rifles only. This left the .45, .54, and .58 crowd wondering why they had been left out of the new propellant generation. Moreover, the fragile construction of the hollow-cored, black powder base of the compressed Pyrodex required precise and gentle loading techniques.

When Knight Rifles, Thompson/Center, and other manufacturers created muzzleloaders to handle three-pellet magnum loads,

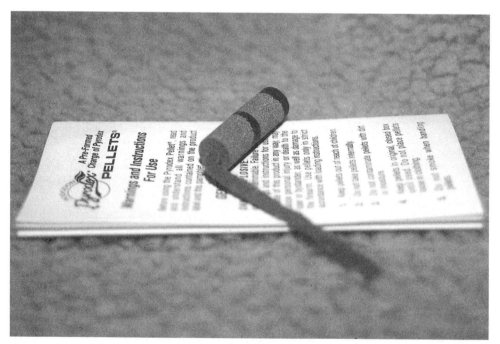

Compressed Pyrodex and Triple Seven powders changed the sport of muzzleloading in a dramatic way.

traditionalists were alarmed by the hype of 150 grains and 2,400 feet per second. Were these ballistically improved guns taking away the challenge of muzzleloading? Would these modern configurations be perceived as just another form of centerfire rifle and eliminate the need for a separate muzzleloading deer season?

Three pellets of Pyrodex didn't always burn inside the shorter (less than 26 inches) carbine barrels. Ignition temperatures were boosted by the Knight Disc System. A 209 shotgun primer took care of the three-pellet ignition problem by increasing the volume of the burning gases. Remington found that the complete burn of the three pellets could be accomplished with the old Civil War musket cap, which was commonly available. CCI created a magnum cap that would throw an increased 3,717-degree temperature at the pellets. Unfortunately, the once simple process of buying caps for the muzzleloader is now clouded with variety.

Into this maelstrom of pellet and ignition problems came the T/C Firestorm. This new muzzleloader solved the external ignition problem with an ingenious breech plug. Incredibly, even a flintlock could ignite the black powder base of the pellet. This was possible because the pellet was lifted by a cone of metal off the face of a normally flat or cupped breech plug. This allowed the heat of a priming powder ignition, as well as an external cap's ignition, to swirl around the base of the pellet.

Another externally ignited, pellet gulping system is the new Thunder Magnum from Traditions. A musket cap directs its fire directly into the rear of the breech, rather than the side, providing sure ignition of the pellet's black powder base.

Primitive shooters, flintlock or percussion, have effectively used roundballs as a projectile for three decades. History has shown this projectile to be efficient as well as the fastest, smallest geometric shape that can be shot accurately in a muzzleloading rifle. But the roundball has a basic weakness: it sheds velocity and energy too quickly to make it effective for game animals past 100 yards.

Magnum velocities pushed the need for better bullet performance. Bullet manufacturers met the challenge with existing lines of pistol bullets. All this was made possible by the advent of the plastic patch known as the sabot.

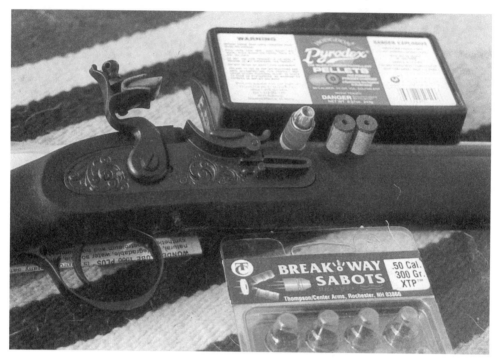

The Thompson/Center Firestorm solved the problem of external ignition for pellets by using an ingenious coned breech plug.

To understand the new bullet technologies, hunters need to start at the beginning. The earliest projectile was a sphere of lead. These lead balls carried the most energy for the longest distances. To ease the loading process, as well as to prevent the lead from stripping off in the barrel, a greased cotton or linen patch was wrapped around the sphere. The sphere shape was chosen because it was the smallest, lightest geometric shape that could fill the bore. Standard rifling twists between 1:48 and 1:72 stabilized the rotation and accuracy of the roundball.

When hunters using nontraditional muzzleloaders began using the roundball, they demanded modern range and performance that the guns couldn't provide. Experimentation with elongated lead slugs began before the Civil War, so minié-type bullets, patched Pickett balls, and, later, Maxi-Balls and similar bullets answered the call for greater retained energy. Although these bullets had greater sectional density for retained energy and better ballistic coefficients

Lead slugs—including Maxi-Balls, Great Plains bullets, Mushroom Express, Buffalo bullets, and others—all derived their original functionality from the success of the Civil War's minié-type bullets.

for shedding the friction of wind, they were handicapped by slower velocities and lead fouling.

As increased loads of propellant pushed bullets to greater velocity, lead erosion clogged the grooves of the rifling, leading to accuracy problems. Bullet manufacturers responded with copper jackets. This harder metal prevented leading of the barrels, but it also prevented adequate bullet expansion. Again, manufacturers responded with serrations in the nose of the jacket, hollow points, and even ballistic tips. But bullet velocity still didn't equal that of the lowly roundball.

Muzzleloaders never achieved high velocity, at least compared with the modern belted centerfire magnums. They never had to. Deer, bear, and elk dropped in their tracks when the roundballs and lead slugs were aimed properly. But the 1990s witnessed an advertising blitz characterized by slogans such as, "to drop one of these [deer], take three of these [150 grains of Pyrodex pellets]. Muzzleloaders never considered going over 2,000 feet per second, but once 2,400 was achieved, it changed the sport forever.

Bullets that could withstand the pressures and velocities of 2,000-plus feet per second had been used for over a century.

This patched roundball has a slow rate of twist . . .

. . . while this sabotted bullet has a fast one.

Vintage calibers such as the .30-30, the .32 Special, and even the .45-70 were legendary for their lead-chucking prowess. But how could these lighter-weight, slender-caliber bullets be used in big-bore muzzleloaders?

The answer was plastic. Plastic sabots around lightweight pistol bullets of .44 and .45 caliber were found to work well in .50-caliber rifles. The only problem that remained was accuracy. Accuracy is not determined solely by velocity; it is achieved by driving a stabilized bullet. In other words, the bullet must be spinning at a rate fast enough to create a gyroscope steadiness, but not so fast that it creates a curveball. Spin a roundball fast at slow velocity, and it shoots accurately; spin it slower at moderate velocities, and it shoots accurately; change the proportion, and only God will know where the ball will go. The opposite ratio works for slugs. Stability for sabotted bullets results from fast-twist rifling.

Most of the in-line muzzleloading rifles are now being built with 1:30, 1:28, and faster rates of twist. These rifles will shoot sabotted bullets well, but don't expect acceptable roundball accuracy unless you shoot low-velocity loads (which are not adequate for hunting big game).

Even the copper solids have gotten into the muzzleloading arena. Barnes Expander MZ all-copper, hollow-pointed, sabotted bullet is attracting attention because of its lower-weight, higher-velocity ballistics compared with lead bullets. Offering optimal

More than half of all 46 states that promote muzzleloading deer seasons have legalized the use of optics, including scopes.

expansion at both ends of the velocity envelope, this premium bullet will be turning many heads in the modern muzzleloading rifle camp.

If some plastic is good, is more plastic better? Aside from polycarbonate stocks that don't warp and plastic sabots that allow for smaller-diameter bullets, T/C's new polycarbonate tip in the top of the Mag Express bullet is stirring excitement. The ballistic tip drives back into the core of the jacketed bullet, creating dramatic expansion (mushrooming) at the slower velocities that muzzleloaders create.

With plastic-wrapped, copper-jacketed, higher-velocity bullets driven by pelletized propellants far in excess of 100 grains, the only logical conclusion was for these modern rigs to use optics for sights. Why bother creating a load that is equipped to hit a deer with lethal energy at 200-plus yards if your sights can't see the animal clearly?

Game officials from densely populated states are beginning to ask how far current technology can move beyond short-range primitive muzzleloaders without creating new problems. For instance, modern muzzleloaders can fire higher-velocity, streamlined bullets just as far as modern centerfire rifles, which are not legal.

More than half of the 46 states that allow a special season for muzzleloaders have legalized scopes. Now the rifles have the same deadly optical advantage of modern centerfires. They also possess the same deadly ballistics as the .30-30 Winchester. And they are as weatherproof as the modern bolt rifle.

The only thing primitive about the current class of muzzleloaders for sale in the discount stores is that they load from the top. State wildlife managers have noted this—sometimes with alarm, sometimes with a quiet nod. Managing the whitetail herd with a single shot, albeit from a compound bow or a front-loading rifle, seems to be the only effective way to curb growing suburban populations with whitetails. But the question that needs to be addressed is: How far can we go from the short-ranged primitive muzzleloader without creating a system that is capable of throwing higher-velocity, streamlined bullets to dangerous distances in the suburbs?

Pennsylvania's Muzzleloading Season

In 2005, Pennsylvania marked 32 years of muzzleloading and deer hunting success. It was one of the first states to sponsor a special flintlock, muzzleloading deer season. Over nearly a third of a century, this noble experiment attracted almost 200,000 Pennsylvania deer hunters. During this time, traditional flintlock rifles have made meat the old-fashioned way, with "ol' DuPont and galena," a mountain man's expression for black powder and lead. These two critical components of a flintlock—black powder and a roundball of lead—have loaded and fired the rifles of our state's hunters since 1974. Certainly, we cannot overlook the contributions of three previous centuries, in which flintlocks provided wild game for the tables of the commonwealth's families.

Pennsylvania's flintlock hunters are now far more experienced and effective than they were in 1974. Back then, only 65 deer (which included only four bucks) were harvested by the 2,064 licensed flintlock hunters. This amounted to a paltry success rate of 3 percent—only three hunters in a hundred connected with a deer.

Those of us who were there that first year remember it well. The weather was unseasonable, too warm and very dry with little snow cover. One of the 30 designated State Game Lands that permitted the experimental season was SGL 110, north of Shartlesville. This first season's attempt at flintlocking bore witness to the confusion posed by the new-fangled old guns as hunters stomped around the brown leaves in the laurels west of the old turkey pens. But in spite of the misfires, flashes in the pan, and questionable accuracy exhibited by these descendants of the pioneers, they sure had a lot of fun. The three-day season, December 26–28, 1974, was most memorable for the hunters who participated, not the harvest taken.

By 1976, the bicentennial year, word of the fun and success of this experimental season had spread throughout the state and to surrounding states; later, it would spread across the country. Licenses soared to 7,626—more than a 350 percent increase. The whitetail harvest jumped to 4.4 percent, and the season was now three weeks long, from December 27 to January 15. Other states had noticed Pennsylvania's success with flintlocks and were joining the bandwagon of primitive hunters. Though still restricted to

Today's flintlock deer hunters are now far more experienced and effective than they were in 1974. Success isn't just measured by how many deer are killed—there is something more, something deeply felt about the sport by hunters.

41 designated State Game Lands, hunters had three years' experience under their belts and were becoming an effective deer harvesting force.

The next two years continued to witness a meteoric rise in flintlock deer hunting interest. Black powder shoots were springing up at every gun club, and "rendezvous" muzzleloading encampments were major tourist attractions. Entrepreneurs were selling "advancements" for the venerable flintlock system, and 25,321 licensed hunters were crowding the 60 designated sites around the state.

In 1979, the Game Commission applied the brakes to the season, calling "the uncontrolled harvest of antlerless deer" a pressing concern. The season was reduced to one week of hunting after Christmas, but this was sugar-coated by allowing flintlock hunters to hunt on both state-owned and private land throughout the commonwealth. The success rate dropped to 3.9 percent from the previous 6.2 percent, and flintlockers complained that their punishment was undeserved because they were still taking less than half the number of deer killed by archers.

Today's muzzleloading deer hunter employs camo, scents, vocalizations, and technology in order to get past the formidable defenses of whitetails.

License sales topped 100,000 for 1980's one-week flintlock season. Once again, the Game Commission's biologist complained that the 11 percent success rate was too high. By 1981, deer hunters had purchased 145,144 licenses, and 8,069 whitetails fell to the white smoke of these muzzleloaders. The Game Commission slammed on the brakes. The 1982 season was shortened to the four days following the regular antlerless deer season—the worst possible time for these short-range rifles, because the deer were scattered and running at the first sound.

Many hunters have forgotten about these dark days when the special flintlock season almost disappeared from Pennsylvania. The main reason why the state has stayed with the flintlock and patched roundball is the potential for the season to be *too* successful. Pennsylvania is the only state of the 46 with muzzleloading seasons that demands a traditional season. Other states allow in-line percussion; scoped rifles; high-tech, sabot-clad, jacketed bullets; and replica powders to improve the lethality of the system. But at what cost—the primitive challenge of the season as it was originally envisioned?

Pennsylvania addressed that issue by creating another muzzleloading season. The October muzzleloading deer season allows any type of muzzleloader, including any ignition, powder, bullet, or sighting system. Regardless of whether you are a primitive longhunter with a flintlock or a thoroughly modern muzzleloader using the most high-tech system available, you will be welcomed to this pre-rut free-for-all in the Keystone State. Moreover, any type of muzzleloader can be used during the other gun seasons in November.

Although most muzzleloading enthusiasts are not considered "trophy hunters" (in fact, most muzzleloaders participate in management hunts for antlerless deer), there is always the possibility that a huge, noteworthy animal may be taken. Because a special status should be awarded to those who handicap themselves with a muzzleloading gun, the National Muzzle Loading Rifle Association has created the *Longhunter Muzzleloading Big Game Record Book,* with more than 500 entries alone for typical white-tailed deer (*Odocoileus virginianus virginianus*). The minimum entry scores are as follows:

Black Bear	18
Grizzly Bear	19
Alaska Brown Bear	21
Polar Bear	22
Cougar (Mountain Lion)	13
American Elk (Typical Wapiti)	255
American Elk (Non-Typical Wapiti)	265
Roosevelt Elk (Wapiti)	225
Mule Deer (Typical)	146
Mule Deer (Non-Typical)	175
Columbia Blacktail Deer	95
Sitka Blacktail Deer	75
Whitetail Deer (Typical)	130
Whitetail Deer (Non-Typical)	160
Coues' Whitetail Deer (Typical)	70
Coues' Whitetail Deer (Non-Typical)	75

Canada Moose	145
Alaska-Yukon Moose	180
Wyoming (Shiras) Moose	125
Mountain Caribou	280
Woodland Caribou	230
Barren Ground Caribou	320
Central Canada Barren Ground Caribou	275
Quebec-Labrador Caribou	320
Pronghorn	63
Bison	92
Rocky Mountain Goat	41
Muskox	80
Bighorn Sheep	136
Desert Sheep	125
Dall's Sheep	132
Stone's Sheep	132

On September 29, 2003, muzzleloading history was made. The Monroe County, Iowa, buck taken by junior hunter Tony Lovstuen rocked the hunting world with a Boone and Crockett score of 307 ⅝.

The main objective is to have fun. Have a blast with your choice of muzzleloader. If you practice and get lucky, you'll be making meat the old-fashioned way. This is a rare satisfaction that only the few and the proud will ever experience.

Buying the Right Muzzleloader

What are the key elements to consider before purchasing a muzzle-loader? Regardless of whether you are buying your first gun or the next dozen, you need to define your needs. Not all muzzleloaders are created equal, but with a knowledge of calibers, rifling rates of twist, barrel lengths, fluting, porting, sighting systems, ignition systems, stock profiles, eye relief, fiber-optics, and assorted furniture, the savvy deer hunter can stack the odds in his or her favor. Turkey hunters face a different challenge. Although rifles and shotguns share many key elements, the smoothbore has an entirely different set of requirements for patterning shot densities at North America's biggest game bird. Smoothbores, trade guns, side-by-side doubles, and modern in-lines will be dissected, defined, and made understandable.

The lonely sound of a distant train whistle dispelled any illusion of being eighteenth-century longhunters. The second-growth hardwoods that surrounded the power-line opening belied any attempt to believe that this muzzleloading hunt was taking place in pristine, virgin forest. Daniel Boone and his Native American neighbors had long passed into history. This special deer hunt was only an honorable reminder of our colonial heritage.

What makes it so special? The excitement is highlighted by pursuing a deer with a single-shot rifle that owes its accuracy and lethality to the custom load—the one that was poured and rammed down the top of the barrel. In a word: muzzleloading.

To get started in this exciting sport, the first step is to buy a muzzleloading gun. However, buying the first gun that comes along, or the cheapest one, is a sure recipe for disaster and a lot of disappointment.

Long after Daniel Boone and his Native American neighbors had passed into history, this special muzzleloading deer hunt served as a reminder of our colonial heritage.

Assuming that you are new to this sport, before you run out to the gun shop and buy your first gun, consider these important questions:

- Where do you hunt?
- Are you a tree-stand hunter?
- How old are you?
- Why do you want to hunt with a muzzleloader?
- Do you need a shotgun or a rifle?

The answers to these five questions will help you choose the right muzzleloader for you. Although hand-me-downs, loaners, and bargain-basement sale rifles might work during an unplanned, hurry-up hunt, they will not make you happy for the rest of your hunting career.

Open hardwoods are ideal environments for hunting deer with primitive flintlock and percussion muzzleloaders. Shots are made at ranges that are usually under 50 yards.

Where do you hunt? If your answer is (a) the open hardwoods of the Appalachians and Alleghenies, (b) the thick underbrush and hardwoods of the piedmonts in the Southeast, (c) agricultural fields and woodlots, (d) the wide open prairie, (e) the tangled dark timber of the Rockies, (f) the open spaces of the southwestern desert, or (g) all of the above, there is a right muzzleloader for you.

For example, open hardwoods allow hunters to shoot at deer throughout the lethal distance envelope with a primitive flintlock or sidehammer percussion. What does that mean? According to the American Hunting Institute, a muzzleloading rifle should deliver a minimum of 500 foot-pounds of energy at impact to humanely and quickly harvest a whitetail. Knowing the energies developed by each caliber and the maximum distance for the rifle-bullet combination allows you to be an ethical and successful muzzleloading hunter.

Another consideration is whether you intend to hunt during all muzzleloading and rifle seasons with the same gun. In some states, those seasons may run from August to March. If you want to hunt in Pennsylvania, any muzzleloader will do in October, but you will need a flintlock in December–January during that state's flintlock-only season. In other states, you will be permitted to use any ignition type, from flintlock to in-line percussion.

Are you a tree-stand hunter? Bow hunters were the first to attain success in the early season by perching themselves high

In most states, any type of muzzleloader ignition system is legal. But mass production and marketing of the in-line system has made this the choice for hunters new to the sport.

above the scent line, which drifts on the wind. You need to ask yourself if this will be your style of muzzleloader hunting. For tree-stand hunting, carbines are the best choice. Their shorter barrels do not telegraph movement the way a longrifle barrel does. In September–October, hunters need to contend with denser foliage than that encountered in December–January. Therefore, heavier calibers are a better choice. Although rifle weight increases when a hunter chooses a .50 or .54 over a lightweight .45, tree-stand hunters do not need to worry about the weight of the rifle being carried. With the gun rested on a lap or tethered to a hook from its sling, weight is not an important consideration.

Is there any disadvantage in carrying a shorter-barreled carbine? Yes. For each inch that a barrel is shortened (from a maximum of 42 inches), flintlock hunters give up about 10 feet per second of velocity. Thus, a 16-inch barrel will be 260 feet per second slower than a 42-inch barrel when both are loaded with the same amount of powder, patch, and ball. Another drawback is the length of the sighting plane between the rear and front sights. The longer the distance, the more precise the aim. Of course, this is dependent on the shooter's eyes as well.

Most carbines, such as the Lyman Deerstalker and T/C Firestorm, are well suited to their role as tree-stand rifles. The barrels produce good velocity, and the fiber-optic sights provide clear pictures. After all, most tree-stand shots at whitetails are close, many less than 25 yards.

Most whitetails are successfully harvested at distances under 50 yards, but open hardwood ravines and ridges may allow for the occasional shot at 100-plus yards. The .54 caliber is a heavier rifle with a huge bore capable of swallowing more powder and lead. Shooting costs are higher, recoil is greater, and rifle weight is considerable. But there are magnum flintlocks that take advantage of the fact that 110 grains of FFg will deliver a 230-grain roundball with 1,465 foot-pounds of kinetic energy. Even at 100 yards, the ball will impart 525 foot-pounds on target.

Bullets carry more foot-pounds of ballistic energy than their sphere-shaped cousins. They also carry more energy farther downrange (even past the 100-yard limit that flintlockers self-impose)

The muzzleloader you'll want to use in a treestand will be different from the one you'd use here, on the ground.

than roundballs do. Hunters need to be aware that slugs are not stabilized in flight by the slow rotation offered by highly accurate roundball barrels. Rates of twist from 1:56 to 1:72 are too slow for slug-shooting accuracy. Barrels with a rate of twist slower than 1:48 will yield optimal accuracy beyond the 50-yard mark. Actually, any rate of twist works well at under 50 yards, even smoothbores.

How old are you? The age of the shooter is an important factor in the choice of a muzzleloader. The obvious concern is weight; the less obvious and more important concern is sight visibility.

Most muzzleloading rifles weigh between 6 and 12 pounds. The newer rifles, with synthetic stocks, are considerably lighter than the older wooden stocks with polished brass fittings that replicate rifles from the eighteenth and nineteenth centuries. I would be the first to sing the praises of a beautiful Pennsylvania longrifle with a curly maple, carved stock and a brass patchbox and inlays, but these guns are heavy. After lugging a 12-pound .54-caliber flintlock longrifle up and down the hills of Bradford County in the icy month of January, this middle-aged longhunter has experienced the aching arms, tired back, and sagging shoulders. Although heavy, long-barreled guns may have an advantage in off-hand shooting competitions, the lighter, short-barreled, modern carbine muzzleloaders do just fine on the targets presented in deer hunting situations.

Older hunters also have another problem: their eyesight. As we age, our eyeballs change shape. As a result, we become farsighted and can no longer see that rear sight as clearly as we used to. When buying a new muzzleloader, consider how well you can see the sights. If the rear sight is too close to see it clearly while focusing on the front sight, make sure that the rear sight can be moved up the barrel to clear the sight picture. Gunsmiths can easily do this for a minimal charge. Wider front sights, larger slots in the rear sights, and even the use of fiber-optics will help older eyes focus. Also, consider painting your sights. A dab of blue on the front sight and an edge of yellow paint on the rear sight will make the sight picture jump out clearly. These two opposite colors stimulate the cones in the eye. This creates a dramatically clear sight picture, especially in the whiteout of a snowstorm.

Why do you want to hunt with a muzzleloader? There are no wrong answers, but your reason will determine the type of gun that will meet your needs.

If you are a traditionalist who takes deep satisfaction from hunting like your eighteenth-century ancestors, then a plastic stocked, fiber-optic sighted, fluted stainless steel barreled, coned-breech, replica powder, pellet-consuming, fast-twist rifled carbine is not going to make you happy. Traditional rifles can be half-stocked or full-stocked, but the stock is usually made of maple, cherry, or walnut; other woods will not look authentic. Traditional rifles have longer barrels than the 24-inch carbines on the rack. Carbines don't have the right "feel" for off-hand shooting, which most deer hunting shots demand. Traditional rifles have octagonal or octagonal to round barrels. Traditional rifles usually have patch-boxes and other brass, silver, or iron furniture (e.g., nosecaps, entry thimble, butt plate). Because of these authentic add-ons, traditional rifles are normally more expensive than their newer synthetic counterparts.

If the muzzleloader is just one more chance for you to tag a deer, then your choice might be controlled by economics. Yet the one area where you should not try to save money is the lock. If the flint doesn't strike spark, if the hammer doesn't quickly snap the cap, or if the striker doesn't immediately punch the 209 shotgun primer, there will be no ignition, and no *kaboom!* Deer can be harvested only when the rifle fires, so be sure that there is a strong mainspring or don't buy it.

Do you need a shotgun or a rifle? Shotguns are different from rifles, both in the way they deliver pellets to the target and in the way they are aimed. Ignition choices are the same as for rifles, and for the same reasons mentioned earlier, be aware of the characteristics that affect lock time and function. Flintlock shotguns are a rarity and are usually produced on a custom-made basis. They are not popular with turkey hunters because the flash of the priming powder on the outside of the barrel alerts the ever-wary gobbler.

Muzzleloading shotguns are different from rifles in the way that they are aimed and used on game. However, they still load from the top—hence the name "muzzleloader."

Also, the longer time delay of ignition can give a cautious bird time to "jump the shot" before the barrel actually fires. Trade guns, basically smoothbore muskets, are historically correct, single-barrel shotguns that can be fired either by a flintlock ignition or by an external hammer striking a capped nipple. "Hammer guns" are popular with traditionalists. Their ignition systems are easier to cap and, more importantly, decap. Double-barrels are typical hammer guns. If multiple shots are important to you—and in turkey hunting, they are sometimes vital—a side-by-side double-barrel shotgun is the most likely choice. In-line ignition systems give the modern muzzleloader the same weather-resistant ignition advantage found in centerfire rifles. However, they are found currently only in single-shot muzzleloading shotguns.

The most important consideration when buying a shotgun is pattern density—in other words, whether the shotgun has a "choke." In shotguns, the choking system constricts the pellets so that they make a smaller pattern of hits on the target. Tight pellet pattern density is vital for anchoring a large bird like a wild turkey. To create a full choke, or a turkey full choke, most manufacturers use a threaded, screw-in choke at the muzzle. This allows the hunter to easily load the wads into the shotgun. It also allows the choke to be modified for pheasant hunting or the use of a cylinder when hunting upland game and wing-shooting doves.

Shotguns are pointed at the wings of most winged game, but turkey shotguns need to be aimed at the head-neck region of this large-boned, feather-armored bird. Shotguns normally carry a bead front sight and no rear sight, and this is satisfactory for wing-shooting flying birds, but it is not the best choice. Fiber-optic rear and front sights, and scopes and optical aiming systems, are better. If the shotgun doesn't come equipped with them, make sure that it can be retrofitted.

In many cases, the bottom line when choosing a muzzleloader is cost. But if the gun doesn't fit your style of hunting, you will never realize the ultimate enjoyment that comes when hunting with a muzzleloader. Not all muzzleloaders fit every hunter. Measure the trigger pull from the inside of your elbow to the second joint of your trigger finger. This should be the same distance as that measured from the butt to the trigger. Most adults measure in the

14-inch range; women and youths may measure 13 or even 12. This distance is critical to an accurate "trigger pull" and makes a difference in shot placement.

Finally, muzzleloading rifles and shotguns, particularly the flintlock, are complex mechanisms, so be sure that the manufacturer guarantees its product. More important, make sure that you will be able to get parts if something breaks or wears out.

CHAPTER TWO

Muzzleloading Gun Types and Tips

Primitive Flintlock and Percussion Rifles

The flintlock is one of the most complicated and demanding rifle systems that any hunter could choose for deer hunting. The percussion Hawken rifle is synonymous with the fur trade and is affectionately used by those following the mountain man lifestyle. But either primitive muzzleloading system can offer a rewarding and fulfilling hunting adventure. A clacking sound of flint on steel, drawing sparks; a flash of fire on the side of the gun; and before you can even react, a loud, thundering boom obliterates the target with a cloud of smoke. Your eyes are stunned, your nostrils fill with sulfur, and your ears fill with the music of an ancient pyrotechnic explosion. Nowhere else in the world of hunting will both your heart and your mind be filled with such rollicking sensations.

To begin this primitive pursuit, spend some time becoming familiar with the system. Once the excitement of making the system work wears off, it will be time to actually think about making it work accurately. You are working with a lot of variables, and the secret to making them work at their optimal efficiency is consistency. And becoming consistent takes lots of practice. That is why success with the muzzleloading system has been described as the Ph.D. of the shooting sports.

Let's begin with the basics: powder, patch, and ball. All primitive flintlock and percussion systems shoot black powder. Black powder is an ancient chemical mixture of charcoal, saltpeter, and sulfur. It explodes very quickly at a lower ignition temperature than modern

The flintlock is one of the most complicated and demanding rifle systems in American history. However, the satisfaction derived from mastering it has no equal.

nitrocellulose, smokeless gunpowder. But it also generates lower breech pressures than smokeless powders do.

Original loads for primitive flintlock and percussion muzzleloaders were described as "powder weight [in grains] for roundball caliber size." In other words, riflemen loaded 50 grains of black powder for a .50-caliber rifle. This load worked for small game and close shots on deer-sized game (under 50 yards). For larger game and distant shots, riflemen adjusted up to a double load (100 grains).

Today's hunter has ballistic tables and manufacturers'

Shooting a primitive muzzleloader offers sensations unlike any in the world of hunting.

From the clacking sound of flint on steel to the loud, thundering boom and the cloud of sulfurous smoke, primitive muzzleloading is a uniquely exhilarating experience.

It's also an effective and immensely rewarding way to hunt wild game.

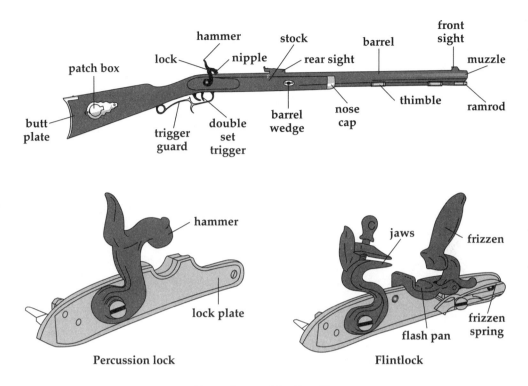

Parts of a muzzleloading rifle

recommendations for accurate and lethal hunting loads. The old saying that you can never overload a black powder gun because it will just blow the unburned powder out the muzzle is a fallacy. Black powder is a class A explosive, and it is quite capable of blowing up you and your rifle and doing great harm to the innocent people around you. You have an ethical responsibility to follow the recommendations of the manufacturer for a safe maximum load.

Part of the fun of primitive rifles is in the acquisition or construction of loading tools. The powder horns that store and carry the black powder are a hallmark tool of the longhunter or mountain man. The carved and scrimshawed cow horns reflect the personality of the hunter who carries them. Names, dates, maps, and mythological and totem animals are inscribed around the large powder horn, while more intricate carvings adorn the smaller priming horns. Leather hunting pouches, sometimes called accoutrements bags, are decorated with pierced designs from nature or animal fur, feathers, and claws. Powder measures and knife

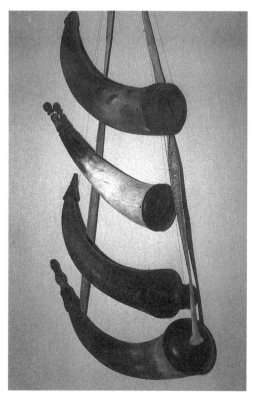

The powder horn that carries black powder is the hallmark of a longhunter or mountain man.

handles made of antlers are also carried by the primitive muzzleloader hunter. These tools are denied to those who choose to hunt with a modern muzzleloader. Their absence makes the heart yearn for an earlier time and system of hunting. A modern powder pellet and a plastic-sabotted, copper-jacketed bullet will never have the warmth and richness of spirit associated with the handmade tools of the primitive riflemen.

Nostalgia will not make you a successful deer hunter, but learning to shoot the primitive muzzleloader will. To do this, you need to understand what makes any rifle, primitive or modern, shoot well. Paramount is an understanding of rifling—those little spiral grooves cut on the inside of the barrel. You need to consider the depth of the rifling as well as the number of turns the spiral creates in one barrel length.

Pennsylvania longrifle gunsmiths didn't invent rifling, but they certainly earned a place in history for their use of this technology. Thanks to them, riflemen of the Revolutionary War were credited with making the British soldiers rethink their tactics. The spin imparted to a bullet acts like the gyroscope that keeps a rocket flying straight. Too much spin, and the bullet turns into a curveball; not enough rotation gives a bullet about as much accuracy as a knuckleball.

Flintlocks originally shot roundballs of lead. Lead spheres were the smallest geometric shape that would fit down the barrel while feeling the effects of rifling. Patches of deerskin, linen, and cotton fabrics were merely a bearing surface that carried lubricant to keep

Leather hunting pouches, sometimes called accoutrements bags, carried pierced designs from nature and may include animal fur, feathers, or claws.

the fouling soft and ease the speed and effort of loading. In fact, the patched roundball was and still is the fastest bullet that a flintlock shooter can load. Speed to target means less time for gravity to cause drop or for the sights to go off target.

Patched rounds fly like baseballs. Very little rotation is required for a ball-shaped bullet that approaches 2,000 feet per second. Good rates of rifling for roundball shooting range from 1:48 (one rotation in 48 inches of bullet flight) to 1:72. Roundballs flying around 1,500 feet per second do well in barrels with a 1:48 twist, while the faster 1,800 feet per second roundballs are more accurate with 1:66. Match the rotation to the speed, and your bullet will be more likely to strike its mark every time.

The depth of the rifling is also important. About four centuries ago, the Swiss noticed that the depth of the rifling groove allowed room for fouling to be pushed out of the way. Patched roundballs shoot better in deep-grooved rifling. Most roundball barrels have rifling grooves at least 0.007-inch deep. This gives the greased patch room to do its job, as well as allowing the necessary space for the folded cloth to load tightly into the grooves. The tighter the patched ball fits into the bore, the more accurate the load will be. Although most manufacturers recommend a .490 lead roundball for their .50-caliber flintlocks, combined with a 0.016- to 0.020-inch cotton patch, you may find that a tighter .495 roundball patched with a 0.010-inch patch yields greater accuracy. Unfortunately, the tighter the fit, the more difficult it is to load, which is why most manuals recommend a looser fit for hunting conditions.

Many of the new muzzleloaders are being manufactured with rates of rotation of 1:38 and even faster. Why? Because these barrels are designed to shoot elongated slugs, copper-jacketed bullets, and plastic-sabotted copper bullets. These pointed cylinders fly like footballs and need increased rates of rotation to stabilize their flight.

To shoot your primitive muzzleloader with accuracy, you must match the bullet to the rifling rate, and therefore to the type of barrel. Is it possible to use one barrel for all types of bullets? Yes, but you must slow down or speed up the velocity at which you are shooting. And remember, slow velocity is no friend to a hunting bullet. Shock, penetration, and a tissue-destroying cone of energy (hydrostatic shock) is dependent on terminal velocities above the speed of sound (1,100 feet per second at sea level).

Roundballs and cone-shaped bullets each have their advantages. Obviously, speed and accuracy under 100 yards favor the traditional roundball. But if longer-range shooting is what your hunting style demands, then energy-retaining bullets are a better choice. Whatever the choice, buy a barrel that is matched to your needs.

Regardless of whether the rear sight is fixed or adjustable, make sure that you can see both it and the front sight clearly. Manufacturers have taken this requirement into account by providing a wide, deep notch in the rear sight and a bold post or bead for the front sight. These sights work well in strong daylight and need no improvement for most deer hunting applications. But if you hunt in dark timber or attempt to waylay a buck in the early-morning mists or the late-evening dews and damps, you may want to use a bright silver or brass front sight to pick up the available light—just like your forefathers carried on their rifles.

To shoot a muzzleloader accurately, match the type of bullet to the barrel. Slow rates of twist are designed to shoot roundballs accurately, while faster rates are designed to stabilize longer and heavier bullets.

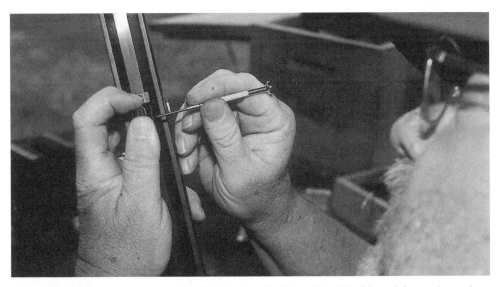

Adjustable sights are a real advantage when changing bullet weights. Fixed iron sights are impervious to accidental movement, but they won't easily change their zero when you change loads.

Fiber-optic sights are incompatible with the philosophy of primitive firearms. But in a hunting context, they definitely provide an improved sight picture.

Fiber-optics are definitely not found on "traditional" firearms. However, these plastic light-gathering and -focusing fibers do increase a hunter's ability to put the sights on target in dim light. Hi-Viz, Tru-Glo, CVA's Illuminator, and other add-on fiber-optic sights can be attached to a rifle for less than $20. And yes, they are legal, even in Pennsylvania.

If you have trouble seeing your sights—iron, brass, or even fibers—you are probably in the over-50 club. Iron sights become difficult to align, which is why the aperture, or peep sight, might be a good choice for your flintlock. Peep sights became popular prior to the Civil War. They evolved as an improved target-sighting system and were particularly well suited for the concentric ring targets found in the popular "meat shoots" and rifle competitions of the nineteenth century. Although they are not legal in Pennsylvania's flintlock season, they are legal for the antlered, antlerless, and special regulations areas, as well as New York's and Michigan's muzzleloader and shotgun seasons.

Peep sights can be economically and easily installed as an add-on to any flintlock. Vernier tang sites are available in many different styles for less than $40. The beauty of this sight is that you can still use the front sight with the peep, or the original rear sight and peep, for a fast fleeing deer. Other rear aperture sights are mounted in place of the original rear sight, but they may offer a sighting system that is more familiar to deer hunters. The Ashley aperture ghost ring hunting sight matches most existing mounting holes and offers adjustability for windage and elevation and a very visible front post that provides a fine white post inside the wider black front sight. This is a good choice for deer hunting applications.

A quick but effective fix for farsighted hunters is to move the rear sight forward. This was common practice during the era of iron-sighted rifles, as evidenced by the many brass nameplates that were installed in the old rear sight mortise, my own muzzleloader included. You will be amazed at how clear the sights become and how your original, dead-eye accuracy comes back when you perform this simple gunsmithing procedure. Simply unscrew or drift out the rear sight, set it atop the barrel, and slide the sight forward as you take aim at a distant object. As the sight picture becomes clear, mark the spot and reinstall the rear sight.

Your rifle can achieve lightning-fast ignition if you remedy a few common problems. They can be summed up as the dreaded sound of *click . . . phfft . . . kaboom!* The deafening *click* of a dull flint striking unproductive steel, or the muffled snap of a percussion cap, sets a rifleman's heart pounding and his brain screaming for answers. This should never happen in a hunt. In the eighteenth century, riflemen simply turned the flintlock upside down and squeezed the trigger. If the main charge fired, they considered the ignition fast enough. Today, with photoelectronic timing equipment, ballisticians have proved that a flintlock is capable of firing in 0.05 second, a sidehammer percussion in 0.02. Quite frankly, that speed makes it too fast for a rifleman to flinch off target.

Before you take that flintlock out for a hunt, check for sparks. With an unloaded flintlock, watch the flint strike the steel frizzen. Productive, white-hot sparks should sizzle as they hit the empty priming pan. Unproductive orange sparks are too cool and too few in number.

The number one reason for the *click* misfire is a dull flint. Your new rifle may have worked perfectly at the range last fall, and after some 20 shots, you cleaned the gun and put it away for deer season. Unfortunately, the new knife-sharp edge of the flint has now eroded to a rounded, worthless edge. Don't be cheap; change the flint. Or, if you prefer the frugal route, use a diamond file for five or six strokes on the flint, every five to six shots.

Hunters can choose from machined agates or knapped flints. Agates are hard stones that saw into a perfectly straight, beveled edge. This is the type of flint that manufacturers include with their flintlocks. But once they dull, they must be replaced. Knapped or chipped flints are naturally occurring stones, mostly from the chalk cliffs of England and France, that can repeatedly be knapped to keep a very sharp, spark-showering edge. These knapped flints are the best choice for hunters. Their glassy composition allows the edge to be knapped or resharpened with a few glancing blows on the edge. The chips create a sharpened glass edge that will reward you in the field with a quick solution to the *click* problem. But before you get cocky, check to make sure that the flint is tightly secured inside the leather wrap that provides the bite for the jaws of the rifle's cock (hammer).

The *click . . . phfft* is the gut-wrenching sound of a "flash in the pan." Humidity is the culprit. Black powder contains potassium nitrate, an anhydrous salt that pulls water vapor into the black powder, increasing its ignition temperature to the point where it can't go off. Increase your chances of ignition by keeping powder granules away from the touch hole as well as inside the barrel. Sticking a bird's feather quill into the touch-hole safely prevents moisture inside the barrel, as well as keeping the powder back from the touch-hole channel. Change your priming powder every 15 minutes in humid conditions. Or, add a little Rain Coat, a fine white powder from Mountain State Muzzleloading (six parts Rain Coat to one part black powder), for an incredibly moistureproof prime. Be sure to keep the pan free of inky black powder before priming. Prime a half pan level with dry priming powder after picking the touch hole, and you will never again hear a *click . . . phfft*.

The number one reason for a click *misfire is a dull flint. This is the first component that needs to be checked before starting out on a hunt.*

Too many deer are missed because of the *click . . . phfft . . . kaboom,* disgustedly referred to as a hang-fire. The delay in tenths of a second causes the sights to drift off target, only to have the bullet fire into a nontargeted area. Check the touch-hole diameter: $1/32$ inch is too small for positive ignition; $1/16$ inch is better. Touch holes also deteriorate over time, with metal-salt crystals growing irregularly in the channel. Install a new one. Another culprit is grease. Cleaning oils and greases have a nasty habit of detouring into the touch-hole channel, preventing a quick ignition of the powder train. Be sure to "clean a clean gun" with denatured alcohol, which will degrease the grooves; then follow with a dry patch.

Primitive sidehammer percussion rifles can avoid the dreaded *snap* followed by silence by ensuring that the fire channel, from the top of the nipple to the right-angle touch hole where the flame ignites the main powder charge, is clear. A thin wire, called a nipple pick, should be inserted after the rifle is loaded. Also, make sure that the caps are stored in a moistureproof container. During humid and wet weather, change the cap hourly. Better yet, don't cap the rifle until you are ready to shoot.

If you do not fire your gun at game during the day and want to keep the load for the following day, do not bring it into a warm house. Condensation will form on the outside of the barrel, and you don't want to take chances. The emptied pan and feather quill in the touch hole will waterproof the breech, as will a patch placed between the hammer and the top of the nipple on a percussion. The greased patch roundball will waterproof the interior powder train. But lead slugs and sabotted bullets do not block water from attacking the black powder. You can remedy this situation by stretching a balloon over the crown of the barrel.

Take the time to look at the lock. No matter how accurately the barrel shoots or how well you fine-tune your sights, if the flintlock or percussion system doesn't fire, the rifle is worthless. Check the strength of the mainspring that powers the cock or hammer of the lock. If it doesn't snap the flint forward into the frizzen, the shower of sparks will be inadequate. If the hammer doesn't squarely strike the nipple with authority, the copper percussion cap won't snap fire into the breech. Check the fit of the pan to the barrel, as well as the frizzen cover over the pan. If either of these have gaps, the priming powder will leak out, leaving nothing for the sparks to ignite.

The trigger assembly is also important. It should function crisply and without undue trigger creep. The question to ask before purchasing a rifle is whether you really need two triggers to shoot one shot. Set triggers have been around for centuries and can give a target shooter an extra edge in accuracy. However, two triggers—one rear trigger called the "set trigger," and a very touch-sensitive front trigger known as the "hair trigger"—can be a liability in a cold environment. Because fingers lose sensitivity in freezing temperatures, and because gloved fingers add bulk inside the trigger guard, hair triggers sometimes fire before the hunter is ready.

Finally, the look and feel of the rifle are determined, for the most part, by the total length of the stock and barrel. Pennsylvania longrifles are beautiful re-creations of frontier art and function. With their long barrels and beautifully carved and figured hardwood stocks, enhanced by wooden or brass patchboxes, they are the ultimate acquisition for any flintlock hunter. But do they meet the needs of every hunter?

Certainly, custom handmade flintlock longrifles and percussion Hawkens check in at the top end of most hunters' budgets, priced in the thousands of dollars. Their style and grace command top prices because gunsmiths spend hundreds of hours carving, inlaying, and engraving the historically accurate arms. Their long sighting plane and balance in the off-hand shooting position make them very accurate in the hands of experienced flintlock hunters. But for new hunters, particularly those used to hunting from tree stands, it might be best to work out the kinks with one of the new high-tech flintlocks. With prices ranging from $200 to $450, Hawken-style rifles sporting 28- to 32-inch barrels will provide most hunters with success and pride. Eventually, however, almost every muzzleloading hunter will want to own one of those fabulous, historic arms, whether to display on the wall or carry on a nostalgia-filled walk through the deer woods.

With more than a dozen models of primitive muzzleloaders manufactured by companies such as Thompson/Center, Connecticut Valley Arms (CVA), Austin & Halleck, Navy Arms, Lyman, Traditions, and Pedersoli, not to mention the many serviceable used guns handed down by former muzzleloading hunters, choosing a primitive rifle should be a challenging and enjoyable quest. Following is a partial list of primitive rifles available to deer hunters (see appendix B for contact information for manufacturers).

The Austin & Halleck gun makers have created a muzzleloading classic for the upscale muzzleloader, but they have also responded to primitive shooters with the Mountain rifle in Flintlock or percussion. The .50-caliber, 32-inch octagonal (1-inch outside diameter) browned barrels, with double-throw adjustable triggers, provide either 1:66 rifling for roundballs or 1:28 twist for conical bullet performance. The fixed rear buckhorn and front silver blade sights are authentic primitive sights. The comparatively lightweight 7.5 pounds of the 49-inch butt-to-muzzle length and the beautiful curly maple stocks make this a rifle to contend with at rendezvous or to show off in the north woods.

Cabela's traditional Hawken rifles are available in flint or percussion ignition. Hefty 29-inch, .50- or .54-caliber barrels with a 1:48 twist rifling carry adjustable iron rear and fixed front sights.

The stock is walnut, and the patchbox, trigger guard, barrel key, and nosecap are brass. The percussion rifle is available in a left-handed version. Fiber-optic sights are available, as are rifle kits. About 43 inches overall, the Hawken weighs 8.75 pounds.

CVA offers a flint or percussion St. Louis Hawken in .50 or .54 caliber. The Hawken has a 28-inch blued octagonal barrel, hardwood stock, adjustable sights, brass trim, and patchbox. It weighs 7.8 pounds and is available in a left-handed model.

Dixie Gun Works has introduced a new reproduction of the German flintlock known as the Jaeger. This 8-pound, .54-caliber rifle comes equipped with a shallow-grooved 1:24 twist rifling, which makes it ideal for a wide array of sabotted bullets. This may be necessary for primitive hunters who need heavy terminal ballistics for large and dangerous game. With the variety of high-performance, quick-expanding, low-velocity sabotted bullets, this replica will be popular with deer hunters. The Jaeger's reputation for ruggedness and accuracy as a military sniper's rifle bodes well for its acceptance as a hunter's rifle, as well as a reenactment piece.

Dixie Gun Works is a giant in the field of primitive firearms. Its large catalog is filled with flintlock and percussion kits, as well as finished rifles. All periods of muzzleloading history—Revolutionary War muskets, frontier flintlocks and Great Plains percussions, and Civil War rifles—are represented.

Jim Chambers Flintlocks fills a unique niche. Jim sells locks, stocks, and barrels for Pennsylvania longrifle reproductions. Just add labor.

Lyman Products Corporation has been in the primitive game for a long time. The Lyman Great Plains rifle in .50 or .54 caliber, flint or percussion, has a case-hardened hammer and lock, blackened steel furniture, and a 32-inch octagonal barrel in right- and left-handed models. It is no lightweight, at 11.38 pounds. Lyman flintlocks are highly regarded for their reliability to spark. Lyman also produces the Deerstalker, a 24-inch carbine with an octagonal barrel in blued or stainless steel. Weighing in at 10.1 pounds, it also is available in right- or left-handed models.

Mowrey Gun Works, Inc., specializes in muzzleloaders designed by Ethan Allen. Its .50-caliber flintlock is patterned after a copy of an early Leman-Lancaster longrifle with a 35-inch barrel, primitive iron sights, brass furniture, and high relief checkered on a curly maple stock; it is also available in nickel silver furniture.

For those yearning for a Revolutionary War Brown Bess musket, Navy Arms Company can accommodate with a re-creation. The .75-caliber Brown Bess has a 42-inch white steel barrel and flintlock ignition and weighs in at 9.5 pounds. A shorter 30-inch barrel carbine is also available. Navy Arms also re-creates the 1763 Charleville musket. Its .69-caliber, 44.63-inch white steel barrel and lock check in at 8.75 pounds.

The Navy Arms 1803 Harpers Ferry rifle in .54-caliber carries a 35-inch round barrel and color-case hardened hammer and lock. Civil War–era Enfields, both two-band and three-band .58-caliber percussions, are another offering of Navy Arms.

Pedersoli, Davide & C. Snc., is a family-owned company that started building muzzleloading guns in 1960. Many of its offerings are carried by retailers such as Cabela's, Dixie Gun Works, Navy Arms, and others. Pedersoli offers a full line of primitive flintlock and percussion muzzleloaders in the American style, as well as specialty European arms.

Thompson/Center has solved the Pyrodex and Triple Seven pellets problem by marketing the Firestorm. The revolutionary, patent-pending Pyrodex Pyramid directs ignition fire 360 degrees around the entire base of the Pyrodex or Triple Seven pellet. As the pellet moves forward, the flame is drawn up through the center of the pellets, creating a "firestorm" in the breech. The .50-caliber flintlock has a 26-inch barrel with 1:48 rifling twist and weighs in at approximately 7 pounds. The rifle is designed to accept a "magnum" charge of three 50-grain pellets, which is equivalent to 150 grains of bulk powder. I have used this system and found it quick to load, accurate, and easy to clean. But hunters need to be cautioned not to hammer the ramrod too hard on the bullet, or the pellet will be crushed, and ignition problems can arise.

T/C has also released the Firestorm in a 209 Cap Lock. This .50-caliber rifle uses a 209 shotgun primer to ignite the Pyrodex pellets. The barrel has a faster twist, 1:28, so that it can effectively use the newer sabotted, jacketed bullets. Both rifles have a black composite stock, aluminum ramrod, and competition click-adjustable rear sights. They also use a coarse-thread, removable breech plug that allows the ramrod to pass all the way through while cleaning.

Traditions Performance Firearms offers flintlock shooters the Buckskinner flintlock carbine. This .50-caliber rifle has a 21-inch octagonal to round barrel, 1:48 rifling, blackened hardware, and a hardwood stock. The Deerhunter rifle is a synthetic-stocked, .32-, .50-, or .54-caliber flintlock or percussion rifle. It measures 40 inches overall and weighs 6 pounds. The Traditions Kentucky rifle is a 33.5-inch-long, .50-caliber barrel rifled 1:66 for accurate round-ball shooting. It is 49 inches long overall and weighs 7.25 pounds.

Uberti, A.&C., S.r.l. was purchased by Beretta in 1999, but muzzleloaders are still produced under the Uberti logo. Its offerings are currently marketed by the same large retailers as Pedersoli.

Kit rifles have always been popular with primitive shooters. Far less expensive than custom-made rifles, their precarved stocks and accompanying lock and barrel provide a lot of help for the new builder. Tennessee Valley Muzzleloading, Inc., offers historically correct kits, ranging from early Jaegers to Pennsylvania, Virginia, and Tennessee longrifles. They come with flintlock or percussion ignition; barrel lengths of 36 or 42 inches, depending on the model; and .32, .36, .40, .45, .50, .54, and .58 caliber.

A great place to see custom-made longrifles from around the country is at Dixon's Gunmakers' Fair. For 23 years, juried rifles, scrimshawed powder horns, and accoutrements have been on display the third weekend in July. The Gunmakers' Fair is located just south of Kempton, Pennsylvania, in the rolling foothills of the Appalachians.

Many hunters who are using percussion locks load their guns with heavier slugs and sabots, and the slower, deep-grooved, slow-twist barrels are not well suited for their needs. So what is a moderate rate of twist? My old T/C Hawken shot great with Maxi-Balls, but only okay with the patched roundballs that primitive hunting in Pennsylvania demanded. The Hawken has a 0.005-inch groove depth with a 1:48 rate of twist. If I kept my powder charge lower than what I liked for hunting, roundballs shot with acceptable accuracy. But lead slugs shot with improved accuracy with heavier loads.

At the time, I couldn't explain the phenomenon. Now, we know. The flight of a long cylinder of lead, such as a conical bullet, even when loaded in a plastic sabot, can be compared with that of a football. If it doesn't have a high rate of rotation, it becomes unstable in flight and flies like an out-of-control football. T/C's Maxi-Ball, CVA's Deerslayer, and Hornady's Great Plains bullets can be twice as long as they are wide. Rifling rates of 1:48 are okay, but accuracy improves as the rate of twist gets faster. Barrels with 1:32 and 1:28 rifling offer better stabilization than does slower-

Alan Roth proved the effectiveness of a cleaned, properly loaded, and well-aimed roundball from his .54 T/C Renegade flintlock on this eight-point taken in Berks County, Pennsylvania.

twist rifling. This becomes increasingly important as the bullets and bearing surfaces of the plastic sabots increase in length.

Regardless of the type of bullet you choose for your muzzle-loader, you need to load it accurately. Manuals warn that the bullet must be seated atop the black powder with no airspace in between. This is important. Airspaces can create dramatic detonation of powder and sky-high pressures that can burst the barrel. Mark your ramrod to the correct depth for the hunting load and make sure that you check it every time you load. For increased accuracy, you might want to try a new tool called the KaDOOTY brass loading–bullet pulling system. It uses a measured force to seat the bullet exactly the same each time, and many of the top shooters in competition are now using this very accurate system. If you are loading conical bullets, consider the Barnes loading tool, which aligns the bullet to the centerline of the bore, as well as matching the bullet ogive. All these aids increase your chances of minute-of-angle accuracy.

The advent of pelletized Pyrodex has caused rifle manufacturers to rethink the percussion cap igniters. To add to the decision-making dilemma, the in-line companies are advertising improved ignition qualities with shotgun primers and musket caps. Does that mean that the old #11 percussion cap doesn't work? Normal loads of bulk black powder and Pyrodex work very well with the 3,024-degree flame thrown by the #11 cap. After all, black powder ignites at 480 degrees, while Pyrodex comes to life at 740 degrees. However, the increased powder charges of 150 grains, or three pellets, don't burn well in short barrels with light bullets. Manufacturers' solution was to increase the volume of burning gas from the cap by going to the 209 shotgun primer, even though the flame temperature was the same. Just recently, CCI began producing a #11 magnum cap with a flame temperature of 3,717 degrees, equal to that of the musket cap. This allows the standard percussion cap rifle to have the same increased performance as the musket, but without the larger musket cap nipple.

Because the nipple, positioned atop the percussion muzzle-loading barrel, is slammed by the hammer each time a shot is fired, it is one of the first mechanisms to wear out. A bad nipple can cause misfires, hang-fires, and reduced velocity. But not all nipples are the same. When a standard #11 percussion cap is struck, the pressure-sensitive primer material explodes, and 6.53 cubic centimeters of 3,024-degree gas roars down to the nipple base. There it is accelerated through a tiny hole in the base. Because of the tremendous heat and pressure, nipples wear out, but not at the same rate. Standard heat-treated, tool-grade steel; hardened bronze-alloy Ampco; and heat-treated stainless steel are the common materials used for nipples. Of the three, stainless steel is the strongest. Some nipples are ported at the top to reduce pressure, and some caps have higher temperatures (the #11 "magnum" percussion cap is advertised at 3,717 degrees Fahrenheit with a volume of 7.59 cubic centimeters). Although higher temperatures and volumes assist in ignition, they have the opposite effect on longevity. You will have to replace them periodically. In fact, I change the nipples on my hunting guns on an annual basis.

Primitive muzzleloaders, flintlock and percussion, have watched their marketplace decline but not disappear. Although

Primitive muzzleloaders using flintlocks and percussions have watched their market share decline—but not disappear. There will always be a place for heritage and nostalgia in the hearts and minds of deer hunters.

modern in-line muzzleloading rifles, complete with scopes and plastic stocks, appeal to those hunters who want to embrace modern technologies, there will always be a place for the longrifle or Hawken. In fact, many muzzleloading hunters who start with the in-line end up hunting with the kind of rifle that started the sport. Why? They want to put the challenge back in the hunt and honor the traditions of this noble sport.

Modern In-Line Muzzleloaders

In-line percussion rifles look different, shoot differently, and need a whole new set of basics to be used effectively on whitetails. The label "modern muzzleloader" arose in 1985 when the Knight Gun & Archery Shop in Lancaster, Missouri, introduced a radically new muzzleloading gun profile, the MK-85. Tony Knight, inventor and

Tony Knight with an eight-point buck from his Missouri farm. He is the inventor and founder of the Knight Rifle family of in-line percussions that have changed the face of muzzleloading.

founder of Knight Rifles (Modern Muzzleloading, Inc.), began the production of "in-lines"—a term that denotes a centerfire ignition system for a muzzleloading rifle that sports a modern stock profile. But there is a lot more to the sport of modern muzzleloading than just shooting the gun.

Muzzleloaders and their guns have changed. Inventors and manufacturers have joined forces to push the envelope of what's legal. While traditionalists decry the changes, the huge market of new muzzleloading hunters continues to fan the flames of "improvements." In-line percussion muzzleloading rifles share one thing in common with flintlocks: they load from the top of the barrel. Everything else—from the lock, stock, and barrel to the scopes that sit atop their fiber-optic sights—is definitely different. Although this is upsetting to many primitive flintlock hunters, it is welcomed by many newcomers to the sport of muzzleloader deer hunting. So, if this new high-tech version of an old-fashioned sport lights your fire, this section covers the in-line basics.

The ignition system of modern muzzleloading rifles is different from those used on primitive muzzleloaders. The in-line percussion system still needs to be capped in order to fire, but the way the primer is struck, the type of primer struck, and even the kind of gunpowder used differ from that applicable to longrifles and Hawkens.

Affordable in-lines can be had for less than most new flintlocks, just under $200. Tradition's Thunder Bolt and CVA's Staghorn, MagBolt, Optima, and HunterBolt, as well as other manufacturers'

The in-line muzzleloader has a percussion system that still needs to be capped in order to fire. But the way the primer is struck, the type of primer used, and even the kind of powder loaded is far different from those used historically in longrifles and Hawkens.

offerings, make it easy to get into the sport. At the other end of the price line are in-lines such as Thompson/Center's Omega, Traditions' Pursuit, Knight Rifles' Disc Elite or Extreme, and Knight Master Hunter, which can lighten your wallet by $400 to $1,000. There are about three dozen other models from various manufacturers that fall in the middle of this price range.

Savvy riflemen know that the price of the rifle should not be the only consideration—performance should be. If the gun doesn't load and shoot accurately, it isn't worth any price. If the gun doesn't disassemble and clean easily, you are asking for headaches down the road. And if the gun doesn't look pretty—well, who cares?

Let's consider what drives accuracy and performance: the barrel. It needs to be understood that in-line percussion rifles are not, and never will be, high-velocity, long-range, repeating rifles.

Compare the best ballistics from a high-performance in-line to the average ballistics of a run-of-the-mill .30-caliber cartridge gun, and the cartridge gun will win every time. My vintage World War I .30-06 is far superior in velocity and accuracy at 200 yards than the best of my in-lines. Don't assume that the in-line muzzleloaders will deliver what a 7mm magnum can. This just won't happen. So if velocity isn't the major ingredient in delivering accuracy and performance in a muzzleloader, what is? Power.

Power with a muzzleloader is the end result of sending a large mass (the bullet) downrange with a moderate amount of speed. In other words, the crushing energy of a muzzleloading round depends on mass, not velocity, to do its job efficiently. "Crushing energy" is the correct expression for muzzleloaders when you consider that heavy bullets can provide the necessary foot-pounds of energy to anchor the biggest of North America's game, let alone a puny white-tailed deer. To adequately fire those big rounds and hefty powder charges, the barrel needs some key ingredients, the first of which is caliber.

Currently, in-line rifles can be acquired sporting .45-, .50-, .52-, and .54-caliber bore sizes. But without a doubt, the .50 caliber has become the most common bore size. Why? It could be attributed to Jeremiah Johnson's favorite Hawken hype or to mass marketing, but this caliber probably gained its greatest popularity during the 30-year roundball era prior to the in-lines. The reasoning was simple: a matter of geometry. The only way a minimum-legal

Most in-line rifles are marketed in .50 caliber for a number of complex reasons, but primarily because this caliber offers a compromise between fast bullet velocity and the power necessary to drop deer and bears in their tracks.

.44-caliber roundball could gain mass, and thus energy, was with a bigger diameter. The .45-caliber roundballs carried enough energy out to 50 yards to quickly dispatch a deer, but some whitetails gave hunters an opportunity at greater distances. Manufacturers watched the market going from the .45 to the .50 and .54 calibers, with most deer hunters opting for the half-inch bore, the .50 caliber.

The late 1990s witnessed the rise of the conoidal slug (pointed bullets). Their longer sectional density and high ballistic coefficients offered higher retained energy at longer distances than roundballs. They also could increase their mass and energy by simply getting longer; the bore size stayed the same. As a result, the higher velocities of the .50s over the .54s, along with their ability to utilize various bullet weights, made them a logical choice.

The second key ingredient is rifling. For an elongated bullet to fly accurately, it needs gyroscopic rotation—in other words, spin from the rifling in the bore. Whereas roundballs need slow rotation to stabilize their high-speed flights to target, bullets need a whole lot more. Look for a rate of rifling twist in the neighborhood of 1:24 (one rotation in 24 inches) to 1:32. This spin stabilizes the bullets in their long flights, which is particularly important when they pass the 100-yard mark.

The depth of the grooves of the rifling is not as critical as the rate of twist, and most in-line barrels are the same. They are button-rifled hydraulically, which results in a shallow groove depth in the 0.005-inch range. This shallow rifling works well with bullets, because the groove doesn't need to allow for the compression of a patch around a ball. But if you are entertaining the idea of using a roundball in that new in-line, then shallow-groove rifling is not your best choice. You will need to look at a barrel that provides a groove cut of 0.008 to 0.012 inch into the bore's rifling.

The third key ingredient is barrel length and composition. Barrel length is not as critical as rifling rates and depths of groove, but marketing has convinced shooters that longer barrels are better. That reasoning owes its existence to Pyrodex and Triple Seven pellets. With many in-line barrel lengths running between 22 and 30 inches, some manufacturers believe that any barrel length under 26 inches will be too short to totally burn three .50-caliber pellets. Although that may be true for pellets, it is not true for loose powder. You lose

A rifle is only as accurate as the hunter's aim. Most in-lines make use of optics for long-range shooting opportunities.

only 10 feet per second velocity for each inch shorter than 26 inches. Longer barrels do give a longer sighting radius for open sights, however; in other words, they can be a bit more accurate. Yet short carbines offer the luxury of lighter weights, many under 7 pounds, whereas their counterparts tip the scales at 8 to 10 pounds.

Barrel composition, regardless of whether you choose blued steel, nickel steel, or stainless steel, has more to do with cosmetics than performance. Fluting—grooves cut into the outside of the barrel—reduce the weight and increase the stiffness, which dampens barrel whip. Porting—slots cut through to the bore at the muzzle—reduce barrel jump, but they can be difficult to clean, even with the cleaner-burning replica powders.

Finally, the fourth key ingredient to in-line barrel performance is the sighting system. Without a doubt, you can shoot only as accurately as you can see the sights. After all, accuracy harvests whitetails, not overwhelming power. Open sights are usually standard on in-lines, but fiber-optic sights will enhance the sight picture in the low-light conditions found in forests. Hi-Viz Sight Systems offers add-on fiber-optic sights. These easy-to-install,

#11 standard cap	#11 magnum cap	U.S. #2 musket cap	#209 shotgun primer	#200 rifle primer
6.53 cc of gas at 3,024°F when fired	7.59 cc of gas at 3,717°F when fired	14.36 cc of gas at 3,717°F when fired	21.98 cc of gas at 3,024°F when fired	11.68 cc of gas at 3,024°F when fired

Percussion caps and primers

light-enhancing fiber-optic sights are low cost but are highly advantageous when it comes to seeing the target. But since scopes are legal for use in many states' muzzleloading seasons, you might want to consider them. Scopes restrict a shooter's field of view, but their magnification can add accuracy for distant targets. Variable scopes may be the best choice, as they allow the shooter to adjust to changes from dense undergrowth to open fields. What is important for barrel choice is that it be drilled and tapped for scope placement and that it allows for proper eye relief (usually 3 to 4 inches from the end to your eyebrow).

The next component that needs consideration is the ignition system. In-line percussion locks are available in five ignition configurations: (1) a standard #11 percussion cap lock, (2) an optional #2 musket cap lock, (3) a 209 shotgun primer ignition lock, (4) Knight disc and full plastic jacket locks, and (5) a small rifle primer. All of

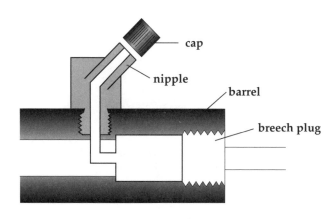

Percussion cap and nipple in place

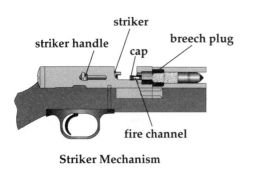

Striker Mechanism

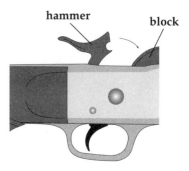

Rolling Block

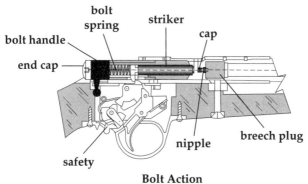

Bolt Action

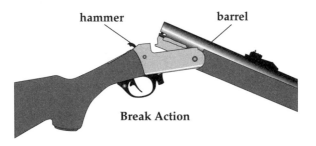

Break Action

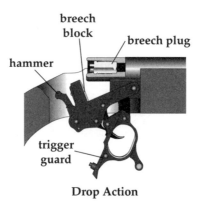

Drop Action

Different types of muzzleloader actions

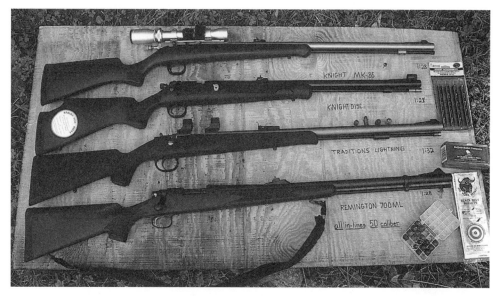

The earliest design—and still one of the most popular in-line actions—is the striker. It features a spring-driven, sliding bolt that moves forward to crush a percussion cap, musket cap, or 209 primer.

them are capable of igniting both bulk black powders and replica powders, as well as the various pellet technologies. But when the chips are down and the weather turns sour, it is nice to have a percussion cap that delivers the largest, hottest volume of powder-igniting gas available. That tips the scale in favor of the 209 shotgun primer, which has quickly become the industry standard.

An important item to remember in all these new "enhanced-ignition" muzzleloaders is that the nipples will eventually need replacement. The U.S. Olympic Muzzleloading Team changes a rifle's nipple after only 25 shots. They believe that the nipple erodes with every shot and will quickly affect the accuracy of the rifle. The touch hole in the base of the nipple widens, velocities fluctuate, and the flame temperature lowers; this may not give positive ignition to Pyrodex, especially in multiple pellets. So remember to examine the nipple and, when in doubt, replace it with a new stainless steel product. CVA is currently manufacturing the Perfect Nipple, Michaels of Oregon offers the Hot Shot, and Mountain State Muzzleloading has the Spit Fire Magnum. Each offers enhanced performance and is worth a look.

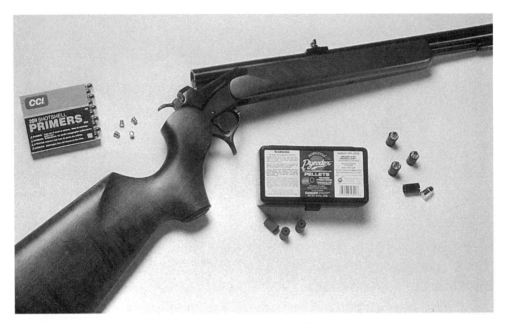

The break action in-line is gaining popularity because of the ease in priming and cleaning.

There are currently five popular types of lock actions for in-line muzzleloaders. The earliest design was the "striker." A sliding bolt is spring-driven forward into the percussion cap. It is a simple design and allows for a double safety, like that found on Knight Rifles. Strikers are found on models from Knight, T/C, Traditions, CVA, Marlin, Lyman, White, Gonic, Navy Arms, Cabela's, Bass Pro, Millennium Designed Muzzleloaders, and others. The second lock system is a rolling block-hammer design. This lock is limited to a few specialty guns made by Pedersoli for Cabela's. Reminiscent of rolling block guns made popular by the Civil War, it is strong and easy to clean. The third lock design is one that is familiar to most centerfire riflemen: the percussion bolt action. Increasingly popular, this strong and safe bolt design is found on Remingtons, Traditions, CVAs, Knights, and other top-of-the-class in-lines. They also are among the most expensive. The fourth design has been very successful for Thompson/Center. The break-action in-line, similar to break-action shotguns, is found on the T/C Encore 209×50, the MDM Buck-Waka, and Traditions' Pursuit. The fifth type of in-line lock design is the drop-down action and the swinging block breech design of Bass Pro's T/C Omega and Knight Rifles' Revolution. This is one of the easiest to clean in-line percussion systems because the entire breech-nipple portion is exposed for easy access.

The last piece of the lock, stock, and barrel trio is the part that holds the other two together—the stock. Although figured wood has long held a special spot in gun collectors' hearts, it apparently does not ignite the imagination of high-tech in-line manufacturers. Synthetic stocks of plastic, fiberglass, and carbon fiber composites are the rule, not the exception. Synthetic stocks do not swell in moisture or shrink in heat. They do not change the accuracy of the barrel in adverse weather, the way wood has been known to

Kevin Bailey used a T/C Omega .50-caliber in-line to take this Maryland seven-point buck. The Omega uses a swinging block action that makes the rifle impervious to weather.

do. But there are a few things that buyers should look for in a synthetic. First, make sure that the stock fits your body size and conformation. If you need a high comb or cheekpiece on the butt stock for proper scope alignment, make sure it is there. Recoil pads are a good idea if you plan to shoot those 150-grain loads behind a 300-grain bullet. Swivels make the whole rifle easier to carry on long walks to the stand or brush-busting deer drives to standers who are a mile away. The stock should also have a good gripping surface on the wrist and forearm. This was once created by checkering wood, but it has been replaced with impressed checkering, or raised contact surfaces. Thumb holes are great for target shooting but are necessary on a hunting arm. But the biggest consideration is weight. The whole idea of synthetic stocks is to reduce the weight of the stock for ease of carrying.

In-line percussion rifles have the ability to use any type of black powder or replica powders. GOEX, which has moved from Pennsylvania to Louisiana, remains the only domestic producer of black powder, but Petro-Explo, Inc., has found a faithful following for its new Swiss and Schuetzen brands. They are all the same black powder—that is, carbon, potassium nitrate, and sulfur—but subtle differences such as grain hardness and dustiness, as well as the source of the carbon, have fans lining up on opposite sides of the cans. But competition always makes a better product, so let's be happy that there is a choice.

Hodgdon Powder has opened up the muzzleloading field to magnum charges with its line of Pyrodex 50-grain pellets. Hodgdon also offers 30-grain pellets for hunters. Originally designed for pistol shooters, the 30-grain weight is ideal for mixing with 50-grain pellets to customize a load of 50-, 60-, 80-, 90- or 100-plus grain loads, something I have been patiently waiting for. The 150-grain magnum loads produce higher velocities than smaller offerings, but my money is on the more accurate, lower-recoil, customized loads. For those who shoot the big bores, .54 and .58, a larger-diameter 60-grain pellet will be produced in the near future.

Even more amazing ballistics and ease of cleaning have been introduced by Hodgdon's Triple Seven. Hunters would do well to try this new propellant in their in-lines, but remember that it is more potent than Pyrodex. Look carefully at the safe loading maximums.

The following list of in-line percussion, muzzleloading rifles barely scratches the surface of the great variety of modern muzzleloaders, but it will give new muzzleloading hunters a taste of what is available (see appendix B for manufacturer information).

One of the most beautiful of the in-line muzzleloaders is the Model 420 from Austin & Halleck. The classic stock profile carved into the high-grade curly maple stock, the 26-inch extrusion-formed barrel shaped from octagonal to round, the match-grade Timney triggers, and the short 0.199 hammer throw create an in-line beauty that achieves ultimate minute-of-angle accuracy at the range. The .50 comes in three choices of ignition: #11 cap, musket cap or 209 shotgun primer. Overall length is 47.5 inches, and it weighs 7.88 pounds. A composite stock is included with each rifle.

Cabela's is the primary U.S. retailer for the Pedersoli muzzleloading rifles. One gun that sets this company apart is the rolling block muzzleloader carbine. Available in .50 or .54 caliber, the 8.5-pound rifle operates on the old Remington rolling block frame, with percussion ignition.

CVA offers in-line shooters the affordable Optima 209 Magnum break-action. Available in .45 or .50 caliber, it has interchangeable-caliber, 26-inch barrels with 1:28 twist rifling. Stocked in composite or Mossy Oak Break-up camouflage, it uses illuminator fiber-optic sights. It is 41 inches overall, with recoil pad, and weighs 8.2 pounds. (In August 1997, CVA implemented a voluntary recall of in-line models with serial numbers ending in -95 or -96. If you have a CVA in-line with such a serial number, do not shoot it or allow anyone else to use the rifle. Call CVA immediately for details on how to return it.)

Knight Rifles has led the interest in in-line percussion rifles for the last decade, and Tony Knight's ongoing research and development efforts are constantly improving an already lethal, long-range system. A new accessory is the Knight Magnum Crossfire breech plug. The breech plug has a crosscut groove on its face that tapers downward into the firing channel. The grooves are wider than the Pyrodex pellet; this channels the ignition gases up the centerline hole as well as around the cylinder. Knight claims that the lock time is faster and that velocities increase by up to 25 feet per second. With more complete burning of the multiple pellets, fouling was noticed to decrease.

The Knight Disc Extreme Master Hunter in .45 or .50 caliber, with a 209 primer ignition system, has a cryogenically accurized, 26-inch, fluted stainless steel barrel. Stocked in black composite or laminated hardwood, it is 45 inches overall and weighs 7.5 pounds. Similarly, the .52 Disc Extreme is a .52-caliber ignited by a 209 primer ignition system with a Power Stem breech plug. It has a bolt action and a 26-inch stainless barrel with a 1:26 twist. It measures 45 inches overall and weighs 7.3 pounds.

The Knight Revolution uses a quick detachable pivoting breech action; its 27-inch barrel, blued or stainless steel, has 1:28 rifling. This .50-caliber rifle has a 209 primer ignition system; it comes in a variety of composite and camouflaged stocks and has an adjustable trigger. The Revolution is 43.24 inches long and weighs 7.8 pounds.

Percussion shooters who take to the modern lines of saddle guns will like the interchangeability of the new Markesbery line of muzzleloaders. The short, 24-inch barrels can be switched from a .36, .45, .50, or .54 caliber by simply dropping in the next barrel. Another new millennium idea is that they are ignited by a choice of percussion caps or the Small Rifle Primer (SRP) system, a bonus when greater ignition volume is desired.

Millennium Designed Muzzleloaders Ltd. offers either a .45- or .50-caliber, break-open action, 209 MDM Incinerating Ignition System in-line rifle with 1:24 rifling. It is stocked in either walnut or choice of camouflage. The rifle uses a transfer bar safety, has a 23- or 25-inch barrel or a 38.5- or 40.5-inch barrel, and is 6 to 6.5 pounds.

Remington Arms Company's Model 200 MLS Magnum is available in .45 or .50 caliber, with a three-way ignition option of #11, musket cap, or 209 shotgun primer in a short-throw bolt action. The 26-inch stainless steel barrel, satin finish, is mounted in a black or Mossy Oak Break-up camouflage synthetic stock. The in-line weighs in at 7.75 pounds and is 44.5 inches overall length.

Savage Arms rocked the muzzleloading world back on its heels with the introduction of a smokeless powder in-line rifle. The Savage 10ML-II features an Accu Trigger, 209 primer ignition, 24-inch stainless or blued steel barrel, composite Realtree Hardwoods camouflage synthetic stock, and recoil pad. The .50-caliber weighs 7.75 pounds and is 44 inches overall.

Thompson/Center took a radical departure from the earlier in-line muzzleloader designs with the break-action 209×50 Magnum and 209×45. Built on the '97 Encore rifle design, which has a break-open action and interchangeable barrels, the new rifle is offered in .50 caliber and is designed for 150 grains of FFg black powder or Pyrodex equivalent. A 209 shotgun primer provides ignition. When firing three 50-grain Pyrodex pellets and T/C's new Mag Express sabot with a 240-grain XTP bullet, the 209×50 Magnum produces a muzzle velocity of 2,203 feet per second and retains adequate energy and accuracy for deer-sized game to at least 200 yards. The 26-inch barrel of 4140 rifle-grade steel utilizes a 1:28 twist to stabilize sabotted bullets. Tru-Glo fiber-optic sights have a click-adjustable rear sight and front ramp sight, but hunters who plan on using the 200-yard terminal ballistics will need to consider adding a scope to this rig. The Encore Katahdin is a 20-inch ported barrel carbine version that weighs in at 6.8 pounds.

A sealed pivoting breech is now offered by T/C in the Omega. A .45- or .50-caliber, 209 primer, under-lever action rifle is taking in-lines to a new level in terms of modern looks. The 28-inch round or fluted barrel (available in stainless steel) is bedded in a Realtree Hardwoods camouflage composite stock. It weighs only 7 pounds, including recoil pad, and is 42 inches long.

Even the in-line muzzleloaders have seen improvements in ignition. Because pellets can be fickle when given an insufficient volume of hot gases, most manufacturers have changed from the #11 percussion cap and its lower volume of 3,024-degree flame to the larger volume of gas from the 209 shotgun primer cap. But the way the flame is delivered to the pellets in the breech of the rifle definitely affects how completely the magnum load of three pellets can be ignited. T/C solved this problem with the Flame Thrower ignition system, which throws a "ring of fire" into the main powder charge, in addition to the central core of fire. This increases the volume of fire to three times that of a conventional #11 cap flame coming through a standard nipple orifice. The T/C Black Diamond .50-caliber rifle employs this radical breech plug with three interchangeable systems—the #11, the 209 shotgun primer, and the higher-temperature flame (3,717 degrees) of the musket cap.

Modern in-lines continue to look and feel more like contemporary centerfires than like the traditional longrifles that started this craze back in the 1970s. Traditions Performance Firearms is offering to this new class of hunters a stainless steel, .50- or .54-caliber, bolt-action, fluted rifle with a screw-on muzzle brake (for reduced recoil), mounted in a high-definition advantage timber synthetic stock with a rubber recoil pad and Tru-Glo fiber-optic sights. This New Age Evolution muzzleloader belches sabotted bullets at better than 2,100 feet per second, again offering hunters a chance to extend their hunt beyond the 150-yard limit that is logical for an open-sighted gun.

Traditions also offers a break-open action in a new in-line called the Pursuit. It is .50 caliber with a 209 primer ignition, 1:28 rifling, and Tru-Glo adjustable fiber-optic sights; it is drilled and tapped for a scope and stocked in Mossy Oak Break-up synthetic with a recoil pad. The Pursuit is 42 inches long and weighs 8 pounds.

Those familiar with the old Sturm, Ruger, and Company, Inc., 77/22 rifles will feel right at home with the 77/50RS. This .50-caliber percussion rifle with a 22-inch barrel in stainless steel has a three-position safety, synthetic stock, and rubber recoil pad. A lightweight at 6.5 pounds, it is 42 inches long.

White Rifles (manufactured by Muzzleloading Technologies, Inc.) offers the Thunderbolt in-line in .451 or .504, with standard #11 (or magnum) percussion as well as 209 shotgun primer. It has a 26-inch straight, tapered stainless steel barrel with 1:24 rifling and

Tru-Glo fiber-optic steel hunting sights, mounted in a composite or laminated stock. A high-end Whitetail Odyssey laser-engraved white-tailed deer or elk scene is available in a thumb-hole stock.

Winchester Muzzleloading (a licensed brand of Blackpowder Products, Inc.) offers the Apex Magnum 209 rifle in either .45 or .50 caliber. The Apex uses a swing-action breech with a 209 primer and a 28-inch barrel. The stainless steel monoblock fluted barrel has 1:28 rifling, mounted in a composite black or Mossy Oak Break-up camouflage stock. Weighing in at 7.75 pounds, the Apex is 42 inches overall.

When it comes to support products for modern muzzleloaders, Uncle Mike's & Butler Creek Muzzle Loading Products have combined to offer a complete line of measurers, wrenches, cappers, short starters, and ramrods. A new offering, the Lightning Loader, is one of the fastest and safest preloaders for muzzleloaders, either roundball or sabotted bullet. It is made of static-proof polymers.

Breechloaders and Cartridge Guns

The breechloader is the last stage of transition between a primitive muzzleloader and a modern, smokeless powder, high-velocity cartridge rifle. Although it conjures up visions of brass shells flying through the air from rapid-fire repeating arms, black powder breechloaders are quite different. Early black powder breechloading rifles, pistols, and shotguns may have won the Wild West, but today they are best known and loved for their re-creation of the West. Cowboy action shooters number 70,000, and their ranks swell annually. Besides being used in a fun sport that re-creates part of our American history, black powder arms are increasingly being used to harvest deer and turkey. Gun actions, cartridge and shell types, and replica firearms are examined here. Their successful use in forest, fields, and prairie is also detailed.

The cowboys are back, and they're shooting old-fashioned, black powder breechloading guns at big game. In fact, the guns they are squeezing had fallen into obscurity, but they are now roaring back with Wild West, black powder fun and accuracy. In particular, the

.45-70 Government is once again grabbing the attention of history buffs, cowboy action shooters, and big-game hunters.

I first noticed this unusual cartridge knocking down iron silhouettes during a long-range cowboy action shoot at Topton, Pennsylvania. An iron gong, 160 yards away, was ringing with regularity as each competitor squeezed off the copper cartridge round, even though the target was obscured by the white smoke of black powder propellant. The huge 300-, 405- (original load), and 500-grain bullets commanded respect down-range, and of course, conversation centered around their telling effect on big game.

Jay Hassler, known to his friends as the "Lost Dutchman," was one of the first buckskinners to make the transition from muzzleloader to cowboy action shooter.

The transition from muzzleloading musket to breechloading rifle occurred as a military necessity. Even in the hands of the best riflemen, a musket could fire only three rounds a minute. The musket–to–trapdoor rifle conversion of the U.S. government Springfield 1861, a .58-caliber muzzleloader, allowed shooters to load and fire at more than double that rate. In fact, the Spencer carbine (personally endorsed by President Lincoln) was described by a Confederate soldier as a Yankee gun that was "loaded in the morning and fired all day." Even black powder's problem with the elements was finally solved. With a self-contained cartridge, weather was no longer a consideration.

Shortly after the .58 conversion to a cartridge, the U.S. Army adopted a new .50-caliber rifle musket breechloader. The Model 1863 became the 1868 trapdoor breechloader. The substitution of a new 36-inch barrel, rifled 1:42 with three grooves 0.0075-inch deep, gave the old rifle new life. The new barrel was screwed into the

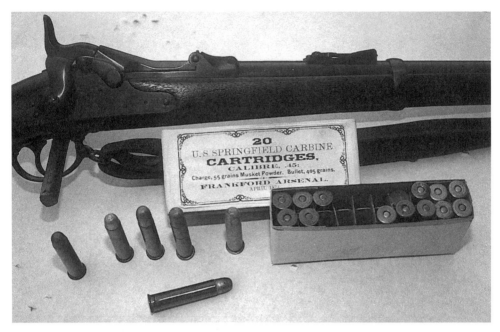

The Springfield .45-70 black powder rifle. This gun was originally made by taking the 1870 muzzleloading Springfield musket and replacing the old iron barrel with a stronger steel one.

receiver, or breech frame, in which the breech block would swing upward and forward for loading and extracting the cartridge.

The cartridge was a U.S. regulation centerfire metallic cartridge consisting of a copper case, 70 grains of musket-grade black powder, a tin plate cup filled with a half grain of percussion fulminate, and topped with a 450-grain, round-nose, all lubed lead bullet. This cartridge was known as the Frankford, as it was made at the Frankford Arsenal. A package of 20 cartridges weighed 2 pounds 2 ounces (1 kilogram). An 1866-patent, Remington pistol .50-caliber rolling block Model 1871 also went into production. It shot a reduced load of 34 grains of black powder and a 460-grain conical bullet.

During the late 1860s, Buffalo Bill Cody used a .50-70 Springfield Trapdoor that he named "Lucretia Borgia" to handle his meat-hunting duties for the railroads. In a shooting contest against a lighter .44-caliber Spencer rifle, Buffalo Bill took down 69 bison in just one day to seal his identity in Wild West folklore.

The .50-70 cartridge was a good round, but its heavier weight and reduced velocity opened the door for the now popular .45-70.

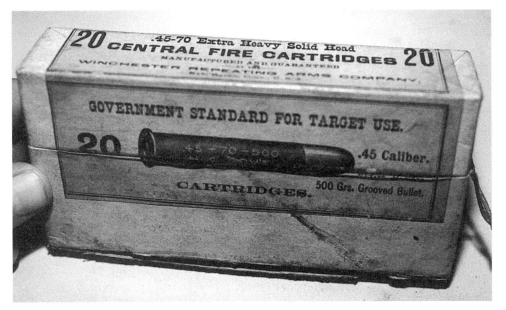

The Springfield .45-70 had a copper case known as the rifle ball cartridge .45.

In 1873, the Springfield .45-70 rifle, which was made from the 1870 muzzleloading Springfield musket, replaced the old iron barrel with a steel barrel. With the caliber reduced from .50 to .45, the three-groove rifling (0.005 inch) had a faster 1:22 rifling for better stabilization of the long bullets. Known as the rifle ball cartridge .45, the copper case contained 70 grains (55 grains for the carbine version) of musket powder, a copper cap with half a grain of percussion fulminate, and a 405-grain lubed lead round-nosed bullet. Later bullets adopted the 500-grain slug. The bullets were cast from 12 parts lead to 1 part tin. They were "compressed 1.11 bullets" with three grease grooves, 0.458 inch in diameter, and the cannelures (grease grooves) were filled with bayberry tallow or Japan wax.

It is interesting to note that these rifles were cleaned with plain old water-soaked rags and lubed with petroleum jelly or sperm oil. By today's standards, the .45-70 velocity seems quite slow, but penetration was impressive. The velocity of 1,330 feet per second (1,150 for the carbine), which was measured at 50 feet from the muzzle and printed on the box, would not fire the imaginations of shooters today. But the .45-70 carried 1,257 foot-pounds of energy (930 foot-pounds for the carbine) to 100 yards and penetrated through 17.2 inches of pine boards (14.5 for the carbine). This made the rifle dangerous on man-sized (or deer-sized) targets out to 1,000 yards.

The .45-70-405 was a cartridge created for the U.S. military in 1873. It was a .45-caliber round loaded with 70 grains of black powder inside its large brass case. Its huge 405-grain, all-lead bullet was impressive for its long-range knockdown power. It was noticed immediately by the buffalo and grizzly bear hunters of the West but eventually found its way into sporting rifles in the East. Trapdoor, rolling block, and falling block single-shots were chambered for this big-bore cartridge in the 1870s, but it soon found appeal in lever- and bolt-action sporting rifles.

About the same time that the 1873 Springfield rifle was being passed out to the U.S. Army, the Remington 1872 rolling block .45-70 was beginning to win acceptance. Hunters soon noticed its long-range performance and were asking for sporting versions.

Although many types of rifles were used by bison hunters, the one name that really stands out is the Sharps Model 1874 (originally designed in 1869). There were 11 cartridge offerings for this famous buffalo gun—from .40-70 on the small-caliber end to .50-90 on the big end—but the .45-120-500 Sharps, according to some experts, was a favorite, along with the less expensive .45-70-500. Most cowboy action shooters and hunters opt for the latter, as there is much less recoil and they are less expensive to operate.

Reproduction Sharps sporting rifles are available from C. Sharps Arms, Inc. The line includes 1874, 1875, and 1877 Sharps, as well as the 1885 Highwall.

The concept of a repeating rifle was made possible by the black powder cartridge, but it took the inventiveness of B. Tyler Henry and the resources of Oliver Fisher Winchester to make the concept a reality. The .44 rimfire, 1860 Henry lever action created a revolution in gun making. What followed was a huge demand for and interest in repeating arms, as well as an explosion in new calibers and cartridge design.

The Winchester repeating rifle, Model 1873, was the first repeating rifle to use centerfire cartridges. Deer hunters love this rifle because it is lightweight, easy to load and fire, and accurate to long distances. One of the most popular calibers created for the '73

Illustrations of the Model 1873 Winchester's repeating rifle system, with the action closed and open, taken from an 1899 Winchester catalog.

is the .44 Winchester centerfire, also known as the .44-40. It contains about 40 grains of black powder and a 200-grain, flat-nosed lead bullet. Accurate up to 300 yards, it was described by Winchester as "sufficiently powerful to kill bear, deer, antelope, and mountain sheep." Cowboy action shooters love this cartridge because there are many pistols chambered for it, such as the Colt Single-Action Army and the Ruger Vaquero.

The Winchester Model 1873 was available in many cartridge sizes that still survive today. The .32-20 and .38-40 calibers were just barely enough for a deer load. The .32-20 Winchester cartridge has been used on deer but is better suited for small game out to 100 yards. Loaded with 20 grains of black powder and carrying a 115-grain, flat-nosed lead bullet, it makes a great rifle for turkey hunting.

The Winchester repeating rifle, Model 1873, was the first repeating rifle to use centerfire cartridges.

A cowboy action shooter works well with the .44-40 because of its accuracy, ease of loading, and compatibility with either rifle or pistol. It is also a favorite among deer hunters using black powder cartridges.

The Winchester Model 94 had two new cartridge choices: the .38-55 and the .32-40. By expanding the .32 and .38 caliber brass cases, additional room for powder gave the bullets greater velocity and terminal energy.

Winchester continued on the path to bigger and better deer hunting cartridges with the Winchester Model 1894. Smokeless cartridges were beginning to elbow the black powder fare out of the way, but Winchester still felt the demand for basic black. The Model 1894 had two new offerings; the .38-55 and .32-40 gave additional power to two existing cartridges in those calibers. By expanding the .38- and .32-caliber brass cases, the additional room for powder boosted velocity and terminal energy.

The biggest surprise to most twenty-first-century riflemen is that the little .22 short and .22 long rimfire cartridges were first loaded with black powder and shot in some of the Winchester '73s. The .22 short used 3 grains of black powder and a 30-grain lead bullet. The .22 long carried 5 grains of black powder and a 35-grain lead bullet.

The Marlin Model 1881 was the first lever-action rifle designed to handle the power of the .45-70 Government cartridge. For a while, it was the most powerful lever-action rifle on earth, and it paved the

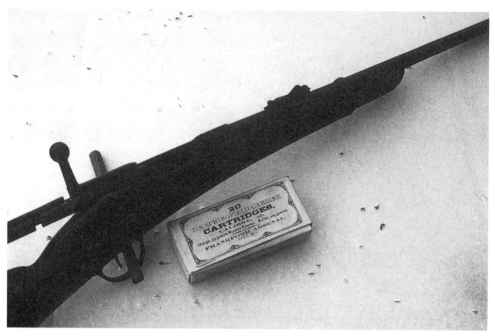

Winchester built the Model 1883 Hotchkiss repeating rifle in a .45-70 bolt action. Not as quick to reload and fire as the lever action, it did possess the accuracy and power that western riflemen demanded.

way for the retirement of the single-shot Remingtons and Sharps. The Marlin was also chambered for the .40-60 Marlin, which is a good choice for deer hunters who want a reduced recoil load.

While manufacturers were feverishly trying to market powerful repeating arms, bolt actions were entering the fray. Winchester built the Model 1883 Hotchkiss repeating rifle in a .45-70 bolt action. Although not as quick to fire as the lever action, it possessed the accuracy and power that western riflemen were demanding. Actually, it wasn't until 1886 that Winchester had a strong enough receiver to support the pressures of the .45-70 and its variants. Still in high demand with hunters, the Winchester 1886 was the only lever-action rifle strong enough to support the recoil of cartridges such as the .45-70-500 and .50-100-450.

So what kind of ballistics can a hunter expect from a black powder cartridge rifle? The table below gives a sample of popular cartridges' velocities and muzzle energies. These measures are approximate because of variables such as (1) Black powder type (e.g., GOEX, KIK, Wano, Elephant, Schuetzen, Swiss) or replica powders (e.g., Pyrodex, Triple Seven, American, Clear Shot, Clean Shot), (2) weight of the bullet, (3) barrel length, (4) primer volume, and (5) seating depth of the bullet.

Cartridge	Grains (black powder FFg)	Bullet (grains)	Velocity (feet per second)	Energy (foot-pounds)
.25-20	20	86	1,304	325
.32-40	40	165	1,385	703
.38-55	55	255	1,285	935
.40-65	55	400	1,195	1,269
.45-70	70	350	1,307	1,328
.45-70	70	405	1,271	1,453
.45-70	70	500	1,179	1,544
.50-95	95	300	1,493	1,485
.50-110	110	450	1,383	1,912

Note: This does not represent a safe loading guide. Please follow the manufacturer's recommendations.

The .45-70 cartridge was America's favorite choice for hunting until the 1900s, when the speed and accuracy of the smokeless powder .30-40 Krag and .30-06 Springfield overshadowed the venerable cowboy cartridges. But like a fine wine, good things improve with age. The interest in this big bore is roaring back, and according to the Marlin Rifle Company, its lever-action Model 1895, the Guide Gun, is one of its hottest-selling models. Remington Arms recently reintroduced its .45-70 Rolling Block Sporter, while Browning, Ruger, New England Firearms, and Thompson/Center feature the cartridge in their modern actions. Custom makers such as Shiloh, C. Sharps, and Pedersoli have provided period productions for years. Even this country's "Big Three" ammunition makers are producing factory loads. Remington even offers the original 405-grain, all-lead slug.

The temptation was too much. I had to try this black powder cartridge on big game, and the black bear seemed an ideal challenge. The trip was arranged.

The first night on stand was quiet, but not the second. I settled into the blind, loaded my black powder Winchester Model 1886,

The bear I took with a .45-70 Government black powder cartridge.

and scanned the dark spruce woods beyond the baited hollow log. I sensed something moving. Instead of a 200-pound *Ursus americanus* lurking in the shadows, a snowshoe hare popped out from under a log. Nearby, a pair of ravens squawked their disapproval. Suddenly, a massive dark object slipped in from the right, using the exact same path I had just walked. Nose to the broken grass, silently as a ghost, the baron of the north woods confronted this intruder's trail—right up to the ladder!

Inside the tree-stand blind, I could only imagine what was happening below me, since the small screened window wasn't designed for watching wildlife below the ladder. Two powerful shakes of the ladder, a muffled *whuff,* and the bear ambled away toward the bait, having established his territorial dominance of this situation. It was only after I regained my composure that I remembered why I was here. The white cloud of smoke from the 70 grains of FFg obscured the black bear. The large 405-grain slug found its mark. The hunt was over in a blinding flash, but the memories, as powerful as the .45-70 Government black powder cartridge, were just beginning.

Rifles aren't the only black powder breechloading guns available to deer and turkey hunters. Pistols have had a place throughout history as a backup weapon, along with a long knife or tomahawk. That all changed with the advent of the powerful cartridge pistols.

In 1836, Samuel Colt visited the Henry Gun Works in Boulton, Pennsylvania, to secure several hundred gun barrels for his new

Pistols have had a place throughout history as a backup weapon, much like a long knife or tomahawk.

factory in Paterson, New Jersey. Even the state of South Carolina contracted for arms from the Henrys, and demand brought additional employees and residences to the area. According to Robert Frick, curator of the Henry Plantation and Gun Works, "When there were government contracts, there were government inspectors, and with all of the work being done by hand, many pieces failed to pass. William made a deal with his brother to sell him the condemned gun parts. He rented work space and hired some twenty workers to assemble usable, but cheap, guns which he sold to South Americans, including the brother of Simon Bolivar, the liberator of South America."

The trade gun business continued up to the Civil War. The high demand led to an increasing use of machines to do the tedious jobs that were once done by hand. But the flintlock ignition system was most often given to the trade gun because it was preferred by the American Indian. James Henry (son of John Joseph) and his son Granville witnessed the demand for percussion rifles from 1836

ABRAHAM HENRY - LANCASTER
1790 - 1811
62 - CALIBER FLINTLOCK PISTOL
FEATURES BOTH A BRASS BARREL AND A
BRASS LOCK ENGRAVED WITH (A. HENRY)
INSIDE A SCROLL UNDER THE PAN &
A DELICATE BRASS SKELETAL SIDE PLATE.
APPEARS TO HAVE BEEN RESTOCKED

The flintlock ignition system was most often used in the trade guns—both pistols and rifles—because it was preferred by the American Indians. But once repeating revolvers became available, the muzzleloaders were quickly discarded.

through 1895. These were years of heavy competition among gun manufacturers during the Civil War and later for sporting arms. But the demand for new innovations in technology is what drove the wheels of the gun makers' industry. Enter the breechloader.

Mass production by companies such as Remington and Winchester brought about the demise of the Henry Gun Works, and by 1907, the last of the Henry guns that were being assembled from old parts were sold. Thus ended six generations of Henry gun makers. Today, the Henry Plantation is located in the small town of Belfast, just west of PA Route 33. It consists of the J. J. Henry home, the William Henry Jr. homestead, and the original site of the Henry Gun Works. The saga of this prolific gun-making family is revealed to visitors of the museum. Ingenuity was the hallmark of the family. It established one of the first assembly lines in the United States to exploit the concept of interchangeable parts. This is usually, but errantly, credited to Eli Whitney. The Henry firearm was not noted for its artistic flair. Instead, it became one of the most desirable weapons because of it durability, accuracy, and low cost.

Cartridge conversion of both Colt and Remington pistols paved the way for the black powder breechloaders. Today, several importers are bringing in these replicas from Italy for both the Single Action Shooting Society's cowboy action shooters and for hunters.

By the late 1860s, Colt began a conversion of the 1860 Army and 1851 Navy pistols. Calibers from .38 rimfire to .32 and .38 centralfire were the first to be offered. As development continued, the .44 Colt and .45 Colt became the heavier and more popular cartridges. Some have said that the invention of the Colt pistol made the saber obsolete. These cartridge conversion pistols are once again available. America Remembers markets 1851 Navy and 1860 Army Richards conversions in .38 special, .38 long Colt, and .44 Colt black powder cartridge models. Navy Arms markets the 1851 Navy Richards–type conversion pistol in .38 special and .38 long Colt.

Although .38-caliber pistols tend to be too low-powered for deer hunting, they are plenty of medicine for turkey. But the larger calibers such as the .44-40 and .45 Colt should be used only in close encounters. By far, the single most popular caliber used by the modern cowboys in their pistol matches is the .45 Colt. The Ruger Vaquero chambered in .45 Colt and .44-40 Winchester is a good choice for hunters. The Hartford Armory markets a classic Remington 1875 in .45 Colt, as well as the .45 Colt magnum. Cimarron, F.A. Co., Inc., specializes in the .32-20 black powder cartridge pistol as well as other calibers.

An interesting conversion pistol is the R&D drop-in conversion cylinder from Taylor's & Co., Inc. A shooter can switch from a percussion .44 to a .45 long Colt by changing cylinders.

Many cowboy action shooters and hunters are using black powder cartridge rifles and pistols from A. Uberti, an Italian firm whose guns are imported by Stoeger Industries.

If you are looking for ammunition to fit your black powder breechloader, one good source is Black Hills Ammunition. A good source of new, unprimed brass for these old breechloaders is Starline.

Black powder cartridge pistols definitely accounted for a lot of tombstones on the boot hills of the West, but they don't have the power to be adequate deer-getters at distances beyond 25 yards. The ballistics in the following table are approximate and apply only to relative energies when hunting smaller game.

Cartridge	Grains (black powder FFg)	Bullet (grains)	Velocity (feet per second)	Energy (foot-pounds)
.38-40	30	175	772	232
.44-40	30	200	756	254
.45 Schofield	27	250	699	271
.45 Colt	33	250	760	321

Note: This does not represent a safe loading guide. Please follow the manufacturer's recommendations.

Shotguns are the third leg of the cowboy action shooters' competition. For turkey hunters especially, there is no greater thrill than to see a bronze-feathered gobbler on the other side of a brass bead dropped in its tracks, thanks to a cloud of swarming lead shot and a cloud of white smoke.

Breechloading shotguns, loaded with black powder–filled brass cartridges, shoot very similarly to percussion muzzleloading shot-

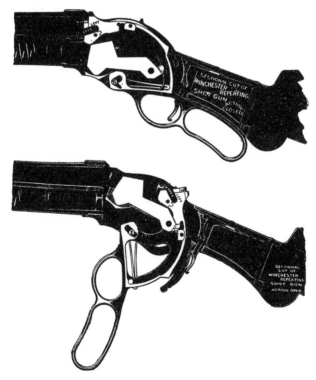

Closed- and open-action illustrations of a Winchester lever-action shotgun, taken from the 1899 catalog.

Shotguns are the third leg of the cowboy action shooters' competition.

guns. The only difference is in the speed of loading the next shot. The brass 10-, 12-, 16-, or 20-gauge shotgun cartridges are themselves muzzleloaders, as they load from the top.

By the late 1860s, while the military and buffalo hunters were focusing on powerful and accurate breechloading rifles, the rest of the nation was buying shotguns. Why? Simply stated, they hit what they were pointed at. Between the Civil War and the end of the nineteenth century, no fewer than 70 manufacturers were busy supplying breechloading black

The hunter with a shotgun will find turkey hunting to be especially satisfying.

Breechloading shotguns, loaded with black powder brass cartridges, shoot with ballistics that are very similar to percussion muzzleloaders.

powder shotguns. Many of these guns were imported, primarily from Belgium, although other European countries added their own flair. Winchester 1879 double-barrel shotguns were actually imports from makers such as Bonehill, McEntree, Redman, and W. C. Scott & Sons. Thirty- and 32-inch barrels were the norm for the brass 2⁷/₈-inch, 10-gauge cartridge shotgun or the 2⅝-inch, 12-gauge shotgun. Sixteen-gauge shotguns had a choice of 28-, 30-, or 32-inch barrels. Whereas rolled steel was used for the normal-grade barrel, Damascus steel barrels were used on higher-grade shotguns. Today, we know that it is inadvisable to shoot black powder, or anything else, through Damascus steel shotgun barrels.

Colt, famous for its pistols, also got involved in the manufacture of black powder cartridge, breechloading shotguns. The Colt Model 1878 exposed-hammer, Damascus-barreled 12-gauge double was one of the many popular stagecoach guard guns (which gave rise to the popular phrase, "I'll ride shotgun!"). It wasn't until the 1880s that "hammerless" models of single- and double-barrel shotguns began to be marketed. With external hammers driving a firing pin into the "centralfire" brass shotgun cartridges, these shotguns closely resembled their percussion forefathers.

The Colt Model 1878 12-gauge was a favorite of stagecoach guards.

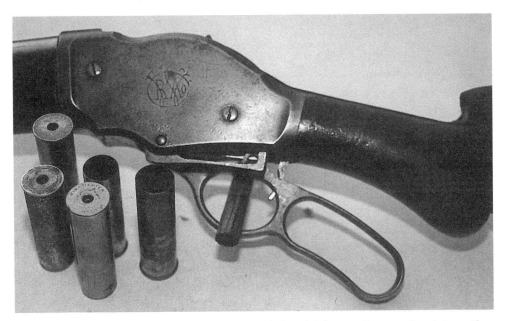

Winchester broke with tradition and introduced a single-barreled, lever-action repeating shotgun, the Model '87.

Winchester once again broke with tradition and introduced a single-barrel, lever-action, repeating shotgun. The Winchester Model 1887 gave shooters the opportunity to put as many as six shots (five in the magazine) into the air before having to reload. The Model '87 was available at first in 12-gauge, but later models were supplied with 10-gauge barrels. Three-blade Damascus bar-

Toward the end of the black powder cartridge era, Winchester began to market the Model 1893 slide action shotgun in response to brisk sales by competitors.

rels were offered for $15 more, while fine Damascus barrels were an extra $20. Full choke was standard but was not stamped on the barrel. Modified and cylinder-bore models were also available. In spite of the new technology, only 64,855 of these guns were made. Many shooters still loved the ease and reliability of the venerable double-barrel. In response, Winchester began using the Model 1887 action for a very powerful black powder cartridge, the .70-150-700, a gun reputed to be a killer at both ends.

Toward the end of the black powder cartridge era, Winchester began to market the Model 1893 slide-action (pump) shotgun in response to brisk sales by competitors. This 12-gauge had barrels in rolled steel, as well as three-blade and four-blade Damascus barrels. Although the receiver was adequate only for black powder pressures, this gun was introduced at the same time as smokeless powder. Winchester pressed hard to keep black powder in the shooting sports. One advertisement read: "To get good results in shotgun shooting it is necessary to have a load that makes an even pattern, gives good penetration and is reliable and uniform in every way. Winchester 'Nublack' and 'New Rival' Black Powder Shotgun Shells are just such loads. The next time you buy, insist upon having them. You can't get better black powder loads no matter what you pay. Ask for the Red W brand." Unfortunately, the higher pressures of the nitrocellulose smokeless powders destroyed many of these fine guns, and Winchester soon recalled many of the '93s.

Black powder breechloading cartridges for shotguns are fun to shoot and are quite capable of taking deer and turkey. But before you take that venerable old shotgun out for a romp, take it to a licensed gunsmith for a proper checkup. Don't be surprised if the gunsmith tells you that the old wrapped steel or Damascus gun should be left on the wall. No Damascus steel shotgun should be shot unless it is certified safe by a licensed gunsmith. The beautiful swirling metal patterns lack the structural integrity necessary for safe shooting because the old welds have degraded with time. But many of the old fluid steels and steel tubes may be safe for shooting black powder only.

During the safety check, the gunsmith can also check for the length of the shotshell chamber. This is important. The 10-gauge was manufactured in $2^5/8$-, $2^3/4$-, and 3-inch models; the 12-gauge in $2^1/2$-, $2^3/4$-, and 3-inch chambers; the 16 gauge in $2^1/2$- and $2^3/4$-inch chambers. You can't force a 3-inch shell into a shorter chamber without dire consequences.

There are several companies that supply components for black powder cartridges. Dixie Gun Works has a huge catalog of black powder guns and shooting supplies. Ballistic Products, Inc., has a full line of reloading supplies for shotshells. Black powder shotshells and reloading supplies are available from Ammodirect. Twelve-gauge black powder cartridges are available in $7^1/2$ shot from Ten-X Ammunition, which also carries other hard to find black powder era cartridges, such as the Spencer .56-50. Circle Fly Wads has been providing Nitro, Overshot, and Vegetable Wads for muzzleloading shotguns for decades and has a full assortment of sizes for shotgun cartridges as well.

The following table of black powder loading data for breechloading shotgun cartridges and shotshells is courtesy of Hodgdon Powder Company. The black powder used was in FFg granulation.

Gauge	Chamber (inches)	Grains/Drams	Shot (oz.)	Muzzle Velocity (feet per second)
10	$2^5/8$	$95/3^1/2$	$1^3/8$	1,057
10	$2^3/4$	109/4	$1^1/2$	1,040
10	3	$123/4^1/2$	$1^3/4$	1,060
10	$3^1/2$	140/5	$1^5/8$	1,150
12	$2^1/2$	82/3	$1^1/8$	1,069
12	$2^3/4$	$92/3^3/8$	$1^1/4$	1,050
12	3	$102/3^3/4$	$1^1/2$	1,044
16	$2^1/2$	$75/2^3/4$	1	1,010
16	$2^3/4$	82/3	11/8	972

The following table gives Pyrodex and Triple Seven data for breechloading shotguns, courtesy of Hodgdon Powder. The Pyrodex cartridge grade (CTG) is loaded by volume in grains, and the internal breech pressure is measured in lead units of pressure (LUP).

Gauge	Chamber (inches)	Shot (oz.)	Wad Column	Volume (grains)	Velocity (feet per second)
10	$3^1/2$	2	Card & filler	140 CTG	1,154
10	$2^7/8$	$1^5/8$	Card & filler	105 CTG	1,115
12	$2^3/4$	$1^1/8$	Card & filler	100 CTG	1,043
12	$2^3/4$	$1^1/8$	WAA12R	70 CTG	1,100
12	$2^3/4$	$1^1/8$	WAA12R	70 "777"	1,187
12	$2^3/4$	$1^1/4$	Card & filler	90 CTG	1,039
12	$2^3/4$	$1^1/2$	Card & filler	90 CTG	1,012
16	$2^3/4$	1	Card & filler	90 CTG	1,128
16	$2^3/4$	$1^1/8$	Card & filler	80 CTG	1,095
16	$2^2/4$	$1^1/4$	Card & filler	80 CTG	1,040
20	$2^3/4$	$7/8$	Card & filler	80 CTG	1,134
20	$2^3/4$	1	Card & filler	70 CTG	1,090
20	$2^3/4$	$1^1/8$	Card & filler	65 CTG	1,052

Any brand shotshell can be used to create these loads. Simply put the correct charge of Pyrodex or Triple Seven (by volume) into the case and adjust the wad column height for a good crimp. Powder charges are measured in an adjustable powder measurer that is designed for black powder. Do not use a powder measurer designed for smokeless powders.

Generally, one .200 nitro wad over the powder and a ¹/₂-inch felt cushion wad will give a column height close to the correct length. The addition of .050 nitro wads to the column will allow for height adjustments for different hulls. A shot collar or shot cup can be used to contain the shot charge with no adjustment to the powder charge. *Caution:* Damascus barrels should be considered unsafe with any powder.

Pistols and Revolvers

Muzzleloading pistols (single-shot) and revolvers have always been part of the muzzleloading sports, but they are increasing in importance as sidearms for the hunt. Flintlocks, percussions, Old Army, New Army, Colt Walkers, and other muzzleloading pistols are commonly seen at ranges. Brass and steel frames, loading levers, and other pistol nomenclature differ from that related to muzzleloading rifles and need to be understood. Target loads, hunting loads, safety precautions, and tricks for sighting a pistol are examined in this section.

When shooters gather at the line during the National Muzzle Loading Rifle Association's national championships, there is little time for conversation. This place called Friendship, a small town in southern Indiana, attracts the most intense, most driven, most focused shooters who ever held a muzzleloader. They are the best, by both reputation and performance.

But after the smoke clears and the line shuts down for the day, conversations turn to "Where are you from?" and "How'd you do on deer this year?" Most of the competitors are also avid whitetail hunters. But anyone from Pennsylvania seems to attract an unusual amount of attention.

Friendship, Indiana, is the home of the National Muzzle Loading Rifle Association. It attracts some of the most driven and focused shooters that ever held a muzzleloader.

One hot topic that caused heads to turn was a possible change in the law that would allow Pennsylvanians to use flintlock pistols for deer hunting. Marty Murphy, an Indiana resident, past president of the NMLRA, and a highly regarded pistol competitor, quipped, "Most pistols don't have enough energy to ethically down a deer, and the well-known inaccuracy of flintlock pistols makes this change a curiosity. Who wanted this law changed, anyway?"

The group of Pennsylvanians who were the focus of this conversation couldn't answer either the "who" or the "why." Sharon Cunningham, retired editor of *Muzzle Blasts* magazine and current marketing director for Dixie Gun Works (the largest retailer of muzzleloaders in the United States), was asked for answers. She said, "I can't think of any production flintlock pistols that would be adequate for deer hunting. We carry a lot of production pistols, both domestic and foreign, and only a very few percussion revolvers or percussion single-shots are up to the task. Isn't a flintlock rifle enough of a challenge for you guys in Pennsylvania?"

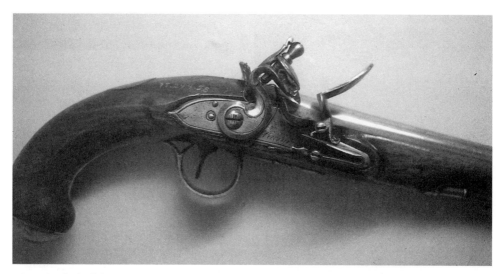

Most pistols don't have enough energy to down a deer ethically, and the well-known inaccuracy of flintlock pistols make their use in hunting questionable.

Is the flintlock pistol ethical for humane deer harvests? If the benchmark is 500 foot-pounds of energy (according to the American Hunting Institute) delivered by a bullet to the deer, regardless of distance, then the answer is no. A study of ballistics for most of the flintlock pistols in .44 or .45 caliber available to Pennsylvania's hunters shows that a normal load of 25 to 40 grains of FFFg black powder will deliver a roundball with a muzzle velocity of 859 to 1,153 feet per second; a conical bullet would be considerably slower. This results in energies between 211 and 381 foot-pounds at the muzzle. When considering how quickly these bullets shed their energy, they are unethical choices.

To achieve the required lethality of 500 foot-pounds, a hunter would need a .58 Harpers Ferry type of flintlock pistol, loaded with 60 grains of FFg and a 525-grain minié. This load recoils very heavily, is less than accurate, and borders on dangerous. The neighboring states of Ohio, Maryland, New Jersey, and Virginia don't allow muzzleloading pistols in their special seasons, and Delaware allows them only for a coup de grace shot. New York allows black powder pistols of .44-plus caliber, as does Kentucky, which requires the load to achieve 500 foot-pounds, but these hunters are using percussion revolvers, not flintlocks.

To achieve the necessary 500 foot-pounds of energy, a hunter would need a .58-caliber Harpers Ferry–type flintlock loaded with 60 grains of FFg and a 525-grain minié-type bullet.

Pennsylvania has prided itself on its impeccable safety record during the special flintlock deer season, which is largely due to the nature of single-shot rifles using low-powered roundball loads. What might transpire with flintlock pistols (which have no safety device other than an unloaded primer pan and half-cock position of the hammer) remains to be seen. How would the pistol be carried? Inside a pocket? (Illegal, since it would then be considered a concealed weapon, requiring a special handgun license.) Inside a belt? By hand? Held like a flintlock rifle? Fortunately, the Game Commission dropped the idea. One might say that it was just a flash in the pan.

But questions remain. What is the role of the muzzleloading pistol? Are there any black powder pistols that can adequately take deer and turkey? How much power do these muzzleloading hand cannons have?

Many muzzleloading pistols of colonial America began their lives as damaged rifle barrels. As gunsmiths rifled the wrought-iron barrels, the cutting tooth that was pulled through the barrel's bore sometimes struck a weak spot in the iron, causing a gouge or imperfection in the rifling. Rather than take a loss on the whole barrel, which was a huge investment in time, the gunsmith took a hacksaw to the good parts of the barrel, and three or four pistol barrels were created. This was a rather inauspicious birth for a handy frontier tool, but it explains why so many early flintlock pistols had almost straight rifling (1:60 to 1:72 was a common twist for flintlock longrifles). Besides, colonial frontiersman used the pistol like a belt knife or a tomahawk in close quarters. It finished the

Many short-barreled pistols in colonial America began their lives as sawed-off pieces of damaged rifle barrel. This did not give them the proper rate of rifling for accurate shooting.

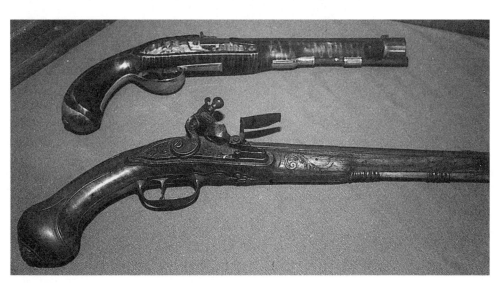

Most flintlock pistols were prone to misfire because of their small flints and locks, though this was not the case with the higher-grade dueling pistols.

hunt; it didn't initiate it. No one really hunted with a single-shot flintlock unless it was used for the coup de grace shot that dispatched a downed animal.

Flintlock pistols were prone to misfire because of the small flints and locks. They possessed too little powder and too light-weight of a bullet to have much energy. They carried poor sighting systems. Some had no rear sight and used only a brass "barley-corn" bead for a front sight. But most of all, they were a real nuisance to carry around. This was not true of the high-grade dueling pistols. But only aristocrats, officers, and gentlemen could afford to purchase these finely crafted, high-end target pistols. Carefully fitted with fast locks and more accurate sighting systems, they were the state of the art at the time.

Single-shot percussion pistols increased the speed of the lock time. They fired faster than the flintlock, were more certain to fire, and made a more accurate arm. The half century of improvements in pistol technology since the Revolution made these nineteenth-century hand cannons a serious firearm. Faster rifling (1:20 was the average) provided better stability for the bullets, which were slower velocity than the same-caliber rifles. This included the expanded offering of both roundballs and the newer conical slugs. Better rear and front sights, and even more ergonomic pistol grips, were causing this new class of pistol to turn heads.

While still an adjunct weapon, chosen for close quarters, the early muzzleloading pistol was not yet ready for the deer woods. It wasn't that large-caliber (.58 to .69) barrels couldn't throw a deadly mass of lead. Instead, the problem that remained was that the large mass of lead had real problems hitting its target.

The following table gives pistol velocities and muzzle energies. These values are approximate because of variables such as (1) black powder type (e.g., GOEX, KIK, Wano, Elephant, Schuetzen, Swiss) or replica powders (e.g., Pyrodex, Triple Seven, American Pioneer, Clear Shot, Clean Shot), (2) bullet weight, (3) barrel length, (4) size of touch hole or percussion primer volume, and (5) depth of rifling and thickness of patching. This table verifies that early flintlock and percussion single-shot pistols didn't possess the energy needed to drop a deer.

Cartridge	Grains (black powder)	Bullet (grains)	Velocity (feet per second)	Energy (foot-pounds)
	FFFG			
.45	20	128 Roundball	920	241
	25	128 Roundball	1,020	296
	30	128 Roundball	1,100	344
	FFg			
.50	25	177 Roundball	780	239
	30	177 Roundball	880	304
	35	177 Roundball	930	340
	40	177 Roundball	980	378
	40	245 Buffalo Ball-et	910	451
.54	35	230 Roundball	790	319
	40	230 Roundball	840	360
	45	230 Roundball	890	405
	50	230 Roundball	930	442
	50	310 Buffalo Ball-et	810	452

Note: This does not represent a safe loading guide. Please follow the manufacturer's recommendations.

Why are so many people enamored with single-shot flintlock and percussion pistols? The answer is multifaceted, but part of it lies in nostalgia. These old colonial and pre–Civil War pistols were carried at Bunker Hill, Sarasota, Valley Forge, and Yorktown. They extended the frontier settlements through the Appalachians and Alleghenies, across the wide Missouri, and into the Rocky Mountains. Without a doubt, they were as much a part of the American saga as the frontiersmen, who wouldn't think of leaving home without one.

There are many replicas of these early single-shot muzzleloading pistols. Dixie Gun Works markets an early colonial style, the Kentucky-Pennsylvania .45 (flintlock or percussion) with a 10.25-

inch barrel made by Pedersoli. The Harpers Ferry .58 flintlock, also with a 10-inch barrel, is a heavy hitter in terms of energy. And for a higher-end dueling pistol, Dixie offers a .45 percussion English dueling pistol with an 11-inch octagonal barrel. Those interested in optimal accuracy may want to consider the Le Page target pistol .44 percussion.

An interesting diversion from the rifled pistol is a flintlock trade pistol in 28, 24, and 20 gauge from North Star West, Inc. With a smoothbore, 10-inch, browned octagonal to round barrel, this pistol has the ability to shoot either a patched roundball or a load of birdshot.

Traditions Performance Firearms offers both a .45 and .50 percussion Pioneer pistol with German silver furniture with blackened hardware, and a .50 percussion Kentucky pistol with a 9.175-inch barrel and 1:20 twist rifling. It also offers a .32 percussion Trapper pistol with double-set triggers and adjustable sights for target shooters. For the gamblers in the crowd, a percussion .31-caliber, 2.25-inch-barrel vest-pocket derringer with a spur trigger is available.

If a single-shot pistol were capable of loading heavier charges, like my friend Dan Brothers's .54 Thompson/Center Scout (now a discontinued model, but the 209×50 in-line is more than equal to the task), then the pistol becomes a true hunting gun. Dan loaded 80 grains of FFg in front of a .50-caliber, 370-grain Maxi-Ball and went hunting. This load generated a velocity of 1,271 feet per second and 1,328 foot-pounds of muzzle energy.

Butch Dill and I were hunting lower Michigan whitetails with a T/C Renegade .58 percussion rifle and a Lyman Great Plains .54 flintlock rifle, respectively. Although we were unsuccessful in our end of the swamp, a muffled shot rang out around lunchtime. It seems that a small six-point buck walked within 20 yards of Dan's tree stand, so he dropped the hammer of his percussion Scout pistol. When the smoke cleared, the six-pointer was down. I don't know who was more surprised at the power of this hand cannon, Dan or the buck!

There are a few modern single-shot pistols that are equal to the task of deer hunting. All of them use the in-line percussion action and 209 shotgun primer. To generate the higher bullet energies downrange, these pistols have stronger barrels and hand stocks that can absorb the recoil. They may not have the style and grace of the colonial sidearms, but they are serious hunting tools.

If a single-shot pistol is capable of loading heavier charges, like this T/C 209 × 50 Encore handgun, then it becomes a true deer-hunting gun.

Mid-Western Outdoor Specialties makes a Model 82 in-line percussion available in 10.5-, 12-, and 14-inch quick-change barrels. Caliber options include a .36, .45, .50, and .54. The barrel is drilled and tapped for scope mounts; Millett adjustable sights are standard.

Thompson/Center markets a powerful single-shot, the Encore 209×50 Model. Available in .50 caliber only, this closed breech, break action, in-line percussion has a 15-inch blued barrel with adjustable rear sights and a front ramp sight. It measures 20.5 inches in overall length and weighs 4 pounds 6 ounces.

Traditions Performance Firearms has a Buckhunter Pro in-line percussion pistol available in both .45 and .50 caliber. Available with a 9.5- or 12.5-inch round barrel or a 14.75-inch fluted barrel and muzzle brake, this high-tech muzzleloading pistol weighs in at 3 pounds 1 ounce to 3 pounds 11 ounces.

Let's take a look at the exponential rise in muzzle energy when a pistol can handle black powder charges from 50 to 80 grains. The following table represents approximate velocities and muzzle energies for a 14-inch barrel. Some of these loads may exceed the safe maximum for a particular pistol. These values are only for comparison with lower-velocity loads found in primitive single-shot flintlock and percussion pistols.

Cartridge	Grains (black powder)	Bullet (grains)	Velocity (feet per second)	Energy (foot-pounds)
	FFFg			
.36	50	65 Roundball	1,780	457
	60	65 Roundball	1,910	527
	70	65 Roundball	2,030	595
	FFFg			
.45	50	128 Roundball	1,330	503
	60	128 Roundball	1,470	614
	70	128 Roundball	1,550	683
	80	128 Roundball	1,630	755
	FFg			
.45	50	200 Buffalo Ball-et	1,180	619
	60	200 Buffalo Ball-et	1,310	762
	70	200 Buffalo Ball-et	1,390	858
	80	200 Buffalo Ball-et	1,460	947
	FFg			
.50	50	177 Roundball	1,110	484
	60	177 Roundball	1,220	585
	70	177 Roundball	1,310	675
	80	177 Roundball	1,400	771
	FFg			
.50	50	240 Hornady Sabot	980	512
	60	240 Hornady Sabot	1,100	645
	70	240 Hornady Sabot	1,170	730
	80	240 Hornady Sabot	1,240	820
	FFg			
.54	50	230 Roundball	1,120	641
	60	230 Roundball	1,230	773
	70	230 Roundball	1,310	877
	80	230 Roundball	1,390	987
	FFg			
.54	50	265 Hornady Sabot	1,050	649
	60	265 Hornady Sabot	1,170	806
	70	265 Hornady Sabot	1,250	920
	80	265 Hornady Sabot	1,330	1,041

Note: This does not represent a safe loading guide. Please follow the manufacturer's recommendations.

What do all these ballistic values really mean to a hunter? To put the numbers into a modern context, compare the muzzle energies in the preceding table to that of a .357 magnum that generates about 1,400 feet per second muzzle velocity with a 125-grain, jacketed, hollow-point bullet and produces about 544 foot-pounds of muzzle energy. Although this is plenty of energy for a wild turkey, this maximum load is just above the 500 foot-pounds of energy necessary for whitetails. (The Illinois Department of Natural Resources has established 500 foot-pounds as their minimum requirement.)

A .44 Remington magnum that generates about 1,170 feet per second muzzle velocity with a 240-grain, jacketed, hollow-point bullet produces about 730 foot-pounds of energy. This makes it a highly effective handgun cartridge for taking down whitetails, much more so than the .357.

In comparison, all three calibers (.45, .50, .54) loaded with 80 grains of black powder and a ballistic underachiever, the round-ball, compete very effectively against the big .44 Remington magnum cartridge. A .54 percussion in-line muzzleloading handgun that is loaded with 80 grains of FFg powder and a 265-grain Hornady sabot actually blows the .44 magnum out of the water in a head-to-head comparison of the two guns' muzzle energies.

Another note of caution is needed: recoil is heavy. If your pistol is capable of safely handling the loads necessary for deer hunting ballistics, you had better use two hands. Shooting from a rest is another way to improve your aim, as it will steady the short sighting plane between the rear and front sights. This works even on the longest of pistol barrels (which are still less than 16 inches).

Revolvers are another exciting type of black powder pistol that attracts plenty of black powder shooters each year. Civil War reenactors, cowboy action shooters, and hunters who feel the need for quick second, third, fourth, fifth, and sixth shots all love the rotating cylinder of percussion power. Although these historic cap and ball revolvers did in many an unfortunate soldier or cowpoke who got in the way of their bullets—and they are, for the most part, effective on turkey and small game—they are not adequate for deer.

The 1847 Walker revolver, designed by Captain Samuel Walker and produced by Colt, was designed for use by the U.S. Mounted Dragoons during the Mexican War. The Walker is the largest historic percussion revolver ever made. With the capacity to consume 55 grains of FFFg black powder and shoot a 141-grain, .44-caliber (.454 roundball) at 1,205 feet per second, the Walker generates 455 foot-pounds of muzzle energy. Powerful? Yes, but not enough for whitetails. The Walker is produced by Palmetto Arms Company and Uberti. It is marketed by Cabela's, Dixie Gun Works, Cimarron F.A., Colt, Navy Arms, and Taylor's & Co.

The Colt Patterson was the first repeating handgun patented by Samuel Colt. This .36-caliber percussion revolver won its fame in the hands of naval servicemen from the republic of Texas and later in the hands of the Texas Rangers. Loaded with 22 grains of FFFg and an 80-grain roundball, the Patterson generates about 900 feet per second velocity and 144 foot-pounds of energy. This will take down a turkey at close range but should not be seriously considered for deer. Many of the importers mentioned earlier also market the Patterson.

The Colt 1851 Navy gained popularity during the Civil War, as well as in the hands of cowboys and lawmen. This .36-caliber percussion revolver shoots an even lighter load than the Patterson, with only 18 grains of FFFg pushing its 80-grain, .376 roundball. This model is available in either a steel frame or a brass frame. The brass frame shoots a reduced load of 15 grains of FFFg.

The Colt 1860 Army .44-caliber percussion revolver became the first pistol to be used in a man's holster, rather than a horse's. This was the favorite revolver of U.S. government troops during the Civil War. Loaded with 22 grains of FFFg and a .451 roundball, the .44 Army generated about 600 feet per second velocity and 112 foot-pounds of energy.

Ruger has pepped up the old Remington New Model Army .44 for hunters. Instead of a safe maximum of 22 grains of FFFg, the Ruger can handle up to 40 grains. This allows the pistol to achieve 984 feet per second and 308 foot-pounds of energy. This strong and accurate revolver is popular with small-game hunters, as well as with cowboy action shooters.

The 1856 LeMat Confederate revolver was patented by Dr. J. A. F. LeMat of New Orleans. This unusual .44 percussion revolver had a single 20-gauge barrel underneath and was the favorite of Confederate generals J. E. B. Stuart and P. G. T. Beauregard. The nine cylinders of the revolver were loaded with 22 grains of FFFg, while the 20-gauge barrel consumed 30 grains of FFg and a .63-caliber roundball. The 350 grains of lead (or shot) produced a velocity of about 500 feet per second and 194 foot-pounds of energy.

Not long after the Civil War, manufacturers began the process of converting percussion revolvers to black powder cartridge guns. Energies generated by both the percussion revolvers and their black powder cartridge progeny never really became serious contenders as deer hunting handguns. It took another century for manufacturers to produce energy-sufficient black powder handguns to change this situation. But these fun-to-shoot replica revolvers are a great way to spend a day plinking at cans, paper targets, or even small game, and they deserve a place in every hunter's pocket or holster.

The following table, courtesy of Hodgdon Powder, shows cap and ball revolver maximum loads for Pyrodex (P) and Triple Seven (777) powders. Some of these loads may exceed the safe maximum for a particular pistol. These values are only for comparison with loads found in primitive single-shot flintlock and percussion pistols and the heavier hunting loads found in modern in-line percussion handguns.

Caliber	Ball Diameter	Grade	Volume (grains)	Velocity (feet per second)
.31	.320 or 0 Buckshot	P	12	580
.36	.375 or 0000 Buckshot	P	28	935
.36	.375 or 0000 Buckshot	777	15	662
.36	.375 or 0000 Buckshot	777	20	832
.44	.451 or .454	P	37	910
.44	.451 or .454	P (pistol pellet)	30	800
.44	.451 or .454	777	20	536
.44	.451 or .454	777	25	763
.45 Ruger	.457 Roundball	P	43	986
.45 Ruger	.457 Roundball	777	30	845
.45 Ruger	.457 Roundball	777	35	987

Note: This does not represent a safe loading guide. Please follow the manufacturer's recommendations.

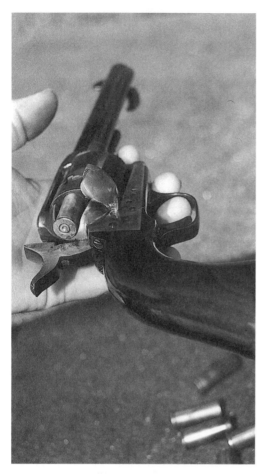

The attraction of a black powder cartridge pistol is its short barrel and ease of transport. But like an earlier age's knives and tomahawks, it should only be considered for short-range use.

Pistols, especially black powder single-shots and revolvers, have never been highly regarded for their long-range accuracy. In fact, in the hands of the average shooter, pistols may have trouble hitting anything more than 25 yards away.

The number-one disadvantage of a pistol is the same thing that makes it an attractive sidearm: it is short (and thus easy to carry). The shortness of the barrel reduces the sighting plane—the distance from the rear sight to the front sight—and this translates into wobble. Wobbling front sights are accentuated when shooters extend their arms and shoot with a one-handed hold. Two hands are steadier than one, but a rest is even better. If you are going to attempt accurate sight-in shots that are reproducible, get a solid rest.

There are several pistol vise products on the market that anchor the pistol to the bench. A more down-home and economical vise can be made from a heavy cardboard box with two V-cuts across one corner. You have to be careful with revolvers, because high-pressure gases are vented at 90 degrees to the face of the cylinder when a shot is fired. You certainly don't want your face or fingers near that spot where the cylinder and barrel meet. You also don't want deflection by the cardboard box back into your eyes. Wear shooting safety glasses and hearing protection.

One method for correcting windage on a fixed sight is to drift it sideways with light taps of a hammer and metal drift.

Never start with a manufacturer's maximum load recommendation. You need to work up to a load that is both powerful and accurate. Once you have settled on the load that shoots with the best combination of power and accuracy, you are ready to establish your sights for the hunt.

Make a three-shot group. If the group centers itself in the black of a 6-inch bull's-eye at 25 yards, you are done. Go home and clean the equipment. Even if all three shots don't cut the 10×, you have a pistol that should not be tampered with for hunting. Tweaking is for paper target competitors. With so many variables such as powder types, batch numbers, humidity, wind velocity, primer types and volumes, lubes, trigger pressure, and ambient temperature, tweaking is not something to mess with when you are looking for hunting accuracy.

If your pistol doesn't group in the black, you have some choices to make. Adjustable sights provide an easy solution. Move the rear sight blade in the same direction that you want your shot to strike. If your shots are hitting low and left of center, screw the windage adjustment clockwise (blade moves right), then screw the elevation screw counterclockwise (blade moves up).

Pistol sights are usually fixed to the barrel however, and are not adjustable. Many of the sights on revolvers are just grooves in the top of the frame, or even a notch in the top of the hammer. This makes them more durable for holstering, but it also makes adjusting them more problematic.

There are several methods for correcting windage (shooting to the left or right) on pistols with fixed sights. First, if the barrel is screwed into the tang or pistol frame, turning the barrel (not an easy matter) sometimes remedies the problem. This is best done by a qualified gunsmith. Remember, you are turning the front sight in the opposite direction that you want the bullet to hit. After turning the barrel, the front sighting may appear to be cocked at an odd angle, but your windage problems will be remedied.

The second method for correcting windage in fixed sights is to drift the sight. This works only with primitive flintlock and percussion sights that have their bases dovetailed into the barrel. Tapping the rear sight in the direction you want the bullet to strike is usually better for aesthetics than drifting the front sight.

The third method is to bend the barrel. Although this sounds extreme, it has been done throughout history as the easiest way to correct windage. But don't try it yourself. This is a serious gunsmithing service that involves the use of an arbor press, where both ends of the barrel are supported as pressure is applied to the center of the barrel.

Elevation problems (shooting high or low) can be corrected by filing down the front sight if the shots are too low or adding more metal if the shots are too high. Again, having a gunsmith bend the barrel is another option.

Many pistol shooters just leave the sights as they are and learn to compensate. In other words, if the pistol shoots to the right, the shooter compensates by aiming a little to the left. If the pistol shoots a little low, a little "Kentucky windage" (aiming a little higher) corrects the problem. This isn't rocket science, especially at 25 yards!

CHAPTER THREE

Powder and Ammunition

In 1248, Roger Bacon wrote, "Thus we may imitate thunder and lightning; for sulphur, nitre and charcoal, which by themselves produce no sensible effect, explode with great noise when closely confined and set on fire." Nearly eight centuries later, the sport of hunting with muzzleloaders is still using sulfur, potassium nitrate, and carbon. With a low ignition temperature and lower pressures than modern gunpowders, black powder still holds a magical allure for the shooting sports and hunters. This chapter explores the different types of black powder, their granulations and applications. Custom load and ballistics tables are included to show the hunter what can be expected in the field.

The warmth of midmorning was melting away the chill of this late-season hunt. Standing on a fallen ancient oak like a minuteman waiting for battle was a hunter toting a .50-caliber flintlock. Forty yards below this position was a young boy waiting for his first muzzleloading opportunity on a deer that he hoped would funnel his way along the creek. My job was to keep watch on this junior hunter while blocking the escape of the driven deer.

Alan Roth has been hunting whitetails for years. Large antlered bucks have fallen to his accurate, scoped centerfires. Management does have graced his table when their numbers needed to be reduced throughout his orchards. Although friends had taken deer in archery and rifle seasons, this year would be different. This would be the year of the heritage hunt: flintlocks only.

Don't be in a hurry to take your one and only shot. Give deer a chance to make a mistake and they usually will.

The rolling hills of southern Berks County are alive with plant diversity. Raspberry canes tangle with greenbrier and poison ivy. Spicebush overgrows arrowwood viburnums, and giant poplars mix with ancient oaks. In this smorgasbord of plant cover, the late-season deer yard. Safe from calorie-draining winds and over-hunted public lands, the deer settle into these hollows to wait out the foul weather of winter.

Earlier that morning, we had waited in a tree stand for the deer to come to us. It didn't work. After a warm cup of coffee and some donuts, a new plan was formed: we would go to the deer. The late season is like that; deer have no need to move much. The easy pickings of agricultural residue are gone; the mast crops from oaks and hickories have been picked clean by squirrels. Food in the form of browse is all that is left. In the thickets of wet areas, food and shelter are one and the same. There is little need for movement.

Ordinarily, a one-man drive is not very successful. But Alan's knowledge of the terrain and his prior experience with orchard-marauding whitetails gave him an advantage. He knew where the deer bedded down, he knew their escape route, and he knew how to sneak along the vegetation-choked creek.

A gray shape hugged the edge of the creek. It was too low to be a human, and no fluorescent orange signaled a hunter. But a vague shape is an unthinkable target. "Give a deer a chance to make a mistake, and it usually will. Don't be in a hurry to shoot," was the advice I had given my son.

Another gray form appeared, and still others. The creek bed was filling up with the motion of growing numbers of deer. Suddenly, a shot rang out from the hilltop, followed by a ghostly apparition of white smoke. Deer scattered in three directions—one group to the orchard past the hunter, who now stood helpless with an empty rifle. A second shot, rumbling from Matt's .54 American Jaeger flintlock, echoed an empty promise. Unsure of the cause of additional white smoke, this band charged past my son's empty gun and up into the blowdown tangle of hemlocks.

Unbelievably, a third group of deer milled around the sandbar at the convergence of the two creeks, one doe offering a perfect broadside opportunity. The third shot was the charm. A patched .50-caliber roundball, powered by a venerable load of 90 grains of black powder, proved accurate.

Alan was the first to the deer, praising the steady aim of the long-barreled, Lancaster-styled Pennsylvania longrifle. "Those things really do take deer, don't they!" he congratulated.

Grins on their faces, Barry and Matt were next on the scene. Missing a deer with a flintlock brings a sense of anticipation for the next try, not remorse. Flintlocks are difficult systems to master, and there is no substitute for practice. Barry's rifle seemed to hang-fire, causing him to aim off-target by the time the main powder charge fired. Matt complained of not being ready when he accidentally touched the hair trigger with cold fingers. Both problems afflict new flintlock hunters, and both are easily solved.

The Keystone State's outdoorsmen have been hunting deer in the late season with flintlock rifles since 1974. It was never conceived as a management tool or even an efficient method of reducing the growing herds of suburban deer; it was established as a way to hunt deer like our forefathers—a heritage hunt. More than a quarter century later, it still has a special ambience and offers the ultimate challenge to those brave enough to hunt in the late season.

The late season is a time of endurance. With diminished whitetail numbers now sensitized to the incursions of hunters during the bow and rifle seasons, these deer are not easily targeted. Deer in January have few urges to move. Forget the rub lines and scrapes, never mind the cornfields and acorns; these animals are in a hunkered-down survival mode. But the 2004 Game Commission statistics prove that flintlock hunters have a great chance to harvest a deer. Almost one in three flintlock hunters took home some venison. This is quite an improvement over the old 1:16 success rate of the mid-1970s, or the 1:11 success enjoyed during the 1980s and 1990s.

"First the powder, then the ball." Those are the words that greet my eyes every time I load my muzzleloader. I carved them into my wooden loading box back in 1974, after making a "dry ball" mistake in the middle of a timed shooting match; they are still good words to live by.

Flintlocks can be very accurate, powerful, and dependable shooting irons if the hunter does everything with consistency and care. But make one mistake in the loading process, and everything becomes a futile exercise in frustration. Such might be the case if you don't load the right kind of powder in the correct volume and the proper granulation. So, let's take a look at black powder, from its most primitive form through the most technologically advanced pellets.

Black Powder

Black powder is a simple mixture of three components: charcoal, saltpeter, and sulfur. The fuel for the mixture is carbon black. The oxidizer for the mixture is a white powder, potassium nitrate. The binder that holds the two together and creates a rapidly expanding gas is yellow sulfur flour. Loosely mixed in a moist environment, the components stick together into a cake. When dried and crushed, the granules of black powder are sifted through a screen to provide the four Fg sizes available to riflemen.

Black powder is a simple mixture of three components: charcoal, saltpeter, and sulfur.

In past centuries, much experimentation took place to create a type of carbon that would ignite easily and burn consistently. Hardwoods such as maple and buckthorn alder, as well as other more exotic species such as eucalyptus, sugarcane, and sugar beets, have been used. They were heated in an oxygen-deficient environment and turned into charcoal. The centuries-old way was to ignite the wood and cover it with earth. A more controlled temperature method is to use an air-restricted oven.

Whereas any old hardwood works to fuel an iron forge, any old charcoal is not satisfactory for creating gunpowder carbon. If the carbon purity is too high, it can autocombust. This is not a good thing for a rifleman wearing a powder horn. If the carbon purity is too low, an insufficient burn rate causes hang-fires and too much fouling. Charcoal carbon consistency is a well-guarded science among black powder manufacturers because good charcoal makes desirable black powders.

Potassium nitrate, also know as saltpeter, forms the bulk (75 percent) of the black powder mixture. This white salt carries the oxygen needed for the instant combustion of the charcoal. Potassium nitrate has come from many different sources throughout history. Minerals mined from the earth, bird guano from South America, and even barn-animal bedstraw have all had a role in creating a potassium-rich salt oxidizer for black powder. And again, the quality and purity of the saltpeter are important in determining the burn rate of the black powder.

Sulfur is an elemental component necessary to form the black powder granule. Though only 10 percent of the mixture, it is necessary to hold the carbon and saltpeter components together so that combustion is instantaneous. But the use of sulfur comes at a price. It melts at a low temperature and is the part of the mixture that smells like rotten eggs when the black powder is fired. Sulfur also leaves behind various sticky sulfates, which hold fouling salts (such as carbon sulfate and ammonium sulfate) tightly against the iron of the barrel. That is why the fouling must be flushed or dissolved from the bore. If you don't remove it without delay, the salts will begin to rust away your accuracy. But sulfur also throws out a dandy cloud of white smoke. Turning black powder into white smoke wouldn't be the same without this odoriferous stuff.

The percentages of the three components of black powder—15 percent carbon, 75 percent saltpeter, 10 percent sulfur—have been the formula for black powder since the days of matchlocks and hand cannons. Today, they may be tweaked a bit by the different manufacturers to produce variations in burn rate.

The time that it takes to mill, or corn, the components into black powder is important. Fine sporting powders, those that burn quickly with higher pressures, are the result of quality components that are milled together for long periods. With black powder, the saltpeter is considered to be the source of calories of heat during the powder's combustion, and the charcoal is the source of gases. According to Bill Knight of Reading, Pennsylvania, an experienced experimenter and student of black powder chemistry, "If one alters the ingredient ratios, the number of calories of heat may be altered, along with the total volume of permanent gases produced. The proportion of carbon dioxide to carbon monoxide is also altered." This is called the "expansive force" produced by the powder. A blasting powder would be expected to exhibit a maximum combustion temperature of 1,800 degrees Celsius, while a sporting powder would produce a maximum combustion temperature of 2,200 degrees Celsius. The theoretical combustion temperature of black powder is usually considered to be 2,350 degrees Celsius.

During the nineteenth century, according to Knight (affectionately known by his friends in the industry as the Mad Monk), "There were three basic types of black powder produced for use as a propellant powder in small arms. These were musket, rifle, and sporting powder—the designation denoting differences in burn rate. Musket powder is the slowest, sporting powder is the fastest. Historically, nineteenth-century sporting powders had a minimum of a 10 percent faster burn rate than rifle powder. Rifle powder was 10 percent faster than musket powder. The differences in velocity were a result of burn rates and ballistic strengths."

According to James Kirkland, an importer of Swiss and Schuetzen brands of black powder, "Black powder is not a chemical explosive such as nitrocellulose (smokeless powder) or nitroglycerin (dynamite ingredient). Black powder is a mechanical explosive. This means no chemical reaction is used to make black powder." Wheel mills weighing up to 5 tons crush the charcoal,

Black powder is a mechanical explosive: no chemical reaction is used to make it.

sulfur, and potassium nitrate together, stripping away the air film that encapsulates hydrophobic (water-hating) particles of charcoal and sulfur. This permits a true, intimate contact between the particles. The amount of time used to mill the powder is critical. If the milling time isn't long enough, the black powder may be cheaper to produce, but the results won't create accuracy. Also, the density of the black powder affects the burn rate and accuracy.

Once the powder has been milled sufficiently, it travels to the powder press, and then to the granulator for sizing. The polishing drums, which are filled with graphite, create a black powder that flows from containers to powder measurers. The polishing drums also give the particles greater strength so that they do not fall apart into dust when rattled around in cans.

Although the process sounds simple, it is far from it. By sticking to small batch sizes, the potential variances in powder quality (known as lot-to-lot variances) are minimized. Too much water or humidity in the powder will keep it from burning correctly. If the grains are too dense, the burn rate decreases; not dense enough, and the granules break apart, causing velocity variances (flyers). Too high a carbon content, and the powder burns too dirty; too little carbon, and the powder burns too slowly.

Competitors who use black powder in their muzzleloaders to achieve minute-of-angle accuracy are very careful about the source of their fuels. They compare rate of burn, volume of fouling, and consistency from load to load. These shooters are very vocal about the attributes of one brand over another. But competition among

In 1974, both domestic DuPont black powder and Curtis & Harvey powder from Scotland were available.

manufacturers has led to very high quality black powder being produced from most plants, both domestic and foreign. Pennsylvanians have watched black powder quality change over the years, and we are now enjoying the best black powders ever produced.

In 1974, there was a sporting-quality DuPont black powder available, as well as Curtis & Harvey. This is what we used during the early days of the flintlock season. Then the Moosic, Pennsylvania, manufacturer sold out to Gerhardt-Owens Explosives. For more than a decade, its rifle grade of black powder (most of the blasting powder went to mines and the military) was the only fuel available. All importation of foreign black powder was stopped when terrorists began using the stuff to blow up airplanes. The only domestic black powder producer left in this country during the 1980s was GOEX black powder.

During the 1990s, Petro-Explo, Inc., began importing a Brazilian black powder. Trade-named Elephant, this stuff set up a competition with GOEX, and experimentation with different sources of charcoal and saltpeter led to a higher grade of black powder. Unfortunately, a plant explosion in Moosic caused GOEX to move to Louisiana, and a flood knocked the Elephant out of production

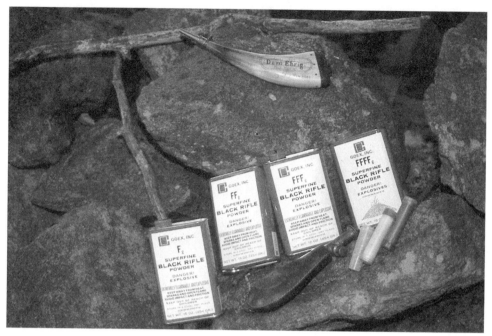

Until the 1980s, Pennsylvania's GOEX black powder plant in Moosic was the only legal source of black powder.

in Pernambuco, Brazil. But then the Europeans got involved with KIK and Wano black powders. Even the Chinese Red Dragon (primarily fireworks grade) found its way into the shooting sports. Today, most gun shops offer the big three: domestic GOEX, German Schuetzen, and premium-grade Swiss.

Swiss black powder is produced in smaller quantities, uses a different wood and charcoaling process, and takes longer to mill. It follows an old sporting powder formula: 78 parts potassium nitrate, 10 parts sulfur, and 12 parts charcoal. It also commands a higher price. But in return, shooters are noticing that it has a faster burn rate and produces 15 percent more energy per volume. It has been described as a true sporting powder, similar to the kind available in the nineteenth century. Loading data from the 1800s seemed to show lower volumes of powder per caliber than what gun manufacturers recommend today. They must have had a different kind of black powder similar to Swiss.

Deer hunters may not notice or appreciate the nuances of each brand of powder. In fact, most people simply buy what is available

Bill Knight, the "Mad Monk," and Dr. Bill Mende were early proponents of importing black powder from Brazil.

or what is cheapest. But they might appreciate the one thing that all black powders share in common: low ignition temperature. Black powder ignites at 480 degrees Fahrenheit. This is the lowest ignition temperature of all gunpowders. It also enables primitive firearms such as a flintlock, with its external ignition, to function. Iron sparks from the flint and steel ignite priming powder, and the flash of radiant heat ignites the powder train inside the touch hole of the bore. Although this ignition temperature is easy to achieve, hunters need to understand granulation sizes so that their flint-locks fire every time.

Black powder is sized according to an archaic system of screen sizes: Fg (from 0.0689 to 0.0582 inch), FFg (0.0582 to 0.0376 inch), FFFg (0.0376 to 0.0170 inch), and FFFFg (0.0170 to 0.0111 inch.) Rather than worry about screen dimensions, concern yourself with comparative size and the pressures they produce.

Fg granulation black powder is about the size of a grain of cornmeal. The largest of the muzzleloading sizes, it is useful for large-gauge shotguns, large-bore breechloader cartridges, and small hobby cannons. Although an 8- or 10-gauge shotgun may be fed Fg, the moment you reduce the gauge to 12, or caliber of the gun to .58, you need to consider loading size FFg.

What is the advantage of a larger grain size? In two words: lower pressure. Black powder is a surface-burning propellant. In other words, the greater the surface area (as in small granule sizes), the more surface there is to burn. Consider an oak log in your fireplace. Light a match to one end, and it won't burn, but cut that log into smaller pieces, down to kindling size, and it will burn with gusto from the same match. Black powder granule size works the same way, but pressures rise significantly with the rate of burn.

FFg granulation is half the size of Fg black powder. Roughly the size of coarse black pepper, it is the recommended size for black powder hunting. Any time a large obstruction such as a lead slug or sabotted bullet is loaded into a rifle, it is safer to load FFg than the smaller and faster-burning FFFg granulation. FFg is recommended for hunting rifles having calibers ranging from .45 to .58.

FFFg granulation is half the size of FFg black powder. This size burns faster than the same volume of FFg, and with more pressure. It also generates less fouling. It is the preferred granulation for many flintlock hunters who use patched roundballs because of its easier ignition. And FFFg, often referred to as "triple F," can double as a priming powder in a pinch. But hunters are cautioned not to use it in rifles, shotguns, or pistols, which are not built to withstand this hotter load. Most manufacturers recommend triple F for calibers .32 to .45.

FFFFg granulation is half the size of triple F. This lightweight, dust-sized black powder is designed for one thing: flintlock priming. Flintlocks need a priming powder in the outside pan that will easily ignite from a couple of sparks dropped into it. "Four F" does this quite nicely at 480 degrees Fahrenheit when the 2,000-degree iron sparks touch the powder. But four Fg has a dangerous side—the small granulation's surface area is huge, which means that it explodes faster and with greater pressure than any of the other granulation sizes. Never load a muzzleloader with four F; it is a priming powder only.

As black powder burns, layers flake off. Incomplete combustion results, and this is part of the reason why a fouling patch must be run through the bore after each shot. Almost 50 percent of the loaded black powder will be expelled as unburned granules. Therefore, there is an increased velocity for FFFg black powder compared with FFg, but at an increased breech pressure. The following table is excerpted from *Lyman's 2nd Edition, Black Powder Handbook & Loading Manual*, using a 28-inch barrel, 1:48 twist, percussion cap:

Caliber	Charge (grains)	Muzzle Velocity (feet per second)	Pressure (pounds per square inch)
.45 (.440 roundball)	70 FFg	1,691	11,100
.45	70 FFFg	1,790	13,300
.50 (.490 roundball)	90 FFg	1,651	7,000
.50	90 FFFg	1,830	9,900
.54 (.535 roundball)	100 FFg	1,592	8,600
.54	100 FFFg	1,683	10,900

Clearly, there is a significant jump of 2,000-plus pounds per square inch when switching from the larger-grained FFg black powder to the smaller-grained FFFg. If your manual calls for a particular granulation, there is a reason for recommending it: your safety.

Black powder burns progressively from the breech ignition point (flash from the priming pan or burning gases from a primer percussion cap). As it burns, it must push unburned granules of black powder, as well as the bullet, out of the bore's muzzle. For this reason, there is not a one-to-one ratio when comparing the amount of powder to the increase in velocity of the bullet. There will be a point of diminishing returns. In other words, as loads increase over 100 grains (or whatever safe maximum charge is stated in the manual that accompanies your gun), pressures skyrocket, but velocity doesn't increase enough to make the extra powder worth the risk of harming the gun or the shooter. You *can* overload black powder! This is a dangerous practice and not worth the risk.

Remember, all muzzleloading gunpowders are hygroscopic. Be sure that they are stored in a waterproof container. The old saying, "Keep yer powder dry, yer nose to the wind, and yer back green" is still good advice. As for my pet rifle, "Alt Blitzen," I'll remember to load first the powder (60 grains of FFFg), then the ball (.445 round-ball in a Lehigh Valley lubed .010 cotton patch), before heading to the dark timber.

Modern Replica Powders and Pellets

Replica black powders are not black powder, but they load the same, shoot with similar ballistics, and produce a lot less solid fouling. They are a different chemical composition from the old charcoal, saltpeter, sulfur mix, but they still produce white smoke. Pyrodex, a household name in muzzleloading, officially came to life in 1976 at the National Rifle Association convention in Indianapolis. A cleaner-burning alternative to black powder, it captured the imaginations of modern muzzleloaders. Loaded in bulk volume, just like black powder, it allowed repeated shots without cleaning. But because the fouling was chemically different, it had to be cleaned chemically, not just with water. Demand for replica powders has come from in-line rifle and cowboy action shooters. The most recent advance in replica powder was the introduction of pelletized powders. In 1996, Hodgdon Powder Company introduced a line of 50-grain Pyrodex pellets that has had an overwhelming impact on the way we shoot muzzleloaders. This section reveals the advantages and disadvantages of choosing the modern alternative powders.

The rifle felt familiar, and the rubber recoil pad fit snugly into the shoulder. Fiber-optic sights glowed fluorescent red and green in the failing light of dusk. A thumb safety slid forward as the whole system pointed toward a group of deer that just appeared a football field away. In spite of the fact that I was hunting with a muzzleloader, this rifle was different from those carried in the 1970s. Only the deer season was the same: a one-shot opportunity.

Four does carefully tiptoed down the deer trail toward the creek. Something followed them, as their constant over-the-shoulder check of their backtrail signaled. The deer's eyes were indistinct at this distance, tipping the fact that they were beyond the lethal range of this hunter. The open sights made accurate shooting

The buck I took with 50-grain Pyrodex pellets.

a problem. Iron or plastic works the same; the sights simply cover the deer's entire vital area, making a sure shot unlikely at that distance. The does were just too far for a good shot.

Slowly, the column of brown shadows became distinct forms of antlerless deer. Halted by the shifting scent line at the creek, the deer lifted their noses into the air, searching for the unknown. Fortunately, the wind moved in my direction, not theirs. But the does were still unsure about crossing the creek.

Suddenly, a new player entered the fray. A buck! Its larger body loped over the crest of the hill and bounded down toward the does. The herd responded by pushing through the water and ascending the opposite hill. Their eyes were now distinct, large circles of white dotted with glossy black. They were under 50 yards, but too much underbrush obscured a clear shot. It didn't matter; the buck was drawing all my attention as they angled away.

The moment of truth was at hand. The buck was now at the tail end of the column, the herd about 70 yards away and chewing up real estate quickly. I made the decision to take any clean shot that availed itself. A loud grunt on the deer call stopped their progress, if only for a moment. That was enough time.

The rifle leaped in my hands as the familiar thump of recoil rocked tightly into my shoulder. Two 50-grain pellets of Pyrodex rocked the stillness of the hardwoods as a 240-grain Hornady sabot left the barrel at about 1,700 feet per second. Carrying more than 1,500 foot-pounds of energy, this was about three times the energy necessary for a quick kill. But the buck didn't react to the shot by flopping to the ground. Instead, it separated from the herd and raced back in the direction from which it had come.

Somewhat confused by the deer's reaction, I decapped the in-line, popped the top of the plastic quick-loader tube, and dumped two new pellets, with their dark bases of black powder, down the bore. With a firm grip on the ramrod, I was surprised at the resistance of the plastic sabot in the fouled barrel. After checking the marked line on the ramrod, to ensure that the bullet was seated properly over the powder, it was time to check for signs of a hit.

Moving down the hill to the spot where the deer had been when I shot at it, I had a chance to rethink the action. The sight picture was clear, no brush in the way. The trigger pull felt crisp, and ignition was immediate. But the deer had been on the move, and I had a lingering doubt that there wasn't enough lead for the 70-yard shot. But unlike the cloud of thick white smoke generated by a black powder shot, the cloud of vapor from the Pyrodex allowed me to watch the buck's escape after the shot.

A clump of grayish-brown hair lay on the ground. This was a good sign, but not a drop of red blood was visible on the wet, brown leaves. Taking up the trail of the fleeing whitetail, at least I knew which direction to follow.

The 10-point buck had crossed two fields and climbed a hill before expiring. It wasn't poor shot placement, just bad luck. The sabotted pistol bullet had slipped through its body without much expansion, or release of hydrostatic shock. Regardless of the type of powder or rifle being used, hunters need to be sure of the entire load, bullets included. There is no substitute for doing your homework before the season. If the bullet doesn't perform at the expected lower velocities past 100 yards, then don't take the shot.

Long-distance shooting for whitetails was not part of the original motivation for the special muzzleloading season, but new

Long-distance shooting at whitetails was not the initial reason for holding Pennsylvania's special muzzleloader season, but new bullets and greater powder volumes are giving hunters increased opportunities with high-powered rifles.

bullets and greater volumes of powder are giving hunters the opportunity to match distances with high-powered rifles. For many muzzleloading hunters, the "third season" has been changed by new technology. Even the gunpowder itself has undergone many changes.

The revolution in muzzleloading propellants began in 1978 when Dan Pawlak came up with a new kind of black powder, a cleaner-burning replica black powder. Pyrodex, created for Hodgdon Powder Company, still had charcoal, saltpeter, and sulfur in its components, but the formulation had changed. Potassium perchlorate and graphite were added, along with a few other trade secrets, to make a substance that seemed to shoot like black powder, but with less gooey fouling.

While competitive shooters shied away from the new replica powder because its variations in pressure were not as consistent as black powder (Hodgdon soon addressed this issue with its Select match-grade powder), hunters loved it. Pyrodex allowed hunters to reload without cleaning, and this was an advantage.

Pyrodex is a propellant designed specifically for percussion black powder and cartridge firearms. It is currently available in three grades. Grade "P" is for all caliber pistols and .45-caliber or smaller rifles with roundball projectiles. Grade "RS" is for all rifles and shotguns. Grade "Select" is a match-grade version of RS that yields greater consistency and accuracy.

To load Pyrodex, you follow the same rules used for loading black powder. Use a volumetric powder measurer, not a scale. If you pour 80 grains of FFg black powder for a particular hunting load, you can pour 80 grains of Pyrodex RS or Select to duplicate about the same ballistics. But it is interesting to note that you will get approximately 30 percent more shots per pound than with black powder.

Pyrodex has a higher ignition temperature than black powder. This is why it does not function well as a priming powder for flintlocks. But it will work as the main powder charge if five grains of FFFFg black powder are poured down the bore first, followed by the main charge of Pyrodex.

Pyrodex causes far less fouling than black powder, and it is possible to seat repeated loads without cleaning. This is sometimes necessary when follow-up shots are required during a hunt. But for

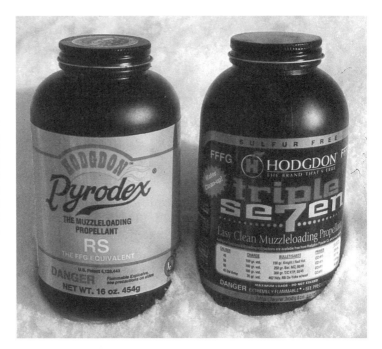

To load Pyrodex or Triple Seven, you measure by volume, not weight. Triple Seven has 15 percent more energy per volume than Pyrodex, so hunters need to be careful when loading it.

the best accuracy, a fouling patch is recommended. A soapy water solution works well for cleaning between shots, but due to the nature of the fouling, a solvent such as E-Z Clean is necessary for final cleaning and storage.

Remember that each gun shoots differently, and densities vary from lot to lot in any gunpowder. Shooters should try various loads to determine the best proportion of power and accuracy. But Pyrodex, like black powder, can be overloaded. The most common sign in an external percussion gun is gas blowback through the nipple. This is what happens when the hammer returns to the half-cock position after a shot. This is dangerous, and the amount of powder in the load must be reduced. Always follow the manufacturer's recommended loads, and do not exceed the safe maximum.

If you plan to load Pyrodex in a metallic cartridge, remember that it will work best in straight-walled cartridges. Never allow an airspace between the powder and the base of the bullet, because this can produce excessive pressures. The loading density must be 100 percent by light compression. You can do this by filling the powder to a level that allows light compression by the seating of the bullet (bottle-necked cases must be filled in this manner). In straight-walled cases, filler wads may be used to buffer and take up the airspace. Card and polyethylene wads should be sized to the internal diameter of the shell so that no airspaces exist. Never use any other type of filler material, because this can lead to barrel obstruction, fouling, and dangerous pressures.

After firing Pyrodex in a brass cartridge case, de-prime and immerse in white vinegar. The acidity of the vinegar neutralizes the corrosive residues inside the case. Hodgdon Powder recommends that the soaking time be limited to 10 minutes. Longer periods of soaking will cause etching in the brass and shorten the life of the case. Immediately rinse the brass and polish the cases in a tumbler with corncob or walnut shell media.

The following muzzleloading rifle and shotgun data are furnished courtesy of Hodgdon Powder. Ballistic data can vary considerably depending on many factors, including components, how they are assembled, degree of powder or lead fouling, type of firearm used, and the loading techniques of the shooter. This is not a recommended loading guide; follow the manufacturer's guide.

MUZZLELOADING RIFLES LOADED WITH A ROUNDBALL

Caliber	Ball Diameter (inches)	Grade	Volume (grains)	Velocity (feet per second)
.32	.310	P	30	1,800
.36	.360	P	43	1,794
.40	.395	P	48	1,751
.44	.437	P	72	1,770
.45	.440	P	75	1,785
.50	.490	RS/Select	96	1,879
.54	.535	RS/Select	120	1,890
.58	.560	RS/Select	100	1,288

MUZZLELOADING RIFLES LOADED WITH LEAD CONICAL BULLETS AND RS/SELECT GRADE PYRODEX

Manufacturer	Caliber	Weight (grains) and Type	Volume (grains)	Velocity (feet per second)
Buffalo	.45	325/HPHB	100	1,409
Buffalo	.45	285/HPHB	100	1,458
Hornady	.45	285/HP	85	1,550
Hornady	.45	325/Solid	85	1,500
T/C	.45	190–200/Maxi	110	1,902
T/C	.45	240–255/Maxi	100	1,735
T/C	.45	320/Maxi	100	1,612
Buffalo	.50	350/HPBT	110	1,370
Buffalo	.50	385/HPHB	110	1,478
Buffalo	.50	410/HPFB	110	1,438
Buffalo	.50`	490/HPFB	90	1,142
Hornady	.50	385/HP	90	1,400
Hornady	.50	410/Solid	90	1,400
T/C	.50	275–320/Maxi	110	1,661
T/C	.50	350–370/Maxi	100	1,525
T/C	.50	460–470/Maxi	110	1,416
Buffalo	.54	390/HPHB	120	1,427
Buffalo	.54	425/HPHB	120	1,536
Buffalo	.54	460/HPFB	110	1,340
Buffalo	.54	510/HPHB	120	1,288
Hornady	.54	425/HP	105	1,400
T/C	.54	360–365/Maxi	120	1,607
T/C	.54	430–435/Maxi	120	1,499
T/C	.54	530–540/Maxi	120	1,396
Buffalo	.58	525/HPFB	100	1,159
Hornady	.58	525/HP	90	1,275
T/C	.58	555–560/Maxi	120	1,331
Cast	.58	315/Mini	100	1,020
Cast	.58	505/Mini	93	880

HP, hollow point; HPHB, hollow point and hollow base; HPFB, hollow point and flat base.

Bullet data provided by the respective manufacturers.

MUZZLELOADING RIFLES LOADED WITH SABOT BULLETS AND RS/SELECT GRADE PYRODEX

Sabot	Caliber	Bullet Weight (grains) and Diameter (inches)	Volume (grains)	Velocity (feet per second)
Muzzleloader Magnum	.45	125–140/.355–.357	80	1,920
Muzzleloader Magnum	.45	145–160/.355–.357	80	1,920
Hornady	.45	158/.357	80	1,800
Buffalo	.50	225/Buffalo	90	1,650
Buffalo	.50	252/Buffalo	90	1,553
Buffalo	.50	302/Buffalo	100	1,524
Muzzleloader Magnum	.50	180–200/.429–.430	90	1,700
Muzzleloader Magnum	.50	210–240/.429–.430	90	1,630
Muzzleloader Magnum	.50	265/.429–.430	90	1,590
Muzzleloader Magnum	.50	185–200/.451–.452	90	1,730
Muzzleloader Magnum	.50	225–240/.451–.452	90	1,640
Muzzleloader Magnum	.50	260/.451–.452	90	1,590
T/C Break-O-Way	.50	200/.429	100	1,730
T/C Break-O-Way	.50	240/.429	100	1,640
Hornady	.50	240/.429	90	1,600
Hornady	.50	300/.429	85	1,400
Hornady SST	.50	250	150	2,250
Hornady SST	.50	300	150	2,130
Buffalo	.54	225/Buffalo	90	1,735
Buffalo	.54	252/Buffalo	90	1,487
Muzzleloader Magnum	.54	180–200/.451–.452	90	1,600
Muzzleloader Magnum	.54	225–240/.451–.452	90	1,550
Muzzleloader Magnum	.54	260/.451–.452	90	1,510
T/C Break-O-Way	.54	200/.429–.430	120	1,871
T/C Break-O-Way	.54	240/.429–.430	110	1,728
Hornady	.54	265/.429	90	1,600
Hornady	.54	300/.429	90	1,400
Mler Mag.	.58	225–240/.451–.452	100	1,450
Mler Mag.	.58	250–260/.451–.452	100	1,500
Hornady	.58	300/.452	95	1,350

Sabot data provided by the respective manufacturers.

MUZZLELOADING SHOTGUNS LOADED WITH RS/SELECT GRADE PYRODEX

Gauge	Shot Weight (oz.)	Wad Column	Volume (grains)	Velocity (feet per second)
12	1¼	.135 Card & ¼-inch filler	100	1,081
12	1⅛	.135 Card & ¼-inch filler	100	1,190
20	1	.135 Card & ¼-inch filler	90	1,070
20	⅞	.135 Card & ¼-inch filler	80	1,115

MUZZLELOADING PISTOLS LOADED WITH A ROUNDBALL

Caliber	Ball Diameter (inches)	Grade	Volume (grains)	Velocity (feet per second)
.40	.395	P	29	840
.45	.440	P	37	820
.50	.490	P	47	790

CAP AND BALL REVOLVERS LOADED WITH GRADE P PYRODEX

Caliber	Ball Diameter (inches)	Volume (grains)	Velocity (feet per second)
.31	.32 or 0 Buckshot	12	580
.36	.375 or 0000 Buckshot	28	935
.44	.451 or .454	37	910
.45 Ruger	.457 Roundball	43	986

The real revolution in muzzleloader hunting took place when Hodgdon converted its Pyrodex to a more convenient form: pellets. With the particles compressed into a sub-.50-caliber cylinder, hunters no longer needed to carry the components for loading bulk powder. But to overcome the higher 740-degree ignition temperature for this class B flammable solid (black powder is a 480-degree

The real revolution in muzzleloader hunting took place when Hodgdon Powder Company began making Pyrodex pellets.

class A explosive), a base of black powder was added to the bottom of the pellet. To load these pellets for optimal ignition, the black base of the pellet must be loaded first into the bore. Care must be taken not to crush the pellet.

To hunt successfully with pellet propellant, it is important that the nipple and breech plug be clean and dry, or proper ignition will not occur. To guarantee an open channel for ignition gases to reach the pellet, use a pipe cleaner to clean the neck of the nipple and a nipple pick to open the flash hole. The same treatment should be given to the breech plug of an in-line percussion system. After cleaning, spray a degreaser through the nipple and breech plug. High-pressure degreasing sprays will flush all solid debris, lubricants, solvents, and moisture from the flash channel, providing an uninhibited path for the flash to ignite the pellet.

Hodgdon Powder also recommends sabots using .45-caliber bullets in .50-caliber rifles. The .45s appear to be more accurate than the .44s, as are one-piece sabots compared with two-piece.

When sabots fail, the results are dramatic. This would not be acceptable for a hunting situation, so be sure to practice shooting the sabot and bullets with which you intend to hunt.

Conical bullet users need to pay special attention to the base of lead bullets when using pelleted powder. A fiber wad is required to act as a gas seal, or accuracy will suffer, leading of the bore will occur, velocity will drop, and the possibility of launching a flaming pellet into the ground cover exists. It is recommended that a soft lube be used around the wad to assist in the creation of a tight gas seal as well as to keep the fouling soft in the bore.

Pyrodex is available in .50-caliber–50-grain equivalent pellets and .50-caliber–30-grain equivalent pellets. This allows loads from light 30-grain practice rounds to 50-, 60-, 80-, 90-, 100-, 110-, and 120-grain hunting load combinations. Even the whopper 150-grain equivalents can be achieved with three 50-grain pellets. But Hodgdon Powder states in its manual that the maximum load per shot should never exceed total pellets containing more than 100 grains volume equivalent. Exceeding the maximum load may cause excessive pressure and could cause damage to the firearm and injury or death to the shooter. Some rifle manufacturers may recommend the use of more pellets than Hodgdon's maximum load. Hodgdon specifically disclaims any and all liability arising out of the exceeding of its maximum load, and the user assumes all risk in doing so.

In-line muzzleloading rifles started pushing the velocity envelope in the 1990s. One hundred grains didn't create enough velocity for "magnum performance." Three pellets, 150 grains of Pyrodex, could push lightweight bullets past the 2,000 feet per second threshold, allowing muzzleloading energies adequate for whitetails out to 200 yards. But three pellets, even with their hollow centers and black powder bases, didn't always burn with consistent pressures in carbine barrels. So, the quest was on for better percussion caps. Thus, the 209 shotgun primer came into vogue for in-lines.

Ignition systems continue to attract the attention of hunters. Even the flintlock has succumbed to a radical change—the Pyrodex pellet. Because Pyrodex won't ignite until the ignition temperature of 740 degrees is reached (260 degrees higher than black powder), most flintlock hunters don't use the propellant. Hodgdon Powder Company solved this problem by coating the bottom of the Pyrodex pellet with black powder. This works great with in-line percussion

The next step in the evolution of replicas took place in 2002, when Hodgdon introduced the Triple Seven.

ignition, but the black powder base sits too low in the breech for most flintlocks to take advantage of it. The T/C Firestorm is one gun that has adapted to the pellet by creating a cone breech plug that raises the black powder base of the pellet in line with the touch hole.

Pyrodex opened up the muzzleloading field to magnum charges, with its 50-grain pellets. Hodgdon Powder also makes 30-grain pellets for hunters. Originally designed for pistols, the 30-grain weight is also ideal for mixing with the 50-grain pellets to customize a load of 50 to 100-plus grain loads. The 150-grain magnum loads produce higher velocities than smaller offerings. For the big-bore .54s and .58s, a larger-diameter 60-grain pellet will be in production soon.

The next step in the evolution of replica black powders took place in 2002, when Hodgdon introduced Triple Seven. Citing better performance, hotter velocities per volume, and cleanup with ordinary tap water, hunters took notice. According to Hodgdon, Triple Seven produces the highest velocities of all granular muzzle-loading propellants when compared by volume. An added bonus

I've had success using Triple Seven in large calibers.

is that the enhanced velocity results in a flatter trajectory and downrange energy. Triple Seven lacks the sulfur odor of powder and is virtually odorless as a residue in the barrel. Because of the lack of sulfur, the fouling is easy to clean up with plain water.

Triple Seven works with all styles and brands of projectiles, which makes it easy to find a load and maintain accuracy. Triple Seven is also a higher-energy replica product designed to provide higher velocities with the same volume of black powder. To duplicate a GOEX or Schuetzen black powder load, you must decrease the powder charge by 15 percent.

But can this class B flammable solid be used in a flintlock? Although Hodgdon does not officially advertise its usefulness in primitive flintlocks and sidehammer percussions because of the higher ignition temperature (around 740 degrees), I have had success with it in large calibers. I have used Triple Seven pellets in a Thompson/Center .50 Firestorm, a bulk powder Triple Seven load in a .54 Dixie Gun Works American Jaeger, and Triple Seven FFg bulk powder in a .58 T/C Big-Bore percussion.

However, smaller-caliber rifles, particularly flintlocks and per-cussions with large nipple snails (right-angle flash channels leading into the bore), may encounter problems. If you are determined to use the new replica powders, be sure to practice at the bench and in cold weather before you take the rifle to the deer woods. Flintlock hunters still need to deal with the higher ignition temperature of Triple Seven by using five grains of FFFFg as a starter charge of black powder. Remember to reduce the main load of Triple Seven by five grains to compensate for the black power starter charge.

Cartridge loads of Triple Seven should be used exactly as spec-ified in the table below (courtesy of Hodgdon Powder). You can safely use a card or polyethylene wad up to 0.03-inch thick to pro-tect the base of the bullet. Loading density should be 100 percent, with light compression not to exceed 0.1-inch. Triple Seven works best when the bullet just touches the powder. Do *not* reduce loads by means of filler wads or inert filler materials such as Grits, Dacron, or Grex, and do *not* heavily compress powder charges. Doing so could create a dangerous situation.

MUZZLELOADING RIFLES LOADED
WITH TRIPLE SEVEN AND A ROUNDBALL

Caliber	Ball Diameter (inches)	Grade	Volume (grains)	Velocity (feet per second)
.45	.440	FFg	40	1,534
		FFg	50	1692
		FFg	60	1926
.50	.490	FFg	70	1,744
		FFFg	70	1,801
		FFg	80	1,842
		FFFg	80	1,873
		FFg	90	1,925
		FFFg	90	1,945
		FFg	100	1,988
		FFFg	100	1,997
.54	.530	FFg	80	1,667
		FFg	90	1,775
		FFg	100	1,846
		FFg	120	1,943

MUZZLELOADING RIFLES LOADED WITH TRIPLE SEVEN AND BULLET OR SABOT

Caliber/Sabot	Bullet Weight (grains)	Volume (grains)/ Velocity (feet per second)	
		FFg	**FFFg**
.45 Knight/Red Hot	150	70/1,963	70/2,041
		80/2,134	80/2,141
		90/2,187	90/2,206
		100/2,284	100/2,295
.45 T/C XTP	180	70/1,916	70/1,936
		80/1,993	80/2,003
		90/2,054	90/2,103
		100/2,108	100/2,225
.45 Knight Lead PT	240	70/1,725	70/1,780
		80/1,792	80/1,843
		90/1,849	90/1,912
		100/1,991	100/2,006
.45 CVA Power Belt	225	70/1,684	70/1,687
		80/1,720	80/1,742
		90/1,784	90/1,799
		100/1,905	100/1,925
.50 Hornady XTP 50/44	240	70/1,578	70/1,566
		80/1,662	80/1,662
		90/1,748	90/1,797
		100/1,820	100/NA
.50 Nosler Shots 50/44	240	70/1,466	70/1,462
		80/1,606	80/1,609
		90/1,645	90/1,651
		100/1,713	100/1,729
.50 Barnes MZ 50/45	250	70/1,609	70/1,594
		80/1,705	80/1,752
		90/1,775	90/1,823
		100/1,847	100/1,971
.50 Speer/Black Sabot 50/45	260	70/1602	70/1,589
		80/1,688	80/1,683
		90/1,757	90/1,794
		100/1,811	100/1,865
.50 T/C XTP 50/45	300	70/1471	70/1,482
		80/1,600	80/1,610
		90/1,659	90/1,671
		100/1,746	100/1,749

(*table continued on page 158*)

MUZZLELOADING RIFLES LOADED WITH TRIPLE SEVEN AND BULLET OR SABOT *continued*

Caliber/Sabot	Bullet Weight (grains)	Volume (grains)/ Velocity (feet per second)	
		FFg	**FFFg**
.50 CVA Power Belt	348	70/1,428	70/1,471
		80/1,465	80/1,500
		90/1,542	90/1,595
		100/1,664	100/1,663
.50 Hornady Conical Wonder Wad	385	70/1,329	70/1,360
		80/1,423	80/1,461
		90/1,517	90/1,541
		100/1,613	100/1,605
.50 Hornady Conical Wonder Wad	410	70/1,276	70/1,383
		80/1,366	80/1,445
		90/1,460	90/1,503
		100/1,508	100/1,594
.54 Nosler Shots 54/45	250	80/1,523	NA
		90/1,625	
		100/1,789	
		120/1,884	
.54 T/C Mag Express 54/45	300	80/1,578	NA
		90/1,632	
		100/1,741	
		120/1,841	
.54 Speer Black Sabot 54/50	352	80/1,531	NA
		90/1,622	
		100/1,692	
		120/1,775	
.54 CVA Power Belt	348	80/1,473	NA
		90/1,564	
		100/1,623	
		120/1,728	
.54 T/C Max Hunter Wonder Wad	360	80/1,439	NA
		90/1,524	
		100/1,604	
		120/1,691	
.54 Hornady Great Plains Conical	425	80/1,354	NA
		90/1,423	
		100/1,499	
		120/1,587	

Effective Loads for Targets and Hunting

Every manufacturer includes a brochure for the care and feeding of its muzzleloading product. But each muzzleloader can be perfected by creating custom loads ranging from accurate target loads to small-game plinkers to crushing big-game loads. Although using various loads with different powders will have measurable effects on pressure and velocity, the real key to muzzleloading power lies in the construction and composition of the projectile. In this section, dependable hunting loads that have been proven in the field and forest are illustrated.

LOADING PROCEDURE

1. Clean the clean rifle bore. The number-one reason for misfires and hang-fires is the dirty tricks that oil plays with black and replica powders. Since oil remains in the grooves of the rifling after the final cleaning, it needs to be swabbed out of the bore with a clean, dry patch. If the oil has been there for a long time and has turned into a viscous goo, use a little rubbing alcohol to dissolve and soak it into the patch.

2. Fire a priming pan of FFFFg powder, or snap a percussion cap. This procedure will burn away any remaining oil from the ignition source and the touch hole and flash channel.

3. Be certain that the flintlock is at half-cock, with the frizzen cover off the pan, so that no accidental sparks can be generated. Insert a feather quill or pipe cleaner into the

Reclean your rifle before shooting, even if it seems to be clean. There is grease and oil that needs to be removed.

Use a separate powder measurer for the black powder going into the gun. Do not use attachments to the horn, flask, or can of black powder.

touch hole. Or, be certain that there is no percussion cap on the nipple that could be accidentally struck by the hammer or any other hard object. Insert a nipple pick into the flash channel, or place a nipple cover on top.

4. Keep the muzzle away from your face as you load. Use a separate powder measurer to measure the volume (not weight) of powder from the container, horn, or flask. Never load directly from a large container like a flask, even if it has a measurer for a spout. If you think 100 grains of powder makes a lot of fire and noise, not to mention damage, just imagine what 7,000 grains (1 pound) could do to your hands and face!

5. Load your powder with consistency. When you pour the powder into the measurer, do it the same way every time. Do not alternate leveling, shaking, tapping, crunching, or heaping black powder into the measurer. The difference in grain volume and load density will affect velocity and accuracy.

First the powder, then the ball!

6. Remember, "first the powder, then the ball." If you accidentally load a "dry ball"—loading the bullet before the powder—you have a choice: either use the screw at the end of the range rod to pull the bullet, or sneak about 5 to 10 grains of priming powder into the breech behind the ball. This can be accomplished easily on a flintlock. Just use a touch-hole pick to push the powder from the pan through the touch hole. On an external percussion, you will need to unscrew the nipple from the snail and sneak powder down through the flash channel with a nipple pick. A third alternative is to remove the breech plug, but this is a difficult operation and may require the services of a gunsmith. Make sure that the breech plug is tightened back to its exact position before loosening. Use a scribe to make a line on both the barrel (underneath, where it won't be seen) and the breech plug, so that you can align them when you refasten.

7. Tap the side of the barrel to shake the granules of black powder out of the grooves of the rifling to allow them to settle in the breech.

If loading a roundball of lead, make sure that the patch is thick enough to fill the grooves of the rifling and prevent gas blow-by.

8. Load the bullet. If it is a patched roundball, use a lubricated patch thickness that fills the bore's grooves. Remember that the patch carries lube to soften fouling. It also creates a gas check to seal the bore from blow-by, preserving accuracy. The tightness of the roundball and patch is critical to accuracy. To illustrate how this works, consider a .50 caliber. With a bore measuring 0.500 inch, and the groove depth an additional 0.008 inch on each side of the ball, if the roundball is .490, the patch (when compressed) must fill approximately 0.026 inch of space. A 0.015-inch cotton patch (pillow ticking) will fill 0.030 inch of space, but compression of the cotton into the lead ball and barrel grooves will make a perfect seal. Use a short starter to begin the ramming process down the barrel. The long length of the ramrod will cause it to bow under pressure, and possibly break. Do not use the wooden ramrods that some manufacturers include under the barrel for loading and cleaning. They break, and the brass ferules slip off the ends when pulled.

Space between the powder and the bullet is dangerous and can cause barrel damage—or worse.

Save yourself some heartache and buy a separate brass, aluminum, or plastic range rod, and let it do the heavy work.

9. If you are shooting competitively for match accuracy, remember to load the tightest patch and ball combination that you can get down the barrel. Some competitors use a ball larger than the bore, such as a 0.501-inch roundball compressed into a 0.010-inch patch. They hammer this load into the barrel, swaging the lead into the grooves. This may work for target loads, but don't consider it for hunting. Difficult loading procedures are no friend in the frigid weather of hunting season. For hunting, stick with a roundball 0.010 inch under bore size.

10. Bullets, including lead slugs such as the Hornady Great Plains, the T/C Maxi-Ball or Hunter, and the many cast lead offerings from Lyman, need special care. They engrave at

Once you have ramrodded the bullet tight to the powder, be sure to mark the ramrod at the muzzle for a future check of proper depth.

loading. This means that they may seat with some difficulty at the muzzle crown, but then slide down the barrel. Lubrication is important. Be sure to use a bullet lube (e.g., Ox-Yoke Wonder Lube 1000 Plus, T/C Natural Lube 1000+, or even beeswax or mutton tallow) in the side grooves (canellures) of the bullet.

11. Keep the bullet seated on the powder. This is very important. Once you have ramrodded the ball or bullet on top of the powder, scribe a mark around the ramrod, flush with the muzzle.

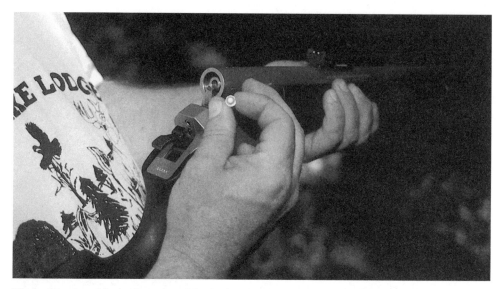

The last step in safely arming a muzzleloader is priming or capping. This should never be attempted until you are ready to shoot.

This visual cue will tell you that the bullet is correctly seated each time you load. And it can be used as a check during the hunt to ensure that the bullet is still where it should be. An airspace between the powder and ball is dangerous and can cause barrel damage, or worse.

12. Remove the flash-hole quill or pipe cleaner to open the fire channel. Prime the pan with a half pan of FFFFg priming powder (FFFg will do in a pinch). Close the frizzen cover over the pan. Keep the primer away from the touch hole for faster ignition. You want the priming powder to flash radiant heat inside the barrel and ignite the black powder charge. You do not want the priming powder burning like a fuse, slowing down the ignition, and possibly even blowing priming powder away from the touch hole. This will cause a hang-fire or flash in the pan.

13. Cap your percussion. Standard percussion caps are known as #11 or #11 magnum. It is a good idea to slightly pinch the skirt to keep the cap securely on the shoulders of the nipple. Musket caps, also referred to as #2s, provide much more ignition gas, but they also can slip off the nipple. The 209 shotgun primers are the tightest fitting percussion caps but are used only on in-line percussions.

Always wear ear and eye protection when shooting.

They will not fit on or inside the nipple of an external percussion system like a Hawken or Plains rifle.

14. Keep the muzzle pointed downrange before you draw to full cock with a flintlock or external percussion or release the safety of an in-line. Align your sights, and gently squeeze the trigger. If your rifle is equipped with two triggers, squeeze the rear trigger until it clicks. This click sets the rear trigger, which has now become the hair trigger because of its sensitivity. For hunting, it is recommended that cold or gloved fingers fire the gun only with the front trigger.

Keep the muzzle pointed downrange before you draw the hammer to full cock or release the in-line's safety device.

Hair triggers tend to go off when the hunter has not yet aligned the sights.

15. If the gun does not go off, wait one minute before you attempt to work out the problem. Damp black powder can sizzle and cook like a fuse before igniting, which is very dangerous.

Shooting a muzzleloader demands practice in loading each of the components, and patience with making the system work.

Today, sabotted, jacketed, hollow-pointed, and even copper solid bullets have been added to the armament of flintlock hunters. Historically wrong, traditionally impaired, but politically correct by marketing standards, the conical bullet in all its myriad types, shapes, and sizes must now be added to the primitive hunter's learning curve.

Does a conical "slug" bullet strike the same spot as a roundball if the hunter uses the same load used in previous flintlock deer seasons? Surprisingly, the answer might be yes, if the shot is taken at a target less than 25 yards away. The real difference between a ball and a slug is evident when the effects of air resistance, wind, gyroscopic rotation, velocity, and mass are evaluated over time and distance.

To make sense of all the math and physics involved when comparing the flight of a roundball with the flight of a conical bullet, think of a baseball. To throw a fastball over home plate, the pitcher adds just the right amount of rotation, learned from years of practice. Too much spin causes the ball to "curve" away from the straight line desired. Too little spin causes the ball to "knuckleball" out of control, veering toward an unknown destination at the plate.

Patched roundballs, like baseballs, need just the right amount of rotation to stabilize them in flight. At velocities under 1,400 feet per second (which are normally generated with very light target loads of powder), a faster rate of twist will stabilize the trajectory of a roundball. But faster velocities (which are generated with hunting loads of powder) require a slower rotation in the barrel to prevent the ball from curving toward the target. Although a 1:48 twist (used by many manufacturers because it allows shooters to use roundball bullets as well as lead slugs) works well under 50 yards or with the slower velocities of roundballs, it becomes very apparent at longer yardages that this is not the optimal rotation.

Slower rates of rifling twist, traditionally 1:60 to 1:72, gave round-balls their historic accuracy to 100 yards. Even slower rates of twist are necessary in heavy rifles that target objects at 200 yards and beyond, since they fire roundballs at a velocity greater than 2,000 feet per second.

The following tables profile commonly used rates of rifling in historic, custom-made, and mass-produced factory barrels. They are meant only as guides.

Caliber	Roundball Diameter (inches)	Standard Rifling Rate of Twist	Minimum Optimal Rate of Twist
.32	.310	1:48	1:40
.36	.350	1:48	1:48
.40	.390	1:48	1:56
.45	.440	1:48	1:60
.50	.490	1:48	1:66
.54	.530	1:48	1:72
.58	.570	1:48	1:84

Footballs, like conoidal bullets, fly differently from baseballs, or roundballs. If the quarterback's wrists and fingers don't impart a high rate of rotation to the football, it won't make a stable spiral straight to the intended target. Low rates of rotation make footballs wobble and fly out of control. The very slow rate of rotation imparted by a roundball barrel would create an unstable flight for a slug. A rifling twist of 1:48 will not shoot an elongated bullet, saboted or not, with the accuracy of a barrel with a faster rate of rifling twist. Barrels, specifically designed for sabotted bullets, are now manufactured with rotations of 1:30 to 1:20. Slugs shot at velocities over 1,600 feet per second need fast rates of rotation to stabilize their performance. Therefore, the longer and faster the bullet, the faster the rifling rotation should be.

Caliber	Lead and Sabot-Jacketed Bullets	Standard Rifling Rate of Twist	Minimum Optimal Rate of Twist
.45	.440–.454	1:48	1:24
.50	.440–.501	1:48	1:28
.54	.450–.541	1:48	1:32

Modern Muzzleloading Bullets

If you have decided to make the switch to slugs, a new barrel may be in order. But first, determine what kind of barrel might be best. Modern muzzleloading bullets can be divided into three groups: lead slugs, sabots, and plastic gas check slugs. Each has its own special barrel requirements.

The first group is best described as lead slugs. The most common ingredient found in all muzzleloading bullets is lead. This is a logical choice, since it is the heaviest nonradioactive metal that is abundantly and economically available. Copper, two and a half times less dense than lead (less kinetic energy at the same velocity), is triple the cost. Bismuth is one proton denser than lead but is basically unavailable, even at four times the cost (except for birdshot in shotguns). Lead is superior to copper in carrying energy downrange, and its high molecular cohesion means that it does a superior job of staying together during acceleration and impact. The mushrooming effect, or obturation, would disintegrate other metals, but not lead. Its greater density gives deeper penetration and more total release of the energy than any other speeding mass.

Lead slugs are marketed under names such as Hornady Great Plains Bullets, Buffalo Bullets, T/C Maxi-Hunter, T/C Maxi-Ball, Buffalo Ball-ets, CVA Buckslayer, and Colorado Conicals. What they all have in common is increased weight, greater sectional density, and a better ballistic coefficient. The heavier bullet increases the

You may need a new barrel if you're moving to slugs.

recoil on your shoulder, results in slower velocities, and increases the cost. These bullets also laminate the bore with lead. But they do have the ability to carry energy more efficiently downrange.

Slugs penetrate better than roundballs because they have greater sectional density. This is a result of their greater weight in relationship to their diameter. This allows the various types of slugs to retain their velocity better than roundballs do. Their ballistic coefficient is higher because of the ratio between their sectional density and their shape. In other words, their pointed noses are aerodynamically more slippery. The same caliber slug comes in different nose configurations, and they are available in different weights. They also have different bearing surfaces against the grooves of the rifling (some designed as lubrication grooves), and even their gas-sealing bases are different.

Slugs are much slower than roundballs at the muzzle when propelled by the same volume of powder, and they too will shed almost one-third of their velocity at the 100-yard mark, but their retained energy is better due to their greater mass. Unfortunately, your shoulder will tell you that you launched a missile heavier than a roundball.

You must take extra care to seat the lead slug on the powder, as well as checking its position from time to time as you hunt. Lead slugs have a tendency to jar loose from their seated position. If an airspace develops, "detonation" could occur. This phenomenon takes place when burning powder is pushed forward from the breech into the airspace created by the loose slug and then detonates at the base of the projectile. Higher-than-normal pressures occur, swelling a good steel barrel into a "walnut," which ruins it for good. The worst-case scenario is a weakened, flawed, or ancient iron barrel that bursts, harming the shooter and nearby spectators.

Another problem inherent to lead slugs is the "laminating" of the bore. Lead is a soft metal that shears off in the deeper 0.008- to 0.012-inch grooves of a roundball barrel. Even on a 0.005-inch slug barrel, lead laminates itself to the lands of the barrel with each shot. If this lead is not thoroughly scrubbed out, accuracy and ease of reloading can be affected. Fortunately, modern solvents and bronze brushes solve this problem.

A new problem that has arisen with lead slugs is "base slamming." I coined this term to describe what happens when a lead slug is loaded on top of a Pyrodex or Triple Seven pellet without the protection of a fiber wad. The first pellet is ignited, and the rest burn progressively down the barrel. The first pellet generates enough gas pressure to slam the second and subsequent pellets into the base of the lead slug. Rather than the normal flare of the skirt or the base of the lead slug filling the grooves of the rifling, gas bypasses the lead base through the rifling grooves. The unburned pellet material becomes a barrel obstruction, and erratic pressures occur. The bottom line is that a grease fiber wad is necessary for the sake of accuracy and maximum velocity.

The second group of slugs is best described under the family name "sabots." Plastic patches around a bullet were introduced in the mid-1970s under the name Poly-Patch. The idea was simple: eliminate the cutting of cloth and the messiness of grease by simply inserting the roundball into a soft plastic gas-sealing cup. In warm weather, it worked. In cold weather, the roundball rolled forward out of the cup, creating a dangerous situation. Plastic patches soon earned a bad reputation, in spite of an improved cup that no longer allowed slippage. Then, in the 1990s, a new idea was introduced: placing jacketed pistol bullets into a larger shoe (*sabot* is French for "shoe" or "sheath") of plastic. The age of the sabot had arrived.

Sabots come in many different forms. Thompson/Center Break-O-Way sabots split into two pieces, releasing the bullet; most others open up their "petals," slits that run longitudinally, to allow the bullet's release. Names like Hornady XTP, Nosler Partition sabots and SHOTS, MML sabots, Swift A-Frame sabots, Silver Lightning sabots, Barnes MZ sabots, and Precision Extremes HPBT, among others, intrigue muzzleloading hunters.

Most sabotted bullets are .44- and 45-caliber pistol bullets that have been "plastic-wrapped" so that they fit tightly into .50- and 54-caliber bores. They possess a smaller diameter and have a better ballistic coefficient and sectional density than roundballs, but their 250- to 500-grain weights are deceiving. They are much heavier than the same caliber roundball, and thus slower with the same volume of powder. But when being shot at really big game or at game animals beyond 100 yards, their retained energy is far more impressive than that of the roundball.

Plastic sabots do not perform with the deeper rifling found on roundball barrels, because exploding gases can bypass the bullet

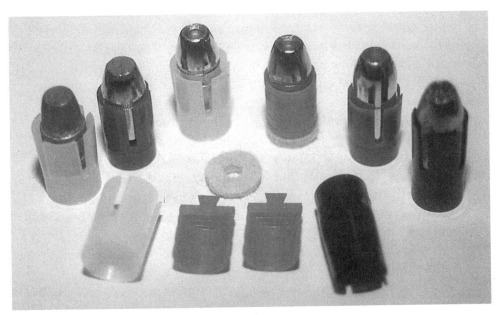

Sabots come in a variety of different forms.

through the deep grooves. The inconsistent pressures lead to inaccuracy. That is why you need a shallow-grooved, fast-twist rifling to shoot saboted bullets effectively. You will need to experiment with different bullet weights, sabot types, and nose configurations until you find the one that works well with your gun. But remember, the soft plastic sabots (not the harder sabots, such as those from Muzzleload Magnum Products) will laminate the lands of your rifling, and this will affect the ease of loading as well as accuracy in future years. To keep the plastic lamination to a minimum, strong plastic solvents and a bronze bore brush are necessary. This lamination problem is the reason for the rise of the third group of muzzleloading slugs—plastic gas check slugs.

The idea of a gas check began at the turn of the twentieth century. Gunsmiths found that the higher pressures generated by smokeless powders would sometimes blow gases by the soft lead of the slug's base. To guarantee consistent velocities, copper was mated to the base of the lead bullet to tightly seal the grooves of the rifling. Today, a plastic gas check is attached to the bullet's base. This provides the advantages of sealing off the blow-by of gases, facilitating ease of loading, and increasing the accuracy of a lead bullet while reducing the amount of plastic laminate on the lands of the rifling. Bullets such as the CVA Powerbelt, Copper Magnum, and Black Belt, have plastic gas checks at their base, but since they do not run a plastic bearing surface between the bullet and the bore, they are not considered sabots.

A thorough understanding of modern muzzleloading bullets would not be complete without a consideration of bullet performance on deer-size game. Bullet performance is the result of several variables: velocity, mass, and the ability to expand (mushroom or obturate). Slow velocities are no friend to muzzleloading bullets. Velocities under 1,400 feet per second are too slow for the bullet to generate enough energy, expand, and penetrate. Since higher velocities are desirable, consider that they are directly related to bullet weight.

Patched roundballs are the lightest bullets per caliber. With a given powder charge, roundballs are faster than slugs. This is important, because it means that they get to the target faster, are more accurate under 100 yards, and expand better.

Why, then, did the jacketed bullet come into existence? The increased velocities of lead slugs caused considerable lead lamination in rifle bores. Any round that exceeded 2,000 feet per second suffered less accuracy with succeeding shots. To remedy this, gunsmiths began to place lead cores in copper jackets. The copper didn't affect the steel bore as much as other metals did, but it created a new problem: copper jackets retarded the mushrooming effect of lead. This caused a huge loss of shocking power. The 11-inch cone of hydrostatic shock that roundball shooters expected from their typical hunting loads was reduced to a 3-inch wound channel. Sure, there was an exit hole, but the deer didn't collapse like they did from the expanding hunks of lead that lethally "shocked" them to the ground.

Overnight, entrepreneurs offered the hunter myriad bullet designs that were supposed to mushroom back with tremendous shocking power, just like the lowly, soft-lead roundball. But the copper jacket prevented that from happening. Bullet designers began to split the jacket at the nose; then they came up with exposed lead tips, the hollow point, and finally, the ballistic tip. However, all these improvements still only added up to what a slower soft-lead roundball could do—expand to 100 percent of its diameter.

The advent of copper solids, albeit hollow-pointed and petaled, introduced another consideration into the mix—metallurgy. Lead has been the traditional bullet metal, but throughout history, iron, tin, nickel, tungsten, bismuth, and other metals have been tried. Is there something new and improved on the horizon? Perhaps, but there is a real problem with bullet expansion when using anything other than lead. The real culprit in bullet expansion is slow velocity. Heavier bullets travel slower than lighter bullets with the same powder charge. Recoil increases proportionately as shooters increase the powder charge to attain the velocities that jacketed bullets need to expand. Felt recoil becomes considerable. For recoil-shy hunters, the soft push of a normal roundball load was an advantage in accurate shooting. But with the advent of slugs, recoil must be considered and addressed.

Following is a sampling of the modern bullets available for muzzleloaders. Barnes Bullets' new Expander MZ sabotted, six-petal bullet is designed to retain 100 percent of its weight on impact. It is available in .50- and .54-caliber packs of 10 or 25 bullets. Barnes also offers an MZ aligner tool that screws into the end of ramrods and has the same shape as the nose of the Expander Bullet.

CVA PowerBelt bullets have a patented snap-on base that provides the benefits of sabotted bullets and none of the problems. The base provides a gas seal, enabling consistent pressures and great accuracy. Unlike sabot bullets, PowerBelt bullets are full caliber sized, are easy to load, and do not require cleaning after every shot. They are available in both copper-clad and full-lead bullets. CVA also offers a Hollow-Point Bullet Starter for maximizing accuracy with any hollow-point bullet.

Hornady sells a 300-grain XTP (extreme terminal performance) magnum bullet inside a black plastic sabot for .50-caliber rifles. They come packaged in 20-bullet cards. Also, Hornady's new Hard Ball is tougher than pure lead. This cold swaged-lead roundball is hardened with antimony and promises deeper penetration than that of the typical roundball. The new SST sabot uses a polymer tip to achieve expansion at lower speeds, as well as preventing fragmentation at hypervelocity.

Hornady is also marketing the Lock-N-Load Speed Sabot SST, which is pushing muzzleloading as close to a cartridge as it can get. Three Pyrodex or Triple Seven pellets are locked onto an extension stem from the base of the plastic sabot. This 150-grain load should be used only in muzzleloading rifles designed to handle this tremendous pressure. A .50-caliber (actually a .45-diameter, 250-grain bullet) SST-ML bullet will generate 2,250 feet per second muzzle velocity and 2,735 foot-pounds of energy. Even out to 250 yards, the bullet will still be sizzling at 1,389 feet per second and smashing home with 1,070 foot-pounds of energy, while losing only 11 inches in trajectory. But make sure that it is a safe load for your particular rifle.

Knight Rifles is offering a line of Knight sabots containing bullets tested in its own rifles. The new line consists of Knight Bonded A-Frame bullets by Swift and Knight Red Hot bullets by Barnes. Designed for 1:28 rifling and higher velocities, they should be great performers in Knight rifles and those with similar configurations.

Nosler partition bullets are famous for their performance on big game. The bullet's soft lead core is separated into two sections and surrounded by a tapered metal jacket for controlled expansion. These bullets have been noted for shooting tight groups at over 100 yards.

Speer is introducing a wide range of bullets for muzzleloaders. Some of the new sabotted offerings include 270-, 300-, and 325-grain weights. Gold Dot and Unicore bullets offer a choice of nose expansion and terminal penetration on various species of small and big game.

Swift Bullet Company offers its highly successful A-Frame bullet in sabots. Famous for deep penetration and superior weight retention, this is a well-regarded bullet known for reliable expansion.

Thompson/Center has introduced the new PTX Power Tip Express and the polymer-tip Shock Wave in Mag Express sabots in conventional and magnum velocities. A polycarbonate tip improves terminal ballistic performance over a wider range of velocities than traditional hollow-points or solid lead slugs.

Traditions Performance Firearms' XTP Hunter sabot hollow-point, a jacketed sabot bullet, offers accuracy and balanced expansion with its .50-caliber, 240-grain load. The company also offers

100 percent wool Wonder Wads for loading prior to the sabot to increase lubrication and protect the base of the sabot. The new T-Shock sabot is a patented expansion technology that uses a sealed hydraulic chamber to ensure expansion and energy transfer at all velocities.

Achieving top performance and reclaiming the accuracy of hot muzzleloader hunting charges behind sabotted bullets may be easier with the new Ballistic Bridge Sub-Base from Muzzleload Magnum Products. It provides an additional gas seal to protect the sabot and bullet from the higher pressures created by hot black powder, Pyrodex, and Triple Seven charges. Available for .50-caliber rifles, the MMP Ballistic Bridge Sub-Base is seated over the powder charge with the ramrod; then the sabot and bullet are seated directly over the sub-base. The domed top of the Ballistic Bridge Sub-Base fits up into the cupped base of all MMPs produced in .50 sabots, as well as most other brands. The additional pressure seal is often needed to tame down the accuracy with some of the hotter smokeless powder loads shot out of the Savage 10ML II muzzleloader.

Power and Accuracy

Can the flintlock rifle, loaded with only a roundball, really develop the kind of devastating power needed to anchor a whitetail in its tracks? The answer may surprise you: yes! Too many modern ballisticians relegate this venerable old shooting system to the attic of outdated mechanisms. The guys who are actually using them and bringing home venison on a consistent basis might be the better authorities. So let's take a look at how to create a devastating flintlock load for your gun.

The following table is courtesy of Thompson/Center; it lists suggested loads for T/C muzzleloading rifles (flint or percussion). These values are for reference only and should not be followed as a loading guide. Follow the manual supplied by your gun's manufacturer. Note that variables such as barrel length, type of powder, thickness of patch, type of lube, and temperature will modify velocity and energy.

A flintlock rifle loaded with a roundball actually has enough power to stop a whitetail.

To down a whitetail quickly and ethically, the hunter must ensure the gun and ammunition provide enough energy.

The first question to be answered is one of lethality. What characteristics must be considered to create a load that quickly dispatches a whitetail? The answer is: energy. The American Hunting Institute back in the 1970s determined that a roundball projectile should exhibit at least 500 foot-pounds of energy to penetrate the 11 inches of vital organs on a mature whitetail. But today's marketing gurus are pushing a minimum of 1,000 foot-pounds of energy, claiming that this is necessary to kill a whitetail. Did whitetails suddenly become stronger and tougher to kill? If the motivation is in-

PRIMITIVE LOAD: PATCHED ROUNDBALLS

Caliber	Bullet Diameter (inches)/ Weight (grains)	Black Powder Charge (grains), FFg	Velocity (feet per second)	Energy (foot-pounds)
.45	.440/127	50	1,605	727
		60	1,720	835
		70*	1,825	940
		80	1,929	1,050
		90	2,003	1,132
		100	2,081	1,221
		Maximum 110	2,158	1,314
.50	.490/175	50	1,357	716
		60	1,434	799
		70	1,643	1,050
		80*	1,838	1,313
		90	1,950	1,478
		100	2,052	1,637
		Maximum 110	2,135	1,772
.54	.530/230	60	1,263	815
		70	1,469	1,102
		80*	1,654	1,397
		90	1,761	1,584
		100	1,855	1,758
		110	1,931	1,905
		120	1,983	2,009
.56	.550/265	80*	1,195	840
		90	1,285	972
		100	1,300	995
.58	.570/279	80	1,302	1,050
		90*	1,373	1,168
		100	1,428	1,263
		110	1,519	1,430
		120	1,595	1,576

*Recommended for optimal accuracy and performance.

creased distance, then I agree that the extra velocity and energy are necessary to kill deer at 200 yards. But most of the deer that I have taken in the last 40 years were at distances under 50 yards.

The following table lists suggested loads for T/C and Traditions rifles. Use it only as a reference; follow the manufacturer's manual as a loading guide. Note that variables such as barrel length, type of powder, thickness of sabot, diameter and grain weight of sabotted bullet, and temperature will modify velocity and energy.

Caliber	Bullet Diameter (inches)/ Weight (grains)	Pyrodex Pellets (50 grains each)	Velocity (feet per second)	Energy (foot-pounds)
.45 ShockWave	.400/200	2	2,035	1,840
		3	2,398	2,554
.50 Break-O-Way	.429/200	2	1,816	1,465
	.429/240	2	1,665	1,478
	.429/275	2	1,611	1,585
	.429/300	2	1,422	1,347
.50 Traditions T-Shock	.451/250	3	2,139	2,540
	.451/275	3	2,086	2,657
	.451/300	3	2,023	2,726

Remember that the greater the distance to the target, the less energy your roundball will carry to it. To understand why, you need to understand two concepts: sectional density and ballistic coefficient. The following table displays how quickly a roundball bullet increases in weight and ballistic coefficient as its caliber size increases. This allows larger-caliber roundballs to slip through the air more easily, as well as retaining energy better at longer distances. These values are also useful when calculating downrange velocities.

Roundball Caliber	Diameter (inches)	Weight (grains)	Ballistic Coefficient
.32	.310	45	.043
.36	.350	65	.049
.40	.390	80	.054
.45	.440	128	.062
.50	.490	177	.068
.54	.535	230	.075
.58	.570	276	.080
.75	.715	545	.097

The geometry of the sphere makes it the lightest-weight, fastest-flying bullet that can fit down the barrel and seal the bore against burning gases. However, it generally sheds one-third of its velocity and nearly one-half of its energy by the 100-yard mark. This is due to its sectional density—that is, the relationship between the bullet's weight and its diameter. Increase the length of the bullet, and it retains energy better; decrease its length, and it loses energy faster. The ballistic coefficient, or the ability to fly through the air with reduced resistance and drag, is also poor on a roundball. The lower the ballistic coefficient, the greater the wind resistance and the faster it loses velocity. If a roundball had a spitzer pointed nose (higher ballistic coefficient), longer body, and boat-tailed back end, it would carry its velocity the same way modern, high-performance jacketed bullets do.

Don't despair. Ballisticians may try to convince you that the roundball is a terrible bullet, based on its sectional density and ballistic coefficient, but remember that tens of thousands of deer and larger game are taken yearly with this lowly orb of lead. There must be a reason.

The reason a roundball can be so devastating is due to its geometry, its plastic nature and tendency to mushroom larger, and its intense density. Specifically, the sphere is an awesome shape. The lightweight .45 caliber checks in at 127 grains, but if you move up only 0.05, the sphere increases almost 50 grains in weight.

CALIBER SIZES

Have you ever wondered how the old caliber sizes used by our military came into being? Turner Kirkland, deceased founder of Dixie Gun Works, did. He made an amazing discovery. It seems that each popular caliber in our country's early history was a result of "half sizing." His chart bears this out:

Caliber	Approximate Number to Pound	Approximate Relative Size
.69 (.68)	13	1
.58 (.57)	25	$1/2$ weight of .69
.44 (.453)	50	$1/2$ weight of .58
.36 (.375)	100	$1/2$ weight of .44
.31 (.320)	150	$1/3$ weight of .44

Bullet Caliber	Diameter (inches)	Weight (grains)	Ballistic Coefficient
.36	.360 Buffalo HP	125	.080
.45	.450 Buffalo Ball-et	200	.067
	.450 T/C Maxi-Ball	240	.078
	.357 Hornady Sabot	158	.177
.50	.500 Buffalo HP Conical	350	.142
	.500 T/C Maxi-Ball	370	.095
	.430 Hornady Sabot	240	.205
.54	.540 Buffalo Ball-et	338	.083
	.540 Hornady Great Plains	425	.163
	.540 T/C Maxi-Ball	430	.150
	.430 Hornady Sabot	265	.189
.58	.580 T/C Maxi-Hunter	560	.123
	.580 T/C Maxi-Ball	555	.120

Move from the 175-grain, .50-caliber roundball to the awesome .54 caliber, and you add 55 grains of weight, up to 230 grains. And if you move up to what I consider the ultimate roundball caliber, the .58, you will be chucking a 280-grain ball of lead. In other words, from .45 to .58 caliber, an increase in bore size of only 0.13 inch, a rifleman can pick up 153 grains of bullet weight.

How does this translate into game-getting power? Consider the devastating energies involved. The .45 caliber (which some hunters consider underpowered, but I have taken 11 deer with it, including my biggest buck ever) sends a roundball to a deer standing at 50 yards with about 500 foot-pounds of energy. The .50-caliber ball dramatically increases to about 725 foot-pounds, and the .54 to 850 foot-pounds at 50 yards. These energies are more than adequate to drop a deer in its tracks, but the hunter must be careful to accurately place the load and, more importantly, to accurately judge the distance to the target.

From all this information, it would appear that only the big calibers are good choices for hunting deer with a flintlock, but it really depends on a number of factors. What style of hunting do you do? How do you feel about carrying a heavy rifle? Do you flinch at the heavier recoil of bigger rifles? What are your chances of using open iron sights and hitting a deer at 100 yards? These answers will determine the best caliber for you.

The most important thing when hunting with a flintlock rifle and a patched roundball is to have confidence. If you load a .45 with 80 grains of FFg, a .50 with 100 grains of FFg, or a .54 with 110 grains of FFg, you will have more than enough devastating energy to kill a deer. These loads have harvested millions of white-tails during three centuries of hunting in North America. You are in good company.

Accuracy is what makes a lethal load, not terminal ballistics. And choice of bullet has a profound effect on accuracy. Accuracy requires that the bullet be accelerated uniformly out of the barrel. This means using a consistent powder charge that causes small group sizes on the target,

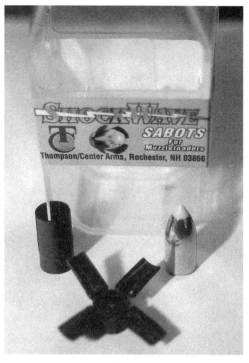

Roundball velocities under 900 feet per second are too slow to create a large wound channel. Velocities under 1,200 feet per second won't allow jacketed bullets to expand.

while ensuring enough velocity for the bullet to cause maximum tissue damage and penetration. This usually happens above 900 feet per second for soft lead bullets and 1,200 feet per second for jacketed. Accelerate the bullet too fast, and it may become unstable; accelerate the bullet too slowly, and "bullet drop" becomes a major nemesis. The three variables in bullet drop are distance, velocity, and deceleration (the rate at which the bullet speed decreases and the bullet falls). In other words, the longer a bullet falls (32.16 feet per second), the faster it drops.

If you hunt with a traditional roundball bullet (powder, patch, and ball), the following information may confirm what you already suspected. A .45-caliber flintlock with a 26-inch barrel can be loaded with a patched roundball (a .440 roundball weighs 127 grains) and 70 grains of FFFg black powder to produce a muzzle velocity close to 1,900 feet per second. This load generates about 1,000 foot-

This roundball has too much rotation, and it curves away from the target.

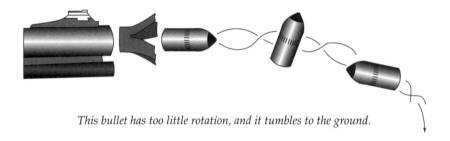

This bullet has too little rotation, and it tumbles to the ground.

pounds of energy at the muzzle—twice the minimum energy needed for a whitetail. But a roundball sheds energy quickly. In just 50 yards, this load will lose half its energy, leaving the hunter with about 536 foot-pounds of energy. This is awfully close to the minimum, but it is still more energy than that of some magnum handgun loads, which are often recommended for deer hunting. The .45 caliber's higher velocity, compared with other calibers, makes it the fastest and flattest shooting of all the flintlock calibers that are legal for deer. It is also a very accurate caliber, and the smaller barrel diameter makes it one of the lightest rifles in weight.

Velocity is important to accuracy. If a deer can run at speeds approaching 40 miles per hour, or 58.6 feet per second, the time it takes for the bullet to reach a deer at 100 yards is critical. The slower the bullet, the greater the possibility that it will impact behind the moving target. Also, the slower the bullet, the less hydrostatic shock will be delivered and in a smaller wound channel. In other words, even though a cylindrical bullet has more retained energy, it may not be as accurate or kill as quickly as a roundball.

When a .50 caliber is loaded with 90 grains of FFFg or 100 grains of FFg black powder, the 180-grain roundball produces a muzzle velocity close to 1,800 feet per second, with about 1,300

Most flintlock rifles have slow rates of twist, which helps make roundballs more accurate.

Velocity is an important consideration when choosing bullets. Too slow a bullet can cause a miss or, even worse, a wounding.

foot-pounds of energy. This is a significant leap in energy over the .45-caliber. It gives the open-woods hunter a distinct lethal-range advantage. In fact, the gun's roundball lethality carries all the way out to 80 yards. Perhaps that is why the .50 has become the nation's favorite caliber and the one that I recommend to all hunters new to this sport.

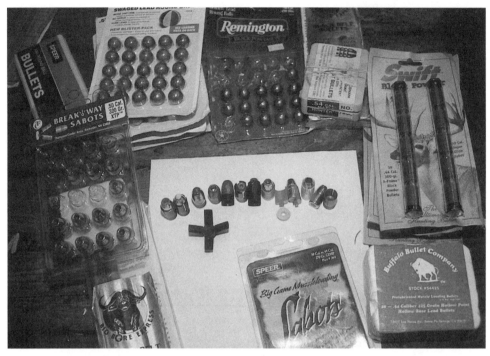

There are two types of roundballs: cast and swaged. Cast bullets must be loaded with the sprue mark up in the patch, while swaged bullets do not have a sprue mark. Both roundballs are equally accurate.

Accuracy changes with the angle of fire. Practice shooting downhill or from a tree stand. Don't count on last year's sight picture shot through iron sights from the bench at a level shooting range to print the bullet at the same spot when it is fired at a 30-degree angle.

Roundballs come in cast and swaged forms. Cast lead ball, both homemade in handheld molds and those commercially cast, can be very good projectiles. But hunters must be aware that casting irregularities can affect accuracy. Mold marks such as parting lines, air bubbles and streaks, and uneven sprue marks can all influence the accuracy of flight. Because the weight of the lead sphere is changed by irregularities of the molded lead, inspect each roundball before you load it.

To take the guesswork out of roundballs, manufacturers such as Hornady, Speer, and Buffalo are marketing swaged roundballs. By compacting a premeasured (by weight and volume) cylinder of lead in a press, the plastic nature of lead allows it to mold into a perfect 360-degree sphere of precise weight and caliber. Remington Gold has taken the swaged lead roundball one step further by plating it with brass. It is important that lead not be allowed to oxidize, because the surface will become abrasive and irregular. Brass plating, a coating of grease or beeswax, or immersion in a lubricating oil preserves the integrity of the sphere's surface and keeps it accurate.

To shoot a roundball accurately, hunters need to load a tight patch-ball combination. The choice of patch material is critical. The cotton or linen material (never use synthetics, because they melt in the heat generated by the exploding black powder) must be thick enough to form a gas seal, carry the lubricant, and hold up to tremendous pressure at the base of the bullet. Examine your patches. If they show holes or burned areas, the patch was not thick enough or was cut during the loading process. Some hunters like precut, prelubed patches like those from Ox-Yoke; some prefer the Teflon pillow ticking available at Dixie Gun Works; and still others like to lube their own cotton patches that they cut at the muzzle. The ideal patch shows a slightly blackened spot where it made contact with the powder, with light streaks where the folds surrounded the roundball. But accuracy, as always, is the bottom line. Only practice and experimentation will give your roundball rig the optimal patch-ball combination.

When choosing your muzzleloading projectile, remember that ballistics change with variables such as powder type and granulation, barrel length, depth of rifling and twist, thickness of patch and lube, and even temperature and humidity. The table on the following page compares different bullets in one rifle.

So which bullet is the best muzzleloading bullet for hunting deer? The answer, as you can see, is both simple and complex. The simple answer is that the best bullet is the one that you can shoot with a combination of accuracy and lethality. The complexity of bullet choice relates to the type of rifle (primitive or modern), length of barrel, rate of rifling, depth of grooves, type of powder, volume of powder, and the distance at which you typically shoot deer. There is no easy answer—just lots of great bullet choices.

.50-CALIBER T/C HAWKEN LOADED WITH 100 GRAINS FFG BLACK POWDER

Bullet	Range (yards)	Impact (inches)	Velocity (feet per second)	Energy (foot-pounds)
177-grain	0	—	1,875	1,403
roundball	50	−1.62	1,387	778
	100	−8.16	1,054	449
355-grain	0	—	1,400	1,566
Maxi-Hunter	50	−2.53	1,153	1,063
	100	−11.6	994	789
300-grain	0	—	1,621	1,750
Barnes Sabot	50	−2.01	1,478	1,455
	100	−6.10	1,349	1,212

Ballistics

A hunter new to the sport of muzzleloading has little time to study the aerodynamics of bullets. But eventually, many muzzleloaders begin to wonder about the perfect load, the most devastating bullet, and how to make the impossible shot possible. This section is for those seeking a Ph.D. in muzzleloading. It provides the analytical answers to the most common question for muzzleloading deer hunters: What would happen if . . . ?

It was the second week of the rifle deer season, and the woods were devoid of the pumpkin-colored army of a million Pennsylvania hunters. The morning had dawned gray and ugly. The steep climb through the brittle squaw wood produced a tinkling sound as each branch snapped from the spruce trees. Steam slowly vented from my overdressed torso. These wisps of vapor only served to remind me that deer would have no trouble avoiding me today. My scent line would obviously arrive far sooner than I would.

The two licenses pinned to my back ensured that I could legally harvest a deer, any deer, with my muzzleloader. But an antlerless deer was not on my agenda. I had far too many days left in the season to want to tag a doe. My home state had decreased

When distance or obstacles make the deer difficult to see, the hunter must establish a good mental picture before firing.

the odds for success on bucks, though, because I had to find one whose antlers consisted of at least three 1-inch tines on each side.

Hundreds of yards away, the straining motor of a school bus whined as it labored uphill. I smiled as I watched its bouncing load of energetic passengers voicing their enthusiasm for arrival at a nearby elementary school. A momentary flashback reminded me of those pleasant days slaving over math equations and physics experiments. Suddenly, a twig snapped up at the edge of the cornfield. A buck! A really nice buck with wide, spreading antlers. One, two, three, four long tines projected from each one. My heart began to pound. Each strong beat rushed another load of oxygen-enriched blood to my cerebral cortex so that I could process all the data that were screaming into my brain from every sensory organ.

"Okay, slow down, take a deep breath," I whispered to myself. Let's see: distance—under 100; angle—40 degrees uphill; temperature—above freezing; barometric pressure—falling at 500 feet above sea level; light conditions—indistinct gloom with a teaser of fog. With the front iron sight covering up much of the deer's front shoulder, I tried to finesse a sharper sight picture by mentally measuring the length of the buck from his brisket to his rump. "Just past the shoulder, halfway up. Squeeeeeeze the trigger," I murmured to myself.

Ka-bang, thundered the big-bore .54 American Jaeger as 100 grains of black powder exploded to life, belching fire and brimstone out the end of its cavernous maw. The thick white cloud of sulfurous smoke hung on the moist air like an eighteenth-century apparition looking for a forgotten Revolutionary War soldier's soul. The second hand of eternity stopped and waited for life to resume after the smoke cleared. But what I saw was unexpected. The big deer with the bragging-sized rack had not moved. His nose twitched, his eyes grew large, and his chest heaved, awestruck by what he had just witnessed. But threatened, he was not!

I was stunned. There I stood with an empty muzzleloader—the same muzzleloader I had taken two caribou with just three months earlier; the same muzzleloader that I had successfully competed with at the National Shoot for the Pennsylvania Flintlock Team. But I had missed—cleanly. The deer eventually lost interest in the apparition as it drifted and dissolved on the heavy downhill thermal. The mighty eight-point buck simply walked away, leaving me in the eerie silence of a missed opportunity.

Have you ever found yourself in this predicament? You will. Given enough time as a muzzleloading hunter, there will be an "oops," followed by an epiphany. In your awakening, you will ask, What would have happened if . . . ?

Since 1888, when Krupp of Germany first accurately quantified the air drag influence on bullet travel by test-firing large, flat-bottomed, blunt-nosed bullets, the science of ballistics has been affecting the way we shoot muzzleloaders. But the modern science of ballistics allows the shooter to understand the variables of bullet shape, velocity, energy, and downrange accuracy. Although ballistics calculations involve some math, mostly multiplying and dividing, this too is simplified with three modern-day tools: an electronic grain-weight scale, an electronic chronograph, and a simple handheld calculator. The effort is minimal, and the results are profound. Understanding simple ballistics calculations will enable you to be a successful hunter, not an also-ran shooter at game.

The modern science of ballistics allows the shooter to understand bullet shape, velocity, energy, and downrange accuracy.

CALCULATING MUZZLELOADING BULLET ENERGY

The first time I heard that the minimum muzzleloading caliber for deer was .45, I was hugely impressed. After all, my earlier hunting days involved .30-30s, .32 Specials, .250-3000s, 7mm magnums, .30-06s, and .308s, and none of these bore sizes came close to the .45. When I looked down the bore of that first .45 caliber, I couldn't believe how big it was. Today, I know better. A 127-grain roundball of .45 caliber just doesn't have the energy to anchor a big whitetail at more than 50 yards.

How much energy is enough? The minimum speed necessary to disable soft tissue (skin and organs) of a whitetail-sized animal with a lead projectile is 163 feet per second. To break bones, accelerate the lead to 213 feet per second. This was why the American Hunting Institute set 500 foot-pounds of energy as the minimum energy required from muzzleloaders back in the 1970s. It stands true today.

You'll need a chronograph to calculate muzzleloader velocities. This electronic device lets you know whether your most accurate load will have the speed necessary to ethically dispatch a whitetail.

But how does one calculate energy? Use the standard kinetic energy (KE) formula given to us by Sir Isaac Newton back in 1667:

KE = (MV × MV) ÷ 7,000 ÷ 64.32 × BW,

where MV is muzzle velocity in feet per second and BW is bullet weight in grains. The figure 7,000 is used to convert grains to pounds (there are 7,000 grains to 1 pound), and 64.32 is the acceleration of gravity.

Let's compare the KE of a .50-caliber roundball, a .50 Maxi-Hunter, and a .50 Barnes sabot:

Data for the .50-caliber roundball (0.490-inch): 177 grains, shot from a 28-inch barrel, 1:48 rifling, 100 grains of FFg black powder, 1,875 feet per second (fps) MV.

KE = (1,875 × 1,875) ÷ 7,000 ÷ 64.32 × 177
KE = 1,382 foot-pounds

Data for the .50-caliber Maxi-Hunter (0.500 inch): 355 grains, 1:48 rifling, 100 grains of black powder, 1,400 fps MV.

$$KE = (1,400 \times 1,400) \div 7,000 \div 64.32 \times 355$$
$$KE = 1,545 \text{ foot-pounds}$$

Data for the .50-caliber Barnes sabot: 300 grains, 1:48 rifling, 100 grains of black powder, 1,621 fps MV.

$$KE = (1,621 \times 1,621) \div 7,000 \div 64.32 \times 300$$
$$KE = 1,751 \text{ foot-pounds}$$

It quickly becomes obvious that the formula for kinetic energy is skewed in favor of higher-velocity bullets. There is an exponential rise in energy with an increase in the velocity of the bullet, but not with its weight. This is why many muzzleloading ballisticians don't accept kinetic energy as the only measure of a bullet's power. In fact, noted author and ballistician Sam Fadala notes that "momentum" might be a more accurate method for calculating muzzleloading bullet performance.

CALCULATING BULLET MOMENTUM

Muzzleloading hunters who have had experience with the devastating power of a big-bore slug of lead, know that an ounce of lead will drop anything in North America. Even at slow velocities, this mighty chunk of heavy metal will destroy bones, liquefy internal organs, and penetrate stem to stern. As already noted, squaring the velocity of a bullet gives exponentially more kinetic energy advantage to high-velocity bullets. But high-velocity bullets, as a matter of course, are smaller in diameter and weightless. They do not have the stopping power of big chunks of lead. If you believe that the weight of a bullet is just as important as velocity, then you should base your power calculations on bullet momentum (BM):

$$BM = BW \times MV$$

Unfortunately, one cannot compare bullet momentum to kinetic energy, but the values generated are useful for comparing bullets. Take a look at the same .50-caliber bullets compared above:

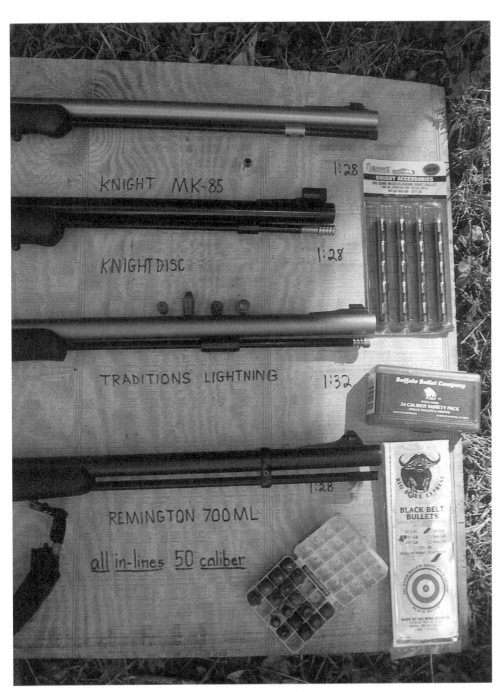

In-lines regularly advertise bullet velocities of more than 2,000 feet per second. But as a matter of course, high-velocity bullets are smaller in diameter and weight. They do not have the stopping power of bigger chunks of lead.

For the .50-caliber roundball: FFg black powder; 1,875 feet per
second muzzle velocity:

BM = 177 × 1,875
BM = 331,875 pounds-feet

For the .50-caliber Maxi-Hunter:
BM = 355 × 1,400
BM = 497,000 pounds-feet

For the .50-caliber Barnes sabot:
BM = 300 × 1,621
BM = 486,300 pounds-feet

When using the bullet momentum formula, it becomes obvious
that the greatest power is exhibited by the heavier .50-caliber Maxi-
Hunter. Although this encourages the crowd of heavy-bullet afi-
cionados, it still leaves questions about whether slow velocity is
desirable in a hunting bullet, particularly at ranges beyond a football field away.

CALCULATING ROUNDBALL MASS
When you buy a box of roundballs, their size and weight are usually
listed right on the box, so it is easy to calculate their kinetic energy,
as long as you can find or measure their velocity. But many times,
cast roundballs, particularly those not of standard sizes, do not have
their weights listed. Use a caliper to measure the diameter of the
roundball, and the following equation will take care of the rest:

Volume of a sphere (VS) = Diameter^3 × the constant 0.5236 ×
2873.5 (the weight of 1 cubic inch of pure lead in grains)

As an example, take a 0.550-inch-diameter roundball used in an
old T/C .56-caliber Renegade smoothbore:

VS = (0.550 × 0.550 × 0.550) × 0.5236 × 2873.5
VS = 0.166375 × 0.5236 × 2873.5
VS = 250.32179 grains

The following table shows the exponential increase in grain weight per volume of lead in relation to a roundball's diameter:

Caliber	Diameter (inches)	Grains of Lead
.22	.220	16
.25	.250	24
.32	.310	45
.36	.350	65
.38	.370	76
.40	.390	89
.44	.430	120
.45	.440	128
.48	.470	156
.50	.490	177
.50	.495	182
.53	.520	212
.54	.530	224
.54	.535	230
.56	.550	250
.58	.570	279
.60	.590	309
.62	.610	342
.69	.680	473
.72	.710	538

Notice that doubling the size of the ball does not double the weight of the bullet. A .36-caliber roundball (actually 0.350 inch in diameter) weighs 65 grains; if the caliber is doubled to .72, it does not weigh 130 grains. Instead, the big colonial .72 caliber throws a 538-grain sphere of lead, a meteoric rise of more than 800 percent in weight! This is why larger calibers, from .50 to .58, exhibit an exponential increase in energy for hunting large game, as well as retaining more energy at longer ranges.

CALCULATING SECTIONAL DENSITY
Sectional density is a calculation applied to bullets; it has no practical value in comparing roundballs. The formula compares

Larger calibers (from .50 to .58) exhibit an exponential increase in energy for hunting large game, as well as in retaining more energy at longer ranges.

a bullet's weight to its cross section. The resulting ratio expresses a ballistic value useful in predicting how the bullet will slice its way through the atmosphere, as well as how it will perform in terminal penetration of a medium. Higher sectional densities are generated by elongated bullets; lower numbers apply to shorter projectiles.

The sectional density (SD) is calculated by dividing the weight of the bullet in grains by 7,000 times the square of its diameter. Using this equation, a jacketed 300-grain Sierra FN .45-caliber bullet (which would be used in a .45-70 Government black powder breechloader cartridge) can be compared with 400- and 500-grain bullets from the same manufacturer:

300-grain Sierra FN
$$SD = 300 \div (7{,}000 \times [.45 \times .45])$$
$$SD = 300 \div (7{,}000 \times 0.2025)$$
$$SD = 300 \div 1417.5$$
$$SD = 0.212$$

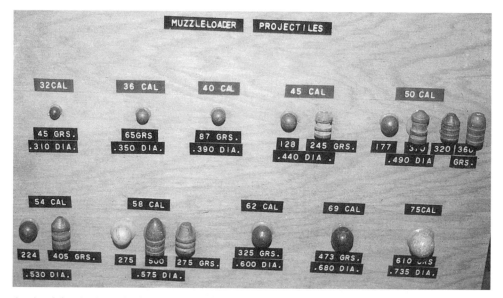

Sectional density is a calculation applied to bullets. It has no practical value for comparing roundballs.

400-grain Sierra FN
$SD = 400 \div (7{,}000 \times [.45 \times .45])$
$SD = 400 \div 1417.5$
$SD = 0.282$

500-grain Sierra FN
$SD = 500 \div (7{,}000 \times [.45 \times .45])$
$SD = 500 \div 1417.5$
$SD = 0.353$

When comparing the three bullets, it is obvious that the longer and heavier 500-grain Sierra has a much better 0.353 sectional density than either the 400-grain or the 300-grain bullet. This number becomes useful when calculating the ballistic coefficient, which determines how well bullets shed air resistance and carry energy to longer distances.

CALCULATING BALLISTIC COEFFICIENTS

The ballistic coefficient is used to calculate trajectories for various bullet designs. It is the ratio of velocity retardation due to air drag (coefficient of drag) for a particular bullet to that of a larger standard model. That model was first calculated in 1874 by the German ballistician Krupp. After testing and tweaking by the military and private enterprise, the standard model, or "G1," became a bullet 1 inch in diameter, weighing 1 pound, and having a flat-base shape. The shape had a two-caliber ogive (the curving point of the bullet) with a length of 3.28 calibers (inches). Thus, any bullet that is 1 inch in diameter and weighs 7,000 grains (1 pound) will have a sectional density of 1.000. A bullet with the same shape as the standard bullet, weighing 1 pound and being 1 inch in diameter, will always have a ballistic coefficient of 1.000. If the bullet is the same shape but smaller, it will have an identical coefficient of drag, with a form factor (shape) of 1.000 and a ballistic coefficient equal to its sectional density.

The formula for ballistic coefficient (BC) is:

BC = Sectional density ÷ Coefficient of form

Fortunately, most loading manuals now list the bullet's ballistic coefficients as well as sectional densities. And, to make life even easier, ballistics tables are available from ammunition manufacturers on-line or in CD form for your computer. It sure speeds up calculating drop, windage, and trajectory for your favorite load.

When comparing the BC of various bullets, it is important to recognize that the higher the number, the less air resistance (drag) the bullet will experience in the atmosphere. For comparison, the following table lists the BCs of some .50-caliber offerings:

Projectile	Weight (grains)	Sectional Density	Ballistic Coefficient
Speer Roundball	177	0.105	0.068
Lyman Maxi	370	0.208	0.095
Buffalo HP Conical	350	0.197	0.142
Lyman Plains	395	0.220	0.160
Hornady Sabot	240	0.185	0.205
Lyman Sabot	335	0.235	0.274
Knight Sabot	400	0.281	0.304
Buffalo Sabot	375	0.263	0.296
Centerfire .30-06	180	0.271	0.431

It quickly becomes obvious that muzzleloader bullets, even the best saboted offerings, do not approach the ballistic coefficients of high-velocity, centerfire cartridge bullets. Although the ballistic coefficient is important in working up efficient loads, it is not the most crucial consideration in choosing an efficient, game-stopping muzzleloader bullet.

CALCULATING RECOIL

Do you remember your science teacher lecturing, "For every force, there is an equal and opposite force"? This explains why your shoulder hurts when you shoot heavy powder charges (150 grains) and massive bullets (over 300 grains.) It is called recoil. Heavy recoil is the number one reason why hunters flinch and miss big bucks. But heavy recoil can be predicted with the following formula supplied by Hodgdon Powder Company:

Recoil energy (in foot-pounds) = $(BW \times MV + 4{,}700\ PW)^2 \div 64.348\ GW$,
where BW is the weight of the bullet in pounds (grains divided by 7,000), MV is the muzzle velocity in feet per second, PW is the weight of the powder in pounds, and GW is the weight of the gun in pounds.

Let's do a calculation based on an average .50-caliber percussion Traditions Hawken Woodsman rifle. Weighing in at 7.5 pounds, it might be loaded with 100 grains of black powder and shoot a 350-grain Buffalo HP Conical bullet out the muzzle at 1,500 feet per second. What will that mean in terms of "felt recoil" against your shoulder?

BW = 300 grains ÷ 7,000 = 0.0428571
MV = 1,500 fps
PW = 100 grains ÷ 7,000 = 0.0142857
GW = 7.5 pounds
Recoil energy (RE) = $[(0.0428571 \times 1{,}500) + (4{,}700 \times 0.0142857)]^2 \div 64.348 \times 7.5$
RE = $(64.28565 + 67.14279)^2 \div 482.61$
RE = $131.42844^2 \div 482.61$

While the ballistic coefficient is important in working up efficient loads, it is not the most critical consideration in choosing a game-stopping muzzleloader bullet.

Recoil increases proportionately as shooters increase the powder charge and bullet weight, but greater velocities are still needed for jacketed bullets.

Recoil is the simple reason why our shoulders hurt when we shoot heavy powder charges and massive bullets.

RE = 17273.434 ÷ 482.61

RE = 35.791703, or about 36 foot-pounds

If this rig generates about 36 foot-pounds of energy against your shoulder with only 100 grains of black powder, what do you suppose 150 grains would do?

CALCULATING RIFLING RATES OF TWIST

Accuracy is a result of many factors, but one of the most important variables that a hunter can control is the rate of twist. As stated previously, slow rates of twist suit roundballs, and faster rates of twist stabilize conoidal bullets. This information is not new. In 1879, Sir Alfred George Greenhill, a professor of mathematics for an advanced class of artillery officers, proposed a formula that we still use today. Following is an example of the Greenhill formula for the rate of twist for a .50-caliber roundball barrel:

Barrel twist (BT) in calibers = 150 ÷ Length of bullet in calibers
BT = 150 ÷ (.500 ÷ .490)
BT = 150 ÷ 1.0204081
BT = 147 calibers

To convert barrel twist in calibers to barrel twist in inches, multiply by 0.457:

BT = one turn in 67.179 inches

One turn in 66 inches is an accepted, time-proven rate of rifling for a .50-caliber roundball barrel.

Paul A. Matthews, in his work on cast bullets, modified this formula only slightly by using 125 for the constant instead of 150. Therefore, the Matthews formula applied to the .50-caliber roundball barrel would be:

BT = 125 ÷ (.500 ÷ .490)
BT = 125 ÷ 1.0204081
BT = 122.5 calibers
BT = 56 inches

My experience is that they both work.

Molding Your Own Projectiles

Part of the fun of hunting with a muzzleloader is the ability to make your own gear. Modern in-line muzzleloaders, with their higher-velocity jacketed bullets, have eliminated the need for cast bullets. Yet many savvy shooters still participate in the enjoyable endeavor of molding their own bullets. Cast bullets add a sense of history, hunting fulfillment, and accuracy to your custom loads. This section details the different types of molds, melting equipment, and casting techniques for roundballs and conical slugs. Casting your own bullets saves money, allows for experimentation in bullet design, and can be a safe and enjoyable way to spend a cabin-crazy winter's evening as the snow swirls in the deer woods.

The spirit of the hunt lives on in the stories that swirl around the campfire, like the pungent smoke generated by the oaken fuel. In front of their eyes glowed a hunter's fire. Behind them and hanging from a stout maple crossbeam was the object of their journey—a white-tailed deer. The circle of life, death, and rebirth was being played out. So, too, the lowly orb of lead was coming full circle in its own way.

The buckskin-clad hunter reached under the deer's hide, opposite the side that had been targeted and struck by the bullet, and there lay a perfect coin of lead, expanded to more than 100 percent of its original diameter. After examination by another Hudson Bay longhunter and a few tall tales about the fantastic shooting prowess of its original owner, the lead was carefully laid into the ladle to be heated. The hunter's fire burned bright with hot red coals and reminiscences of past hunts, as the orb of lead relaxed into a shiny, silvery, molten state. It would live again as a new bullet, carefully cast, and painstakingly loaded. A new bullet for the next hunt was reborn.

If this northern adventure lights your fire, then you are ready to take the next step in muzzleloading. Molding your own bullet is a simple job, but one of satisfaction and honest heritage. People have been casting projectiles of lead since the days of the Roman Empire, and bullets since the 1400s. But here in North America, the campfire casting of galena bullets was a weekly necessity, as there was no corner gunshop, supercenter outdoor emporium, or 1-800-catalog to order from. If you didn't cast 'em, you couldn't shoot 'em!

Why cast lead bullets? Isn't lead dangerous? Aren't sabotted and copper-jacketed bullets better for hunting and easier to use? Wouldn't it be less expensive to just purchase a couple of boxes of bullets? Who shoots cast lead bullets?

Perhaps the simplest reason to cast your own lead bullets is because you can. This commonly available element is used in plumbing, electrical, radiological, metallurgical, boat-building, fishing, and hunting applications, to name a few. With a very low melting point of 621 degrees Fahrenheit, it can change from solid to

With a low melting point of 621 degrees Fahrenheit, you can liquefy lead with the simplest of heat sources.

liquid with the simplest of heat sources. A rendezvous campfire, Coleman gas stove, propane torch, and even modern electrical furnace and melting pots make short work of changing the state of this elemental metal.

The second reason to cast lead bullets is economics. It costs about three cents worth of lead (unless you get the lead for free) to make a .50-caliber roundball, maybe a nickel for a larger conical bullet. Buy that same bullet as a jacketed sabot, and you can multiply the price by 20 to 30. If you do any amount of target shooting, are involved in black powder competition, or participate in the cowboy shooting sports, you really can't afford to ignore the savings.

Although there are other personal reasons for casting lead bullets, such as the profound connection to American history, I believe that the most satisfying reason for melting lead is the visual pleasure of watching the liquid galena solidify into a shiny orb or the even more defined shape of a spire-pointed, gas-sealing, bearing-ribbed, grease-grooved conoidal bullet. This vision becomes even more appealing when you picture yourself harvesting that big buck with a bullet made by your own hand.

There is something fundamentally satisfying about molding a shiny orb of lead.

There are thousands of shooters who enjoy the process of casting bullets from lead. Many of these hobbyists are organized into the Cast Bullet Association.

One common concern is that handling lead may be dangerous. The possibility of burns, vapors, and ingestion exists, but with the proper safety equipment, the danger is minimal. With temperatures ranging from the melting point of 621 degrees for pure lead to over 800 degrees for lead alloys, it is important that you always wear gloves, safety glasses, long pants, apron, and shoes to prevent accidental splash-burns.

Lead does not vaporize until it reaches 1,100 degrees. This is not a danger for electric home production pots, but if you are using a hotter propane or acetylene burner, a high-temperature thermometer is necessary to prevent excessive heat. In reality, lead at this extreme temperature doesn't cast well, and amateur bullet casters rarely, if ever, encounter this problem.

Many amateur casters have had their blood tested for lead contamination. Their results come in at around 5 micrograms, compared with the average city dweller's range of 8 to 11 micrograms. The federal standard established by Occupational Safety and Health Administration is 40 micrograms per 100 grams of blood; this is the danger point at which monitoring is necessary. At 50 micrograms, a worker can no longer be exposed to any lead substances. The National Rifle Association's publication *Cast Bullets* reports that lead poisoning caused by casting bullets is very uncommon. The real problem is dust exposure.

Ventilation is the key to a safe environment where lead is present. Regardless of whether you are casting lead bullets or shooting them at an indoor range, exhaust fans that carry any possible lead vaporization away are a necessity. The greatest source of particulate ingestion occurs from the "dross," which is scooped off the surface of the molten lead. Dross is a layer of solid particles, sometimes alloys of tin, antimony, and even zinc. These particles are toxic when inhaled, but the lead oxide in the mix is also of concern. A good safety precaution is to skim the dross and place it in a metal container with a lid. This effectively reduces the safety hazard.

With temperatures climbing to 800 degrees Fahrenheit, it is important to wear glasses and gloves when molding bullets.

Although it may be convenient to cast lead in the basement, this is not the best location. Because of the dangerous level of heat and possible vapor contamination, it is advisable to do your casting outdoors under a protective canopy. Overhead protection is needed to keep water away. When water from rain or from an accidental spill (such as coffee) contacts molten lead, there is an instantaneous explosion of steam. Water expands 1,600 times its volume when it changes from liquid to gas (steam). The burst of steam energy carries with it molten missiles of lead, which can be very dangerous.

The danger of lead ingestion is highlighted by media reports about kids having high lead levels in their blood just from being around lead-based paint. But this is because they are eating paint chips that they pick off the walls in older houses or apartments. Hunters don't eat lead bullets, they shoot them! But if a bullet

Another good safety precaution when molding is to skim off the dross and place it in a sealed container.

caster handles scores of lead bullets once they are cooled, his or her ungloved hands can become contaminated with lead. To be safe, it would be wise (and common sense) to wash your hands before touching or consuming food. This eliminates the ingestion concern.

The next concern of hunters is efficiency. Aren't sabots with their pure copper or copper-jacketed lead bullets more efficient missiles for high-velocity in-line rifles? When lead (not patched roundballs) exceeds 1,500 feet per second, it begins to laminate the bore and needs the stabilization of a copper gas check. Copper (Brinnell hardness number 40) does this very efficiently, but it leads to other problems when the lead is fully jacketed: obturation (mushrooming back and releasing energy). Pure lead (Brinnell hardness number 5) does not need to be accelerated to velocities over 2,000 feet per second to be efficient game-harvesting bullets. Hypervelocity leads to hyperproblems. Lead bullet casters are quite satisfied with the accuracy and terminal bullet performance of their homemade bullets.

According to Norm Johnson's "Match Wheelgun and Load Preparation" in *The Fouling Shot* (September–October 1989, p. 81), the following velocities are required to expand or deform various hardnesses:

Brinnell Hardness Number	Minimum Terminal Velocity (feet per second)	Hollow Point* (feet per second)
30–50	2,400	
20	2,200	
18	1,900	
14–15	1,500	
10	1,400	900
8	1,300	800
5 (pure lead)	1,200	700

*The size and shape of the hollow point, as well as the nose shape of the bullet, will affect the terminal velocity necessary. These numbers are only approximations.

Would a hunter spend more on bullet casting equipment than on buying a year's worth of bullets? The answer is probably yes. For an average hunter, it would likely take many years to recoup the costs of the equipment. Obviously, a hunter-shooter who needs thousands of bullets to get through the year's target shooting and hunting season, would save money in a shorter amount of time. But, as with any hobby, cost is not the primary factor.

Now that the joys and concerns of bullet casting have been addressed, let's take a look at the equipment necessary for success.

CASTING EQUIPMENT

The basics of lead bullet casting involve heat, a crucible of some sort, a mold, lead, and a way to transfer the molten metal into the top of the mold. In a primitive situation, like the one depicted at the beginning of this section, a hunter needs only the hot coals of a wood fire, a ladle, some lead, and a bullet mold. The total costs for this homespun adventure might amount to less than $20. A single-cavity Lee roundball mold in .490 (for a .50-caliber rifle) is about $14, and the Lee ladle is available for about $4 (although an old tablespoon would also work). As we become more demanding as home bullet casters, higher-quality equipment becomes desirable and is readily available from various supply houses (see appendix B).

As you become more experienced as a bullet caster, you'll begin to want higher-quality equipment.

Good electric furnaces for melting lead range in price from about $28 to more than $300. As you upgrade your production pot, you will begin to enjoy larger heating elements, bottom pouring spouts, larger volumes, and variable temperature controls. All these features make the casting experience more precise and increase your rate of production.

When bullets other than roundballs are cast, you may find it desirable to alloy the lead with other metals such as tin and antimony. This requires a precision tool like a hardness tester, which can cost from $36 to almost $100. A lead thermometer is also critical for measuring optimal casting temperatures for production. Casting thermometers that measure from 200 to 1,000 degrees range in price from about $30 to $50. Another important addition to your lead-alloy mix is the fluxing agent. Beeswax and paraffin are two old standbys, but graphite and other more high-tech products such as Brownell's Marvelux casting flux help keep the tin and antimony in the correct proportion to the lead. Flux products generally run under $10 and are well worth the price.

Although lead is generally available from inexpensive sources, it is sometimes desirable to purchase ingots that are already mixed to the correct proportion. Alloy ingots that weigh about 7 pounds command about $10.

The following table will give you an idea of the approximate hardness levels for commonly available lead alloys:

Beeswax and paraffin are two old standbys for fluxing, but graphite and high-tech products like Brownell's Marvelux casting flux help keep the tin and antimony in correct proportion.

Alloy	Brinnell Hardness
Pure lead	5
Soft lead	5–8
Lead/tin (2% tin)	8
Lead/tin (4% tin)	10
Lead/tin (10% tin)	11
Wheel weights	11–12
Wheel weights plus 2% tin	13–14
#2 alloy	15–16
Linotype	22
Pure copper	40

BULLET PRODUCTION

The first step in the casting procedure is to bring the lead up to the production temperature, which is normally 120 percent of the lead or lead-alloy melting point. Pure lead needs a production tempera-

While lead is inexpensive and available from many plumbing and electrical sources, it is sometimes desirable to purchase lead-alloy bars to ensure a correct proportion.

ture of about 750 degrees, the alloys between 750 and 850. It may take 20 minutes to bring the lead up to the correct temperature before you are ready to cast.

The second step is to degrease and smoke the mold. The mold always needs to be cleaned of grease and oil, or wrinkles will occur in the cast bullets. This is easily accomplished with denatured alcohol or a can of ether starting fluid. At this point, the cleaned and dry mold needs to be "smoked." This involves applying a layer of carbon to the inside of the cavity to facilitate the lead's dropping from the mold. Smoking the surface of the aluminum or iron mold provides an insulating surface that slows down the freezing of the molten lead. You can accomplish this smoking process with soot from a butane lighter or by applying a mold spray such as Mold Prep or Action Magic II. It is also important to lube or smoke the sprue cutter hinge and sprue cutter surface so that they can function with the least lead stickage.

A cleaned and degreased mold needs to be "smoked" before the first cast bullets are poured.

Step three is to set the mold on top of the furnace to bring its temperature close to that of the melting lead. This allows lead to flow freely inside the mold, which is particularly important when you are casting minié, maxi, and conoidal bullets, with their irregular cannellure grooves and air vents inside the mold.

Begin the casting process by stirring the lead with the dipper or ladle inside the pot. Use a flux to mix the tin or antimony back into the lead alloy. Be sure to scrape across the bottom of the pot to knock loose any dirt or lead oxides, which will then float on the surface. Skim off any dross and discard it properly in a lidded can. Now the lead should look as shiny as a mirror and ready to pour into the mold. Plan on recycling the first dozen bullets, because they will probably have wrinkles and voids. This is normal, as the interior of the mold has not yet reached the critical temperature for perfect bullets. Also, wrinkled bullets are a good indication that the lead in the production pot is not yet hot enough for optimal casting.

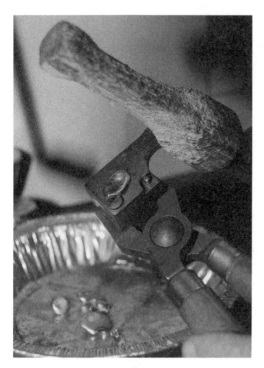

After watching the sprue freeze back into solid form, you'll see a dimple on the lead surface.

After watching the excess lead atop the mold, known as "sprue," freeze back into a solid, you will notice a dimple form as lead is contracted into the mold. Count to three before cutting off the sprue and dumping the bullet onto a soft, nonflammable surface (leather or cotton or linen cloth, but definitely not synthetic fabrics, which will melt and stick to the bullet). As the mold heats up, the cavity diameter can grow as much as 0.003 inch. This is another reason for being patient with your bullet production. If you spot a frosty-looking surface on the bullet, the temperature of the lead may be too high. This is due to a metallurgical change at the cooler surface of the bullet.

Be sure to flux and stir the pot every two to three minutes, and skim off the dross as it appears. If you add lead to the pot from discarded bullets or a new ingot, you will need to wait another 15 minutes for the molten lead to get back to casting temperature. This is where an accurate casting thermometer comes in handy.

Also, be careful that no foreign objects melt into the mix of lead and alloy. Aluminum and zinc will ruin the casting properties of the lead. The higher the proportion of antimony alloy in the mix, the larger the bullet diameter will be from the same mold when compared with lead (see below). Antimony hardens the mix and provides a better gas seal for slugs, but it inhibits obturation when bullets are used for hunting. Roundballs perform better without antimony, even though they can shrink up to 1 percent in the mold, whereas slugs with antimony do not. Following is an example of the results with a .36-caliber bullet mold:

Count to three before cutting off the sprue and dumping the bullet onto a soft, nonflammable surface.

Bullet Alloy	Diameter (inches)	Weight (grains)
Pure lead	0.3578	215
Wheel weights	0.3584	212
Lyman #2 alloy	0.3590	206
Linotype	0.3594	200

As the table shows, the bullet diameter increases but the weight decreases as the percentage of antimony (a lighter element than lead) increases. This is a good reason for not using recovered bullets from shooting ranges, as their composition is unknown.

Tin is not necessarily a bad alloy for roundballs, as long as the percentage stays low. Tin increases the fluidity of the mix and helps cast bullets fill out the mold. Tin was the earliest recorded alloy added to lead, being listed as nineteenth-century alloy for the improvement of cast bullets.

If you are using a high tin-antimony-lead alloy, be aware that this alloy will soften with age. Slugs made from this mix are best

Tin-antimony-lead alloys will soften with age. Slugs made from this mix are best kept in a freezer.

kept in a freezer to preserve their "hard lead" quality, which is desirable in some types of slugs that are shot at higher velocities. Lead bullets can even be "tempered" in an oven. Bake the lead at 400 degrees for 1 hour, and then drop it into cool water. Be sure to wear eye protection, gloves, and protective clothing if you pursue this procedure.

Weigh your bullets. You can use the formula for calculating the mass of a roundball (given earlier in the ballistics section) to measure the difference. If your bullets are not within 1 percent of the same weight, discard them. I like to lube all my best weighed bullets to prevent oxidation, as well as to provide the lubrication necessary for lead slugs.

There are many good choices for conoidal bullet lubes. Generally, bullet casters use a paraffin-beeswax-oil mix or an Alox-beeswax "sticky" mix. Others like the hard coating of molybdenum sulfide, commonly known as "moly." A third group prefers the Alox-based liquid lubes that are commercially available. I use plain old vegetable oil on my bullets and stick them in an airtight container.

Casting bullets is a great way to spend some time sharing your sport with others. When done in a safe and protected environment that is well ventilated, it will produce hours of enjoyment, a chance to share hunting stories, and an inexpensive way to shoot your favorite muzzleloader.

CHAPTER FOUR

Preparation, Care, and Maintenance

Sighting In

From the time of Roger Bacon to the present, barrels loaded with black powder and bullets have been pointed at targets. By the eighteenth century, accuracy was demanded by riflemen so that they could consistently hit deer at under 100 yards. An early barleycorn type of front sight was seated in the open notch of the rear sight of the longrifle for amazing accuracy. But today, a vast array of open iron, fiber-optic, globed aperture, and telescopic sights have captured the imagination of muzzleloading deer and turkey hunters. This section details easy methods for sighting in open sights and scopes and explains how to allow for Kentucky windage and other vagaries of ballistic flight.

Deer tracks were everywhere. The fresh coating of snow was making it easy to see that the deer had collected in the shelter of the hemlocks by Junk's Pond. This looked like it would be an easy hunt.

Having hunted this land in Bradford County for the last three decades, the four of us had come together, once again, for our traditional post-Christmas hunt. What a collection of diehard muzzleloaders we were: all over 50 years of age, veteran flintlockers with a haphazard history of success on late-season deer, and each carrying a different gun—a Thompson/Center Hawken .50, a Traditions .50, a Lyman Deerstalker .54, and a Dixie American Jaeger .54.

Whitetail deer near Junk's Pond

Though none of their stocks and barrels matched, they all performed with deadliness on whitetails.

Anticipation for a quick kill was running high as the two drivers walked with the wind toward the two standers, who watched for fleeing shadows of brown. The first two drives proved that there were plenty of whitetails around, and the tracks in the snow provided numbers and direction. But the first glimpse of deer didn't take place until later in the morning.

With the temperature hovering close to zero, it was ironic to see the steam rising from the hats of the hunters. Walking the Endless Mountains of Bradford County will do that for the body: frosted mustaches and steaming heads, tired feet and numb fingers, achy joints and a burning desire to see deer.

The third drive was the charm. Bob and Gary retraced their steps from the first drive. Deer tracks showed that the whitetails had escaped the hemlocks, just as we had predicted they would. Rather than following their normal trails to the top of the hill, they broke to the right into the deadfalls left by some recent lumbering activity. And that was exactly from where they broke cover.

The drivers watched the explosion of brown as the fleeing deer kicked up their heels and crashed through the brush. Though their flintlocks were drawn to full cock and mounted to their shoulders, the whitetails' quick escape through the thickening branches didn't allow for an ethical shot.

Suddenly, deer appeared to the standers. Both the fleeing deer and the unprepared standers were caught off guard. Bill and I had not reached the agreed-on area to set up for the hunt when the deer rocketed through. The animals seemed surprised that anyone without "four-hoofed drive" would invade this rough terrain.

Four does burst from the treetops and were heading straight at us. Calling out to Bill to shoot, I shouldered the Jaeger. Normally, a deer gives a hunter three seconds for a shot: one second when you first spot the quarry, the next second when the animal is standing broadside in your zone of fire, and the third second as it flees and quarters away. These four does didn't follow the rules. In less than three seconds, they had come and gone, allowing only a quick shot that intercepted more brush than deer. My tag would stay in my license that day.

Whenever a hunter misses a shot at a deer, a second-guessing, soul-searching process begins. Did I sight in the rifle correctly? Are my sights accurate, or would my old eyes be better off with the newer fiber-optic sights? Could I see a buckhorn iron sight more clearly than the V-notch? Did I sight in the rifle at the wrong distance?

There are basically four styles of open sights for eighteenth-century-style flintlocks, an untold number of inserts for aperture or peep sights for nineteenth-century-styled sidehammer percussions, and myriad reticules for scopes on the newest twenty-first-century in-line percussion muzzleloading rifles. All of them work as advertised.

FIXED VERSUS ADJUSTABLE SIGHTS

Because fixed sights don't have screws or ratcheting wheels to turn, many new muzzleloading hunters are afraid to deal with them. But fixed sights offer one huge advantage: once they are sighted in, they stay sighted in. To adjust the windage (left or right on the target),

There are basically four styles of open sights for eighteenth-century-style flintlocks, along with an untold number of inserts for nineteenth-century-style percussion peep sights.

you need to "drift" (tap) the rear sight's beveled base in the direction that you want the bullet impact to move. The front sight can also be drifted. But remember to drift the front sight in the opposite direction that you want the bullet impact to move. To adjust the elevation, the front sight is normally filed down to bring up the point of impact. If the rifle shoots high, you will need to deepen the notch in the rear sight. Once the sights are exactly the way you expect them to shoot, tap down on the barrel with a punch, above the sights' bevels, to make them tight and unmovable.

Adjustable iron and fiber-optic sights are the norm on most assembly-line-manufactured rifles, both flintlock and percussion. Because they can easily change the bullet's point of impact by turning them left or right (for windage) and up or down (for elevation), it also means that they can go out of adjustment. A spring, either coil or leaf spring, controls the elevation screw, and sometimes the plane of the sight "sticks" inside the sight, throwing accuracy right

Adjustable iron and fiber-optic sights are the norm on most production rifles, both flintlocks and percussions.

out the window. Make sure that you do a visual inspection, followed by a one-shot sight-in session each year before the hunt starts. Any time we increase the mechanical advantage to a procedure (such as sighting in), we also increase the opportunities for the mechanical parts to malfunction. Be diligent for the sake of accuracy and ethical hunting.

THE SIGHTING-IN PROCEDURE

Before any sight-in session, check the rifle, particularly the sights, to verify its accuracy. Little gremlins such as loose sight bases, wiggly rear adjustable sights, and untightened scope mounts all contribute to "missed deer."

Although bore sighters, collimators, and lasers are great aids in getting close on that first shot, they do not guarantee accuracy. They are no substitute for zeroing a gun on the range.

Muzzleloaders need to control the variables of powder and bullet, as well as the ignition. Be sure to use the same brand and lot number of black powder or replica powder for the entire sight-in session. Each batch of powder will have small variations in burn rate, as the mixing and milling of black powder is not an exact science. Do not switch between FFg and FFFg grades of black powder. FFFg powder generates about 10 percent more velocity than the same volume of FFg. Load volumetrically, not by weight.

Always sight in your rifle on a solid rest. This could consist of sandbags atop a bench or table, a notched cardboard box, or a

Always sight your rifle from a solid rest.

sight-vise rifle rest. You will never be sure of your shot placement if you cannot control the variables of a moving sight picture in a wobbling off-hand shot. From this solid rest, carefully squeeze off three shots with a dead-center hold. This means that you level the top of the front sight with the top of the notch in your rear sight, and hold that picture in the center of the target.

Begin your shooting close to the target. I like to start at 13 yards. This not only puts my first shot on the paper target; it also immediately shows me if I am in vertical alignment. It is easy to make future shots hit higher or lower by varying the elevation of the sights, but horizontal alignment, particularly off the paper at hunting distances, is a lot more difficult. Also, at 13 yards, I can predict that a shot 1-inch high at 50 yards will be dead-on at 75 yards and about an inch low at 100 yards. This system works with rifles in calibers of .45 to .58 if the muzzle velocities are between 1,800 and 2,000 feet per second—typical velocities for the "hotter" hunting loads of 90 to 120 grains of black powder pushing a patched roundball. If you are shooting a heavier lead slug, such as the T/C Maxi-Ball, or one of the many sabotted rounds, your

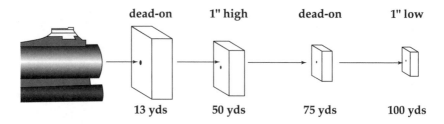

dead-on   1" high   dead-on   1" low

13 yds   50 yds   75 yds   100 yds

The 13/75 Sight-in Method

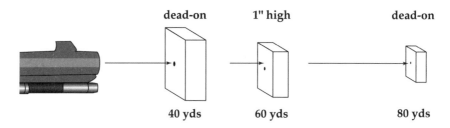

dead-on   1" high   dead-on

40 yds   60 yds   80 yds

The 40/80 Sight-in Method

ballistics will be similar if your muzzle velocities are above 1,500 feet per second.

Another method for sighting in, which has been handed down through generations of black powder competitors, is to sight in at 40 yards so that your bullet strikes the same spot at 80 yards. This is a result of the trajectory of a bullet climbing through 40 yards, hitting an inch high at 60 yards, and then descending to the same line of sight at 80 yards.

If your group sizes at short ranges—13 to 40 yards—are more than 2 inches, there are a few things that you can adjust. Begin with the ignition sequence. Flintlocks should fire with a *bang*, not rattle with a *klank-sis-boom-bah!* This slow ignition will affect accuracy, even on a solid rest. Try to pick the touch hole with a straightened paper clip after you load the barrel. Then, prime the pan with half the FFFFg black powder primer that you normally use. A half pan of primer pushed away from the touch hole will result in much faster ignition than a full pan of primer clogging the opening to the powder train. Also, be sure that you are ramrodding the load with the same pressure each time you load. Bouncing the ramrod on the bullet does nothing to help accuracy and in fact can defeat it. A good product for accurate shooting is the Ka-DOOTY loading rod. Its sliding weight gives the same exact pressure to the load every time, producing ultimate accuracy.

Check that the load is seated at the same spot each time, as evidenced by the mark that you made on the ramrod the first time you loaded the clean gun. Any airspace between the powder train and the seat of the bullet will spike pressures, lead to inaccuracy, and could even be dangerous.

Do not switch bullets. Once your flintlock is sighted

Once you've sighted in with a particular bullet, changing weights and bullet types will change the trajectory.

in, it is sighted in for a particular bullet. If you decide to use a lead slug or sabotted bullet, you must sight in with that bullet. Confidence in your gun can make all the difference when shooting at deer. Doubts about the powder and bullet will never allow you to be a successful hunter.

SIGHT PROBLEMS AND REMEDIES

One of the big problems that older hunters encounter is the inability to see their open sights clearly. The rear sight that is standard equipment on muzzleloading rifles, whether open iron, aperture, or fiber-optic, is placed in a position for the average hunter with 20/20 eyesight. When farsighted individuals look through these sights at a distant target, the rear sight becomes fuzzy to the point of uselessness. This can be remedied by simply moving the rear sight forward. This cleans up the sight picture and does not make the rifle less accurate. Alternatively, put a stroke of blue paint on the front sight. This is the part of the sight picture that focuses on the animal, and blue is a color not found in the forest, field, or coat of a deer. The stripe of blue—particularly in snow, when iron sights

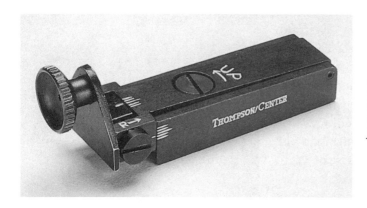

Aperture sights make it easier for shooters to center the front sight, but they are illegal in some primitive firearms seasons.

are more difficult to see—will improve your chances of a successful shot. Adding a thin swipe of yellow along the top of the rear sight will help your eyes center the front blade in the rear notch, and the discrimination of the edges will be vastly improved.

With fiber-optic sights, bundles of tiny plastic fibers gather ambient light and transmit it to the end of the sight, creating a startling bright dot that looks almost battery powered. There is no contest between a fiber-optic sight and an open iron sight: the fiber-optics are much easier to discriminate in low light. But there are problems. Fiber-optic sights do not provide the minute-of-angle accuracy that open iron sights do. This is particularly true when shooting in the bright daylight, when the edges of the green and red fibers are more difficult to discriminate. In strong daylight, the top of the fiber-optic is difficult to judge, many times forcing the shot to go low, under the intended target. But in the subdued light of the forest, and particularly in hunting conditions, fiber-optics are definitely an advantage. Fiber-optic sights absorb the low light of dawn and dusk and create a more visible sight profile than iron sights do. Today, there are many aftermarket brands of sights that will fill a dovetailed sight on your octagonal barrel or bolt fast to your rounded barrel. Hi-Viz, Truglo, Williams and RMC are some of the popular optics suppliers (see appendix B).

The lethal area of a whitetail is about a 12-inch-diameter zone, roughly the size of a paper plate. Any sighting system that allows accuracy at that 12-inch zone out to 100 yards will be sufficient for the late-season, muzzleloading-only deer season. If your rifle needs to take whitetails beyond a football field distance, the only practical answer is the scope (discussed later).

The bottom line is knowledge. Know your rifle; become familiar with its feel and function. Know your powder and bullet; understand its limitations and lethal distance. Take only ethical shots, and shoot straight, having the confidence of zeroing in the system back at the bench.

The table on the following pages gives some common recommended muzzleloading loads and ballistics from Lyman's 2001 *Black Powder Handbook and Loading Manual*. It contains figures for bullet drop, which will help you to sight in your rifle, depending on what your distance from the target is.

When comparing the Lyman data with the Knight

Fiber-optic beads gather ambient light and transmit it to the end of the sight, creating a startling bright dot that looks almost battery-powered.

Rifles data, note that there are two different "zero" or starting points for bullet drop. This must be carefully considered when comparing different bullets' ballistics. These ballistic data should be useful only for understanding the differences in bullet drop with typical muzzle-loading rifles (flint, percussion, or in-line percussion). None of these are suggested as safe or optimal deer hunting loads for your muzzle-loading rifle. Follow the manufacturer's recommendations for safe loading of the firearm.

SPECIAL CONSIDERATIONS FOR THE HIGH-VELOCITY MUZZLELOADER

Once a muzzleloading rifle fires a bullet at a velocity greater than 1,800 feet per second, you are entering the realm of centerfire ballistics. You also have a new set of concerns related to sighting in.

RECOMMENDED LOADS AND BALLISTICS

.45-caliber, 28-inch barrel, 1:48 twist

	Zeroed at Muzzle	25 Yards Trajectory	50 Yards	75 Yards	100 Yards
70 grains FFFg .440 (128 grains) roundball, 1,790 fps muzzle velocity, 911 foot-pounds muzzle energy	0.0"	−0.36"	−1.67"	−4.27"	−8.66"
70 grains FFg .45 (245 grains) Maxi, 1,511 fps muzzle velocity, 1,002 foot-pounds muzzle energy	0.0"	−0.52"	−2.29"	−5.63"	−10.89"
70 grains Pyrodex Select, 200-grain Lyman sabot, 1,502 fps muzzle velocity, 1,002 foot-pounds muzzle energy	similar to 245 Maxi	similar to 245 Maxi	similar to 245 Maxi	similar to 245 Maxi	similar to 245 Maxi

	50 Yards	100 Yards	150 Yards	200 Yards	
100 grains FFg or RS, 180-grain saboted Red Hot Bullet, 1,718 fps muzzle velocity, 1,248 foot-pounds muzzle energy*	+1.2"	0.0"	−5.2"	−14.97	

.50-caliber, 28-inch barrel, 1:48 twist

	Zeroed at Muzzle	25 Yards Trajectory	50 Yards	75 Yards	100 Yards
90 grains FFFg .490 (177 grains) roundball, 1,694 fps muzzle velocity, 1,128 foot-pounds muzzle energy	0.0"	−0.40"	−1.82"	−4.59"	−9.15"

	50 Yards	100 Yards	150 Yards	200 Yards	250 Yards
90 grains FFg, .50 (370 grains) Maxi, 1,297 fps muzzle velocity, 1,382 foot-pounds muzzle energy	0.0″	−0.68″	−2.91″	−6.97″	−13.15″
100 grains FFg or RS, 250-grain saboted Red Hot Bullet, 1,590 fps muzzle velocity, 1,403 foot-pounds muzzle energy*		+1.60″	0.0″	−6.89″	−19.75″

.54-caliber, 24-inch barrel, 1:48 twist

	Zeroed at Muzzle	25 Yards Trajectory	50 Yards	75 Yards	100 Yards
100 grains FFFg, .535 (230 grains) roundball, 1,759 fps muzzle velocity, 1,581 foot-pounds muzzle energy	0.0″	−0.36″	−1.60″	−3.99″	−7.91″
100 grains FFg, .54 (430 grains) Maxi, 1,390 fps muzzle velocity, 1,845 foot-pounds muzzle energy	0.0″	−0.57″	−2.41″	−5.73″	−10.69″
100 grains FFg, .535 (240 grains) Buffalo sabot, 1,527 fps muzzle velocity, 1,243 foot-pounds muzzle energy	0.0″	−0.49″	−2.10″	−5.01″	−9.39″

*Knight Rifles ballistic for comparison.

First, you need to learn hyperspeed ballistics. The following values are courtesy of Modern Muzzleloading, Inc. (Knight Rifles), for a gun with a 26-inch barrel, 1:28 twist, loaded with 100 grains FFg or 2 Pyrodex pellets:

Bullet	Range (yards)	Impact (inches)	Velocity (feet per second)	Energy (foot-pounds)
.45/150	0	1.50	2,086	1,884
Red Hot	50	0.47	1,879	1,529
Sabot	100	0.00	1,687	1,232
	150	−3.57	1,511	988
	200	−10.98	1,354	794
.50/220	0	1.50	1,910	2,308
Knight	50	0.69	1,737	1,910
SBT	100	0.00	1,577	1,573
Red Hot	150	−4.26	1,431	1,295
Sabot	200	−12.61	1,302	1,072

The following values are for a gun loaded with three Pyrodex pellets (150 grains) with a 209 shotgun primer:

Bullet	Range (yards)	Impact (inches)	Velocity (feet per second)	Energy (foot-pounds)
.45/150	0	1.50	2,417	2,529
Red Hot	50	0.16	2,192	2,080
Sabot	100	0.00	1,979	1,695
	150	−2.39	1,779	1,370
	200	−7.50	1,594	1,100
.50/220	0	1.50	2,144	2,500
Knight	50	0.39	1,958	2,086
SBT	100	0.00	1,783	1,728
Red Hot	150	−3.09	1,618	1,425
Sabot	200	−9.60	1,468	1,173
.52/275*	0	1.50	2,091	2,091
Knight	50	0.55	1,825	2,033
Red Hot	100	0.00	1,584	1,531
Sabot	150	−4.08	1,373	1,152
	200	−12.55	1,203	883

*Knight's .52 rifle has a 26-inch barrel, 1:26 twist.

Second, you really need a scope (discussed next) to adequately use the improved ballistics presented by these high-velocity bullets.

SCOPES

What a morning! Wind swept out of the northeast during the night, driving rain and sleet through the remaining oak leaf canopy. As the wind slowed and shifted to the north, a dismal fog followed. I was wet to the first layer, my boots squished as I walked down along the edge of the field, and the skin on my fingers looked like a cross between a drowned nightcrawler and an anemic prune.

The only thing worse than the weather was the fact that this was the first day of the early muzzleloader season, and it seemed impossible to "keep yer powder dry!" Sure, the muzzle was down, and I had a balloon stretched over it. I kept the breech area under my armpit, but I also knew that black powder and Pyrodex have the uncanny ability to absorb moisture from the atmosphere, even on a good day.

While I was feeling sorry for myself, listening to the cadence of my slogging boots, something made me stop in mid-puddle. It was that sixth sense that every hunter gains from experience. There were eyes staring right at me—eyes focused from inside the fencerow at the careless hunter walking out in the open. Four deer, one with headgear, were holding a full house of poker cards, and I had a kangaroo straight: 2-4-6-8-10—and worthless! As expected, the deer were absorbed by a swirl of fog as they headed for the security of the forest. Now miserable, embarrassed by my mistake, and trying to figure out how I could make the best of this predicament, the only silver lining in this dark cloud was that the deer had not winded me.

Backing off from the encounter, I headed for a neck in the woods that the deer might funnel through. I had no sooner sat down on my Breedlove cushion than I noticed deer—the same four. The buck was nosing his frolicking harem forward, and they totally ignored me as I reached for my MK-85. Once again, I was worried about the gun.

The deer were at least 150 yards away. A shot with a flintlock or sidelock percussion loaded with a patched roundball would have

The enhanced optical clarity and magnification of scopes produce increased accuracy.

been totally out of the question. But I was using new technology, an in-line percussion loaded with two Pyrodex pellets and shooting a sabotted, jacketed bullet. More important, I had the advantage of a Burris 3×7 scope on top of this outfit.

Fortunately, the deer didn't give me time to second-guess. I had to take the shot. The three does reversed field and went back in the direction they had come from, and the buck bolted straight ahead. As he angled down the creek toward me, I picked up his chest in the crosshairs. Just as he stopped to look back, I felt the recoil against my shoulder.

Confident of a hit, I reloaded and paced over to the spot where I hoped to find the deer lying. I counted off 119 paces! But there was no prize on the ground, and no sign of a hit. It took a half hour's tracking job to finally locate the deer. Scant drops of blood led to the 10-pointer, but a quick check of the hide revealed that the load was not the problem, the shooter was. The Barnes bullet had performed admirably, punching a good wound channel clear through both sides, low on the neck. My shot was almost a foot forward of my aim point.

Was it damp powder or slow ignition? Maybe, but I'd rather blame the shot on the distance, the wet weather, the wind, and my

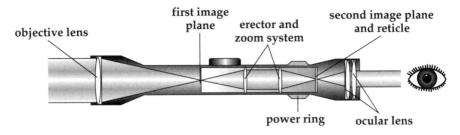

first image plane   erector and zoom system   second image plane and reticle

objective lens

power ring   ocular lens

Parts of a scope

Crosshair view

anticipation of the buck bolting across the creek. I was very lucky and happy that I hadn't lost the buck to an errant, wounding shot. All things considered, I owed this buck to technology.

An important question for muzzleloaders is to scope or not to scope. There are good reasons to consider this option. Obviously, the more clearly you see the sights, the greater the accuracy you can achieve. Their enhanced clarity, their ability to gather dawn's early light, and the magnification of the target are all valid arguments for optical sights.

An in-line topped with a scope allows better accuracy, particularly at targets past the 100-yard mark. This is important to riflemen who are trying to take advantage of the increased energy retention made possible by sabotted bullets driven at higher velocities by load equivalents over 100 grains.

Choosing a scope takes some serious thought. A muzzleloader should not be thought of as just another rifle. Because the mounting rings tend to be farther back on the receiver, eye relief is a major consideration. Most scopes have an eye relief distance of less than 4 inches. This means that the distance from the scope to your eyebrow may be too close to avoid injury with a heavy recoiling rifle. Scope companies such as Bushnell, Tasco, Thompson/Center, Burris, Simmons, and others have recognized this problem and are delivering scopes designed just for muzzleloaders. I like the 5-inch eye relief that many of them provide.

Scope overmagnification can be a real disadvantage for muzzleloaders. When deer are close or in thick cover—that is, normal muzzleloading conditions—magnification greater than 3× can be a real nightmare, as the normal aim point disappears into a sea of brown hair. See-through mounts (scope bases) force you to raise your head to see through the scope, but they allow you to use your fixed sights for really close shots or give you the ability to pick up a running deer.

In-line rifles discharge gases underneath the scope. In fact, a lot of smoke exits the breech area when massive 150-grain loads are touched off. To prevent your scope from suffering the dirt and erosion of this fouling, be sure to buy a scope protector, or at least wrap some electrical tape under the scope's tube.

Before you take that first shot with a scoped muzzleloader, check your equipment. Be sure that the screws in the scope bases are tight. In fact, it is a good idea to degrease the screw threads in the base, then add a tightening agent such as Loctite to the screws as you finger-tighten them. Bore sighting is the best way to get that first shot close. This is a quick, low-cost procedure for any gunsmith and shouldn't be overlooked.

Now that you are ready for that first shot, lay the gun into a benched cradle or gun rest. Do not sight in off-hand. Keep the target close—25 yards is too far, 10 yards is better. At this point, your first bullet hole will be on the target somewhere. And that is good enough, because it allows you to put the second shot "on the money."

After cleaning the bore with a fouling patch, reload the rifle. Back on the rest, aim at the same point you used for the first shot, but don't shoot. Instead, turn the reticles up or down for elevation, left or right for horizontal correction, until the crosshairs or reticle dot is now centered on the first bullet hole. Shoot!

The second shot should now be where you want it, and you can move on to longer distances. If this rig is expected to shoot accurately out to 200 yards, take note from the ballistics tables—zero the muzzleloader at 100 yards so that all the deer will be hit in the 12-inch lethal zone from close to long range.

RANGE FINDERS

Quick and humane kills are the ultimate desire of every ethical hunter. Muzzleloading hunters accept the handicap of one shot and the limitations of range imposed by the system. To fully exploit the accuracy and lethality of any hunting load, hunters need to understand ballistics. But to apply that knowledge, they must be able to accurately guess the range to the target. To eliminate one of the main reasons why hunters miss or wound game, learn to use a range finder.

Learn to use a rangefinder to reduce the number of misses and woundings you have.

It is a matter of record that after the Gulf War, a group of trained military specialists evaluated their ability to judge various distances to within 10 percent of the actual distance. They were correct only 30 percent of the time. Now the military won't leave home without a laser range finder. Should you?

Range finders, most of which are now laser range finders, are an affordable accessory for any type of hunt. Muzzleloader bullets, like arrows, shoot a rainbow trajectory throughout their effective range. You need to know the ballistic drop of the bullet, as well as the range to the animal, to be effective. I use my Bushnell Yardage Pro any time I can't see a distinct whitetail eyeball or must guess the yardage on a boss gobbler. Laser range finders from Bushnell, Brunton, Simmons, Swarovski, Tasco, and others, as well as the lower-priced optical range finders from Ranging Rangefinders, will make you a more effective and ethical hunter.

Tuning

Every muzzleloading rifle has the ability to shoot more accurately and perform more reliably on the hunt if some commonsense tuning practices are applied. Finicky flintlocks have more moving parts and need more care than other ignition systems. Flint choices, flint knapping, lock tuning, and priming tricks are just some of the easy-to-apply strategies. Cantankerous percussion rifles also need tender loving care. As well as tuning the lock, the fire channel in the nipple assembly needs attention, and the choice of percussion cap makes a difference. High-tech in-lines have fewer moving parts, but tolerances are more critical to performance. This section tells you how to take a run-of-the-mill gun and turn it into a real game-getter.

FLINTLOCK GUNS

Hunters can blame their lack of success on bad luck, superstition, or other people, but we all know the real reason: carelessness. If you want that flintlock rifle to be a real tack driver, you need to pay attention to details. With more moving parts in its lock mechanism than any other gun action, this means that muzzleloaders have

SUPERSTITIONS

Abrown shape rocketed from the golden cornstalks, silhouetting itself against the blue autumnal sky. The young hunter, shocked at the noise and movement, regained his composure and led the deer with his .50-caliber muzzleloader. The rifle thumped against his shoulder as orange fire and white smoke blasted out of its bowels. The ivory antlers gleamed as the deer bounded into the safety of the woodlot. Only the telltale white smoke hung on the morning thermal as the boy finally exhaled with disappointment.

An hour later, another brown form emerged, and still others. The herd glided through the goldenrod and submerged into the tall weeds of autumn. Through the frosted tall grass the rifle spoke a sulfurous song. "Darn," the boy yelled to his friend, "this muzzleloading gun couldn't hit the broad side of a barn even if I was standing right aside of it!" As the boy and his friend continued down the old dirt lane toward the abandoned farmhouse, an owl hooted, a wisp of fog moved off the lake, and the boys realized that this Halloween hunt was getting spooky.

Berks County, Pennsylvania, has enjoyed a long history of superstition and legend. Indian myths have joined with Pennsylvania Dutch culture to provide a wealth of hunting superstitions and a shopping list of spooky things to worry about. The following, gleaned from a half century of hunting with ears wide open, is offered for the Halloween hunter who can't always explain why things went the way they did.

For starters, the boy should have listened to this piece of advice: "To make a *Freischutz* (a gun that never fails), always load it with a bullet cast on a crossroads at Christmas Eve, and it will hit the mark or bring down the game without fail." Of course, I doubt if Hornady, Speer, or Nosler could guarantee which bullet was made on Christmas Eve.

Have you ever missed a deer? To prevent this heartache, one superstitious remedy from the ages was to "pour some rabbit blood down the barrel." Alternatively, one could simply "swab the shotgun's bore with the heart of a bat and then shoot the bullet of bat hair so that the gun will always strike its mark."

I have had some strange experiences in the dark and dank hemlock forests near Hawk Mountain, but I have never met a witch there. Apparently, our forefathers did. They advised the hunter to lay his gun down in a moving stream to remove the spell of a witch. Then, "the witch who cast the spell wouldn't be able to pass her water until she begged the owner's forgiveness."

Many an old stock carried carvings or inlaid pins in the shape of crosses. This would prevent the gun from ever carrying a hex or curse. Even so, it was widely known that the first shot from a new gun would never hit its mark or kill its game. (Maybe this admonition was devised to make the young or inexperienced practice first, then hunt.) (*continued on page 236*)

Hearing an owl hooting over your left shoulder or shooting at a rabbit sitting quietly under an elderberry bush were considered bad omens. If this should happen, immediately stop hunting and go back to bed, lest the spirits find you. Also, never count your bullets, or the spirits will resent your overconfidence and deal with you accordingly.

Hunting dogs have always been a source of companionship while hunting. But sometimes a wild scent causes even the best of hounds to run astray. Remember, "a good hunting dog will never run away if you feed it bread warmed under your armpits."

And finally, "never shoot an albino deer or they [the spirits] will resent your arrogance at such an easy mark, and one of your family will be made to pay for the mistake."

more things that can go wrong. To be successful, you need to understand the equipment.

Flintlocks should fire with a resounding bang when you pull the trigger, not the often heard *tick, click, kabooom!* of reenactors on the History Channel. Ignition should happen in 0.050-second, which is much faster than you can blink. To prevent your flintlock from performing like a "flinchlock," begin by disassembling the lock.

Use a screwdriver that correctly fits the slot in the head of the screw. An undersized screwdriver will torque the slot and leave a blemish, an unsightly burr, and is also likely to slip out of the slot and dig into the stock. Remove the bolts and carefully remove the lock plate from the stock. Visually inspect the lock mortise. If there are any rub marks on the wood or synthetic, that is a sign that something is not functioning as it should. Use a scraper or chisel to relieve the high spot so that the tumbler, spring, trigger lever, or any other moving part is free of friction.

Lubricate the moving parts with a light machine oil. Grease will thicken in cold weather and slow down the lock time. Lubrication is especially necessary behind the bridle, where the tumbler rides against the lock. Make sure that the lock plate is smooth and free of rust. The main spring, sear spring, and tumbler all ride against this flat piece of iron, and it needs to have as little friction as possible.

John Getz explains the beauty and effectiveness of one of his company's custom flintlocks to visitors at Dixon's Gunmaker's Fair. The flintlock has more moving parts than any other gun lock and requires vigilant tuning for optimal effectives.

The lock and parts of a flintlock require cleaning and lubrication in order to function at their best lock speed. If tuned properly, a flintlock can fire in $1/500$ of a second—faster than a person can blink.

All too often, when rifles are cleaned after a practice session or hunt, the innards of the lock are overlooked. This leads to rusting and dysfunction or, at the very least, a slowdown of lock time.

Remove the lock. Check the tolerances between the barrel and the base of the frizzen (the flat steel struck by the flint). The metal surfaces should not rub, and some filing may be in order if this is the case. Lubricate the top flat of the frizzen spring so that the frizzen cam (the U- or V-shaped projection that rides on the small leaf spring on the outside of the lock) slides easily. A drop of oil on the frizzen bolt will also allow the frizzen to rotate more easily. But don't overdo the oil, because any excess will find its way into the pan and contaminate the priming powder.

Now turn your attention to the cock. This rotating hammer device was given its name because it looks like a cock rooster with a stone in its beak. Any looseness in the cock, and the flint stone will not strike the steel frizzen forcefully and produce sparks. The cock is given rotation by the tumbler on the inside of the lock. An extending bolt shoulder of iron projects through the lock plate, and this must rotate smoothly. Again, check for rust, and lubricate. The square hole in the base of the cock slips over the tumbler bolt and is anchored with a large-headed screw. Be sure that it is tight. If the cock wiggles where it attaches to the tumbler, a gunsmith will need to add or upset the metal to take up the space and make it tight. Any looseness here will cause poor spark production.

Before you check for tightness of the top screw above the flint, turn your attention to the stone itself. The number-one reason why flintlocks don't fire is that the owner is too cheap to change the flint. Flints do tend to get dull, for obvious reasons: friction against the steel erodes the knife edge into more of a rolled edge. The bevel on the agate may still look good to your eyes, but if the edge doesn't feel as sharp as the edge of broken glass, do something about it. Most agates that come equipped on rifles have two beveled edges, one on each side. Simply turn the flint around and you'll be back in the game of making sparks. Or, if you prefer a more modern ceramic flint, take a look at one with a better-sparking saw-toothed "hunting edge" by Tom Kyper of Kyper Rifle Flints.

There is a simple test for flintlock sparking ability. Take an empty flintlock (check this by measuring the ramrod's depth in the

If you are unhappy with the shower of sparks that is thrown by a sawed-agate flint, try using a fine-grained English or French model.

bore along the outside of the barrel) into a dark room, turn it upside down, and dry-fire the lock. Count the number of sparks. If you don't have at least seven sparks, your flintlock is not ready to go hunting.

Usually, a reversed or a new flint will take care of the problem. If you are unhappy with the agate flint's performance, you may want to try a fine-grained, silica-rich glossy black English, amber French, or milk-glass-looking German flint from Track of the Wolf. In fact, my flintlocks never leave home without one. These ethnic flints have a different rock composition that gives them sharper edges, and most important, they can easily be resharpened while they are still in the jaws of the cock. This is a very important feature when hunting.

To sharpen a flint, known as "knapping," support the flint under the lower jaw of the cock with your finger and chip away at the old edge. A glancing blow is lightly struck at a 90-degree angle to the edge of the flint with a piece of brass (so as not to make sparks that could accidentally discharge a loaded gun or deliver a crushing blow to the brittle stone, causing it to be split and become worthless). A specialty accessory known as a flint knapping tool (resembling a miniature brass hammer) is a handy item for the leather hunting pouch.

The knapping process causes "spawls," or semicircular flakes of flint, to detach from the main stone. This produces a very sharp edge similar to that of broken glass. With the ability to be knapped several times, these true flints produce more sparks than agates do and will last two to five times as long in the flintlock.

Flints take a lot of abuse as they smack into the steel frizzen, producing hardened and tempered iron sparks and send sizzling igniters into the pan of priming powder. If they are not tightened into the jaws of the cock with good pressure from the top-jaw screw, they will not produce good sparks and will likely shatter. To help absorb some of the shock of contact with the steel, American flintlocks normally sandwich the piece of flint inside a folded piece of leather. European military muskets and German Jaeger flintlocks were normally equipped with thin sheets of lead around the flint. They both work.

The proper size of flint for your rifle is determined by the width of the frizzen and the depth of the jaw's throat, as well as the distance to the frizzen.

Does it matter whether the flint is installed with the bevel up or the bevel down? No. What does matter is that the flint is the correct size and is mounted properly. The size of the flint is determined by the width of the frizzen and the depth of the jaw's throat. Under-sized flints cut fewer sparks, while oversized flints strike the side of the barrel and break, as well as causing unsightly cuts in the barrel. If the flint is too long, it will push up the frizzen at half-cock, accidentally releasing priming powder. A flint that is too long will also strike the frizzen too high, increase lock time, and actually cause the sparks to be driven away from the priming powder by the slope of the frizzen face. Flints that have uneven thickness or are too thick will never tighten properly. When they don't hit the flint squarely across the frizzen face, poor ignition takes place.

A properly mounted flint leaves just enough room between its edge and the face of the frizzen. The flint strikes the frizzen in the middle with great speed and force and drops the sparks straight down into the priming powder. Correct installation also leads to longer flint life, faster ignition, and happy hunting memories.

PERCUSSION GUNS

Primitive percussion rifles ignite their main powder charges in less than half the time that it takes a flintlock to do the same. The percussion cap evolved out of the need for a weather-resistant ignition system. One might think that they have fewer problems than flintlocks, but actually, percussion rifles experience many of the same problems.

Lock time is a function of spring strength, friction, hammer speed, and flash channel distance. As already discussed, friction inside the lock reduces lock time, promotes flinching, and leaves the hunter with a good deer tale instead of a hanging deer tail. So begin the tuning process inside the lock mortise and lock plate. Lubrication with a light oil is vital.

The hammer on the percussion lock has some of the same problems as the cock on the flintlock. Make sure that it is attached tightly to the tumbler, or it won't deliver the solid smack to the percussion cap that is necessary for ignition.

There are additional problems that arise with percussion systems. Because you are dealing with temperamental little #11 percussion caps, which tend to fall off the barrel's extension tube,

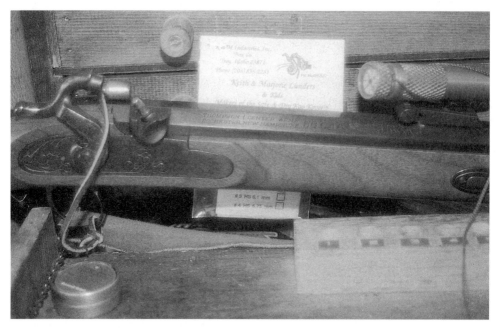

Primitive percussion rifles ignite their main powder charges in less than half the time that it takes a flintlock.

(the nipple), you need to pay extra attention to details. Since the flash channel is longer than the flintlock's, the gases tend to cool, and because moisture can totally jam the system, the system tends to be persnickety.

Nipples are not a permanent piece of the percussion puzzle. They wear out just like flints and need to be replaced periodically. So always check the shoulders (the top) of the nipple to make sure that they are not bent or mashed. Unscrew them from their base in the snail or drum and inspect the base. If the tiny flash hole has opened up from the heat of repeated use, or if the metal has crystallized irregularly, replace the nipple. Rusty and loose-fitting nipples are dangerous. When replacing a nipple, consider using one of Uncle Mike's Hot Shot Nipples. They are coned for ease of capping and decapping, and the nipples seem to stay attached longer. The Hot Shots are also vented to prevent blowback and ensure a hotter flame reaching the powder charge. They are a good choice for Pyrodex and Triple Seven powders.

AMPCO nipples are made from a tough alloy with a tensile strength of 118,000 pounds per square inch. This is stronger than most steels used in muzzleloading barrels. It resists repeated hammer blows better than other nipples and withstands the erosion of hot gases better. Its small 0.028-inch base orifice intensifies the jet of burning gases, and some claim that it has better ignition properties. But even these nipples will wear out in time.

A necessary evil of shooting percussions is dealing with the 90-degree angle of the flash channel. Use a nipple pick to ensure that the base orifice is open. Repeated shooting drives unburned percussion particles into and around this hole, which will close up in time. It is also a good idea to use the hottest cap you can buy for your rifle. Standard #11 caps give irregular ignition to the replica powders; a magnum #11 is better. Those who retrofit to a musket cap can expect even greater volumes of hot gas and more dependable ignition. The following table, courtesy of CCI/Speer, lists the temperatures and volumes of gas that are expected with each type of percussion cap:

Primer	Flame Temperature (°F)	Gas Volume (cc)
#200 large rifle	3,024	11.68
#250 large rifle magnum	3,717	11.97
#209 shotgun	3,024	21.98
#10	3,024	6.53
#11	3,024	6.53
#11 magnum	3,717	7.59
U.S. musket cap	3,717	14.36

When fulminates of mercury were discovered to work in percussion rifle systems, they changed the gun industry. But with these original pressure-sensitive particles or percussion caps, which were used in rifles and muskets until the end of the black powder era (the close of the nineteenth century), highly destructive fouling was a real problem. Today, this is not the case.

According to Dynamit Nobel-RWS, Inc., the invention of Sinoxid priming compound in 1926 revolutionized the ignition process and completely eliminated the problems of instability and deterioration associated with earlier forms. Fulminating mercury was replaced with organic substances, namely, trycinate and tetranzene. The oxidizing agents borium nitrate and lead dioxide, together with sulfur antimony and calcium silicide, were added to produce a highly combustible but smooth-burning mixture that is characterized by outstanding anticorrosive properties.

Percussion caps must balance sensitivity with safety in storage and transit. It is worth noting that Sinoxid priming compound is not hygroscopic. It is resistant to climatic influences and has unlimited shelf life in stores.

HIGH-TECH IN-LINE GUNS

At first, the early in-lines caused hunters to pursue a new type of cleaning procedure. Disassembly of the striker, nipple, and breech plug, as well as the trigger assembly, required specialized tools. Compared with the primitive flintlock and percussion guns, cleaning was a labor-intensive task. Escaping gases from the percussion caps dirtied the bottoms of scope tubes, and special covers soon appeared.

Improvements followed through the 1990s as more manufacturers attempted to grab a share of this new market. Each ignition system was new and improved, but regardless of whether the company switched from #11 caps to musket caps to 209 shotgun primers, the problem remained. Vented percussion gases and gunpowder blowback fouled the striker mechanisms in the breech.

Safety improvements involving striker locks, trigger locks, and other disruptive mechanisms added safety to the hunt but caused muzzleloaders to rethink the firing process. It is still a good idea not to cap the rifle, regardless of cap type, until you are ready to take a shot.

Many of the new high-tech in-lines utilize synthetic stocks with free-floating barrels. This concept is borrowed from modern centerfire companies, but it does work. What you need to understand is that the tension you put on the forearm anchoring bolt must be the same each time, or it will affect the barrel whip harmonics and change the point of bullet impact. Place a tiny witness mark on the forearm to line up the slot of the bolt slot, and you will be in good shape.

In-line muzzleloaders began to impact the muzzleloading market in the mid-1980s.

The latest break-action in-lines are making the 209 shotgun primer the igniter of choice. But these primers put fouling into the flash channel that needs to be cleaned if misfires are to be avoided.

Many hunters are now attaching bipods to their rifles. Again, be reminded that this will affect barrel harmonics and change the point of impact. So, if you plan on using the bipod, sight in the gun with it attached.

Muzzleloading Accessories

Part of the fun of being a muzzleloading hunter is in the creation or re-creation of original eighteenth-century equipment. While buckskins may be a stretch for modern muzzleloaders, scrimshawed powder horns, leather possibles bags, short starters, bullet boards, and patch knives are all worthy of creative effort, and they add distinction to the rifle that hangs above the fireplace. This section examines both old and new muzzleloading accessories for the hunt and for competition.

October is both a time and a state of mind. For muzzleloading hunters, it is a special blend of the best of all things natural—a Kodachrome spectacle of scenery, crisp mornings, balmy afternoons, and heartwarming friendships.

Into this natural mix of heightened sensory adventure, enter stalkers of white-tailed deer. This is the season of the longhunter, so named because of their extended absence from the frontier farm after the crops were in and a supply of firewood was laid up for the winter. This group of farmer-hunters donned their hunting pouches and scrimshawed powder horns and took up their trusty longrifles. Two hundred years later, our spouses still refer to us as longhunters, even though we spend only hours, not weeks, away from home. Deer season is here when the hickories go golden, the maples turn vermilion, and the oaks burn a brilliant bronze.

Two weeks of deer scouting and squirrel hunting with a Cabela's .36-caliber Blue Ridge percussion proved to me that the bucks were not following their normal trails from the cornfield up into the hardwood ridge. Perhaps the warmth of 70-degree days coupled with a post-summer dryness had moved the resident deer from the top of the oak ridge to the cornfield valley. Or perhaps it was the increasing

A MUZZLELOADER'S CHECKLIST

IN OR ON YOUR BACKPACK

☐ Hunting license and special stamps
☐ Wallet and identification
☐ Cell phone and radio
☐ Fluorescent orange
☐ Emergency kit
☐ Camera
☐ Binoculars
☐ Laser range finder
☐ 25 feet of cord
☐ Butane lighter
☐ Flashlight
☐ Knife or saw and sharpener
☐ Pencil and paper
☐ Repair kit
☐ Cleaning kit
☐ Hand warmers
☐ Large plastic bags

☐ Topo map
☐ Compass
☐ GPS unit
☐ Water
☐ Candy or granola bar
☐ Scent dispenser
☐ Toilet paper
☐ Disposable rubber gloves
☐ Glasses and sunglasses
☐ Rain poncho
☐ Whistle
☐ Multi-tool
☐ Duct tape
☐ Fluorescent ribbon
☐ Keys (car, house, cabin)
☐ Waterless soap

IN OR ON YOUR HUNTING POUCH

Primitive Rifles

☐ Bulk container of black or replica powder
☐ Powder measurer
☐ Primer (flintlock) horn or flask
☐ Frizzen cover
☐ Extra flints and leather wraps
☐ Bullet board with patched roundballs
☐ Cleaning patches
☐ Flint knapping tool
☐ Vent pick and pan brush
☐ Patch knife
☐ Small belt ax
☐ Patch puller or worm
☐ Cleaning jab
☐ Sight paint and small brush
☐ Pin or wedge puller

Modern In-Lines

☐ Pyrodex or Triple Seven pellets
☐ Percussion caps or 209 primer
☐ E-C Loader or Speed loaders
☐ Capping tool
☐ Extra sabots and bullets
☐ Lubricant or wax
☐ Small bottle of solvent
☐ Decapping tool
☐ Small screwdriver
☐ Nipple pick
☐ Nipple wrench and spares
☐ Ball or bullet puller
☐ Breech plug wrench and tools
☐ Allen wrench
☐ Scope covers

(continued on page 248)

A MUZZLELOADER'S CHECKLIST *continued*

OTHER ACCESSORIES

- ☐ Range rod or spare ramrod
- ☐ Cleaning kits and small bucket
- ☐ Extra clothing (particularly socks)
- ☐ Insulated under- and outerwear
- ☐ Deer glide or drag or cart
- ☐ Ammunition box with lock and key
- ☐ Camouflage blind or tree stand (with cable lock and key)
- ☐ Plane tickets, passport, itinerary

- ☐ Face mask and gloves
- ☐ Decoys and scents
- ☐ Trigger lock and key
- ☐ Walking staff
- ☐ Spotting scope
- ☐ ATV and keys, locking cable
- ☐ List of names and phone numbers

pressure of grouse hunters that pushed the herd farther into the woods. Even before the bow hunters clanked up the trees to their stands, weather and human encroachment had changed the deer patterns from an early-morning or late-evening hunt to a nocturnal "no contest." Early-season deer hunting is like that in the Appalachians.

Having watched a young Y-buck nose into the wind just below my false scrape, followed by a maternal doe and her yearlings, I began to think that this year's early muzzleloader season would be over by the end of the first day. But the appearance of a red fox quickly put an end to that thought. As the days wore on, morning and evening hunts were proving to be more entertaining than productive.

October is the season of the longhunter. Endless flocks of goldfinches, towhees, yellow-shafted flickers, and raucous bluejays punctuated the stillness of the canopy with their seed-searching and constant chatter. Even a resident gray squirrel, whose second-story tree I shared, became a familiar face. I smiled as I looked down at the powder horn I was carrying, a bold, bushy-tailed gray artistically scrimshawed into its ivory surface.

Change was necessary. My treetop strategy wasn't working. It was time to climb out of the golden canopy and start hiking over hill and dale. A ground assault was the only answer, a frontal assault into the edge of the deer's bedding and security areas. I knew that these foliage-rich areas had been skirted by hunters with tree stands.

The problem soon became apparent. I was the driver, but there were no standers. The deer certainly were not at risk from this tactic of still hunting in the leafy brush of early October.

October 13 was the earliest date that I had ever primed a flintlock for deer hunting in Pennsylvania. In the predawn stillness, the clinking sounds of ramrods seating lead roundballs, copper slugs, and plastic sabotted bullets must have seemed alien to the ears of the already treetop bow hunters. For the past two weeks, camouflage clothing in the canopies ruled the hardwoods. Now, a new type of orange-vested army, more than 180,000 strong, was on the move. Though still in the minority when compared with the archers, the flintlock hunters were determined to make an impact on the antlerless herd. After all, the Pennsylvania Game Commission's Dr. Gary Alt had asked for our vigilance in cropping the abnormal ratio of does back into balance. We longhunters were not only consumers of venison; we were now part of the management strategy.

That first Saturday morning witnessed a longer-than-normal procession of cars funneling out of town and onto the dirt roads that crisscross the rural sections of the state. A "new tradition" in deer hunting seemed to be marking its place on the natural calendar. A new season had dawned. But unlike the rifle season, which catches whitetails out in the open of the harvested grainfields of November, the primitive flintlock, percussion, and in-line hunters were greeted with a much leafier situation—unharvested fields and fully clothed trees. There would be no easy shots and quick hunts today. The muzzleloaders would need to take the hunt to the woods.

My 14-year-old son sat in an ancient, truncated black birch tree. His aluminum ladder stand was swallowed by a cluster of gnarly old limbs. Fully confident with his high-tech, scoped T/C Black Diamond, two Pyrodex pellets, and a T/C Break-O-Way sabot, Matt believed that his modern rig would give him the edge to score quickly on a doe and have the rest of the day to join his friends in a game of soccer.

As the sun pierced the eastern horizon, it brought with it a familiar but unseasonable warmth. Unlike previous mornings when I had held a bow in my hands, the deer did not make an appearance. Only the familiar buzz of grasshoppers and the high-pitched whine of mosquitoes kept my senses on edge. Three hours of watching squirrels, cardinals, and chickadees, punctuated by the lonely whining of a locomotive's distant horn, were enough excitement for one morning.

There would be other mornings. The pan of my flintlock was emptied of priming powder; a feather quill was pulled from my leather hunting pouch, along with a leather frizzen cover. Now that the rifle had been rendered safe and unable to draw sparks, I inserted the quill into the touch hole to prevent moisture from sneaking in. Civic responsibilities were calling.

Everyone seeks the serenity of the forests for their own personal reasons, but they usually leave because of the demands imposed on them. Although reluctant to climb down from the old black oak, I felt the need to help the community, particularly in the aftermath of the 9/11 tragedy. As a Boy Scout scoutmaster, I had responsibilities to the boys from my Troop 510. They were "Scouting for Food," an annual event that replenishes the community larder for those in need. The boys supplied the legs and the enthusiasm, the residents happily donated the cans and boxes of foodstuffs, and Trinity Lutheran Church supplied the location. A real feeling of hope pervaded the whole experience, and if there ever was a good reason to stop hunting for a few hours, that was it.

As the abnormally hot weather persisted, each day's routine ended with a few minutes in the tree stand. With each setting sun, daily reports from friends told stories of opportunities, some ending in clicks, flashes, or no bangs. But that's why we enjoy the season so much; muzzleloading hunters never know when they will end up with a buck or a buck's worth of problems. Reaching into my double-yoke elk-skin hunting pouch, I felt the buttery-smooth doeskin bag of flints. A buck's worth of insurance, I mused. A new flint ensures success. And so it was for a neighbor's 15-year-old son who shot his first deer with a flintlock and hasn't stopped talking about it for days. It seemed like everyone was seeing deer but me. The week was ending, and something had to change.

"The last Saturday is always the best Saturday." My enthusiasm was contagious over the phone as I tried to convince by flintlock buddy Bill to come over to the farm. "You just have to be here at 4. After all, it's the last day!"

Bill responded, "Is that A.M. or P.M.?"

We agreed that a late-afternoon hunt worked best for both our schedules. We also agreed that short-sleeved shirts were in order for the 80-degree, unseasonable weather, but the threat of ticks and flies made us quickly dismiss that idea.

Late in the afternoon, Matt headed for his ladder stand up on the ridge, while Bill and I walked to the hillside above the swamp. Deer sign was noticeable everywhere. A well-used trail showed evidence of recent hoof marks, fresh scat, and rubbings. With my friend's .50-caliber Hawken covering the funnel between Matt and the swamp, I knew that my silent, one-man drive along the ridge should produce some results. What I didn't appreciate was the heat.

Toting a flintlock rifle, dressed head to toe in camo and orange, perspiration began to take its toll. My powder was dry, but I wasn't. Spying a good resting spot along an ancient, toppled white oak tree now completely devoid of bark, I settled into a good ambush and snoozing spot. Evening approached, and Venus began to glow in the southern sky, soon to be joined by the conjunction of Jupiter and Saturn. My thoughts wandered as I mused about those early Paleolithic Indians—the Leni Lenape, Delaware, Seneca, and Iroquois. They, too, hunted this same ridge, carrying arrows pointed with knapped jasper and quartzite inside their own bags of deerskin.

A quick glance down at the handmade jasper flint in my lock created a sudden connection with those spirits of past woodland hunters. Even though the hands of time will continue to turn for each generation, all hunters share a special bond with those who came before them, a moment in time that draws us inexplicably together, propelled by the primordial need to hunt. We may hunt for different reasons—for sport, food, or camaraderie—but the need is undeniably there and always will be. Like the stone that tips an arrow and sparks a flintlock, our primitive pursuit is ageless.

A distant thunder from a flintlock rifle brought me back to reality. Deer were on the move, and it was time to pay attention. A flock of twittering chickadees began their annual harvest of black birch seeds by flinging the seed pods to the ground and then descending on them to eat. Apparently, I was too well concealed by my camo, and I was soon covered with the lightweight chaff of their endeavors.

Suddenly, movement from across the power line diverted my attention from the bird antics. All became still except for the constant chirp of crickets. Deer have an uncanny way of disappearing before the naked eye, even when they are standing out in the open. Not 30 yards away, a Y-buck, antlers gleaming in the setting sun, stared directly at me. Thirty yards is an easy shot, even with a flintlock. But this management season was designed for antlerless deer, so this buck would be spared.

As the buck walked away, stopping to stare back at my intrusion into his personal rub line, another deer emerged. A mature doe, nose to the ground, wandered onto the same path from the opposite direction. But the hot scent of the buck caused her to stop, snort, and jump off the deer path. Apparently, the doe wasn't ready for what the hormonal buck was advertising during this pre-rut period. Sidestepping away from the path, she retreated to the security of the raspberry cane and grapevine thicket.

With only 15 minutes left in this October flintlock season, it looked like the hunt was over. Dumping the hours-old priming powder in the pan of the flintlock, I reached under the flap of my pouch and felt the familiar chip-carved neck of my engraved Skip Hamaker priming horn. As I began to stand up to reprime the lock,

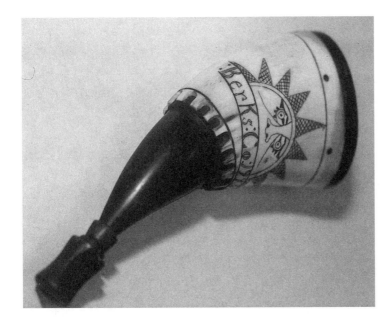

My engraved Skip Hamaker priming horn.

another deer popped into view. Again, a doe stopped at the buck's path, smelled the strong buck scent, and snorted. But this time, the rifle was ready, drawn to full cock, and the open iron sights quickly came into alignment with the deer's shoulder.

One hundred grains of FFFg GOEX black powder shattered the stillness with a thunderous roar. A sulfurous haze smoked the presence of the deer like a ghostly apparition claiming its victim. But when the smoke cleared, the doe was gone. Knowing which way the deer didn't go was the only clue I had to work with. No hair or blood from the .54 roundball was visible at the place where I thought the deer had been standing. Red dots littered the leaves, but they were not droplets of crimson blood; they were red pigments in the yellow leaves that had recently fallen from the trees.

Wondering if I had missed, I replayed the shot in my mind, noting my location, the deer's position, and her possible escape routes. A quick swabbing of the big-bore with a spit-moistened patch allowed me to reload and be ready for a follow-on shot, if the opportunity presented itself. Slowly taking up the trail, signs of overturned leaves and crushed vegetation soon began to tell the story.

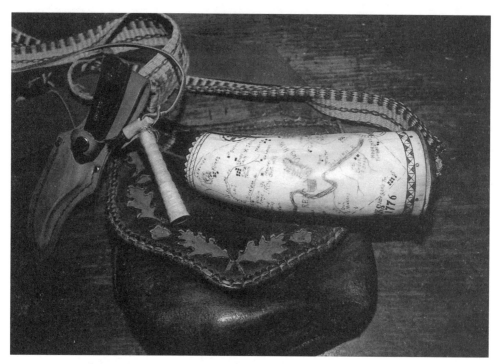

The hunting pouch has historically played an important role in the maintenance and loading of a rifle.

In less than 30 yards, a glimpse of brown body hair signaled that the shot had been true. The .54-caliber flintlock American Jaeger had made meat the old-fashioned way. And the crickets continued to greet the evening with their chirping chorus.

HUNTING POUCHES

"Without the means of care and loading, the gun becomes merely a club," Madison Grant eloquently stated back in 1977 in his book *The Kentucky Rifle Hunting Pouch.* Although clothing pockets seem to have replaced hunting pouches for modern muzzleloaders, I still feel a utilitarian need for these venerable bags. "By 1825, the hunting pouch had begun to serve two masters without favor: the flintlock and percussion. The sparking stone was being challenged by the fulminate cap and was to give ground grudgingly like an old herd bull in the face of a more youthful antagonist," Grant added.

Regardless of whether they are called hunting pouches, possibles bags, haversacks, or accoutrements bags, one fact remains true: these bags are an indispensable repository for tools. Moreover, they are pieces of American folk art and serve as a connection to our heritage.

Why continue using an obsolete bag of leather, fur, or cloth? In a word: organization. Although pockets are convenient for carrying plastic vials of powder and sabot, the other tools that are needed to correct or clean a rifle tend to get lost as they languish unnoticed and unlocated from season to season. Hunting pouches serve as the repository for the necessary, a home for the indispensable, and they hang ready to go at a moment's notice.

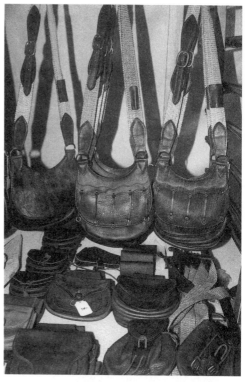

As American riflemen left the militias and embraced the solitary lives of frontiersmen, the hunting pouch became smaller.

Reenactors are very careful about the style of bags they hang from their shoulders or belts. From the highly ornate European military accoutrements bags to the plain, utilitarian pouches of the frontiersmen and the brightly decorated bead and quill bags of the Amerindians, the bag has had a storied past. But unfortunately, while the rifles survived, the leather and cloth bags didn't. There are a few relics now carefully maintained in museums and private collections, but most of our popularized ideas about how a bag should look have come from the movies. So, if you are looking for the correct bag to hang with your primitive rifle, you'll need to generalize.

Reenactors of the French and Indian Wars carry a fairly large, square-shaped bag. The leather bag, perhaps a tougher version of the German cloth haversack (sack for horse food), carried more than tools for the flintlock musket. It carried salt horns, cups, spoons, mirrors, and other tools needed for frontier military life. But as riflemen left the ranks of the militia and embraced the solitary lifestyle of Appalachian frontiersmen, the hunting pouch got smaller. From that time until the end of the black powder era after the Civil War, hunting pouches generally took on one of five shapes—D-shaped, double-pouched, heart-shaped, square-pouched, and kidney-shaped—and were 6 to 8 inches wide and 7 to 9 inches deep.

The D-shaped bag was a deepened semicircular design that seemed to be the workhorse bag of the hunting fraternity. From the strap of this small bag hung a vent pick and brush, a powder measurer, and a loading block. Knives were either hung in a scabbard on the strap or attached to the back of the bag.

The double pouch, which was a modification of the D shape, offered more room and better organization of contents. The two pouches kept metal tools from rattling and spooking game or giving away the hunter's presence to hostile enemies.

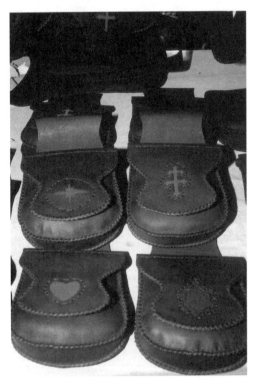

The heart-shaped bag forced the contents to settle in the center at the bottom. This prevented spillage of the tools while running over rough terrain or hitting the trail at full gallop on a horse.

The square pouch seems to occur in every stage of muzzleloading rifle development. From the earliest Plymouth Rock Pilgrims to the end of the Rocky Mountain fur trapper era, the square-shaped bag was used. This is probably because it was the easiest of the shapes to make from one sheet of leather or cloth. It provided the greatest depth and volume for the money.

The square pouch seems to occur in every stage of muzzleloading rifle evolution.

Shorter flaps of heavier design removed the need for buttons or buckles.

The kidney-shaped hunting pouch accommodated longer items. Long handles on lead melting ladles, buffalo-skinning knives, long-handled bullet molds, and other lengthy utilitarian tools needed the room, and the kidney shape provided that without becoming too bulky.

The flaps on all these shapes varied greatly. Shorter flaps were made of heavier designs, which included the fur-faced fox, bobcat, or bear. Long flaps of leather afforded closure without the need for a button or buckle. In many instances, the weight of a hanging powder horn kept the contents firmly inside the bag. Without a clasp, the hunter could gain faster entry for reloading or repair.

Leather piercings didn't appear until after 1820. Cutouts in the shape of acorns, oak leaves, hearts, stars, and other folk art motifs revealed a splash of color from the underlying fabric or leather. But by 1850, elaborate designs disappeared as the demand for utilitarian "percussion" tool bags increased.

Throughout the hunting pouch's history, calfskin was used most often. The skin of deer, elk, and moose was also used, but it didn't possess the durability needed to resist the abuse of metal tools. Fur-bearers such as the raccoon, possum, skunk, bear, fox, coyote, and wolf also entered the mix, but there are few survivors left for us to examine. Today, many of these fur-adorned hunting pouches are popular with rendezvous reenactors.

It is noteworthy that most hunting pouches were hand sewn with sinew or linen thread. The sewing machine was not in general use until the 1840s, but even then, most hunting pouches were not machine-stitched. The Civil War changed that. In fact, cartridge belts for military arms began to lessen the need for the venerable pouch. Many of today's pouches are machine sewn, but there are still a few leather artisans who produce hand-sewn replica bags.

Today, hunters have many bags to choose from, ranging from replica bags to belt pouches to museum-quality reproductions. There are many good hunting pouch craftsmen attending state and national rendezvous, as well as the national championship in Friendship, Indiana. But three artisans stand out for their re-creations of eighteenth- and nineteenth-century hunting bags: Known as the "Leatherman," Gary Fatherree has been creating hunting bags for decades. Although he makes many different styles, he is well known for his Germanic-style hunting bags typical of Pennsylvania. Another respected leather pouch artisan is Harry McGonigal, known to buckskinners as Reverend Harry. He is a noted seminar speaker and creator of historically correct hunting pouches handmade in the old way. Ken Scott's leather hunting pouches were featured in the *Book of Buckskinning, Muzzle Blasts, Muzzleloader,* and *Dixie Gun Works Black Powder Annual.* He has a national reputation for leather and cloth pouches in styles including eastern, western fur trade, French and Indian War, Revolutionary War, and Pennsylvania German.

POWDER HORNS

> "I Powder with my Brother ball . . .
> A Hero like do Conquer All."

The flintlock longrifle is the most famous example of folk art produced in colonial America, but the lowly scrimshawed powder horn is a close second. No early American fireplace would be com-

Along with the flintlock longrifle, the engraved powder horn is one of the finest examples of colonial folk art.

Cow horns have been the weatherproof container of choice for thousands of years. They rose to prominence in America when they were elevated to the status of art by engravers.

plete without a lowly cow horn of powder hanging above the leather hunting pouch. Pouches and horns take their proud place aside the rifle. They are a team; each is a strong individual component, but none can complete its task without the other two.

Cow horns have been the weatherproof containers of choice for thousands of years. They took on a specific chore in the fifteenth century when musketeers needed a way to store and moisture-proof their black powder stores. But cow horns truly rose to prominence in America when their utilitarian nature was elevated to the status of art by engravers. India ink, sometimes even black powder ink, was incised into the shell of the horn. Maps, city renderings, animals, and owners' names were all inscribed into the riflemen's horns. Crude carvings, important dates, scripture, poems, and verse all took their places on powder horns.

One bit of verse scrimshawed into a powder horn in the private collection of Rich Nordi stated to the ages:

> *Arouse jolly Bacchus the horn to embrace*
> *It will cheer up the spirits to follow the chase*
> *It will brace up the nerves the game to pursue*
> *And cause the bold huntsman to sound the halloo.*

Paul "Skip" Hamaker is a nationally known powder horn builder and engraver. He creates accurately detailed round, flat, and screw-tipped black powder horns for reenactors, muzzleloading competitors, and hunters. They are styled after those from eighteenth-century colonial America but take on new life in the hands of this twenty-first-century master scrimshander. The April 1997 cover of *Muzzle Blasts* magazine featured a Hamaker powder horn alongside a custom reproduction flintlock, leather pouch, and knives. Hamaker was asked by the National Muzzle Loading Rifle Association to create a period powder horn to be raffled off as part of a fundraiser. The money raised is being used to construct a colonial block house and stockade fence on the primitive range at the NMLRA's national headquarters in Friendship, Indiana. More recently, Hamaker created a set of engraved powder horns for the Ned Smith rifle, which honored this noted American artist's life. Hamaker's work is also on display at the Rockwell Museum in Corning, New York.

Paul "Skip" Hamaker is a highly regarded engraver of powder horns. His horns are accurately detailed and evoke the round, flat, and screw-tipped horns of colonial America.

Walnut plugs are turned and carved from local hardwoods. The completed horns are soaked in rapeseed oil.

A Hamaker powder horn begins as a raw cow horn that is hand-sanded, boiled, and soaked multiple times in onion skins. He carefully uses authentic colonial methods to create the golden hue found on the original horns that he studies in museums. Walnut plugs are turned and carved from local hardwoods, and the completed horn is soaked in rapeseed oil. Once the horn is completed architecturally, Hamaker adds his special touch—engraving. This is accomplished by drawing and scratching into the horn with sewing needles, then rubbing diluted India ink into the design. On one particular horn—a 1758 replica of one carried by a Scottish French and Indian War officer, Farquar Emdombbein—Hamaker engraved *Nemo me impuna lacesit* (No one attacks me with impunity). Embellished with a Scottish coat of arms and a thistle, this period replica will once again see life on the hip of a living historian.

Another member of the Honourable Company of Horners (HCH) and scrimshander of note is Orville "Spark" Mumma. He specializes in small, flat, scrimshawed priming horns. Four of his powder horns were recently featured in the movie *The Alamo*. Billy Bob Thornton, who played Davy Crockett, carried one of Mumma's bone-tipped, southern-style screw-horns into the fray. Mumma has been a horn maker and scrimshander for almost three decades. His priming horns are as small as 2 1/2 inches or as large as 5. His powder measurers range from 20- to 200-grain capacities. His museum-quality powder horns are much in demand by collectors and hunters.

Past guildmaster and cofounder of the HCH, and noted horn maker and scrimshander is John C. Proud. Many of his horns have

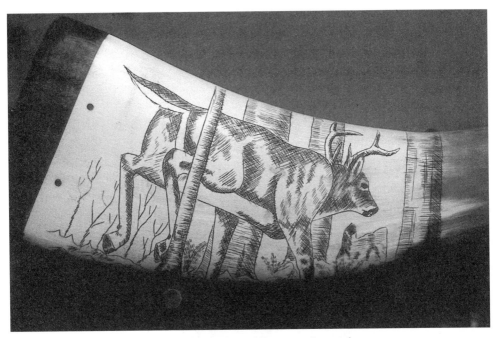

Hamaker's horns have their own unique style.

They are not only recreated from historic horns but also embody game animals, historic maps, and the personalities of their owners.

The author with his powder horn and other assorted longhunter gear.

won blue ribbons and best of show at Dixon's Gunmaker's Fair and have appeared in all of the major muzzleloading magazines. Proud is well known for his engraved horns from the French and Indian War period. Proud's work was featured in the August 2004 *Muzzle Blasts* magazine.

Other talented horn makers include Roland F. Cradle, Lee A. Larkin, Steve Lodding, Arthur J. DeCamp, Mark Thomas, Mike Small, H. David Wright, and Ron Ehlert. (See appendix B for contact information for all the artisans mentioned.)

METAL FLASKS

The arrival of the fulminating percussion cap changed the face of muzzleloading in the early nineteenth century. The Civil War signaled its death knell. The metal flask evolved in this environment, and despite its short life, it too has a significant history.

Pockets were fast taking the place of hunting pouches. Priming horns were not needed with the percussion rifles. Coat pockets and flasks seemed to be made for each other, and they signaled the end of the horn maker and the engraver. Eli Whitney's invention of interchangeable parts and the assembly-line construction of rifles was employed to stamp out the metal halves that were soldered together into a flask. They soon became as common as the copper penny. Stores such as Tryon of Philadelphia and the Great Western Gun Works of Pittsburgh made it possible to purchase these flasks for $1, while the more artistic varieties commanded up to $14.

Flasks were constructed of tin, copper, zinc, brass, and German silver (nickel brass) and were decorated with patterns of game, patriotic symbols, or hunting scenes embossed in their metal surfaces. They were shiny, colorful, and easy to carry, but they didn't last. Cartridges made short work of the flasks, and their existence was short-lived.

Today, flasks are associated mostly with pistols. Their small size and long, pointed spouts make loading the cylinders easier than working with a powder horn. Unlike the watertight shell of a powder horn, flasks are not nearly as weather resistant. Be sure to keep the flask concealed during bad weather, but I am not sure that I would want to keep it in my pocket.

Civil War reenactors may carry the flask as a powder reservoir, but a rifle should never be loaded directly from the flask. This is a safety hazard. A glowing spark left behind by the unburned black powder carbon could ignite the powder being dumped from the spout of the flask. An ignited half pound of black powder can make a devastating impact.

RELOADING AIDS

A rifleman of the Revolutionary War epoch was expected to load and fire his musket three times in one minute. Although this rate of fire wouldn't impress a modern soldier holding an M60 machine gun, it was a real challenge for a militiaman holding a muzzle-loader. To improve his rate of fire, the minuteman kept his powder measurer, usually the tip of cow horn, hollowed-out deer antler, or cone of brass, tethered to a lace above the powder horn. Once the powder was poured down the bore, the loading of a greased, patched roundball could be hurried by using a bullet board.

A bullet board was a half-inch-thick board with a hole drilled to ball size. The rifleman laid a greased patch across the opening, pressed a roundball into the hole, and then cut the patch. This early American speed-loader allowed the rifle-man to simply poke the patched ball out of the board and down the bore in a single stroke. Having participated in many speed matches with muzzleloaders, I can attest to its efficiency. I carry a three-shot bullet board tethered to my hunting pouch strap, along with a short starter sleeved inside my pouch.

Those who hunt with modern muzzleloaders will probably choose a different approach—the plastic speed-loading tube.

The bullet board, an early American speedloader, carries a prepatched and prelubed roundball for decreasing the time it takes to load a rifle.

Back in the 1980s, flexible plastic vial-like tubes were preloaded with powder and bullet. They worked, but the resistance of the bullet to the expanding vial cylinder left shooters looking for something else. Plastic 35mm film cases were tried, then plastic plumbing conduit was cut to size for various calibers and loads. In time, efficient Speed Shells, Quik-Loaders, and Lightning Loaders were combined into a revolving-cylinder, multiple-loading tube such as the EC-Loader.

Although they speed up the loading process, they do not provide a quick second shot when a hunter misses with the first one. It is far better to run a fouling patch up and down the barrel, carefully reload, and then take a well-aimed second shot. But if you are looking for modern convenience, the EC-Loader is worth a look.

For Pyrodex and Triple Seven pellets, RMC makes a molded plastic quick-loading flask that holds 22 pellets and dispenses 2 pellets at a time. The flask is designed for .50-caliber, 50-grain pellets. The RMC Hunter Model pellet flask holds only 12 pellets, for lighter weight and pocket convenience.

Today, Speed Shells, Quik-Loaders, and Lightning Loaders have joined the EC-Loader to enable modern muzzleloaders to reload with greater speed.

Plastic sabots need care so that the bullets don't slide out of alignment in the plastic, which will adversely affect accuracy. This is one of the reasons that I like the Speed Shell tubes for pellet or sabot loads.

OTHER HUNTING ACCESSORIES

Because these items need to be carried in the hunter's pockets, backpack, or hunting pouch, think in terms of practicality and light weight.

Regardless of whether you are loading from a powder horn and bullet board or a plastic-tubed reloader, you will need a short starter. These 6-inch rods made of wood, brass, or aluminum are attached to a handle containing another short nubbin to facilitate bullet loading at the muzzle. Long ramrods are impractical and might bend or break when used as a starting rod. Short starters are useful and easy to make yourself if you want to save some money. Besides, an antler-tipped short starter looks mighty impressive in the hands of a primitive hunter.

If you are loading from the horn, make sure that you have a volumetric measurer. There are many styles of plastic and brass adjustable measurers, but the powder measurer that I carry dangles from my powder horn strap and is made from a deer antler. It not only looks right; it does a quick job of measuring powder without having to look at it.

One tool that you definitely don't want to leave home without is a good knife. Hunting pouches usually have a patch knife scabbard sewn into the bag or up on the carrying strap. For those who carry everything in their pockets or on their belts, there are many great folding and straight knives that can be used for cutting patches or skinning deer. But choose wisely. A knife without a good spine or tough steel that holds an edge when plowing through the sternum or pelvic bones isn't worth a hoot to a deer hunter.

Another essential tool is the belt ax or tomahawk. It is small and lightweight but is far more effective in camp when it comes to gathering kindling, field-dressing a big buck, or quartering and butchering the meat than any knife. Lewis and Clark made sure they didn't leave home without pipe tomahawks (which were made at the Harpers Ferry Federal Armory from old damaged rifle barrels). They carried 36 tomahawks on their Voyage of Discovery because they knew that the iron hawks would be prized as trade goods. Today, tomahawks and belt axes are readily available. The one that I carry fits into a scabbard on the back of my hunting pouch and is sharp enough to serve as a knife in a pinch.

Hunters who use flintlocks need a vent pick. This can be as simple as a straightened paper clip or as fancy as the wire pick, pan brush, and flint knapping combination tools that dangle from the shoulder strap. Sidehammer percussion shooters need to keep a nipple wrench, an extra nipple, and a nipple pick handy as well.

Ignition for a flintlock is a spark from flint and steel, so it is a good idea to keep a couple of spare flints and small squares of leather wraps in your hunting pouch. And don't forget the small screwdriver that fits the slot of the screwhead on top of the cock. A small priming horn can be either suspended from the strap above the main powder horn or separated and stored in the pouch.

Percussion caps, regardless of size, are best kept in a capping tool rather than carried loose in a pocket or bag. This makes them easier to handle, even with cold fingers, and it is easier to cap the nipple when using a capper's extension. I have been carrying Ted Cash's brass cappers for decades, and they have always performed admirably; they even look historically correct.

Names can be deceiving. An "in-line" capper is shaped in a straight line. This is difficult to use on an in-line gun, which requires a "goosenecked" capper with a curved shape that allows easier insertion of the cap inside the breech. You should also be aware that musket caps and 209 shotgun primers will not fit into normal #11 cappers.

In another small leather pouch, it is important to keep a cleaning jag, worm (patch puller), fouling scraper, and ball or bullet puller (screw base). These don't take up much room or weigh much, but when you need them in the field, there are no substitutes for these tools that fit on the end of your ramrod.

It is also a good idea to buy a range rod, instead of stressing and possibly breaking the ramrod that came with the gun. Range rods come in brass, aluminum, resin-inpregnated wood, carbon fiber, nylon, and plastics. Their extra length, plus the easier grasping handles, makes them a more useful tool. Look for a range rod equipped with a muzzle protector. These metal or plastic cones fit into the muzzle crown and protect the rifling from abrasion, preserving accuracy. Make sure that your range rod has a thread size in the attachment connector that matches your cleaning jag, worm, scraper, and ball puller. A common thread size is 8 × 32. The "8" is the thread diameter, and the "32" means that there are 32 turns to the inch. The 10 × 32 is commonly used on Thompson/Center ramrods. On some foreign guns, the metric measurement is 6 × 1 millimeters. Other thread sizes fit only one manufacturer's accessories (e.g., Hoppes).

I also recommend a shooting stick. It can be a heavy, bore-sized range rod or any of the popular folding sticks used with modern rifles. I like a heavy "Moses" type of stick, which I use to lean on when going up slick, icy hills; to test the thickness of ice when I cross a creek or the depth of mud when I skirt the edge of a swamp; to move wild rose and raspberry stickers out of the way as I walk through a tangled thicket; or to steady my rifle when I am out in the open and need a rest for an accurate shot.

Slings are a good idea. They free the hands for climbing and clearing brush, and, when slung on the shoulder, they safely point the muzzle away from companions. Modern-styled muzzleloaders come equipped with sling attachments and even nylon straps. Rifles not equipped with slings can benefit from the leather or nylon "quick slings" that are available from many gun manufacturers. Good padded nylon slings can be bought for less than $20.

Bad weather demands a piece of waterproofed "cow's knee" (linseed-oiled deerskin works well) to protect the flintlock or percussion lock from moisture. There are plastic versions of this elbow-shaped affair, but I like to be able to fold the knee and put it in my hunting pouch. It is like carrying a raincoat for your gun.

Round toothpicks and small feather quills should be carried along to stop up the touch hole when you need to change or knap the flint. This is also a good way to keep the powder dry when you overnight a loaded gun. Pipe cleaners work well for drying moisture out of a nipple and are handy items to stick in the bottom of the pouch.

Remember, seeing is believing. And if you can't see it, you can't shoot it. Compact binoculars improve your chances of finding deer and discriminating their headgear from the bushes. And once you have safely determined that the buck is a shooter, wouldn't it be nice to know how far away it is? Range finders give you the exact distance, allowing you to determine whether that animal is within the lethal envelope of your hunting load.

It is also important that you carry a small compass and a first-aid and emergency kit. Fog, nighttime, and bad weather have a nasty habit of turning a pleasant walk into a directionless nightmare when you are without a compass. I have to admit, I have succumbed to the electronic world of the global positioning system (GPS), but when the batteries drain, it is nice to have a compass to fall back on.

A first-aid kit need only contain some Band-Aids, antibacterial lotion, and rubber gloves. You would be amazed how many times you nick yourself while hunting, and this little kit can prevent infection if you are away from home.

The emergency kit can be a lightweight affair. A space blanket provides warmth and dryness, and its reflective Mylar coating will help rescuers find you. A small vial of iodine tablets allows you to consume surface water; it won't taste great, but you won't get violently sick either. Waterproof matches or a butane lighter allows you to start a fire and stay warm, preventing hypothermia. A small LED (light-emitting diode) flashlight provides an intense beam of light in a compact unit. The LED bulbs uses less battery power than a metal filament bulb. By staying warm and dry, and by having the ability to consume water and signal your position, you increase your chances of survival when lost or injured. Don't leave home without this kit.

SHOOTING AND COMPETITION ACCESSORIES

Before you buy any accessories, you need a way to organize them. Here we can learn from fishermen. Like a tackle box, a shooting box should have plenty of drawers and dividers, a large tray, and a handle for portability. My wooden shooting box dates back to the early 1970s, but many competitors now use plastic boxes. Plastic doesn't warp, splinter, or swell in bad weather. The trays glide more easily, and plastic costs less than wood.

If you intend to load from the box, you will need spouts for the cans or plastic bottles of black powder or replica powder. Make sure that the spouts have caps so that they are closed during firing, even though the box should be a safe distance behind you when you are shooting.

Volumetric powder measurers come in brass and see-through plastic materials, but what is most important is how accurately they measure the powder. At the very least, they should measure powder accurately to within five grains.

A caliper may not be a critical piece of equipment when you first start muzzleloading, but in time you will find yourself measuring bore rifling, bullet diameters, and critical tolerances of everything. A small, accurate grain-weight scale will increase your shooting accuracy, allowing you to measure the weight of bullets so that they are consistent from shot to shot.

If you are shooting roundballs, you need patches and lubricant. Cast bullets such as miniés and maxis also need special lubricants for their grease grooves. Between shots, you will want to run a fouling patch down the bore. Special solvents are designed to clean replica powders, as well as lead, copper, and plastic. The box is the place to organize these chemicals and keep them out of the hands of children.

Special tools that you normally wouldn't carry on a hunt have a place in the shooting box. Vise grips, needle-nose pliers, slotted and Phillips screwdrivers, mainspring vises, clamps, pin and wedge drifts, files, plastic or brass hammers, magnifying glass, ramrod puller, sight paints, breech plug wrenches, nipple wrenches, Allen wrenches, and ratchet drivers with various inserts need to be organized so they are available at a moment's notice.

I am a great believer in a spotting scope and a chronograph. The scope prevents a lot of wasted time walking from bench to target as you sight in a new load or new rifle. An inexpensive chronograph can instantly tell you whether the amount of powder, thickness of patch, type of lubricant, or bullet-rifling match is correct. Shot-to-shot variations less than 10 to 20 feet per second should be expected. If your velocities are not consistent, your accuracy won't be either.

Safety equipment such as safety glasses (always carry a spare for friends and spectators), ear protection (disposable earplugs are good, but earmuff types are better), and a range officer (someone who ensures that no one walks downrange during live fire) will go a long way toward making this an enjoyable and safe hobby.

GUN CARE ACCESSORIES

Muzzleloading guns are finely tuned tools, and as such, they need protection—in other words, a gun case. Soft gun cases are the rule for transporting muzzleloaders by vehicle. They should be padded to protect sights and scopes. If you plan to use air transportation or ship the firearm by common carrier to a distant location, you definitely need a hard gun case. Hard plastic cases are less expensive and do an adequate job, but aluminum cases provide maximum protection when the firearm is roughly handled. Make sure that a high-density foam is used inside the hard case to absorb the bumps. For both plastic and metal cases, be sure that they have the capacity to be locked. Airport security personnel will inspect the gun to be sure it is unloaded and then ask you to lock it up to their satisfaction.

Gun locks, such as the trigger locks and cable locks available at sporting goods stores, are a great safety device for modern guns, but they may not fit all muzzleloaders. Trigger locks won't fit double-set triggers, and most muzzleloader actions can't be opened for the insertion of a cable lock. The only way that you can truly be sure that the gun is unloaded is by measuring the bore with the ramrod. Airport security personnel may not be familiar with this type of gun, so be patient and explain the situation; logic usually prevails if you are polite.

Gun safes are the ideal way to store a muzzleloader safely and the best way to protect your investment. But make sure that you buy a safe with enough vertical height for your longer-than-normal muzzleloading rifles and shotguns—26- to 44-inch barrels added to a 14-inch butt stock make for a mighty long gun. Your gun safe should have a minimum inside height of 60 inches, but 72 is better. Moisture has a nasty way of sneaking into basements, and also into gun safes. You can purchase a dehumidifier for the downstairs, but a drying device like a Golden Rod, or even a low-wattage lightbulb, does a more efficient job. Make sure that there is a way to get an electric cord into the gun safe.

Inventory all your muzzleloaders and modern guns. Photographs, bills of sale, serial numbers, and descriptions are necessary for any homeowner's insurance claim if they are stolen. The National Rifle Association also offers additional insurance for personal firearms, which is a great idea if you have started collecting more than a couple of firearms.

Cleaning Techniques and Products

Muzzleloading rifles shoot more than bullets out of the bore. Sometimes, as much as 50 percent of the black powder does not totally burn. This leaves a foul-smelling, sticky residue of corrosive chemicals clinging to the rifling. Pyrodex, though cleaner burning, also leaves a chemical soup behind that can destroy a barrel if it is not chemically neutralized. This section tells the truth about cleaning between shots and its effect on accuracy and longevity of the barrel. It also explains the effective cleaning techniques for preserving your investment.

Ka-chunk. Click, ka-chunk. Click, ka-chunk! These are dreaded sounds that chill the soul of a flintlock-toting hunter. Not 40 yards away stood four deer, and the flintlock wouldn't fire.

Full cock: *click.* After a quick check of the priming powder, the sights were aligned one more time. A slow squeeze of the trigger released the power of the mainspring, and a *ka-chunk* echoed one more time as the flint smacked into the frizzen. These are the agonizing sounds that reward the owner of a dirty gun.

When I got back to the barn for some morning coffee and doughnuts, Alan greeted me with a long face and a dysfunctional flinter in his hands. "Everything worked fine except the gun," he remarked. "I had deer in front of me all morning. They couldn't see me or smell me, but they sure could hear my rifle clicking and ka-chinking. And they just stood there!"

When I looked at the lock mechanism on the old T/C Renegade .54, it was immediately apparent that this flintlock needed a major makeover. The touch hole was cemented shut with fouled black powder, the bore was rusty, the mainspring had a hard time rotating the tumbler, the broken and dulled flint barely knicked the bottom of the frizzen, and the pan cover hardly lifted above the pan as one pathetic spark slid past the fence. There was no chance that this rifle would fire in its present condition. Unfortunately, this wasn't the first muzzleloader I've seen with ignition problems because it wasn't cleaned properly.

FLINTLOCK CLEANING PROCEDURES

1. Make sure that the gun is *unloaded.* Use the witness mark on your ramrod that you use to be sure that the bullet is seated. If the witness mark goes down the bore where you can't see it, you know that it doesn't have a load in it from the last hunt. Or, put the ramrod down the barrel, grasp it right at the muzzle crown, and pull it out. With your fingers at the same spot, measure the ramrod on the outside of the barrel to make sure that it reaches all the way down to the vent.

2. For a hooked patent breech, remove the wedge from the forearm by tapping lightly with a wood or brass hammer and pull it the rest of the way out with pliers. Lift the muzzle from the forearm of the stock

Before loading that first shot, make sure that the rifle is unloaded. Check the witness mark on the ramrod to be sure that there is no possible load or obstruction in the bore.

until the hooked patent breech is clear of the tang. Place the breech of the barrel into a container of cold water (I use an old toilet downstairs. It is easier to flush away the fouled water than to carry it in a bucket.) Place a clean patch over the cleaning jag, which is screwed into the threaded end of the ramrod. I like to use a separate range rod and allow the ramrod to perform a cosmetic function under the barrel. Slush-pump the bore with the cleaning jag and cotton patch piston. This action will draw water through the vent or flash channel on the upstroke and then expel the dirty water on the downstroke.

For pinned longrifle barrels, the procedure is different. Most longrifle shooters do not remove the pinned barrels from the full stock unless there is a reason to do so. Instead, remove the lock by turning out the two lock-plate bolts on the opposite side of the stock. You can use one of the many soaked cleaning patches to remove the fouling from the bore, or you can use an E-Z Flintlock Gun Cleaner (Dixie Gun Works) tool, which holds a rubber gasket to the touch hole and clamps down on the barrel. This tool has an attached flexible tube that is inserted into the container of water or cleaning solution.

3. Clean the bore thoroughly with cold water for black powder, solvent for replica powders. Triple Seven is the exception; fouling from this replica powder can be dissolved with water. Don't forget to swab the outside vent or touch hole. A pipe cleaner does a good job for thoroughly cleaning the touch hole's flash channel.

4. Dry the bore with clean patches.

5. Heat the barrel with hot (140-degree) water or a heat source such as a wood stove, radiator, or hair dryer. If you use hot water, be sure to repeat Step 4.

6. Swab the bore with grease patches (nonpetroleum). I like the lube from Lehigh Valley Patch Lubricant. This micronized beeswax solution does an outstanding job as a rust preventative, as well as a patch lube for roundballs and a fouling patch lube for between shots.

7. Wipe the barrel with a greased patch.

8. Clean the lock mortise with a dampened patch or toothbrush. *Do not* spray with gun oils; this weakens the wood fibers. *Do not* pack it with grease, as this will gum up the interior lock parts in cold weather.

9. Clean the interior lock parts with a water-displacing oil. Again, I use the Lehigh Valley lube for flushing dirt out of the tumbler, sear, and detent. Light oils are a better choice for preventing rust in this area. Clean the exterior of the lock, particularly the pan area where black powder fouling contaminates the frizzen, cover, cam, spring, cock throat, and jaws. When you lube this region, be sure to keep the oil or grease off the flint and frizzen face, or you will experience a misfire.

Be sure to clean the bore thoroughly.

10. Replace the lock, stock, and barrel. Lube the triggers. Clean the wood with a light coat of wood cleaner or preservative. I like Old English because it replaces vital wood oils and also tends to cover up dings from bumping or scratching the stock.

Use cold water for black powder and solvent for replica powders.

If you store your gun for long periods, it is important that you run a greased patch up and down the bore from time to time, particularly if it is kept in a moist basement environment. You will never clean 100 percent of the sticky sulfur fouling from black powder arms. This stuff turns to sulfuric acid in the presence of moisture and will steal the function and accuracy of your shooting iron if you don't pay attention.

PERCUSSION CLEANING PROCEDURE

1. Be sure the gun is *unloaded.*

2. You have a choice: slush-pump, as for the patent breech procedure; wipe the bore with dampened patches; or screw out the nipple and replace it with a threaded cleaning tube such as the Ox-Yoke Muzzleloader Black Out Flush Cleaning System and slush-pump the bore without removing the barrel from the stock. Just insert the tube into the container of water or solvent. Replace the jag with a breech plug scraper. A square face for flat breech plugs and a rounded scraper for coned breech plugs are available.

3. Clean the lock. If you didn't remove the nipple in the previous step, it would be a good idea now. The right-angle flash channel and the nipple port in the base are ideal spots for fouling buildup, which generally results in a misfire just when that big buck steps in front of your sights. Use a toothbrush to clean the threads, and put a dab of grease on before reinserting. Be sure to clean the cup under the hammer. Many times, a cap will squash and stick inside the recess. This cushions the hammer blow to the percussion cap, resulting in a misfire.

4. Heat the barrel as stated previously.

5. Grease the bore and barrel flats and lubricate the lock and triggers.

6. Clean the stock.

7. Run a lubed patch up and down the bore every couple of months.

IN-LINE CLEANING PROCEDURE

1. Make sure the gun is *unloaded.*

2. Remove the bolt, striker, or rolling block. Disassemble as needed. Clean with solvent and lubricate. Clean and lube the trigger-safety assembly.

3. Remove the nipple and the breech plug. Clean with a pipe cleaner through the flash channel, and use a toothbrush to clean the threads. Lubricate with the special breech plug grease recommended by the manufacturer. Remember, Pyrodex takes a special cleaning solvent such as Knight's E-Z Clean to neutralize the perchlorates in the fouling. Sabots leave plastic laminate in the bore. To clean it out, use either a shotgun solvent that dissolves plastic or this homemade recipe for NMLRA "Racing Oil": In a 1-gallon plastic jug, mix 1 pint each of isopropyl (rubbing) alcohol, hydrogen peroxide, and Murphy's Oil Soap. Keep this mixture out of sunlight, because the peroxide degrades in light.

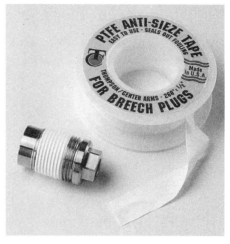

Reassemble and lube all of the parts in the action and the barrel. Use a specifically designed thread lube or teflon tape for the breech plug threads.

4. Run solvent-soaked patches through the bore, from the breech end to the muzzle. This pushes any particulates out of the muzzle rather than back into the action-trigger assembly. It also creates less wear on the rifling at the muzzle crown, thus preserving accuracy.

5. Reassemble and lube the action and barrel. Use a thread lubricant or Teflon tape (as directed by the manual) when inserting the breech plug into the barrel.

6. Synthetic stocks need nothing other than water or solvent to clean them. Do not use oil; this will only attract dirt, as well as making the gun slippery to hold. Wood stocks, even laminated wood, require wood-enhancing oils. Unscented furniture polish works well. Do not use machine oils, which soften the wood fibers.

7. If you have a scope, you have several additional responsibilities. Clean the barrel of any fouling on the bottom of the scope tube, just above the bolt, disc, block, and striker (commonly called the action). Scopes get fouled on their glass lenses too, but *do not* use solvent on the glass. There are special solutions and brushes

---

FOULING CORROSIVE CHEMICALS LEFT INSIDE THE BARREL

Potassium carbonate (K_2CO_3)
Potassium sulfate (K_2SO_4)
Potassium sulfide (K_2S)
Potassium thiosulfate (KNCS)
Carbon (C)
Sulfur (S)

FOULING GASES EXPELLED FROM THE BARREL INTO THE AIR
Carbon dioxide (CO_2)
Carbon monoxide (CO)
Methane (CH_4)
Hydrogen sulfide (H_2S)
Hydrogen (H)
Nitrogen (N_2)

made for optics. If you use a regular patch, it may erode the special coating that inhibits moisture and enhances light. Be very gentle when cleaning your optical equipment.

8. If you have a muzzle break, barrel porting, or barrel fluting, you have an extra job. Use cotton swabs and cleaning solution to remove fouling. If you do not clean thoroughly, rust (even in stainless steel) will degrade the barrel.

9. Clean and lubricate the bipod and sling swivels. They can get dirty and squeak, and you don't want a big buck hearing that.

CLEANING PRODUCTS

You do need to clean between shots. Regardless of whether you are hunting, practicing, or taking part in a muzzleloader frolic, cleaning is the secret to barrel life. For black powder, Shooter's Choice

Regardless of whether you are hunting, target shooting, or reenacting, cleaning is the secret to rifle longevity.

BP Cleaning Gel, Lehigh Valley Shooting Patch Lubricant, Ox-Yoke/Wonder Lube, T/C #13 Bore Cleaner, Birchwood Casey BP Solvent, Knight Rifles, BP Solvent, as well as others can be used effectively. Using a spit patch is not a great choice if there will be a prolonged period between shots. Spit can lead to rust. Keep solvent-moistened patches handy, and ramrod one up and down the bore. Use each side of the patch, reload, and go on with the hunt. A more thorough cleaning will be necessary at the end of the day.

A fouling patch ramrodded between shots will remove 90 percent of the dirt left behind and provide the shooter with consistent friction that allows minute-of-angle accuracy. If you don't clean before that second shot,

While only a fouling patch is needed between shots, a thorough cleaning at the end of the day is absolutely necessary.

your gun will still have sufficient accuracy for a deer-sized target, but don't push it. Consecutive uncleaned shots may cause the bullet to get stuck halfway down the barrel. This scenario is not only frustrating but also dangerous. Thorough cleaning with a water bath is not necessary between shots, but it must be done at the end of the day, or barrel life and accuracy will suffer.

If you use Pyrodex, whether in the form of loose powder or pellets, Hodgdon Powder recommends that you use a product such as E-Z Clean to neutralize the highly corrosive chlorine compounds.

Triple Seven cleans up with plain old water. But as with any other exploding chemical, you need to be vigilant about cleaning between shots. Thoroughly clean the rifle at the end of the day if you hope to maintain an accurate barrel.

To clean the residue of smokeless nitrocellulose powder, you need to use a modern centerfire rifle solvent that is designed to clean up the by-products generated by the 209 shotgun primer, as well as the residue created from the ignition of the nitrocellulose powder.

Water is a polar solvent, capable of dissolving and flushing out just about every metallic salt known to our sport. When it comes to black powder and Triple Seven, it is the best cleaning solvent there is. Hot soapy water was once the standard method of degreasing and cleaning muzzleloaders. But with experience, most competitive shooters realized that the soap wasn't necessary. In fact, it was stripping valuable rust-preventing oils from the metal pores in the bore. Hot water opened the pores even more effectively, but this trapped water inside the metal as it cooled. All these factors led to major cases of rusting days after the gun was cleaned. Today, many knowledgeable shooters stick to plain cold water. It dissolves the salts and flushes the fouling without opening up the metallic pores of the bore. Then, after drying the cold bore, they apply heat from a hair dryer, wood stove, or radiator to totally eliminate moisture.

If you are shooting lead or copper slugs, you will need to run a lead-copper solvent such as Birchwood-Casey's Black Powder Solvent or Hoppe's Bench Rest #9 down the bore to remove the buildup of tiny metal particles. Plastic sabots also leave behind a laminate that needs to be cleaned. CVA's Advanced Sabot Solvent addresses this need.

After cleaning the bore, apply a natural grease to it; do not use a petroleum-based oil. Petroleum oils change to tar in the presence of the high temperatures generated during the explosion of powders. T/C's Bore Butter, Wonder Lube's 1000 Plus, and even Crisco vegetable shortening work better.

CLEANING TOOLS

- ☐ Screwdriver (to exactly fit the slotted head)
- ☐ Nipple wrench (percussion guns)
- ☐ Breech plug wrench (in-lines)
- ☐ Small wood or brass mallet
- ☐ Toothbrush
- ☐ Pipe cleaners
- ☐ Screw, bolt, pin container
- ☐ Needle-nose pliers
- ☐ Drift pin (longrifles)
- ☐ Wedge drift or puller
- ☐ Separate cleaning rod
- ☐ Cleaning jag
- ☐ Patch worm (to retrieve patches)
- ☐ Bore brush

Basic cleaning of a muzzleloader is time-consuming and messy, but it is a great time to get together with a buddy, talk about the hunt, and dream of future adventures. Besides, it pays big dividends. Just ask Alan. A week later, at the same location, he dropped an eight-pointer with one shot from his cleaned-up T/C Renegade.

Practice

Tulip poplar seeds floated to earth like the rotors of a gnome's helicopter. High in my tree stand, which was 20 feet off the ground in an ancient black cherry tree, I watched a flock of wild turkeys as they began the morning entertainment.

Hens and teenager poults noisily cackled as they did a fly-down from their treetop roosts to the edge of the cornfield. Their exit from the giant poplars was a comical affair. Branches crumbled and fell while the turkeys ducked and squawked at their mistreatment by Mother Nature. Reflecting on how many times we hunters are outsmarted by these savvy birds, I could scarcely believe how careless the turkeys were. Debris fell on their bronzed feathers, and they jumped and flapped their displeasure, but they really didn't try to get away from the bombardment.

With so much wildlife activity happening around me, it seemed incredible that the deer woods were so empty of hunters. Here I sat, alone, in my favorite hunting season, the late muzzle-loading deer season. Gone were the stealthy bow hunters with their mechanical bows prowling the scrape lines, gone were the orange-clad armies of shotgun- and rifle-toting gun hunters noisily driving the frenzied herds of whitetails. In their place was a group of hardy hunters who choose to brave the worst weather of the deer season with the least prospect of bringing home venison. These were the muzzleloading hunters, responding to the challenge of the season for one major reason: it's fun!

The muzzleloading fun factor is actually quite complex because it has many influences. Obviously, we all feel good when we share time with friends. We are in the low-pressure, healthy environment of the outdoors, doing something that makes us smile at our own shortcomings. But quite frankly, we all feel a greater satisfaction

Set 20 feet above the ground, a treestand can be a daunting place for a muzzleloading deer hunter to load and troubleshoot a gun.

when we actually accomplish what we set out to do: harvest a deer. Let's consider how we can improve our odds of doing that.

One key to success is practice, but how much practice is enough? According to a recent survey in *Deer & Deer Hunting* magazine, the average gun hunter takes 84 shots before hunting season. My experience is that the average muzzleloader can get off about 20 shots during a normal three-hour practice session. This means that at least four days of shooting practice are necessary to fine-tune your system.

Practicing with a muzzleloader is fun. Whereas those who hunt with modern guns or bows simply zero their sights and start hunting, the muzzleloader must shoot various loads to find the one that performs best. Practice not only allows you to determine the best loads; it also teaches you tricks for accurate shooting (trigger squeezing and breathing techniques), sight enhancement (painting iron sights with black or fluorescent paint), consistent velocities, cleaning short-cuts, and new ideas from shooting with friends who use different equipment.

Later that "day of the turkeys," I had a chance to find out whether my practice would pay off. Four does followed the creek to the torn-up leaves where the turkeys had been feeding on poplar seeds. I picked out the lead animal, aligned the sights, and sent the roundball about 40 yards from my .50 flintlock. "Ol' Phoenix" had shot true, and the doe piled up on the fencerow in less than 20 yards.

Safe Storage and Legal Transportation

Black powder is classified as a class A explosive. It has a low ignition temperature, detonates in improper containers, and generally cannot be kept safely in large amounts in the home. Replica powders are classified as class B flammable solids and are much safer to store and transport. But muzzleloading hunters need to be aware of state and federal regulations governing their transportation. Air transportation since September 11, 2001, has become extremely tricky for hunters carrying guns, bullets, and propellants. This section details the risks, safe storage, and legal transportation of muzzleloading components.

SAFE STORAGE OF BLACK AND REPLICA POWDERS

The ignition point of black powder is 480 degrees Fahrenheit; that of Pyrodex, Triple Seven, and other replica powders is about 740 degrees. That means that black powder ignites at an oven baking temperature, and the replicas ignite at temperatures used to melt lead on a stove. Never forget that these temperatures are easily attained. Moreover, during a house or car fire, these muzzleloading propellants have the ability to do a lot of damage and put a lot of people at risk.

Federal law allows individuals to keep up to 5 pounds of these propellants in a home or car. That is 35,000 grains of explosive. So, if you are like the many hunters and muzzleloading shooters who keep a couple of cans on hand, it is time to rethink where you are keeping them. A rule of thumb for storing black powder is to keep it in a cool, dry place. Wooden gun cabinets are okay, but steel gun safes are better. My personal choice is to keep extra cans of powder in my basement freezer. The reason for this choice is simple: safety. Where would you expect anything to survive the temperatures of a house fire? That's right, the freezer. Frozen meat and vegetables will maintain low temperatures even in a fire, and if they do thaw, the water that results will only boil at 212 degrees, providing time for firefighters to extinguish the fire before the critical ignition point of the black powder can be reached.

A freezer will not cause condensation and contamination of the powder if the container is sealed. I take the precaution of putting the can in freezer bags, so that condensation can contaminate only the outside of the can, not the contents.

TRANSPORTING MUZZLELOADERS TO CANADA

Like many other sportsmen and -women from Pennsylvania, I love to hunt in Canada. Over the years, Anticosti whitetails, black bear, caribou, ptarmigan, spruce and ruffed grouse, grizzly bear, and moose have beckoned hunters to leave their suburban homes for the unbroken, pristine boreal forests of the north. There is only one problem: border crossings.

Leaving the United States for Canada used to be easy: stop at the patrol booth and give a few simple answers as to citizenship, place of birth, intention of visit, and length of stay.

Since January 1, 2001, nonresidents must declare their firearms in writing and must pay a nonrefundable fee. This buys you a temporary license and registration, but you must reregister and pay the fee each year. You need to fill out a Non-Resident Firearm Declaration (Form JUS 909 EF). You can get one at the border, but to save time, you can call and have one sent to you ahead of time (1-800-731-4000) or you can download it from the Web (www.cfc-ccaf.gc.ca). Make two photocopies of the completed form and present all three forms to the customs officer at the border. Leave the signature block empty. The customs officer must verify your firearms and witness your signature. You must also pay the $50 Canadian fee before you receive a confirmation number and a copy of the confirmed declaration, which you must carry with you at all times while possessing your firearms in Canada.

Alternatively, you can apply for a Canadian possession and acquisition license (PAL), which is renewable every five years and costs $60 Canadian for nonrestricted firearms. But first you must take and pass the Canadian Firearms Safety Course. Once you obtain a PAL, you should verify and register those hunting guns that you intend to use. This costs an additional $18 Canadian. You also need the PAL to buy ammunition in Canada, but you are allowed to bring up to 200 rounds with you when you cross the border.

The Canadian Firearms Safety Course was developed in partnership with the provinces and territories, national organizations with an ongoing interest in firearms safety, and firearms and hunter education course instructors from across Canada. This past April, a friend and I traveled to Ontario to tackle the safety course and the two-hour test. Each of us was given a different written test, but the practical gun handling and safety portion was the same. Common sense is always a major part of any hunter education course, and the same can be said for the Canadian course. Although there is a rather large book available for study (and for sale), we found that our knowledge from Pennsylvania's Hunter Safety Education Test and years of experience were more than adequate preparation for the examination.

The course covered the evolution of firearms, from matchlocks to centerfires; gun parts, such as bolts, levers, safeties, locks, stocks, barrels, and sights and scopes; the major actions (break, bolt, pump, lever, semiautomatic); basic firearms safety practices, such as safe storage and transportation; field carries and obstacles; and types of ammunition (rimfire, centerfire, gauge versus caliber). Firing techniques, procedures, and responsibilities of the firearms owner were also major topics covered.

TRAVELING OVERSEAS WITH A MUZZLELOADER

As soon as you decide to leave the country on an adventure with your muzzleloader, you need to contact the U.S. Customs Office and fill out a short Form 4457. A customs official will verify the gun as described and sign and date the form. You keep a copy of the form and present it to foreign customs agents to prove that the gun is legally yours. If you forget it, they can legally confiscate your muzzleloader.

You can contact U.S. Customs for a "Certificate of Registration" at www.cbp.gov or by calling the nearest customs port location. Hunters are strongly encouraged to contact the embassy or consulate at their destination to inquire about specific laws and firearms regulations. Many foreign countries limit the number of guns per entry (usually two), and knowing this information in advance will prevent hassles.

International travel requires a hard-sided gun case with full-length hinges and secure locks or padlocks.

Bear in mind that some international airports in New York and New Jersey have local regulations prohibiting firearms on airport property. It pays to call ahead and ask questions concerning the transportation of firearms.

TRANSPORTATION OF BLACK AND REPLICA POWDERS

If you are traveling by car, truck, or motor home, you need to pack your powder in such a way that heat, sparks, or impact from an accident can't ignite it. The Bureau of Alcohol, Tobacco, and Firearms mandates that an individual may keep only up to 5 pounds of black powder in a habitable environment, and that technically includes a car. But you need to be aware that enclosed highways, such as mountain and waterway tunnels, totally ban this class A explosive, so plan your travel route accordingly. Public transportation vehicles such as buses and trains have their own set of rules, so check with the carrier before you buy a ticket and step on board.

Transporting a muzzleloading gun with its propellants and bullets takes a lot more thought than taking a modern gun along on a hunt. You need to be aware of the federal, state, and local laws wherever you hunt—no exceptions. You need to do some homework, and it may be wise to enlist the aid of a travel agent or outfitter.

The transportation of black powder and its replica powder alternatives is a confusing issue. In all modes of transportation (car, boat, rail, airplane), the primary federal governmental agency is the U.S. Department of Transportation (DOT) and its hazardous materials regulations. According to Arthur L. Fleener, the DOT's current hazardous materials program specialist and special agent, DOT regulations state that any individual can carry up to a 25-pound case of black powder in a personal vehicle anywhere in the United States for personal use. (Apparently, the BATF is more concerned about home storage, and the DOT is of course more concerned with transportation.) DOT's hazardous materials regulations do not apply unless the powder is being carried for resale or any other form of commerce. Black powder, loaded cartridges (black, replica, or smokeless), primers, and percussion caps are all considered hazardous materials. If any individual or commercial enterprise attempts to ship such materials (through carriers such as FedEx or UPS), it becomes subject to DOT regulations.

Loose black powder is strictly forbidden for transportation aboard a passenger or cargo aircraft—no exceptions. But the regulations are mute as to the type of propellant used. The regulations do not differentiate between ammunition loaded with black powder and that loaded with smokeless powder. In addition, the airlines dictate how many pounds or rounds of ammunition is allowed in checked luggage, not the DOT. Therefore, call your airline ahead of time to find out its restrictions and suggestions for how to safely transport your muzzleloader, as well as your powder and primers.

For more detailed information, you can contact DOT at 800-467-4922 or go to www.hazmat.dot.gov/rules.htm. For packing tips and other suggestions that may assist you during your next trip aboard an aircraft, get in touch with the Transportation Security Administration at 866-289-9673, visit www.TSATravelTips.us, or e-mail TellTSA@tsa.dot.gov.

CHAPTER FIVE

Hunting Deer

Defeating the Big Three Deer Defenses

Trophy bucks grow to their tremendous size because they know how to survive. If you would like a crack at an animal of this caliber, you need to learn how to defeat its main defense mechanisms: scent, sight, and sound.

The most powerful defense that any whitetail has against predators is its nose. Once you understand why a deer relies so heavily on the olfactory glands in its nostrils, you will become a far more effective hunter.

Deer are plant eaters, primarily browsing on low-growing forbs and waist-high bushes and overhanging limbs. As an herbivore, a deer's head points straight into the ground or bush as it browses its way through life. Not being able to keep its head up to look for danger is a real liability when predators are sneaking around downwind; add in the noise generated by grinding on browse with the molars, and it is clear why eyesight and hearing take a backseat to the deer's ultrasensitive nose.

A deer's sense of smell is controlled by chemoreceptors that send messages to the limbic system at the base of the cerebrum. More simply, molecules given off by various sources are sensed in the nose and interpreted by the brain. At what distance a whitetail can smell a human is open to debate, but most whitetail guides put the distance beyond 100 yards. Of course, other factors such as wind, temperature, and moisture can modify that distance.

A whitetail's sense of smell is operating at peak efficiency when the weather is warm, moist, and still. Balmy days put

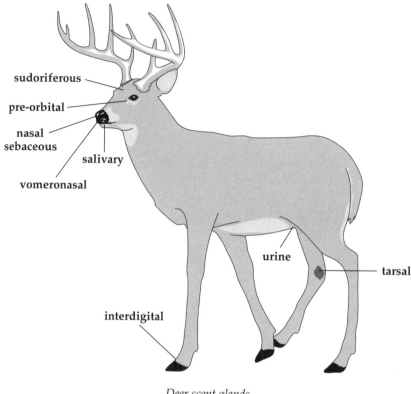

Deer scent glands

hunters at their greatest disadvantage when they are stalking on the ground. (This is one of the reasons why tree stands are so effective in the early season.) Warmth causes hunters to perspire, and the higher temperatures cause the odor molecules to move around more freely. Moisture allows the olfactory organ in the deer's nose to be a better receptor of odor molecules. With no wind to disperse these molecules, whitetails can accurately judge the direction of a threat, as well as its distance. In contrast, snow and rain dilute a hunter's scent, and wind makes it very difficult for a deer to pinpoint a threat. That is why foul weather can be very lucrative for muzzleloading deer hunters.

Hunters can use different tactics and equipment to reduce their scent. Carbon fiber clothing, masking scents, and deer lures are effective at preventing odor and distracting a deer's nose. It is common knowledge that a successful hunt begins the day before you leave home. The reason for this is that the food you eat, the clothing you wear, and the kind of personal hygiene you use determine the amount of scent you spread around on your hunt.

The day before you set out to harvest a deer, rethink your diet. Stay away from foods that produce detectable body odor, such as spicy foods with garlic and oregano. Deer can easily pick up this strong scent from any exposed skin, which includes your face and hands.

Foods high in cholesterol cause a surge in body temperature, and this leads to perspiration. Alcoholic beverages such as beer and wine have a similar effect. Tobacco, regardless of whether it is smoked or chewed, produces a strong aromatic gas that sticks to your lips, exposed skin, hair, and clothing, making you a marked man (or woman) the next day.

To prevent the body from creating telltale odor molecules, cleanliness begins with a shower on the morning of the hunt. Unscented soap is a must; perfumed soaps leave a telltale scent marking you as "unnatural." If you don't have unscented soap, just use baking soda to cleanse your hair and body. This stuff is amazing, and it is one of the cheapest insurance policies against scent-alert that I know of.

It is important that your clothing be as free of human scent as your body. Wash your clothes in Sport Wash or baking soda, but don't dry them in a machine that was previously contaminated by dryer sheets. Just let the clothing drip-dry in the air. After drying, it's a good idea to place the garments in a plastic bag with the addition of a masking scent. Oils of pine, acorn, apple, earth, and other natural scents (be sure that it matches the environment where you'll be hunting) work well in masking any telltale scent molecules from civilization. In a pinch, just grab a handful of leaf litter and humus from the surrounding woods and throw it into the bottom of the bag before you put in your hunting garments. Be sure to seal the bag until you are ready to hunt.

Finally, on the day you intend to hunt, be sure to wear rubber boots as you walk from the vehicle to your hunting site. This will prevent your feet from leaving a strong scent trail of gasoline, dog, and other civilization odors. Even sweaty feet can ooze molecules of odor through leather boots and tip off the deer.

Native Americans used masking scents to their advantage long before they taught the European immigrants how to feed their fam-

The eyes of a deer are very good at discriminating movement and noticing when something new has been added to their backyard.

ilies with wild deer and turkey. By wearing branches of strong-smelling cedar, spicebush, or pine or sacks of the targeted animal's droppings or tarsal glands, the native hunters became nose-invisible to whitetails. My favorite Indian tactic that I have used effectively is a lure-scented white handkerchief. This trick fools both the deer's nose and its eyes. A urine- or lure-soaked white handkerchief hung waist high on a branch signals to a buck that a doe is in the area. With a slight breeze, the handkerchief does a great job of simulating a twitching deer tail, and the buck's instinct takes care of the rest. This trick is so effective that it should be illegal!

The eyes of a deer are very good at discriminating movement, as well as noticing when something new has been added to its backyard. Don't be misled by misinformation about deer being color-blind or having terrible eyesight. Recent research, as well as four decades of deer hunting experience, has convinced me that deer can see very well.

Although the whitetail retina (the lining in the back of the eye on which the image focuses) doesn't have the same number or sophistication of color-sensitive cones that the human eye possesses, it has an effective number of rudimentary cones that are especially sensitive to the blue-green spectrum of light. A deer's eyeball is larger than a human's and is packed with specialized rods that are sensitive to short-wavelength light. This provides them with great low-light vision, which explains how they can see to jump over wire fences at night. This also enables the deer to pick up movement faster than a human can react to it. The lens of the deer's eye lacks the yellow filter found in the human eye, a pigment that blocks ultraviolet light. Deer also have a unique reflective layer of pigment (the tapetum lucidum) that doubles their ability to gather light once it passes the retina.

Jay Neitz, studying the effects of color on deer retinas at the University of Georgia in 1992, made a startling discovery: deer are much more sensitive than humans to the shorter wavelengths of light. Deer have been found to have a blue cone with a peak sensitivity at 455 nanometers (nm), which is very close to the 440-nm peak of spectral power caused by laundry brightening agents. This 440-nm light is seen as bright blue in the dichromatic eye of the deer. It occurs on garments of any color from camo to blaze orange if brighteners are present. Because of this landmark study, UV-Killer and other ultraviolet treatments are now popular on commercial hunting clothes.

All this adds up to one thing: don't wear blue jeans or a green shirt, and don't move. Even in subdued light, deer will pick up on any unnatural movement by a hunter.

When a deer perceives something as new or out of place, it immediately reacts with alarm. A new tree stand, a standing hunter, or even vegetation that was recently cut down will cause deer to avoid an area. Deer are creatures of habit, as evidenced by their well-used deer trails, but if anything looks unusual to the deer, they will be gone before the hunter even knew they were there. This is the main reason for making any changes to your hunting spot weeks before you intend to use it.

Stealth is a vital tool in the hunter's attempt to get close enough for a lethal shot. It can be accomplished in many ways, but camouflaged clothing is a primary tool to try to reduce your presence. If you hunt in a state or province that does not require fluorescent orange, match the camo pattern to the environment you are hunting in. Be careful of patterns that use too many dark colors too close together, or the deer will quickly pick up this dark silhouette, especially in tree stands. Open patterns that distract the eye from picking out the human shape are especially good for tree stands, as the light and dark patterns resemble tree limbs against the sky.

The ears are equally as important as the eyes when it comes to alerting deer to danger. The average deer's ear possesses a 24-inch

Deer hear around five times better than humans do. The Game Ear offers one way for muzzleloaders to level the playing field.

reflecting surface that funnels sound down into the auditory canal. Whereas a human can hear sounds that measure from 250 to 8,000 hertz (human speech range is from 500 to 2,000 hertz), a deer hears sounds from 20 to 20,000 hertz. Deer can hear that same high-frequency dog whistle as your favorite retriever, or the snap of a branch, or the click of a set trigger. The bottom line is that deer hear about four to five times better than humans do, according to Bob Walker, who operates Walker's Game Ear.

Normal sounds generated in the woods, such as the rustling of leaves (2,200 hertz), the chattering of squirrels, and the twittering of birds, do not alarm a deer. But the slamming of a car door, the snapping of a tree branch (4,000 hertz), the ripping sound of Velcro fasteners, the vibration of a zipper, and the click of full cock will definitely send a whitetail to the alert position.

Because I like to hear the deer before the deer hear me, I have come to rely on my Game Ear (a hearing-assist device). Deer hoofbeats on leaves, low-volume deer vocalizations, and even the sounds of brush being swept aside by an oncoming whitetail can alert a hunter to the location and distance of the deer. This gives you more time to aim and be ready for the shot, which is a huge advantage for a muzzleloading hunter.

NOISE LEVELS GENERATED WHILE HUNTING	
Breathing	10 decibels (db)
Rustling leaves	20 db
Whispering	20 db
Snapping branch	40 db
Normal talking	60 db
100-yard rifle shot	100 db
25-yard rifle shot	140 db

Deer concentrate on movement. This is why a deer may try to coax a hunter to move by dropping its head into a false feeding position and then quickly popping its head up to stare at the intruder. One trick when moving in on a feeding deer is to watch its tail. A twitching tail is a warning signal that the deer is about to lift its head, and a hunter can time his or her movement to this visual clue.

Another misconception is that deer do not look up. This is not true. If you move quickly, cause an unexpected sound, or create too much human odor, deer will look up, stare a hole right through you, snort loudly, and wave good-bye with their tails. Tree stands generally offer the advantage of being above the deer's normal line of sight, but mistakes in the tree stand can alert deer, no matter how high you climb.

The defense mechanisms offered by the deer's noses, eyes, and ears are more than a match for most hunters. Even though muzzleloading whitetail hunters are usually an experienced group, because we need to take our shots at a closer range, we really do need to overcome the deer's big-three defenses.

Pre-Rut Strategies

Some states, such as Pennsylvania, schedule management hunts before the whitetails' breeding season. This pre-rut season demands muzzleloading strategies that deal with the heavy foliage, food preferences, and pre-mating-season concentrations of deer. If you are looking for a trophy at this time of year (October), consider hunting like a raptor—a bird of prey that swoops down on the unsuspecting. Tree-stand hunters do this as they pattern deer to move in close beneath them. Muzzleloading hunters in the treetops have special needs, and this section lays out the blueprint for success.

A patchwork quilt of amber poplars, crimson maples, and bronzed oak leaves were shimmering in the quickening wind of the afternoon. Although the stillness was beginning to be interrupted by wakening crickets and the erratic buzzing of grasshoppers, it was no longer summer. A chill was descending with the sun, which slowly settled into the clouds on the western horizon. The only warmth for the rest of this season would be generated by the slow pace of hunting boots, as well as the effort required to carry a 9-pound muzzleloader. This was, indeed, the October country that for many years could be enjoyed only by archers. But now, for just one week, the brilliant autumn foliage would be shared by those who had one smoky shot at venison.

The afternoon hunt was a necessity. The demands of working for a living came first. A quickening pace along the logging trail generated a lot of steam, but I had to get to my favorite spot at the top of a 2-mile-long ravine. Whitetails have pretty accurate biological clocks; they know exactly what time to move, even if the hunters don't. If the deer moved from their beds for an evening foray in the fields down in the valley before I could settle into this ridgetop position, only insects and birds would fill the evening's venue.

It was exactly nine months ago that I sat in this same spot. A foot of snow crusted the boulders while a vicious wind tore at my layers of clothing. Hunkered down in a wool cap with tingling fingers gripping the handwarmer, it had sure looked like a different place from where I was hunting now. A broad vista of hillside benches and deer runs had been clearly visible without the interference of underbrush and tree leaves. Even the snow telegraphed where the deer had been and where the hunter should be. Somehow the hunt seemed easier in the harsher conditions of January. But this was October. The weather was different; the clothing was different. Even the equipment and tactics would need to change in order to be successful during this management hunt. A Berks County antlerless tag rode on my back.

During the first five days of the season, I briefly glimpsed four deer as they loped through the tangle of spicebush, alder, and viburnum. The rich underbrush was a real problem for hunters hoping to spot deer. The colorful leaves also made it difficult to determine if other hunters were in the background of a shootable deer.

Four deer in five days? I knew from experience that I should have bumped into five times that number, but my aimless walking and fumbling tactics were not working. With only two days left in this early muzzleloader season, I knew that it was time for a change.

Patterning a deer herd can pay big dividends. Unlike the scattered deer herds of January, October whitetails can be reliably patterned. Hunters should focus on mast crops, particularly white and red oak acorns, beech nuts, and hickories. This does not mean that agricultural offerings of corn and soybean or hayfields will not be visited. But it does mean that deer activity will be primarily nocturnal as they venture forth in their farmland raids. Daylight success will be contingent on locating the primary daytime forage hotspots of mast crops.

Muzzleloaders in trees may sound like an oddity, but it is a useful tactic in October. Hunters need to set up their stands between the food areas and the bedding areas, paying special attention to the prevailing wind and thermals in the area. Remember, a tree-stand hunter's

Muzzleloading hunters perched high in trees have many advantages, including scent dispersion, greater visibility, and the safety afforded by shooting into the earth.

tactics are similar to those of a hawk or owl. These birds of prey set up in predictable areas, that is, the places where their prey eat or need to funnel through. The secret to success is camouflage, as well as the ability to detect sound and motion. Camo patterns that work well on the ground may be too dark for the tree limbs. Also, the location of the tree stand should never silhouette the hunter against the sky. Stealth is critical.

When muzzleloaders hunt from a high perch, the angle of the shot becomes critical. On level ground, roundballs normally create an 11-inch cone of tissue-smashing hydrostatic shock from the point of entry. That translates into a "double-lunger," putting the animal down for the count in less than 20 seconds. Shot placement within a paper plate-sized lethal zone is easier on level ground. When the hunter is elevated, the lethal zone shrinks. Not only is the target smaller, but factors such as deflection from bony material (shoulder, ribs, spine) become paramount. A shot placed just beneath the spine might result in the immediate drop of an animal, but since only one lung is impaired, the deer will escape with a good likelihood of survival.

Accuracy changes when a hunter shoots downhill. Don't count on last year's sight picture shot through iron sights from the bench at a level shooting range to print the bullet at the same spot when it is fired at a 30-degree angle. Although you may find it difficult to practice from a tree stand, you need to do it. Ask any bow hunter—the angle of fire really makes a difference. Regardless of which ignition system (flintlock, sidehammer percussion, or in-line percussion), which type of powder, which bullet, or even which type of sights you choose, the bottom line is that they all take practice.

If you decide to pursue whitetails with an old-fashioned deer drive, consider that the dense foliage of October will play an important role. Ground shrubs such as spicebush, autumn olive, and viburnum will prevent a clear picture of your quarry. Woody-stemmed forbs such as goldenrod, wild roses, and ragweed will deflect roundballs. Nettles and poison ivy will leave rashes on your skin. But more important, all these plants will telegraph your presence to deer, sending them into flight long before you see them. And consider the fact that you won't see the standers as you approach the end of the drive, any more than they can see you. Flu-

Accuracy changes when a hunter shoots downhill. Practice this type of shot before hunting in a high perch.

Some states do not require hunters to wear fluorescent orange during the muzzleloader season, but this can make for an unsafe situation, as deer drivers can't easily see standers at the end of the drive.

orescent orange—250 square inches of it—is not just a good idea; it can be a lifesaver.

A safety consideration for tree-stand hunters is bullet seating. Although a rifleman can firmly seat a slug over the powder when loading with a ramrod, lead slugs have a nasty habit of sliding forward. If an airspace forms between the powder and the base of the slug (because the barrel was pointed downhill at a deer from the tree stand), detonation can take place when you squeeze the trigger. Detonation—or the exploding of powder—is exactly what happens every time you fire a gun. But an airspace between the powder and the bullet changes breech pressures dramatically, with the bullet forming an obstruction. Higher-than-normal pressures at the base of the bullet can deform the barrel or, worse, cause a disastrous explosion. In either case, the rifle (but hopefully not the shooter) will be damaged beyond repair. Be sure to check the bullet seating, marking a ramrod before you bounce around while getting into the tree stand. Then measure again with the marked ramrod to see if the slug has moved forward. Historically, many of the early slugs, such as the Pickett bullet, were patched with cloth to prevent this movement. Later, oiled paper was the preferred patch.

As a matter of safety, tree-stand muzzleloaders should never be primed or capped until the hunter is ready to shoot. A dropped muzzleloader, even at half-cock, is dangerously ready to discharge accidentally. Sparks fly from frizzens, and fire snaps from caps when struck by a rock. On a flintlock, keep the frizzen open, keep a feather quill in the touch hole, and keep the cock in the fired position. Also, if a rifle is tethered to a rope and hauled up into the stand, always tie it so that you raise the rifle butt first.

Now that you've pondered the calendar and other factors, it is time to answer the question of where to set yourself up. Without a doubt, the top choice would be near agricultural areas that are adjacent to hardwood ridges. Save the swamps and nasty tangles for the late flintlock season. You are now in competition with the bow hunters for the same piece of the antlerless pie. Private land usually holds the best chance for success, but October is the perfect time to hunt the public lands for unpressured whitetails.

An acorn-fattened doe surprised me only 15 minutes before legal shooting hours ended, and a well-placed round from a .54 flintlock Pennsylvania longrifle dropped the deer to the ground. My revised strategy had worked. My family would enjoy October country deer roast, not just another deer tale.

October is a month for flaming colors of foliage and falling leaves. It also is a great time for challenging deer to show themselves. Deer are curious. If a hunter does something to get their attention, they will come.

In a doctoral study at the University of Georgia, Mickey Hellickson observed radio-collared deer to document their reactions to antler rattling. His research showed that antler rattling works, is predictable, and is a method that hunters should employ. Hellickson, who is now the chief wildlife biologist for the 825,000-acre King Ranch in south Texas, found that buck responses tended to be lower during the pre-rut period than during the rut, but not by much. He also noted that older deer, from $4^1/2$ to $7^1/2$ years of age, were more inclined to come in response to rattling than were younger and older deer. But what was astounding was the distance: the average distance that a buck moved 30 minutes after responding to the rattling was almost a third of a mile.

What does this mean for an early-season muzzleloading deer hunter? It means patience. When you begin a rattling session, don't go at it full force for a couple of minutes, look across the field, give up, and go somewhere else. Successful rattling demands that you rattle loudly, pause, rattle again, and use deer calls to bring in the wariest of deer. If you spot a buck coming to your position and keep rattling, the deer will hang up, look you over, and disappear downwind. Persist. You need to begin the rattling session every 30 minutes and have confidence that deer on the move will eventually hear the enticing music.

Hellickson's study determined that loud rattling attracted nearly three times as many bucks as quiet rattling, and that the length of the rattling session was not that important. The study also found that morning rattling (around 7:30 A.M.) was more productive than midday or afternoon rattling. Cloudy days with light winds and warm temperatures were more productive than sunny and cold weather.

Prior to the rut—usually occurring around the second week of November in Pennsylvania, earlier in more northerly states and provinces, and later in the south—I like to hunt the home range of whitetails. October is a great month for this hunt.

Scout an area that has these two components: food and bedding cover. Feeding sites are not always as predictable as looking for the nearest cornfield. In agricultural areas, corn and soybeans are heavily fed upon by whitetails, but once the acorns begin to drop from the branches, deer quickly change their feeding priorities. Whitetails instinctively know that the carbohydrate-rich meat of white oak, chestnut oak, and red oak acorns (in that order of preference) will allow them to put on the fat necessary to survive the long winter.

The whitetail's home range is an area where you have seen deer feeding on agriculture in the summer or on mast-laden white and chestnut oak, beech, and other nut-bearing trees in September. These feeding places are usually close to their traditional bedding sites. You will notice early scraping activity along field edges, some halfhearted rubs, and lots of deer tracks near certain areas of creek beds. If you are lucky, you might find some "deer candy," or soft mast crops, that are particularly attractive to deer: apples, blueber-

A buck rub reveals where and when the buck is traveling.

ries, grapes, pokeberries, thornapples, persimmons, rose hips, Osage oranges, staghorn sumac, and mushrooms.

Next, you need to identify the main trails that funnel deer into these food sites. If your goal is a buck, pay close attention to his calling cards: rubbed saplings. Whereas does create obvious trails into the edge of an agricultural field or favorite stand of oaks, bucks show you the exact way they're coming, as well as when. They also show you the trail that leads back to their bedding area. Look closely at where the antlers scraped the saplings. If the rub is on the side away from the food source, the rub tells you that this is the direction the buck is using to go back to the security of his bedding site. If the rub is on the opposite side of the sapling, away from the field, the buck is telling you that this is the path you should hunt in the evening when he is headed for the field.

This is the most predictable time of year to harvest a deer. Because the foliage is so thick, you need to get close to their travel lanes, and definitely get some elevation. Tree stands allow you to see over the thick weeds and underbrush, and they put your scent column above the deer's nose.

Tree stands pose special problems for muzzleloaders. Foremost is the loaded rifle. It should not be primed or capped when you haul it up a tree. Be sure to remove the #11 percussion cap and have a cover over the nipple to prevent dirt from the tree bark getting in there. Plug the touch hole with a toothpick or feather quill, and put a leather cover on the frizzen. With in-lines, you need to remove the cap and protect the flash channel from dirt. I always tie a cord around the gun's wrist so that the weight of the barrel makes the muzzle point down at the ground as I pull the rifle up to the stand.

Placement of the tree stand is crucial. Remember, the advantage of stealth is lost if you are silhouetted against the morning sun or evening sunset. If the morning thermals carry your scent to the ridgetop trails, the game is over before the first move is made. To avoid this, stay on the north side of the hill. This is usually where deer relax anyway. The north side allows the thermal-carried scent to reach them as it rises up and over the ridge from the south side. From this location, their eyes and ears are scoping the hillside of the less densely vegetated north side. Also, avoid oak trees for tree-stand placement. If you happen to choose a nesting tree for a gray squirrel, or its favorite acorn-bearing tree, the constant scoldings will alert every deer in the neighborhood.

Downdrafts can work against the perfect tree-stand setup. The hunter's scent is normally not a concern from high above the ground. But it is wise to take precautions against the possibility of cooler air coming off a ridge and dropping your scent to the ground. This is why it is so important to practice scent control or use a cover scent. Although fox or deer urine is effective for most situations, the tree stand is not one of them. When was the last time you saw a red fox or a whitetail climbing a tree? Raccoon scent is a more natural choice. And if you are perched in an apple or pine tree, those scents provide a free natural cover.

Back on the ground, you want to entice a deer to stop to provide you with a good shot, but you don't want it looking up at you. You can make that deer position itself for the perfect shot by using a curiosity scent, a deer decoy, or even vocalization from your deer call. Whichever method you choose, practice. If you use an apple scent in a pine forest, place a doe decoy facing you, or blow an aggressive buck grunt, you will be signaling the wrong message and cause the deer to notice you.

Deer constantly vocalize. Does make soft contact grunts; yearlings bleat in return. If you give an aggressive buck call, you may cause confusion and flight. Save those lusty buck grunts and snort-wheezes for the rut. During this pre-rut period, you only want a deer to stop and ponder why another deer vocalized.

With each passing day, leaf cover will diminish, and you will need to elevate your stand so that your silhouette can't be seen by deer traveling beneath you. Deer will also become increasingly nocturnal with the cooler temperatures, so the prime time for intercepting these deer will be one hour after first light and one hour before. Use the afternoons for scouting, when the deer will be least likely to be moving or feeding.

Deer will be predictable if you did your scouting. Shots will be close, and deer will disappear as fast as they appear in the thick underbrush. Be patient; don't shoot through brush. A well-aimed shot will avoid a tough tracking job in red-spotted oak and maple leaves. This special early season allows muzzleloaders to hunt deer when the animals are at their peak populations and at their most predictable. If you are looking for a trophy, be it a big buck or a trophy doe, this is the time of year to hunt like a raptor—like a predatory bird that swoops down from the sky with black powder and white smoke. So sit back and enjoy this best of all seasons to be in the hardwoods.

Rut Strategies

November is a special month for northern deer hunters. It is the breeding season for white-tailed deer. Muzzleloading hunters need to adapt to the changing conditions of the rut. Equipment, clothing, decoys, scents, and deer calls all come into focus for a two-week period. Muzzleloaders can increase their chances of success by keying into ground blinds within the traditional breeding areas. Calibers, powder charges, and bullet selection all play a part in the muzzleloading formula for success.

There is magic in the air. It is the kind of too-good-to-be-true feeling you get when you win the lottery, inherit millions from a long-lost relative, or discover gold in your backyard. For muzzleloading deer hunters, the magic is having a deer season in November. This is the season when the herd is still relatively unscathed, and the big bucks lose their typical wariness of daylight and people. This rut season, the breeding season for whitetails, is a season when shots under 50 yards are the norm, not the frozen exception typical of special muzzleloading seasons in January.

The advantage of this November season for muzzleloading hunters is in the numbers. When all the harvest figures for the year are totaled, 82 to 85 percent of the deer harvest will be taken in November. That translates into 320,865 fewer deer for the January hunt in Pennsylvania and most other states with late muzzleloading seasons. But how does that affect the way muzzleloading hunters put themselves into position to be successful?

Unpredictability is the hallmark of the rutting buck. His agenda is cleared to do only one thing: pursue receptive does. Traveling on those old deer trails that so clearly mark deer movement between food sources and bedding areas is no longer the best option for bucks. Traditional breeding areas, if you can locate them, are the new hotspots. However, finding deer even in these areas is a roll of the dice at best.

The peak of the rut varies with latitude. In the Canadian provinces, the rut usually occurs earlier in October. Pennsylvania and other states located along the 40th parallel can expect the first three weeks in November to exhibit rutting activity, with the peak of the rut occurring during the second week of November. Rutting activity is modified by weather, dryness, and availability of food supplies. In the southern states, such as the Carolinas, expect the rut to peak anywhere between late November and the second week of December.

When the leaves are gone from the hardwoods' canopy, deer change their travel patterns. Their agenda changes, and tree stands lose some of their advantages. It might be a good idea to get back

Usually, 82 to 85 percent of the total deer harvest takes place in November.

on the ground and hunt like a mountain lion in ambush. Stalking, ground blinds, scent suppression and lures, camouflage, decoys, and vocalization are the key elements needed to put the unpredictable buck puzzle together.

STALKING

Stalking is a favorite method for seasoned veterans. "Keep yer nose to the wind and yer back green" is an old saying that merits a hunter's attention. Although most of us will never approach the skill level of the Amerindian in stalking close to game animals, some elements of stealth are easy to learn. Although their deerskin moccasins allowed them to move more quietly than our rigid-soled hunting boots do, and they could read from the spoor whether they were on the trail of a buck or doe, Native American stalking techniques can be adopted by muzzleloading deer hunters with little effort.

"A downwind buck is a gone buck," is another old saying that I have learned to pay attention to. The biggest buck that I ever saw while hunting stood broadside across an open field. The distance was more than my muzzleloader was capable of handling, so I just waited as the big whitetail started to walk in my direction. About the time that he reached the edge of my lethal shooting envelope, his nose suddenly went up in the air, followed by that big flag of a tail. In less time than it takes to tell the tale, he spun around and was gone, leaving me with a stunned expression on my face. The wind had shifted and had given me away.

Remember this important rule of hunting: wind currents change when you least want them to. Although most hunters in North America deal with a westerly wind, a low pressure cell from the south can cause the wind to rotate out of the southeast or northeast. Also, morning thermals carry wind from the valley to the ridge and then reverse direction as the evening downdrafts bring scents off the ridges to waiting whitetails, who know the drill better than the hunters do.

The only time that I can count on stalking as a productive method is during bad weather, particularly snow. By walking into the wind, I can ambush deer that have taken to their beds. Not only is there very little noise when walking in fresh powdery snow or rain-soaked leaves, but scent molecules are pushed back down to the ground by the falling precipitation. Visual acuity for deer is reduced in the moving curtains of rain and snow squalls, and a muzzleloader can actually see more deer as they jump out of the security of their bedding area.

GROUND BLINDS

Tree stands work well in this season, but ground blinds may be even better. The reason for staying on the ground is foliage. The autumn leaves are on the ground, not in the canopy. Any tree-stand hunter in a deciduous oak or maple will be silhouetted, appearing as a huge dark blob against the sky.

Ground blinds are the best way for waylaying deer when you need an immediate ambush site. Unlike tree stands, which depend on a suitable tree being in the right spot and at the correct yardage from the expected deer, a ground blind can be erected exactly where you want it to be.

When the leaves fall off trees, hunters become a scary silhouette against the sky for deer. This is a good time to get into a ground blind for maximum concealment.

There are two basic types of blinds: natural and artificial. A natural blind is constructed from those things that God put there. A rock outcropping is a great place if it is in the right location. A log deadfall can be just as deadly. Some hunters like to cut vegetation and stick it in the ground like a palisade around a fort. But cutting plants can cause two problems: legality and wilting. Some states allow hunters to use natural and existing material but not to cut or damage anything in the construction of the blind. Wilting is another problem that signals to a deer that a change has occurred in his backyard. If you need to use cut vegetation and it is legal to do so, stick with evergreens. Cedars, pines, and spruces provide cover as well as natural scent masking and won't wilt in the noonday sun. The needles won't send up a red flag the way that wilted deciduous tree leaves will.

My favorite natural blind material is dead branches. Find an old stump, an upended root system, or a large rock for a foundation. Position a comfortable stool (rocks are not soft enough for my butt) and sit on it so that you can estimate the height of the ground blind, and then place branches so that they will break your silhouette at least to the top of your hat.

Remember, a ground blind should not be solid wall. You want to be able to see and shoot through it. A good blind simply breaks up your solid form, making you indistinguishable from the foreground clutter. Part of the beauty of dead branches is that they never wilt and will be there for many future hunts. These natural blinds also change naturally with the seasons, catching fallen leaves and snow, and they even have future foliage growing up through them.

Artificial blinds are made from cloth, gilly mesh, and other manufactured materials such as plastic and metal. Their advantages are impressive. They provide immediate concealment and a minimum disturbance to the rocks, trees, and underbrush. They also act as a scent well, which prevents the hunter's scent from drifting on an unexpected swirl in the wind. And they help muffle sounds from the cocking of the gun or any fabric noise produced during the aiming process. The opaque material screens movement, unless you have the sun behind you. You don't want to telegraph your presence like a shadow box, so be aware of the location of the rising and setting sun when you pick your ground blind site.

Be careful about the type of camouflage you choose for a ground blind. Although some hunters swear by their photographic background or army type of camouflage, I prefer a camo that uses a lot of black, brown, and tan. More than 50 percent of the forest floor will be composed of these three colors. Tree trunks, rocks, and branches are usually what I construct my ground blind from, so a good camo for this situation is any pattern that uses light and dark lines to break up the solid form of the blind. Once inside the blind, you still need to wear a face net and gloves. The glare of skin is enough to send any deer packing, particularly when you move to take the shot. And it is a lot easier to hit a stationary target than one running 40 miles per hour.

Your face can warn deer of your presence in another way. I believe that a deer can feel a predator's stare. When a deer comes into my lethal zone, I do not stare at the animal until I'm ready to sight and shoot. Once a deer's eyes make contact with yours, it reacts, and sometimes you miss an opportunity simply because of that predatory stare.

The location of ground blinds must be planned so as not to interfere with the normal travel patterns of whitetails. Deer notice everything in their environment. If you change the area they live in, they will immediately become suspicious. Keep the blind at least 30 yards away from the food and bedding trail that you are keying into. Better yet, stay 50 yards away if you can see through the undergrowth.

If you plan a morning hunt from the ground blind, keep the blind above the trail where you expect to intercept the deer, but be careful that the deer can't silhouette the blind against the skyline. Morning thermals will cause the wind to rise up the hill, and you don't want your scent carried up to the deer. In the evening, the wind drift reverses. Then, keep your blind beneath the deer trail to take full advantage of scent drift.

The reason that some hunters are more successful than others is that they place their ground blinds at natural ambush points. Remember that the rut is a time for whitetail romance, so forget the food plots. Instead, look for bucks to be chasing does on the first bench of a hillside above a field; a saddle depression between two fields; the edge of a large rock outcropping; the edge of a mountain meadow or blowdown; a natural creek crossing; a woods opening beside a field where the canopy of tall trees has prevented vegetation from growing on the forest floor; low areas where creeks feed into pond and lakes; any constriction caused by a fence, stone wall, or the like; and most important, near the breeding scrapes left by dominant bucks.

SCENT SUPPRESSION AND ESTROUS LURES

As stated earlier, the nose of a whitetail is its main line of defense against predators. Personal hygiene and the use of scent-suppressing sprays and garments will go a long way toward getting you within the lethal range of a muzzleloading gun. Rubber boots and carbon-fiber scent-suppressing garments are great when you first take them out of the airtight bag you stored them in, but after a sweaty day afield, they lose their ability to keep you scent free.

Scent management is a daily affair. After a hard day walking to and from the blind, stalking the buck, or just loading and unloading the equipment from the car, you need to recharge your gear. This can be done in any hot environment, but you need boiling temperatures to drive out your old scent. But beware, modern synthetic fabrics and synthetic rubber have a nasty habit of shriveling into a hardened lump of plastic when the temperature gets higher than boiling. So please read the label precautions or manufacturer's warranty information before you start toasting and baking your equipment.

Though not as effective as a very warm, dry environment, but better than not attending to your clothing or boots at all, you can hang your things outside to air out and dehydrate. After a few hours in the outdoors, stuff them into a garbage bag with fresh leaves and earth to restore the masking qualities. You won't be invisible during a close encounter with a whitetail, but at normal shooting distances, you will cause the buck less alarm.

Estrous lures can be an important part of your setup during the rut. Be sure that you buy fresh doe urine that has been refrigerated and kept out of the sunlight. One whiff will tell you whether it has become nasty ammonia or has retained its urine essence. An ammonia fragrance may not frighten the deer, since it is a normal by-product of decomposition, but it certainly won't attract them either.

Don't put deer lure on your clothing. Put it on the ground, just like deer do. Estrous lure has powerful pheromones that bucks can zero in on quite accurately. You don't want a buck to key in on your location; you want him to key in on the false scrape, decoy, or other spot where you want to make the killing shot. Therefore, if you are using a scent trail to that spot, saturate a foot pad with lure at the spot and then walk away from it; this gives the deer the impression that the hot doe is down the path to your ambush. Take off the foot pad after you have walked 50 yards away. You can then saturate the foot pad and use it as a scent target back at the scrape

Estrous lures can be an important part of your setup during the rut.

where you want the deer positioned. All these precautions will pull deer in, not leave them suspicious 50 yards away.

CAMOUFLAGE

"Don't choose a book by its cover," your elementary school teacher advised. Later in life, particularly during your hunting years, you learned, "Don't choose a buck by its cover"—you need to look at its antlers. But we must choose to cover up with camouflage if we expect to have close encounters with big bucks.

The upright human silhouette is particularly noticeable to whitetails. Though we may look like rather tall, upright tree stumps, movement is what gives our presence away. Breathing, turning your head to locate deer, blinking, moving your hands in the process of aiming, moving your legs for locomotion, and every other little nervous twitch telegraph *predator* to deer.

To dissolve the human silhouette, particularly the moving appendages, we need to use light and dark colors to distract a deer's eyes from our solid form. Many camo manufacturers are doing this with patterns that employ light-colored tree limbs and darker green or brown-gray leaf patterns to break up the solid human silhouette. Die-cut leafy, three-dimensional patterns have taken camo to the next level. Whenever the wind moves, so does the camo pattern. This enhances the hunter's ability to disappear into the woods, weeds, or grasses.

Muzzleloaders don't need to get as close to their quarry as bow hunters do, but we still want the advantage of shots under 50 yards. A good camouflage suit can do that for just a small investment. Many of the popular styles are now available in coveralls that cost less than $100, and with a little care, this clothing should last for years.

DECOYS

Many states allow muzzleloading deer hunters to hunt during the rut, and this makes decoys an invaluable tool. While hunting in Virginia during the second week of November, I found out just how useful a deer decoy could be for enticing a buck to come closer. I built a ground blind 30 yards uphill from a forest opening where I had found massive buck rubs and a lot of scraping activity. After constructing the blind and ensuring that it would blend in with the forest floor, I placed a decoy set of a buck and doe near an artificial scrape I had made, facing away from the blind. In the waning light of the day, I left the area with a positive feeling for the next morning's hunt. Sleep was difficult that night due to the anticipation of a close encounter with a big buck.

What I found when I came back to the ground blind the next morning was devastating. The Y-buck decoy was lying in pieces about 20 yards from where I had positioned it. The fluorescent orange antlers had been yanked from its head, and the head had been gored and pulled from the body. Visible tine marks told the rest of the story. The doe decoy was flipped on its back, and the 3-foot artificial scrape had been pawed into a 6-foot rectangle. The urine-soaked ground had a very distinctive "this is *my* turf" aroma, left by the enraged buck. Besides a new buck rub beyond the scrape, several of the surrounding saplings had actually been bent over and broken. This big boy was obviously upset by the intrusion of the decoys. Although I didn't see the buck that morning, he was shot by another muzzleloader in that same spot only one day later—a massive eight-point monarch.

Decoys become an invaluable tool for muzzleloaders during the rut. This visual stimulation puts the buck in a predictable spot for optimum shot placement.

Decoys, curiosity scents, and deer calls (doe and fawn bleats) can be a real advantage. I have watched deer veer away from their traditional trail to check out the Feather Flex doe decoys I had placed beneath my tree stand, just 20 feet from a mock scrape. Deer are curious. If you set the stage with visual (decoys), olfactory (deer scent), and auditory (doe bleats) enticements, deer will drop their guard, forget their intended focus, and come into a predictable shooting situation. This means that you will settle the front bead of your muzzleloader into the open iron rear sight and onto a fat doe that is less than 30 yards away.

When you set up your decoy, make sure that it is upwind of your blind or tree stand. That way, a swirling downdraft can't accidentally give away your location before the decoy has had a chance to perform its magic. Don't hide the decoy in underbrush or under a rise in elevation; deer need to see it. In fact, the main reason that you are using a decoy is to confirm to a curious buck, that a doe is in the area, ready to breed. So put that decoy or decoy herd out in the open, and always facing away from where you are sitting.

Bucks always try to move in from the rear of the decoy. It is a good practice to place some estrous scent where nature intended it to be found. Besides, this distracts the buck from looking around for danger—namely, you. As stated earlier, a white handkerchief laced with estrous lure provides movement, a visual cue, and a tantalizing "come hither" scent to entice that buck into gun range.

DEER VOCALIZATIONS

Big bucks are solitary animals within their normal range. The rut reverses that solitary existence and turns a buck into an aggressive, wild-eyed stalker. As these heavy-bodied and antlered whitetails begin their search for receptive does, they become quite vocal. Their sense of hearing comes to the forefront as they strain to hear doe bawls.

Deer vocalization is real, and hunters need to learn the language. Deer calls can make the difference in bringing deer in for a closer shot.

Properly used and not overused, a doe bleat will attract attention, curiosity, and even concern on the part of a group of does. It can bring animals into a spot that they wouldn't normally have checked, but beware of the deer's uncanny ability to pinpoint a sound. When a deer is coming into muzzleloader range, stay off the deer music, or you will give your location away.

Vocalization becomes even deadlier during the rut. Properly used, a lusty grunt or snort-wheeze vocalization will attract bucks from their normal trails to your location. Stop calling once the buck has keyed into your area, or he will accurately locate you. The idea here is to feed his aroused state with a little curiosity that makes him vulnerable. Remember, those huge ears give a deer an uncanny ability to pinpoint sounds, and since you don't look like a doe, bewilderment usually quickly turns to flight.

Tennesseean Jerry Peterson, owner of Woodswise Products, believes that hunters need to master three calls in order to be successful in deer season, particularly during the rut. Peterson calls them the "ABCs." The "A" call is an attention grunt. It represents a maternal declaration to her fawns: "Pay attention." The "B" call is twofold. The first part is the standard doe bleat that the female uses to answer any other deer's vocalization. The bleat, in essence, says, "Here I am." But the second part of the bleat occurs in breeding season. Known as the estrous bleat or the breeding bellow, this is the vocalization that drives bucks into a frenzy. Now the doe is saying, "Here I am, and I want to breed *now!*" What male of any species could resist that? This loud and long bellowing sound can be repeated anywhere from 3 to 12 times, pausing for 5 seconds between calls. The pause allows the doe to listen for a responding grunt from a suitor. The "C" call is a contact call, which rises and falls in the manner of a lost deer looking for the rest of the family group. This call can be used during any season, as the deer is basically saying, "Come to me."

When does the buck's grunt or grunt-snort-wheeze call come into play? This is a call that one mature buck vocalizes to another as a challenge. It works well when your plan of attack is to call out a challenge to any bucks in the area to see who is the biggest and baddest—the one who will win breeding rights. This call is effective in the pre-rut season. But once a buck's hormones start surging, his neck swells, his eyes bulge, and he has only breeding on his mind, not sparring.

OTHER CONSIDERATIONS

The prime time for hunting rutting bucks is in the late morning. Why? If you were a buck and wanted to look over the willing ladies, where is the best chance to hook up? The answer lies in the rub lines and scrapes adjacent to food sources. Here the does are coming back from their nocturnal raids on agriculture or finishing up the acorns missed by squirrels. By waiting until midmorning, bucks can scent-check every deer that fed in that area.

Rifle choice for this season boils down to which gun you shoot most accurately. A .45 caliber has plenty of roundball energy out to 50 yards, a .50 caliber to 80 yards, and the big-bores past 100 yards. If you hunt like a hawk high up in a tree stand, stick with the easier-handling carbine. For those of us who like to keep our noses to the wind and our backs green, the Pennsylvania longrifle holds better in the off-hand position. The choice is personal, and there is no one best gun.

The rut places different demands on muzzleloaders. Shots at game will be a bit farther away than those taken from a tree stand. If you are a roundball shooter, stay with the larger calibers like .50 and .54, because they retain more energy for greater distances than smaller calibers do. For traditionalists, this is a good time to use that longrifle. The longer sighting plane can be a real advantage for accuracy on these 50-yard and longer shots. If you are using an in-line, caliber isn't much of an issue with a lead slug or sabot bullet, but the sights are. In states that allow scopes, they provide a huge advantage over open sights. Rifle weight is not critical, since the gun will not be carried for any great amount of time. This is why the heavier-barreled Plains rifle style might be a good choice for ground blinds.

Remember, a mountain lion hunts by ambushing its prey, and successful deer hunters would do well to mimic these feline predators during the midseason whitetail rut.

Deer are changing their agendas, and you need to change yours. Daily forays to fields of corn and soybean give way to nocturnal raids, and midday snacks include acorns and other mast crops. But as whitetails become increasingly obsessed with the rigors of the rut, unpredictable bucks dash out of their normal range toward does in estrus. Muzzleloading hunters can increase their chances for success by keying their ground blinds into traditional breeding areas.

Post-Rut Strategies

December is the most challenging time of year to be a hunter. December–January weather patterns become unpredictable, with strong winds and snow for most of the country. In the North, subzero weather challenges the function of muzzleloading equipment, as well as human stamina. The frozen conditions not only affect the choice of clothing and equipment; they also call for a change in strategies. Deer will no longer pattern easily for food or procreation; they now retreat to sheltered thickets and survival yards. Tree-stand and ground-blind ambushes become less effective tactics. The old-fashioned solitary stalking technique and the multihunter deer drive become more effective strategies at this time of year.

Christmas brings out the best in friends and families, but opening day of the late-season hunt is the one that many muzzleloaders wait a whole year for. It was tradition for Jeff Hester and his friends to head for their Lycoming County cabin the day after Christmas. There was a special magic about the four-by-four pickup truck clawing its way through the snow-drifted logging road. That first wood fire in the stove and that yellow glow of the gaslight warmed the spirit more than it did the cabin. A feeling of anticipation heightened the senses as each new deer track was spotted dimpling the snow on Pewter Bough Mountain.

The six friends set out for the first of their morning "spook hunts," or what others call scent drives. It was their method of slowly driving deer from the impenetrable mountain laurels that choked the snow-laden hillsides of Pine Creek. Once fresh tracks were located on the State Forest Land logging roads, the standers would take positions on cross-trail locations. The spookers would then fight their way through the tangled laurels and scrub oaks. By walking slowly and letting the wind carry their scent, deer would slowly be moved toward the standers.

It was on one of these drives that Jeff had a chance to test the new Green Mountain barrel he had fitted on his T/C Hawken stock. The first deer of the drive was a small doe, but the nervous look back over her shoulder toward the laurels signaled that other deer were following. In fact, a whole herd of deer suddenly busted cover like hot popcorn from a skillet. Suddenly, a large deer stopped and stared at Jeff just long enough for the blue-painted front sight to align with the yellow-painted rear sight on the deer's front shoulder.

Sparks leaped from the frizzen to the primer, and the snowy boughs of the chestnut oaks dropped their burden as the roar of black powder echoed across the ridge. The whitetail dropped her tail, spun around, and headed back for the security of the laurels as Jeff quickly reloaded. For five long minutes, all was quiet except for the soft crunch of Jeff's crutches as they slowly took him along the hillside trail. Soon, he spotted red dots scattering to the right side of the trail. A well-defined blood trail took him straight to his deer, not 50 tangled, snow-laden, mountain laurel–choked yards from where he had shot it. This disabled Pennsylvania hunter, paralyzed by polio since age three, had proved the effectiveness of a .490 roundball propelled by the power of black powder, as well as the perseverance of a dedicated late-season hunter. (For information on hunting aids and organizations that assist disabled and handicapped hunters, contact the Pennsylvania Game Commission at www.pgc.state.pa.us; the Disabled Hunters of North America at www.dhna.org; or the Safari Club International at www.safari-club.org.)

Of the 46 states offering a special muzzleloading season for deer, 23 of them schedule hunts during the late season. This time period, December and January, is also known as the post-rut. Whitetails change their priorities away from the rigors of the breeding season and concentrate on only one thing: survival. Their metabolism slows down in reaction to the lack of food and the lower nutrition found in browse. Food is still important, particularly to the bucks, who need to replenish the fat reserves they squandered while sparring for breeding rights, as well as the rigors of the rut. Conservation of the precious calories found in their remaining fat reserves, though, is paramount, and necessary to their survival through the harsh winter.

Why is a working knowledge of whitetail biology necessary for creating a late-season strategy for muzzleloading success? In a word: agenda. Since the deer have a different daily agenda from the one followed in November, you need to change yours if you want to be at the right place at the right time. Whitetails no longer make morning and evening forays along scrape and rub lines. Horn rattling and mock scrapes no longer appeal to bucks. Ridgetop acorns will still be sought, but because the squirrels have buried most of them, these highly prized carbohydrates will not be

GOOD REASONS TO HUNT THE LATE, POST-RUT SEASON

- It provides a "third" deer season.
- Holidays mean school or work vacations, allowing hunting with family members.
- There are a lot fewer hunters.
- Deer are unpressured and return to their old pre-rut agendas.
- This single-shot season provides a perfect "school" for teaching young hunters.
- Snow provides a blackboard of deer activity.
- Low evaporation and frequent precipitation keep the leaves soft and the walking quiet.
- Deer are concentrated into thickets and feed in a few calorie-rich food sites.
- Underbrush has fewer leaves, making visibility greater.
- The bucks that survived the bow and gun seasons are usually bigger and smarter than their naive siblings who were harvested earlier.
- This is a fun season, and the pressure for the harvest has abated. Success is measured by the number of funny whitetail encounters and log-burning cabin stories.
- What other season has such great challenges as finicky ignition, howling snowstorms, and fruitless close encounters? And what group of hunters smiles and laughs more at those challenges?

a regular attraction. Instead, deer are thinking about finding the densest cover, staying out of the wind, and staying alert to the intrusion of hunters. Because it is far more difficult to replace the calories lost when running from danger, deer opt to conserve calories by simply holding tight to the cover. They may circle back on the hunter and return to their beds, or many times, they simply don't get up.

Since deer are glued tight to their cover in the late season, the tree stands that paid such dividends during the regular buck and doe season are of little value. Since deer are not moving randomly in response to the mating season, ground blinds are also less effective. With little doubt, the most successful strategy for taking venison at this time of year is to hunt like a canine. Coyotes and wolves hunt by pursuit, and so should you. In other words, learn to use

Coyotes and wolves successfully pursue their prey on foot in the late season, and so does the savvy muzzleloader. This is a good time for the deer drive.

the deer drive to push the whitetails from the precious security of their cover.

DEER DRIVES

There are several types of deer drives. Successful muzzleloaders will tailor their strategy to the type of terrain that is being hunted. If you are hunting a thick area of brushland, the old-fashioned pan-banging, beagle-baying, yodel-yelling noisy drive is a surefire tactic for unnerving whitetails, but it is not the best tactic for a single-shot muzzleloader. This type of drive usually results in wild-eyed deer galloping out of the cover and passing by the standers like Superman on his way to a bank robbery. This is a bad idea. The problem presented is how to shoot accurately at a running deer with a smokepole. In other words, how does one estimate the lead on a running deer with a bullet that is moving only around 1,600 to 18,000 feet per second? The bottom line is that you can't ethically call this shot with accuracy.

Deer drives can be highly effective in making deer visible. However, the fast-moving deer running through heavy brush is not an ideal target for a single-shot muzzleloader.

Whitetail distance and speed are critical to the hunter's "guesstimation" of lead, before the shot is fired. Deer lope at around 18 miles per hour, but they can run at speeds up to 40. If you take a shot at a running deer that is 75 yards away, your bullet could impact more than a foot off-target. Hypothetically, consider that if the deer is running 25 miles per hour (37 feet per second), the bullet will take 0.02 to 0.03 second to get there, thus allowing a 9- to 13-inch margin of error. If the whitetail is traveling at 40 miles per hour, the bullet would be off-target by 22 inches at 75 yards and by 44 inches at 100 yards. Also, consider the fact that deer do not run on the level, or in straight lines, to their destinations. They jump over obstacles, leap across depressions, and generally bounce along rather than moving at a steady gait. Based on this knowledge, what ethical hunter would take a running shot? There is a much better way to deal with deer drives.

The second type of deer drive is the silent drive. In this type, hunters allow the deer to see the human silhouette (usually dressed in fluorescent orange contrasted against camouflage or other contrasting colors) and react to the invasion of a predator. If the wind is in the hunter's face, or blowing laterally from side to side, this slow-paced silent, visual drive usually provides drivers

The second type of deer drive is the silent drive. When deer are allowed to see the human silhouette, they'll flee in the direction of the standers.

the opportunity to take shots at stationary deer. This type of drive won't work in underbrush where the foilage is so thick that you can't see through it, but it works well in the moderate underbrush of maturing hardwood forests. Quick-handling, half-stocked Plains rifles and Hawkens in the heavier .54-plus calibers are a good choice for these conditions, as the shots to the deer are usually more than 50 yards. If your state allows an in-line, be careful of those high-powered scopes that reduce your field of vision. Open sights, fiber-optics, large-aperture peep sights, and nonmagnifying 1× scopes are better choices for quick aiming and shooting at moving deer.

The third type of drive is the scent drive. This involves slow movement by the drivers while the wind over their backs carries their scent and alerts the deer in front of them. This is one of my favorite types of drives, particularly on snowy mountain laurel, rhododendron, or honeysuckle hillsides. More often than not, the drivers get more shooting than the standers as the whitetails attempt to circle back into the cover or when they surprise deer in their beds.

Regardless of the type of drive you choose, keep the distance traveled during the drive to a minimum. Many small drives are better than one giant half-day affair, because the deer will slide sideways at 90 degrees to the drivers. If you drive into the wind, the drivers have just as good a chance at a shot as the standers. This keeps everyone happy. But be sure to keep at least one stander downhill of the drive, because this is where the deer are going to squirt out the side of the drive.

Fluorescent orange cloth-ing is a necessity for both driv-ers and standers. Even the American Indians practiced safety during their own deer, elk, and buffalo drives. Al-though they didn't possess orange clothing, they knew enough to distinguish them-selves from game. They accom-plished this by wearing a headdress and clothing that included both feathers and fur. Since there are no animals that grow both, the moment one Indian saw this inconsistency, he knew that only a man could wear such garb. Today, we rely on bright orange to keep us out of harm's way, but the safest

Many times, the deer driver is the one who gets the opportunity to shoot: deer aren't as likely to flee in panic and burn valuable calories in the late season.

course is not to shoot in the direction of the standers, or back into the drivers. Common sense can go a long way toward making us safer hunters.

SOLITARY STALKING

Snowy weather plays an important role in any type of hunting, but it is particularly valuable to the late-season hunter. Visibility is reduced, scent swirls on the wind, and deer movement is recorded by the snow, which acts like a blackboard. It records size, shape, direction, number, and freshness of the tracks. Bed sites record urine stains (does stain the edge of the bed when they stand; bucks urinate in the center) and piles of droppings, and the tracks lead in a direction where the animals are watching their backtracks for predators. All this information gives a real edge to muzzleloading hunters who know how to use it.

Whenever it snows, I enjoy a game of one on one. Putting my nose to the wind, I slowly sneak toward the hillside bedding areas. These are often found one-third of the way down from the top of a

Snow is perfect for stalking deer. Stalk into the wind slowly and be ready for deer to rise from their beds.

hill or ridge in mountainous terrain. In the southeastern rolling farmlands, the deer bed closer to the fields, where any rise in the topography allows them better visibility and the opportunity to read scent on the thermals. Many times the deer are not alerted to the presence of the hunter because the snow reduces visibility and creates unpredictable downdrafts that make scent direction unreliable. If you can find standing rows of corn and have the landowner's permission to hunt, deer often concentrate in the middle of such a field. But this situation usually works better with two or more hunters because shots inside the stalks are difficult, and "walking" the deer out of the field results in easier, open shots at the deer as they exit.

Whitetails will not leave their beds in secure cover unless they know the exact location of the intruder. With the wind in your face, you have overcome the scent problem. Now, you only need to worry about your silhouette. Snow camouflage, which uses limb and leaf patterns to break up the solid white, really gives an advantage to the hunter. As you move slowly, following deer tracks, you often catch the deer off guard, unaware of your presence. This is why many of my shots are under 50 yards, which is ideal for my .45 flintlock longrifle.

What happens to the late-season, post-rut strategy when the weather just does not cooperate and give muzzleloaders a good tracking snow? The combination of dry, cold weather and dead leaves makes the forest floor as crunchy as a bag of potato chips. This is a difficult environment. Sound can work against you, or

SNOW TACTICS

- As snow depths increase, deer bed down closer to their feeding areas in order to save calories expended on travel.
- Deer can smell an acorn through a foot of snow. Find an area where the deer have been digging, and they will most likely return the next day.
- Wear snow camo, because anything else will form a dark silhouette.
- Low areas such as creeks and ravines are favorite places for bucks to turn around and face their backtrail for predators.
- Antlerless deer usually bed as family groups. If you are looking for a buck, it will usually be the only bed, and larger than a doe's.
- Travel across the wind when approaching bedding areas. Binoculars will help you find the rounded brown lumps lying in the snow. Does and yearlings lie motionless, but bucks usually turn their heads looking for danger, and this is a great time to spot antlers.
- Expect the unexpected, and have your muzzleloader at the ready when stalking through snow. Deer reluctantly leave their beds in deep snow, but once they do, they pop out of the snow like a ruffed grouse taking flight. Shots will be close and furious.

you can turn this disadvantage into a winning strategy by getting together with a friend for a two-man drive. Place the stander on a predictable or known escape route, but instead of having the driver walk in a straight line toward the stander, use a long zigzag or unpredictable circular route to unnerve the deer. Move slowly, and don't be afraid to backtrack, because whitetails often try to sneak around the driver once they know the position of the stander.

OTHER CONSIDERATIONS

Clothing is an important part of a flintlock hunter's late-season strategy for success. Deer drives can work up a sweat, and wet clothing chills the skin 23 times faster than the cold air does, and this can lead to hypothermia. Good moisture-wicking long underwear should be worn beneath insulated clothing. Since the heart-pumping hills will take care of keeping drivers warm, don't overdo the insulation. If you plan on standing during all the drives, then warmer jackets with hoods are a good idea. I like to carry hand and toe warmers for these situations. They are light and inexpensive and can make the long waits tolerable.

The same intensity that you put into locating whitetails during the pre-rut and peak rut seasons for bow and rifle should also be applied now. You will be more successful in driving deer when you key in on the following late-season hotspots: hillside thickets, old clearcuts now overgrown with raspberry cane and redbrush, tangled ridgetop scrub oaks, alder swamp edges, and storm-ravaged blowdowns—in other words, the thickest, nastiest, cover available.

Remember that late-season whitetails hate the wind. It robs heat and steals precious calories that they can't easily replace from browse. Wind also makes it difficult for deer to hear predators entering their security zone. This may be why whitetails like to bed down on the leeward side of a mountain or hill. In this position, the wind brings any predator's scent over the hill, freeing the deer's other two defense senses (sight and hearing) to concentrate on anything coming from below their beds. Cone-bearing trees such as pines, spruces, and hemlocks can reduce wind speeds by 50 to 75 percent and are excellent sites for deer to yard up in heavy snows. Look for the deer to be about one-third of the way down the leeward side of a conifer hillside.

A great time to hunt is just before or after a major storm system moves through. Deer have an uncanny built-in barometer that senses pressure changes. As the air pressure drops, deer leave their bedding areas and head for the highest-calorie agriculture or browse that's still available (staghorn sumac is very high in fat and protein). They sense that they need to stock up on food to sustain them during a multiday storm. As soon as the bad weather abates, watch for deer movement as they go back to refill their empty stomachs.

If you are going to vocalize or rattle to attract whitetails, keep it soft and slow. This is the season for saying "hello," not "hey baby." If you get aggressive, the deer will bolt, spending calories it can't afford to lose. Many times, a hunter can get a whitetail to stop and investigate a sharp noise, if only for a split second. Some hunters whistle. I prefer a doe bleat for a curiosity stopper. A stationary deer allows better shot placement.

When winter snow depths pass the knee-deep stage, look for deer tracks leading toward swamps. The green grasses that normally clump up in these soft, mucky areas are an easy food source for whitetails. Deer still need water in the winter, and marshes and swamps usually have a trickle of water draining the wetlands that stays liquid through the late season.

Once a morning silent or scent drive is over, don't automatically head for a new area. Whitetails choose a bedding area for good reasons, and they don't abandon them easily. When deer take flight, they usually take a circuitous path back to their original bedding area. Give the whitetails a chance to settle back in, and then repeat the drive in the same area. Now that you know their escape routes, the odds are in your favor.

The care and maintenance of muzzleloaders require some adjustment in cold weather. Oils and greases thicken into semi-solids when the snow flies. It is best to degrease the cams, springs, and bearing surfaces with alcohol and lubricate with a dry graphite

To be successful during the post-rut and late deer season, modify your strategies to include the changing agenda of the whitetail.

lube or high-viscosity oil designed especially for cold temperatures. Beware of set triggers. When the rear trigger is set, the front hair trigger may be fired prematurely by cold, numbed fingers or glove-covered fingers. It is better to stick with the front or single trigger that fires with a positive let-off of about 2 pounds.

The most challenging whitetail season is the post-rut late season. To be a successful muzzleloading hunter, redesign your strategies to include the changing agenda of the deer. Deer no longer pattern for food or procreation; they now retreat to survival zones. December–January weather patterns become unpredictable, brutally cold, and treacherously white. This frozen foul weather affects clothing and equipment choices and calls for a change of strategy. Tree stands and ground blinds become less effective, while the old-fashioned stalk and drive techniques become the most effective methods of finding groups of whitetails. Learn to read the snow and the deer trails like a canine hunter on the prowl. Your success with a flintlock will add venison to the list of wild gourmet delicacies that grace the family table.

Shooting Strategies and Recovery After the Shot

The shooting conditions that hunters face once they leave home are a far cry from the ideal conditions of the practice range. This section details what happens when shots are taken up- or downhill, through brush, or at deer standing behind trees. Deer do not always drop in their tracks when shot. Strategies for recovering the animal, based on whitetail anatomy and hunter experience, are also covered here.

Smoke from a cabin down in the hollow was curling up through the hardwoods like a snake stalking a mouse. The chill of the November morning was being replaced by a gentle thermal rising from the valley below my stand, carrying the scented smoke with

The buck I took in November, moving through the brush in the distance.

it. As I thought about the hickory smoke's effect on sausage and bologna, it suddenly struck me that smoke is actually the essence of a muzzleloading hunt.

Black powder hunting is different from every other kind of hunting. We burn simple chemical substances—carbon, sulfur, and potassium nitrate—to produce the energy necessary to shoot a bullet. But it is the smoke, like an important afterthought, that people really notice. The larger the volume of powder, the greater the cloud of white smoke. Our mission, to quickly and humanely harvest a whitetail, is dependent on that smoke. It is our responsibility to smoke deer ethically.

A young buck suddenly burst out of the raspberry canes. At first, he was nothing more than a brown shadow winding his way through the treetops and brush left behind by loggers. But as the buck leaped onto the logging road, a glint of ivory betrayed his escape from the hunters below, down in the swamp.

Here the smoke obscures the nearby goldenrod and staghorn sumac, the bullet's flight, and the impact on the deer.

Seventy-five yards is a long shot for an open iron-sighted flintlock. But in a mere second, the distance closed to 50 yards. The six-pointer was in full flight and moving fast. As the flintlock clicked into full cock, the deer broke stride, stopped, glanced over his backtrail, and then departed headlong into the high goldenrod weeds under the power line.

No rifle is the rumored "brush-buster" that some hunters profess to owning. Even the huge-caliber, slower-moving muzzleloading bullets do not possess the magic that allows them to slip through weeds, vines, and saplings in a straight line. Poor accuracy and depleted energies make a brush-buster shot an unethical choice for hunters.

"Give a whitetail a chance to make a mistake, and it usually will," I noted to myself. But the deer cut across the weeds, quickly putting time and distance between us. Without a break in stride, the buck turned 25 yards into 50. Noting the opening ahead of the deer, I settled the iron front post just in front of the shoulders as I swung the long barrel in time with the deer. "Time and distance," I muttered as I quickly calculated the risky shot.

I never felt the trigger's tension against my finger. Smoke! Lots of smoke roared toward the deer, obscuring the bullet's flight, the goldenrod, the staghorn sumac, and the impact on the deer. Smoke hung on the air like a ghostly apparition, consuming all that it blanketed.

Had the shot been true? Was the deer hit? Had my subliminal calculations for distance and time been effective? Or did an overeager imagination delude this rifleman into thinking that he could make an impossible shot, regardless of its ethical costs?

I descended the black oak tree, reloaded the .54, and fought my way through the greenbrier thorns and goldenrod. The ground didn't reveal what I had hoped to see—a swath of red. Chastising myself for attempting the risky shot, I knew that ethics demanded a thorough search for the deer's escape sign. Back up in the tree, the rifle again aimed toward the opening, it suddenly struck me that I had been searching in the wrong place.

Once again, a tug-of-war between my camouflage pants and the greenbrier slowed my progress. But this time, the effort was rewarded with a fat six-point buck that lay exactly where the flintlock had been aimed. Noting that the animal had fallen instantly to a spinal shot in its lower neck, I made a mental note that this was not where I had aimed. Again and again I came back to the thought that smoking a running deer is not an easy or even a good opportunity. Only luck had prevented me from merely wounding this animal, and although I was happy for the recovery, there was a strong sense of guilt for having taken the foolish shot at all.

RUNNING DEER

A running deer shot is not a good choice for muzzleloaders. The pie-plate-sized vital area of the deer is a difficult target to hit, and the "guesstimation" time is critical. Moreover, it is extremely difficult for a hunter to see who else may be in the background of that running deer. If it is a house, a car, or worse, another person, the result could be tragic. But there are a few situations in which a running deer might need to be anchored, after examining the backdrop and deeming it safe. One that comes to mind is finishing off a wounded deer beneath a tree stand or downhill from the shooter.

When smoking a deer on the run, the estimation of distance and time is critical when taking a shot with a muzzleloader. If you decide to shoot at a 75-yard running deer, consider the consequences. A whitetail escapes cover by loping along at 25 miles per hour, or about 37 feet per second. This puts the animal about 0.02 to 0.03 second past the bullet-sighted impact zone—in other words, 13 inches off-target. When you factor in a full-flight whitetail crossing an open area at 40 miles per hour, or 60 feet per second, your

Consider the variables in taking a shot at a distant, running deer. At 75 yards, your impact may be off by 13 inches or more.

bullet would be 22 inches off-target at 75 yards and 44 inches at 100 yards. A piece of good advice is to take your shot when the deer is standing still.

When estimating time and distance, the type of bullet is not as critical as its velocity. The slower the velocity, the greater the amount of time it takes to get to the target. Also, the slower the bullet, the less hydrostatic shock will be delivered in a smaller wound channel. In other words, even though the cylindrical bullet has more retained energy, it may not be as accurate or kill as quickly as the roundball. Faster bullet choices make sense for reducing lead time, but slower, more massive slugs carry their velocities better past the 100-yard mark—too far to take a shot at a running deer.

Slow ignition adds to the difficulty of estimating the distance and time of a muzzleloader bullet's accuracy. The fastest ignition is from in-line rifles. Although less than a second elapses from the time you squeeze the trigger until the propellant blasts the bullet from the barrel, that 1 second is significant. Multiply the ignition lapse time by a factor of 2 (with an external percussion gun) or 5 (with a flintlock), and it becomes almost impossible to accurately place a shot on whitetails that are in full flight. This is especially true at distances greater than 75 yards.

Temperature, particularly temperatures below freezing, can have a profound effect on bullet velocity. If you sight in on a 75-degree day, your rifle will lose about 102 feet per second when the mercury dips to 15 degrees. This will adversely affect your bullet placement.

JUDGING DISTANCE

Judging distance without a range finder is a real coin flip, and a wrong guess can produce a miss or, worse, a wounded animal. But I have found a method that is fairly accurate. Over three decades of hunting for deer, I noticed that deer less than 50 yards away have distinct facial features, particularly the eyes. Up to 50 yards, the deer's eye is a glassy black, surrounded by a ring of white hair. If you sight your flintlock in at 40 yards, it will print at exactly the same spot at 80 yards, and 3 inches low at 100 yards. A 50-yard shot should be dead center. When a deer reaches 75 yards away, the eye is not wet and glassy looking but instead appears as a black dot in that white ring around it. At 100 yards, the eye is not distinctly visible; only the white appears on the head, within a ring of brown. Using this simple trick can really help a hunter bring home the venison.

What about shooting uphill or downhill? Newton's law of gravity provides that answer. Gravity pulls a bullet down to the ground with the same velocity-time formula, regardless of whether you shoot uphill or down. In other words, a 50-yard uphill shot from a ground blind will have the same bullet drop as a 50-yard downhill shot from a tree stand or a 50-yard off-hand shot across a cornfield. Know the ballistics for the gun you are using, and compensate accordingly.

APPROXIMATE DROP OF MUZZLELOADING
BULLETS (IN INCHES)

.45- to .58-caliber roundballs at 1,800 to 2,000 feet per second

0 Yards	50 Yards	100 Yards	125 Yards
−8	0	−5	−12
−8	2.5	0	−6

.45- to .58-caliber conical bullets at 1,400 to 1,600 feet per second

0 Yards	50 Yards	100 Yards	125 Yards
−8	2.3	0	−8
−8	5.2	5.8	0

Note: These are only approximations that are affected by bullet shape and density. Pointed bullets with narrower diameters and greater density have less drop. Lighter bullets and those with blunt noses are more affected by wind.

Shots at whitetails beyond 100 yards demand a new tool, the laser range finder. Slow-velocity muzzleloading bullets do not possess the flat trajectory of high-velocity centerfires. So ethical hunters must know the distance to game, the energies of the bullet throughout its range, as well as its trajectory's drop beyond 100 yards.

When I am hunting open ranges, be it a large field or a prairie, I rely on my Bushnell Yardage Pro Legend laser range finder. This small optical device emits invisible, infrared energy pulses. Digital technology and a high-speed clock are used to instantaneously calculate distance by measuring the time it takes for each pulse to travel from the range finder to the target and back. The ranging accuracy is plus or minus 1 yard under most circumstances, and the maximum range is a lot farther than I will ever shoot at a deer with a muzzleloader—about 800 yards. Deer can't sense the infrared pulses, and its small palm size doesn't make it any more visible to a deer than the movement of your arm. But what really impresses me about this unit is that it is totally waterproof; it even floats if you drop it in a stream or pond. For those of us who foul-weather flintlock in the late season, this is a real plus.

BULLET PLACEMENT

Every muzzleloading hunter knows that there will be no quick second or third shot. This is why many muzzleloaders use the tactics of bow hunters to get closer than the average rifleman would. Regardless of whether you hunt from high in the trees or low in the bush, you need to think about shot placement. Slower-velocity bullets from muzzleloaders do not possess the penetration characteristics of smaller-diameter, high-velocity centerfire bullets. Hunters need to look for the broadside or quartering-away shot to properly strike the vital organs of the whitetail.

There are only two ways that a muzzleloader can quickly and humanely dispatch a deer. The bullet must disrupt either the "electrical system" or the "plumbing."

In your house, if you turn off the electricity, the lights instantly go out. In a whitetail, the electrical circuits are controlled by the nervous system. A bullet striking the brain or spinal cord will instantly disable a deer. This is the famous "flop" situation that some successful hunters like to remark about. But this electrical system, which controls muscle and thought processes, is so small (a target less than 3 inches for the brain, and only 1 inch for the spinal cord) that it is not a wise choice for a running-deer shot.

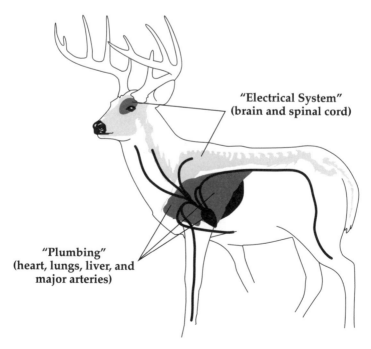

Ethical deer hunting requires that you aim for the nervous or circulatory system.

Broadside shots are the best bet for muzzleloaders: less penetration is required to reach the vital organs than in any other body position.

The only logical aim point for a running deer is the "plumbing," or the circulatory system. The circulatory system can be compared to the water pipes in your house. If a tiny aquarium filter hose is nicked and begins to leak, it would take days to flood the kitchen floor. But if there is a crack in the water main coming into your house, the basement would be flooded in seconds. This analogy holds true with whitetails, whether standing still or running. When your bullet creates a hole in the circulatory system, blood pressure immediately begins to drop. If your bullet strikes the heart, the aorta, the carotid artery in the neck and head, or the femoral artery that runs under the backbone and down both hind legs, rapid blood loss is imminent. Vital organs such as the heart, lungs, and liver also open the flood gates to blood loss and in most cases cause the animal to expire in less than 20 seconds.

Broadside shots are best for muzzleloaders. They require less bullet energy and penetration to reach the vital organs. The best target area is the chest. This 12-inch-diameter "pie-plate" vital zone

A whitetail running directly at you makes for a poor body position for taking a shot. From this angle, the two-inch-wide spinal column is in constant motion, and the heart and lungs are protected by the sternum and ribs.

contains the heart and lungs. Damage to both lungs causes immediate suffocation, and the animal is usually recovered less than 50 yards away. Damage to the heart causes immediate loss of blood pressure and oxygen deprivation to the brain, and recovery is usually less than 40 yards away. In both cases, the deer is dead in less than 10 seconds. Aim one-third to halfway up the side of the deer just behind the front shoulder.

Quartering-away shots are also good choices for muzzleloaders. Besides taking out both lungs or the heart, the bullet's impact usually strikes the opposite shoulder and "flops" the deer in its tracks. Aim behind the shoulder facing your sights.

Head-on shots are not a good choice for muzzleloaders. Although hunters may brag about head and neck shots, and though they are immediately disabling, the small 2-inch lateral vital zone comprising the brain and spinal cord is not easy to hit, particularly when the deer is moving. A chest shot above the sternum will strike the aorta or one lung but will also drive back through the stomach and intestines, leaving a horrible mess for field-dressing and meatpacking. A low chest shot is likely to only wound the animal because of the body armor presented by the sternum, shoulder, and rib cage.

Quartering-toward shots are not good choices for muzzleloaders either. You might get lucky and strike the 2-inch zone of the spinal cord and brain, but a higher percentage of shots will strike the sternum (chest), scapula (shoulder), or rib cage and deflect away from the internal organs. This shot is chancy at best and unethical at worst.

Rear-end shots are also a poor choice. If shot high, they might strike the spinal cord or brain and be immediately lethal. But anywhere lower is going to drive the bullet through the "guts." Recovery is usually more than 70 yards.

Elevated shots from tree stands need to take into consideration the closeness of the shot. Most hunters have never sighted in a rifle at 15 yards or less, and this is important. Most bullets strike lower than expected because they have not risen to the plain of the sights or the crosshairs of a scope. Therefore, you need to compensate by aiming somewhat lower on the deer than you normally would. This guesswork is not a good thing when trying to pick out the vital zone of a deer seen from above, which is half of that available in a broadside shot. Pick a spot just down from the spine and right behind the shoulder. This shot does not have a high percentage of success.

RECOVERY AFTER THE SHOT

Always know where you are hunting and how to get back where you started. For many, hunting is just a walk in old, familiar territory. But for more adventurous hunters, hunting may involve an expedition to some far-off destination. Learn to use a topographic map. A good source for topo maps is the DeLorme Mapping Company's *Atlas and Gazeteer*. Each state map is bound into an easy-to-read set of topo maps that detail public hunting areas, natural features, and primary, secondary, and gravel road accesses. For computer-savvy hunters, waterproof, 36- by 44-inch wall maps (which I fold up and keep in my hunting pouch) can be ordered from www.mytopo.com. These are custom-made topo and aerial photo, high-resolution, U.S. Geological Survery maps, equipped with navigation grids.

The critical moment in tracking a wounded whitetail is right after the shot. It is often difficult to see a running deer's reaction to a shot from a muzzleloader. The cloud of smoke from the burning propellant fogs the area between the hunter and the hunted. Factor in interference from weeds, shrubs, and trees, and you have a very difficult environment for viewing anything. But you need to be able to see the deer's reaction, or the "flop" versus the "wiggle." When a lead ball or conical bullet strikes a heavy bone mass like the shoulder or spinal cord, so much shock is applied to the nervous system that the deer "flops" straight down. But if the bullet strikes soft tissue between the ribs, low in the neck, in the liver or stomach, or in the hams, the deer may kick, jump up, or not show any reaction at all. A bullet that disrupts the circulatory system results in more of a "wiggle." Both flops and wiggles can be signs of a lethal hit, but the type of reaction signals how fast you should set out to recover the deer.

Before you leave the tree stand or ground blind where you made the shot, mark your location. I like to use biodegradable toilet paper for this purpose; its whiteness contrasts with the surrounding colors of foliage, and it's something you usually carry in your pack anyway. Now, take a bearing with your compass or, better yet, mark your waypoint with a GPS.

There are two schools of thought on how fast deer should be recovered. The first, led by Dutch Wambold, a famous archer, believes that all wounded deer

Before you leave your shooting position to trail a wounded deer, mark your location. White toilet paper, an orange piece of ribbon, or (best of all) a GPS will make your return trip much easier. A GPS also helps you predict where the deer may be going.

should be followed immediately because this pushes the deer and hastens the loss of blood. A deer's heart beats three times faster when running, and this increases blood loss and causes the animal to expire faster. This group also believes that a deer has a remarkable ability to stop bleeding and recover its strength when it is given time to lie down.

RECOVERY TIMES BASED ON BLOOD AND FUR EVIDENCE

Evidence	Body Part Struck	Waiting Time to Begin Recovery
Blood		
Bubbly, pink	Heart or lung (bubbly)	Immediate
Red, decreasing	Liver	1 hour
Red/brown with vegetable matter	Stomach/intestine	2 hours
Pink/red with large volumes	Arteries	Immediate
Dark red, decreasing, with fibrous matter	Muscle	Immediate/ questionable recovery
Dark red, decreasing, with bone chips	Leg bones	Immediate/ questionable recovery
Fur		
Brown/gray, long hair	Body	Immediate to 2 hours
Brown/gray/white, short hair	Legs	Questionable recovery
White	Throat, low belly, tail	Questionable recovery

The second school of thought on game recovery believes that an animal hit in the chest should be trailed immediately. But if the deer is struck anywhere else (liver, stomach, intestine), it should be given time to expire.

According to William Monypeny Newsom, if a deer were running when a bullet struck its heart, the high blood flow to the muscles and brain could allow the deer to run for 15 seconds before

TRAILING TIPS

- Mark the deer's location when it was shot. White toilet paper is visible and biodegradable, but fluorescent orange and pink ribbon is easier to see.
- Note the deer's posture when shot.
- Check for blood sign and hair type (see table).
- Use your compass, topo map, or GPS to take a bearing before you begin trailing.
- Mark your backtrail at the edge of visibility for the last marker.
- When the blood trail is difficult, get down on your hands and knees to read the scant sign of hoof marks and dots of blood. But make sure that you are wearing fluorescent orange safety clothing and hat.
- If you lose the trail, back up and circle the last sign. Injured deer usually head into the heaviest cover, or toward a source of water, to elude predators.
- Don't give up. Go get a buddy. There is a distinct advantage in having an extra set of eyes and experience.
- Use a spray of hydrogen peroxide on wet or red-spotted leaves to determine the presence of blood. Blood will foam, even when wet.
- Night trailing requires a Coleman lantern or fluorescent light to make the blood glow. Remember to mark your trail with reflecting tape or tree tack so that you can find your way out.

succumbing to the wound. At an easy lope of 18 miles per hour, the heart-shot whitetail could travel about 150 yards; at 30 miles per hour, it could easily travel more than 200 yards. An animal that is immediately pursued will put as much distance as possible between the predator and itself before stopping to evaluate the situation. Blood loss may be faster, but so is its retreat.

If your shot was less than lethal and you give the deer a chance to stop, the recovery distance my be shortened. Why? A wounded whitetail's first reaction is to escape danger, and then lie down to recover. When the deer lies down, internal bleeding from marginal hits may take a while to stop, if ever, and blood pressure continues to drop. Low blood pressure means that a reduced oxygen supply begins to affect muscle groups, as well as the brain. The deer will be in no condition to attempt another long dash when you approach it with a reloaded muzzleloader.

A long drag back to the truck or camp can be hard on older hunters who are already toting the weight of a muzzleloader and gear. An easily seen orange nylon drag makes the job safer and easier.

Once the recovery of the deer has been accomplished, the next daunting task is getting it out of the woods or field. When I was younger, a stout piece of cord was all that I carried along for the deer drag. As I got older and bolder, and the distances from home got farther, the drag became a major task. At that point, I decided I needed help. A lightweight product that can be thrown in a backpack came to the rescue. Known as the Deer & Bear Glide, it was the invention of another older deer hunter, Jack Curlee. This strong, lightweight synthetic, slick-bottomed body sled wraps around the animal, protecting the hide, and makes the drag almost effortless. It is available through Cabela's, or you can contact Curlee's company, Biowerk, USA.

Many hunters never get a chance to weigh their deer after they harvest the animal. With only a simple cloth or steel tape measure and the following table (developed by the Penn State University Department of Animal Science in conjunction with the Pennsylvania Game Commission, Division of Research), you can estimate its weight.

Heart Girth (inches)	Live Weight (pounds)	Field-Dressed (pounds)	Hide Weight (pounds)	Edible Lean Meat (pounds)
20	49	36	1.9	23
21	53	39	2.3	24
22	56	42	2.6	26
23	60	45	3.1	28
24	65	49	3.5	30
25	69	53	4	31
26	74	57	4.5	34
27	79	62	5.1	36
28	85	67	5.7	38
29	91	72	6.3	41
30	97	77	7	44
31	104	83	7.7	47
32	111	90	8.5	50
33	119	97	9.4	53
34	127	104	10.3	57
35	136	112	11.2	61
36	145	120	12.3	65
37	156	129	13.4	69
38	166	139	14.5	74
39	178	149	15.8	79
40	191	160	17.1	85
41	204	172	18.6	90
42	218	184	20.1	97
43	234	198	21.8	103
44	250	212	23.5	110
45	267	228	25.4	118
46	286	244	27.4	126

Most hunters use the venison and antlers from their trophies, but deerskin is one of the finest leathers around, and it is a shame to waste it. Buckskinners take pride in their fringed shirts and pants, hunting pouches, and flint and bullet bags, but modern muzzleloaders can have gloves, jackets, car seat covers, purses, and footwear made from tanned hides. Just the touch of the creamy soft leather will bring back the details of that memorable hunt. We owe it to the sport and the game animal to use all that it has offered us.

Foul-Weather Techniques

To be a successful hunter when the mercury bottoms out and the sun doesn't shine, you need to be prepared to deal with foul weather.

It had not been an easy morning. The gang at Whitetail Camp had pursued the normal first-day ritual for this late-season muzzleloading deer hunt. Bob went to his favorite tree stand, Gary to the other, Dennis to the overlook at the pines, and Bill made tracks everywhere else. But the lack of coordination didn't produce a single deer encounter. Even though this seasoned group of muzzleloaders knew better, old first-morning habits die slowly. What this group needed and reluctantly put their legs to was an old-fashioned deer drive, the single most effective way to hunt deer in the late, great season.

Snow was hanging on everything. The puffy dry crystals had created cotton fields in the shrubs and high weeds, cutting visibility

This frosted cabin, typical of many in Pennsylvania's northern tier counties, is once again occupied by late-season deer hunters during the Christmas holidays. Vacation from work and school provides the opportunity for renewing old friendships.

down to 10 yards or less. Fortunately, the fluffy snow that had fallen overnight also worked in the hunters' favor. Size, direction, speed, and number of deer in each small herd were easily known by anyone who cared to read the symbols in the snow. Since the tracks were leading out of the hemlocks by the creek, they predicted that the herd would probably be feeding on the hillside browse.

They decided to push the deer out of the raspberry thicket that had taken over the clearcut near camp. Bill picked up the trail and immediately saw fresh tracks heading straight up. The point on the ridge that the hunters call the fish hook is an unusually good ambush point, since five logging trails funnel the deer into that spot. Bob headed off to the west through the nastiest tangle of horse-high briers and stump sprouts that the northern tier country could produce. Just minutes into the silent drive he heard Bill yell, "There they go. Four of them. Dennis, coming your way!"

The deer were reluctant to leave the security of the thicket, but their shadowy forms were not a safe target. Bill shouldered his .50 Hawken several times with the deer only 40 yards ahead, but the brush and snow made shooting impossible. Suddenly, the herd broke cover and headed straight across the logging road. Anticipating a shot, Bill and Bob stopped and listened. But instead of the expected earth-shattering boom, they heard the all too familiar and always agonizing *phffft!* "Darn, darn, darn!"

The deer stopped to look back at the wisp of smoke that hung on the side of the rifle. Predictably, the lead doe snorted, and the family group loped uphill to escape this sulfurous smoke apparition.

"What happened?" hollered Bill as he broke out of the cover, pulling thorns from his clothing. Dennis's red face and white beard made him look like an embarrassed Santa Claus as he tried to explain away the misfire. "Maybe I didn't keep my powder dry," he chuckled. But a quick check of the touch hole revealed the real culprit. The vent on the side of the barrel was so tightly plugged with greasy-looking powder that an acetylene torch could not have ignited the load of black powder.

A plugged touch hole or flash channel is the number-one problem that prevents flintlock hunters from bringing home the venison. The first step in preparing for foul weather begins when you with-

A plugged touch hole or flash channel is the number one problem that prevents muzzleloaders from bringing home the venison.

draw the flintlock from the gun safe, cabinet, closet, or case. You need to clean that clean gun. Most ignition problems occur because the grease and oil used at the end of the cleaning process turn into gremlins in the wintertime. As temperatures decrease, so do the lubricating qualities of grease and oil. Heavy oils and grease thicken and slow down the lock time, making shots inaccurate. To remedy this, take the lock out of the mortise in the stock and degrease the tumbler, sear, detent, spring, and any metal surfaces requiring movement. Rubbing alcohol works well for this. After degreasing, lubricate the metal parts with a very light machine oil, or even kerosene, which will not slow down the metal-on-metal movement.

After degreasing the lock, turn your attention to the barrel. Cold, thickening grease has a nasty way of plugging the touch hole. Lubricating oils also thicken, but they have another nasty side effect—smothering the black powder and raising its ignition temperature. In extreme cases, the black powder turns into a gooey paste that will never ignite, rendering the barrel useless until it is thoroughly cleaned—a time-consuming process. A simple cleaning patch with rubbing alcohol can prevent this problem.

Before you ramrod a load down the barrel, turn your attention to the ignition system—the flint and steel. A flintlock in 20-degree temperatures reacts differently from the one you practiced with at 50 degrees. Without sparks, there is no fire. As temperatures go down, the steel becomes more difficult to work with. One of the reasons for this is the presence of water inside the pores of the frizzen. Drying the frizzen pays big dividends and is easy to do. After ensuring that the barrel is not loaded, apply the flame from a butane lighter under the base of the frizzen. Do not smother the flame on the steel, or the incomplete combustion will leave carbon black on the surface. As the frizzen heats up, a layer of "sweat" will appear. At this point, remove the heat.

After drying the frizzen, cover it. There is no point in having a ready-to-spark, dry frizzen if you are going to tote it around all day in foul weather. A fingertip cut from an old glove and slipped over the top is a great way to cover it up.

Even if the steel frizzen produces 2,000-degree sparks, these white-hot steel pieces won't shower the pan of priming powder unless your flint is sharp enough to scrape them free. Remember that the cold makes it harder to rip sparks loose from the steel, so you need to take extra measures to ensure that the flint is sharp and solidly mounted in the jaws of the cock.

After all the commotion on the hillside, the hunters regrouped and decided to go up on top. This Bradford County ridgetop is typical of many—the trees are regenerating and fairly open, but the mountain laurel is thick. They decided to push to the south end of State Game Lands 36. Even though it was the first day of the flintlock season, December 26, there were no other cars in the parking lot, and it seemed like the thousands of acres were unhunted.

The strategy was simple. They used the wind to their advantage as they slipped along the north side, hoping to walk deer up to the standers in the laurels. One of the problems the drivers

Cover your frizzen. There's no point to having a dry frizzen, ready to spark, if you are going to tote it around all day in foul weather and get it soaked.

encountered was snow in the lock. Dollops of puffy snow fell from the branches as they waded through the stuff.

I always walk with the muzzle down and the lock area tucked under my armpit. This keeps the lock dry, even in rain, and the rifle is positioned for a quick snap to the shoulder when needed.

Alternatively, a wax or thickened grease dam applied between the side barrel flat and the stock mortise will cause the water to drip harmlessly down the forearm. Placing a grease bead along the flashpan and then carefully seating the frizzen cover atop it completes the waterproof seal of the pan. But it doesn't hurt to change the priming powder every half hour just to ensure ignition.

A good idea for percussion rifle shooters is to put a small piece of leather between the hammer and nipple to stop moisture from going down the uncapped flash channel. If you already have the percussion cap on the nipple, cut a small piece of plastic aquarium hose and slide it over the cap and nipple. This nipple collar does two things: it prevents moisture from slipping under the skirt of the percussion cap and dampening the primer compound, and it holds the cap tight to the steel nipple so it can't fall off.

"Keep yer powder dry!" is far more than an amusing old saying; it is a vital piece of advice. Flintlockers have two problems with wet guns—the powder train and, more typically, the priming powder. The powder train, or the powder, patch, and ball inside the bore, is usually not affected by water coming down the muzzle unless you are using a loose-fitting sabot or a patchless lead slug. The greased, tightly swaged patch and ball are a fairly effective water seal. This is not to say that water, or a plug of snow or mud, is not worrisome; it is, in fact, downright dangerous and must be prevented. This is easily accomplished with plastic wrap and a rubber band or a tightly stretched balloon.

The other opening in the barrel—the touch hole or vent—is often the culprit when the powder train becomes damp, contaminated, and useless. To prevent water from entering, I simply plug the flintlock vent with a toothpick or bird's quill until I'm ready to prime and fire. On a sidehammer percussion, use a brass cap cover, a leather patch, or even a rubber eraser. In-lines pose their own problems, and you will need to get creative to keep the moisture out. There are plastic and flexible rubber lock covers that can also be stretched over the entire lock area, regardless of lock type.

The best priming powder is obviously the one that stays dry and ignites at the lowest temperature. Ordinarily, dry FFFFg works the best, but the larger grain size of FFFg works better in foul weather and still ignites at the same temperature—480 degrees.

"There they go!" yelled Bill. "There's a buck. I think one of them's a buck." More than 100 yards away, the deer scrambled out of the logging residue. Rather than running to the safety of the laurels up on the ridge, they took off directly into the wind.

Meanwhile, up on the ridge, two flintlocks tattooed the morning stillness. Unknown to the drivers, two antlered deer were circling back when Bob and Gary intercepted them. Shooting across a small ravine and into a tangle of downed timber, their shots had no telling effect. After a thorough check of the ridgetop, as well as

While it's tempting to reload and pursue fleeing whitetails, resist the urge. A quick fouling patch run up and down the bore will make sure that the second shot is an accurate one and prolong the life of the barrel.

their trail, which led back to the original morning hunt in the hemlocks, the lunch bell sounded.

While the party of hunters relaxed over warm soup and sandwiches, plans were made for the afternoon's hunt. The guns were kept outside to prevent condensation, they were deprimed, and toothpicks were placed into the touch holes to prevent moisture from slipping inside, but the fired and reloaded guns would still need cleaning.

A big mistake that causes muzzleloaders to misfire is allowing a reloaded gun to go uncleaned for a day. When black powder is fired, the fouling left behind is full of carbon, sulfur, and metal salts. Almost 50 percent of any charge is left unburned and blown free of the bore, but much of it remains in the grooves of the rifling, drawing moisture and turning into a thick, corrosive, gooey mess. Although a second load can be ramrodded through this mess and fired successfully, if a hunter waits too long, the load will eventually become dampened by the hydroscopic nature of the fouling.

The warm afternoon sun had melted most of the snow from the previous night's storm. As the puffy snow liquefied and dripped from the treetops, the hunters from Whitetail Camp had a new problem. While walking back to the ridgetop, droplets from the overhead branches were striking their barrels. Slowly, the moisture was creeping down the barrel flats between the lock, stock, and barrel, quietly turning the priming powder into ink. But to prevent this, they had put wax dams between the barrel and stock, just ahead of the lock, as well as using grease to seal the priming pan on the lock.

As luck would have it, the fifth hunt of the day produced a close encounter of the flintlock kind. At less than 40 yards, two does stopped in the laurels, broadside to the hunter. Bob raised the .50 caliber, and the 80 grains of FFg sent the patched roundball true to its mark. The doe bounded twice and collapsed in the laurels as the other stood motionless. The smoke cleared, and meat had been made the old-fashioned way, with black powder, a cast lead round-ball, and a flintlock rifle.

After the successful hunt, the happy but tired hunters collected back at the pot-bellied stove to dry out.

While some hunters are fond of shooting their rifles at the end of the day, this is a waste of powder and lead and can be dangerous in the absence of a receptive backstop that doesn't produce a rico-chet. The powder train won't go bad as long as the touch hole is sealed (a toothpick works well, as does a feather quill), and if they don't shoot the guns, the hunters won't need to spend the next half hour cleaning them.

The morning hunt on the Jackson farm was a season ender. Bob and Bill had already been successful, Gary was hunting back home in Montgomery County, and Dennis had left for a Texas goose hunt. But persistence found me back in my old tree stand overlook-ing an old apple orchard. A threatening sky and dropping ther-mometer foretold the January snowstorm, but the falling barometer had another effect. Deer! Magically, the empty woods was full of the sounds of whitetails moving about.

My tree stand was located in a giant poplar, next to a stand of oaks. Over a decade of memories had convinced me that this was a productive area. A quick check of the lock (degreased for the cold

A bleat can convince a doe to put her head up and come closer to your stand.

weather, as light oil speeds up the lock time), looseness of the primer (FFFg doesn't cake up as fast as FFFFg and ignites just as well), and sharpness of the flint assured ignition. But time was running out.

The herd of eight does was feeding on acorns, but just a bit too far away. As snow began to fall, I grunted a doe bleat. Instantly, the lead doe lifted her head and walked toward my stand as she chewed on a morsel. She came to 80 yards, then 50. "Keep coming," I mumbled, as the painted blue front sight nestled into the yellow rear, centered on the doe's shoulder. At 25 yards, the doe stopped, stomped her front feet, and slowly turned.

The frizzen cover slipped off, the hammer was drawn to full-cock position, and the trigger clicked backward. A bright light lit up the canopy, followed by a thunderous clap of fire and brimstone. The deer jumped backward as a telltale tuft of brown hair floated to the ground.

Taking a doe in winter with a Pennsylvania longrifle.

Suddenly, the forest floor was alive with brown forms scurrying in all directions, crashing through the brush, snorting their alarm—all but one. A mottled brown form lay motionless, gathering snowflakes. The deer had given up its earthly existence so that others could eat and live on.

FOUL-WEATHER STRATEGIES

- Degrease the lock and barrel.
- Use a light oil on moving lock parts, particularly the frizzen spring and cam.
- Make sure the hammer is tight.
- Make sure the flint is sharp and tight in the jaws.
- Use brand-new percussion caps and 209 primers.
- Create a wax dam along the side of the barrel and stock in front of the lock.
- Avoid a "hair trigger" on double and set triggers.
- Slide a plastic hose collar around the nipple and #11 caps.
- Place a leather patch between the hammer and nipple channel.
- Use a greased leather "cow's knee" or other waterproof lock cover.
- For flintlocks, ensure a "dried frizzen" by covering it with a waterproof boot.
- Use FFFg black powder, which won't cake as fast as FFFFg primer in the priming pan.
- Place a wooden toothpick or feather quill in the touch hole.
- Use a grease gasket around the edge of the priming pan.
- Keep priming powder and rifle loads in waterproof containers.
- Avoid condensation by keeping the rifle in a cold environment.

CHAPTER SIX

Hunting Wild Turkeys

As the white shadbush lends a blush of excitement to the bare branches of spring, mountain ridges come alive with the music of wild turkeys. Success comes to those hunters who do their homework and are in the right place at the right time. A white cloud and thunderous roar from a muzzleloading shotgun add spine-tingling excitement to the hunt, and there is no finer way to smoke a longbeard than with black powder. Wild turkeys are truly big-game animals worthy of a muzzleloader's passion. This chapter details the specialized muzzleloading guns and loads that are necessary for anchoring these big-winged trophies.

Spicebush and wild grapevines blocked all but the silhouette. Anticipating movement into a shooting lane between two lichen-covered boulders, I eased the 12-gauge Traditions Turkey Pro shotgun into position. This bronzed longbeard and I were head-to-head at 30 yards. For want of a clear shot, the safety was slipped back.

Dilemma: The bird was too close for any telltale movement from the slate call and too obscured by brush for a clean shot. Apparently, this gobbler had not yet spotted the Buckwing hen decoy placed on an open, flat area that once served as the foundation for a charcoal kiln used by woodsmen of an earlier era.

The thought of colliers heating hardwoods into charcoal suddenly struck me like the thunderous gobble of a bird just belted out into the morning mist. Charcoal is the fuel of black powder.

Spicebush and heavy grapevines prevented a 30-yard shot in this instance.

The better the charcoal, the better the black powder performs. And there I sat, trying to coax an eastern wild turkey into a shootable spot so that I could let loose the power of black powder, fueled by charcoal.

More than a century ago, the colliers and their trade disappeared. But unlike the colliers, the black powder shotguns that once depended on the charcoal makers knowledge and skill continue to play a role in today's hardwood forests. These charcoal-burning shotguns are still harvesting wild bounty—the wild turkey.

Hunting the wild turkey with a muzzleloading shotgun is a real blast. It is also the ultimate challenge for those looking to put the thrill back in the hunt. Good calling techniques will bring a bird within 40 yards, where a modern buffered load is lethal. But handicapped by a muzzleloader, you need to get that bird another 10 yards closer. This thrilling close encounter of the feathered kind also takes far more attention to details, but the reward is worth the effort.

Muzzleloading shotguns feature many shapes, sizes, and types of ignition, but they all burn charcoal.

The first question that must be addressed is where to get a muzzleloading shotgun. Unfortunately, with the low demand for these guns, small shops rarely carry any in stock. The same is true for many of the big discount chains, but this is slowly changing. Some of the manufacturers that are building high-quality and affordable sidehammer singles and doubles, as well as in-line singles, include Thompson/Center, Traditions, CVA, Navy Arms, Knight, Dixie Gun Works, Cabela's, and Pedersoli.

The next question is, should a turkey hunter buy a single- or double-barrel shotgun? Three decades of turkey hunting have provided lots of opportunities to observe the results from shots ranging from 5 to 35 yards. Many of these birds flopped to the ground, rolled around, and then were anchored by my foot. Two birds in particular got up and escaped because I couldn't get to them in time. All hunters want lethality with that first shot, but that isn't assured every time you squeeze the trigger. Because muzzleloaders cannot provide that quick second or third shot like modern autoloaders, some hunters believe that the logical conclusion is to carry a bigger bore or, better yet, a second barrel.

SHOTGUN BORE SIZES

Gauge	Diameter (inches)	Millimeters	Weight of Bore-Sized Lead Ball (grains)
28	0.550	13.88	208
20	0.615	15.6	293
16	0.662	16.8	370
14	0.693	17.6	432
12	0.729	18.4	493
10	0.775	19.6	601
8	0.835	21.2	771
6	0.919	23.4	1,048

Note: A shotgun's gauge is determined by the number of roundballs cast from 1 pound of lead; for example, a 12-gauge bore-sized ball will cast 12 roundballs to 1 pound.

I love double-barrel shotguns. Having grown up with Ithaca, Fox, and Franchi side-by-side shotguns in the Southeast's bountiful pheasant fields during the 1960s, I learned that these guns were quick to point, shoot, and take game. As I made the transition to original cylinder-bore, muzzleloading, double-barrel shotguns, I found that these guns didn't provide the tight shot patterns needed for the larger, sturdier, heavier, game bird of the 1970s. Those big 18- to 20-pound wild turkeys take real knockdown energy. This demands that the gun provide multiple pellet hits in the inch-wide brain and spinal cord region. The only practical way to attain this is with an external choke added to the gun.

Mark Bansner, a gunsmith from Adamstown in Berks County, gave one of my early muzzleloading shotguns that choked advantage. He took a Thompson/Center New Englander 12-gauge, cylinder-bore shotgun; threaded the end of the barrel; and added a Remington Extra Full turkey choke. It made a big difference in tightening the pattern. With the choke removed, I could easily load and slide the wads down the barrel.

This would be impossible with a fixed choke system. With the choke tube back in place, the extra full choke was ready to pattern a dense swarm at 30 yards. It takes extra work to load and shoot multiple shots, but how many shots do you get at a wild turkey?

Double-barreled shotguns give turkey hunters a valuable second shot. Unfortunately, they are not aimed as accurately as a single barrel with open sights and a scope.

Unfortunately, one shot is all you can expect from one muzzle-loader barrel. But a single, well-aimed shot is usually all a hunter needs. To make sure it is a good one, however, you need some kind of aiming device. A bead on the front of the barrel is sufficient for wing shooting, but turkey hunting demands a more accurate shot. To aim the shot column, get a good set of rifle sights. Better yet, add fiber-optic sights to your gun. They really enhance the shooter's ability to aim a load of shot in low-light conditions. The 1990s witnessed the rise of shotgun scopes for turkey guns. These low-powered, 1× to 3× magnification scopes provided a distinct advantage for aiming at small targets like a turkey neck. I put a Bushnell Trophy 1.75-4×32 Mossy Oak Break-up Camo scope atop a Traditions Firearms 12-gauge Turkey Pro shotgun and was amazed at how accurately this outfit could chuck a load of #4s. When I added Cabela's MAD Turkey Choke to the outfit, the gun shot more like a rifle than a shotgun. This definitely gave me the

One well-aimed shot is usually all that a turkey hunter needs.

confidence to try shots up to 40 yards on any turkey unfortunate enough to respond to a call and a decoy.

What about two shots? There is no question that having a backup, second shot is sometimes necessary. But pointing a double-barrel muzzleloader changes the way you shoot. Forget a scope; it does not mount easily on a side-by-side. Even rifle sights are difficult to add to the barrel rib. Another problem is that hunters must become familiar with the accuracy of each barrel because they do not shoot to exactly the same spot.

Shot density is regulated by choke, and if an external choke is not used, the "modified" choke is as tight as the barrel can be constricted in order to ramrod overpowder cards and shot wads down it. Fortunately, many of the new double-barrels are available with screw-in chokes. Fiber-optic sights can be added to the central rib between the barrels, but most guns are simply used with the stock bead and no rear sight. The lack of a rifle sight or scope is a handi-

A tightly choked, scoped shotgun is an accurate and lethal gun for wild turkey. This type of rig is particularly effective on birds at ranges beyond 30 yards.

cap, limiting accurate shooting to under 30 yards. But losing 10 yards is not a major handicap when turkey hunting. All the turkeys I have killed have been shot at less than 30 yards, and only one turkey needed a second barrel to anchor it permanently—but I was sure glad I had it in reserve.

The most important consideration in determining whether a single or double barrel is best is personal preference. Both systems have advantages and disadvantages.

What is the best load for 20-pound turkey? That depends on your shotgun. Muzzleloading shotguns are commonly available in 10 and 12 gauge, with most of the single-barrel outfits sticking to 12-gauge bores. They all shoot black powder, regardless of manufacturer, quite well. But the higher ignition temperatures of Pyrodex and Triple Seven powders demand a hotter cap. So, if you are using a traditional, externally mounted, sidehammer gun, I would stick with the easier-igniting black powder in FFg granulation. In-line shotguns use the popular 209 shotgun primer. Outfits from Traditions, Knight, and others work well with either black powder or Pyrodex or Triple Seven, though I haven't had good success with pellets. Stick to the bulk powder for best results.

The secret of successful pellet penetration with any load is the correct proportion of powder and shot. Without the ability to slam home a hornets' swarm of shot into the brain or spinal cord of a heavy-boned turkey, everything else becomes meaningless.

Shotgun Basics

SHOTGUN PELLETS AND PENETRATION

Penetration of shot is determined by three pellet factors: velocity, size, and hardness. Pellet velocity is a direct result of the volume of powder used and the amount of resistance generated by the pellet's mass and friction. Slow velocity is no friend of a shotgun pellet, since it loses velocity and energy very quickly. Turkey are big game birds, and the load that worked well on upland game won't be adequate for a 20-pound, feather-armored, trophy game bird. Regardless of the gauge of the shotgun (10 and 12 are good choices for muzzleloaders), you need to keep your pellet velocity faster than 1,000 feet per second at the muzzle.

Grains FFg	Shot (oz.)	Velocity (feet per second)
10-gauge, 28-inch barrel		
90	1¼	969
100	1¼	1,031
110	1³⁄₈	1,109
12-gauge, 28-inch barrel		
70	1	997
80	1	1,040
80	1¼	997
90	1	1,049
90	1¼	1,092
90	1³⁄₈	1,000
100	1¼	1,196
100	1³⁄₈	1,112

Besides the obvious factors of distance and accuracy, penetration is a result of three factors: velocity, pellet size, and hardness.

Wanting real-world results, and being skeptical of advice from armchair experts, I decided to test the effective penetration of various loads on real turkey necks procured from a local processing plant. Testing began with a Navy Arms T&T (trap and turkey) 12-gauge muzzleloader, because this double-barrel was choke modified and full choke, which seemed typical of the guns commonly in use. A friend and I set up some turkey necks on a line about 30 yards downrange. We began with a light load of 70 grains of FFg black powder. We used the same volume of #4 shot, since this was the commonly accepted standard (volume for volume) touted by shotgun shooters at the National Muzzleloading Rifle Association's national matches. The velocities recorded by my chronograph averaged close to 900 feet per second for both the modified and full-choked barrels. Since modern shotguns chambered for 3-inch magnums produce velocities around 1,400 feet per second, the 70-grain load in this muzzleloader seemed way too wimpy for turkey.

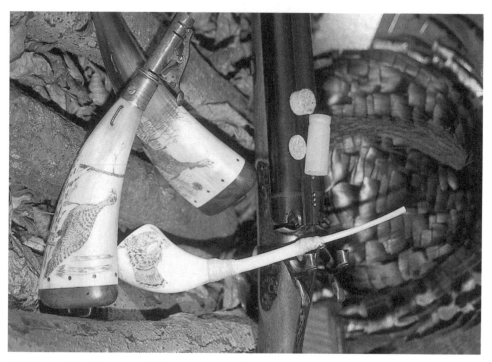

Field tests with a Navy Arms T&T 12-gauge revealed that a "century load" of FFg and #4s were the best mix. It's been my favorite load ever since.

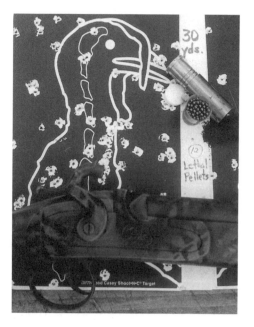

Higher velocities usually cause holes in pellet pattern density. Sometimes it is wise to back off the hot loads in favor of a denser pattern.

Pellet size is an important variable in determining the amount of lethal energy necessary to kill a turkey.

To increase the velocity, we raised the volume to 80, 90, 100, and even 110 grains of FFg black powder. The last load was at the limit of safety for this gun, and for my recoil-sore shoulder, but it did record 1,290 feet per second. The #4s proved devastating on the turkey necks, with smashed and separated vertebrae illustrating the energy in these large pellets. But the very few hits revealed a problem—pattern density.

Compromise was in order. By dropping back to 100 grains of FFg, the load was still racing across the chronograph at 1,250 feet per second, and the hole in the center of the pattern was reduced. At that point, it appeared that the "century load," (100 grains of FFg black powder propelling the same volume of #4s) would become my perfect 12-gauge turkey load.

Pellet size is the second variable in determining the amount of energy imparted to the neck of a turkey. The larger the pellet, the greater the amount of energy and penetration your gun will

Broadside   **Full Strut**   **Moving Away**

Lethal shot areas for turkeys

deliver. In a penetration study by ballistics expert Tom Roster (commissioned by Winchester-Olin Company), data revealed that at least 3 pellets (of any size) must strike the turkey's brain and spinal cord area. One of those 3 pellets must penetrate bone and smash neural tissue. Data also revealed that an average of 13 pellets must strike the head or neck to get an average of 3 pellets in the lethal area. Shots under 30 yards favor a hunter using #5 or #6 pellets, because of the increased number in a load, but shots longer than 30 yards require the energy of #4s.

Pellet Size	20 Yards	30 Yards	40 Yards
#7 $1/2$ (0.095 inch, 338 oz.)			
Velocity (feet per second)	940	790	670
Energy (foot-pounds)	2.5	1.8	1.3
#6 (0.110 inch, 218 oz.)			
Velocity	980	840	720
Energy	4.2	3.0	2.3
#5 (0.120 inch, 168 oz.)			
Velocity	1,000	860	750
Energy	5.6	4.2	3.2
#4 (0.130 inch, 132 oz.)			
Velocity	1,020	890	780
Energy	7.4	5.6	4.4
#2 (0.150 inch, 86 oz.)			
Velocity	1,050	930	820
Energy	12.2	9.5	7.5

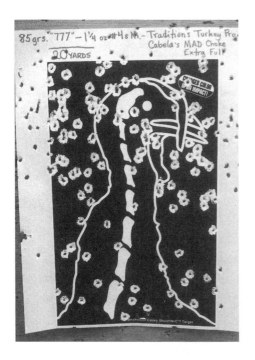
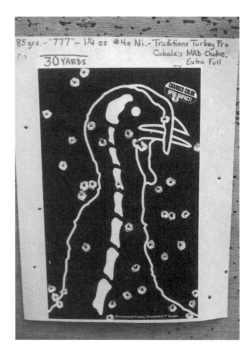
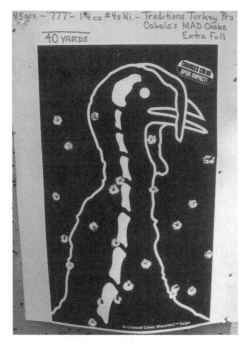

Pellet pattern density quickly decreases as the shooter moves back. These three practice targets make it as plain as the waddle under the turkey's beak: 30 yards is okay, but 20 yards is better.

In my tests, the #7 $\frac{1}{2}$s flattened out on the bony vertebrae with good pattern density, but they didn't penetrate. Some of the #6s penetrated between the vertebrae, but not through the vertebrae or skull at 30 yards; they did have a winning pattern density, however. I decided to stick with the fewer pellets in a #4 load, betting on increased penetration.

One of the simplest ways to tighten a shotgun pattern is by using a plastic shot cup. The plastic saves the bore from friction with the shot, and it restricts the expansion of the shot as it exits the muzzle, giving an overall increase of 5 to 10 percent in density.

Pellet hardness, the third variable, affects deformity, both during acceleration inside the barrel and during penetration of feathers and bone. The harder the pellet, the better the chance of reaching the goal of brain or spinal cord impact. Round, hard pellets also increase pattern densities. But hardness should not come at the expense of less weight, which leads to a decrease in penetration. Therefore, muzzleloading shotgunners should stick to pellet materials such as lead, bismuth, and tungsten or iron.

Material	Density (grams per cubic centimeter)
Tungsten	10.4
Lead	11.1
Steel	7.9
Bismuth	9.4

Now that I had defined my choice of velocity and size of the shot, the question of hardness still needed testing. Soft lead flattens out too easily to be a good choice for penetration. Hardened lead is better; this is referred to as chilled shot and is commonly available. Copper-plated chilled shot is even better, and steel shot is the best in the penetration department. Steel shot, however, lacks the mass of lead, necessary to retain energy, which means that you may want to limit your shots to 30 yards. My tests with steel proved that the hardened-iron pellets give excellent patterns, but you need a modern barrel that is designed to handle the stresses generated by this hard pellet load.

Although my tests did not include the latest in shot technologies (bismuth and tungsten) because they were not available over the counter, it would not surprise me if future muzzleloading shotguns take advantage of their heavier masses and retained energies. But a word of caution is in order: older muzzleloading shotgun barrels may not be equipped to handle anything other than lead shot.

What occurred one foggy spring morning some two decades ago was a disappointment that still stings my hunting memories. As fate would have it, a big bronze-feathered boss gobbler responded to the soft yelps of my guide. Noted outdoor writer Shirley Grenoble had worked her magic and pulled the bird to within 25 yards. A big red, white, and blue head periscoped above the mayapples to take a "look see." Orange fire, red hot sparks, and the breath of a dragon blew the swarm of pellets straight to the target, slapped the turkey to the leaves. As the roar echoed down the valley, the downed gobbler shook its head, oriented itself and set its wings over the edge of the ridge as my empty smokepole and I stood speechless.

If the stock is too long for a young hunter, measure your trigger pull and cut off the stock. This may be a job you'd rather trust to a qualified gunsmith.

Only the right barrel of this big 10-gauge was needed to bag the bird.

Butch Dill and I celebrate after downing this turkey, which serves as further proof of the effectiveness of muzzleloaders.

That gobbler had absorbed a good percentage of a 10-gauge, $1^1/_2$-ounce load, fired at approximately 1,100 feet per second, and lived to gobble another day. Why? The answer is penetration. I had unwisely opted for the dense pattern of the #7$^1/_2$ pellets, but they just didn't have the oomph to penetrate the turkey's vertebrae. Every hunter has the moral responsibility to learn from his or her mistakes, and I set out to learn from mine.

The first bird to test my load the next spring was a "silent Sam." Clearly, I intended to correct my mistakes from the previous hunt. This gobbler had spoken only once while on the roost, and as soon as he joined up with his flock of ladies, the woods filled with sounds of songbirds and squirrels, not turkeys. Having worked silent Sam the week before, I knew where he was headed. Lower on the ridge was a grassy field, abandoned by a bankrupt dairy farmer and waiting for another wildlife-endangering housing project. There was only one logging road that crossed the shallow stream at the bottom of the hill, and this was my destination.

My friend, world-champion turkey caller Butch Dill, and I did an end-around football maneuver, set up the FeatherFlex hens, and waited for Sam. He heard the diaphragm yelps, spotted the hen decoys, and, anxious to take advantage, made a beeline to our trap.

I barely had time to pull the hammers back to full cock before his blushing, wrinkly head appeared over the brass beads on the top flat of the shotgun. *Boom!* The 10-gauge, loaded with a century load (100 grains of FFg and a 100-grain volume of pellets), roared to life, silent Sam did a backflip, and two hunters did a back-slapping jig to celebrate their success. I felt redeemed with this new load of #5 pellets.

LOADING

The years since that hunt have seen a number of improvements in the sport of muzzleloading smoothbores. Plastic shot cups, lube-impregnated wads, shotgun quick loads, and even new types of propellants have all made an impact. But the process of loading a smokepole is still the same. You need to start with a clean barrel, devoid of oils as well as fouling. Snap a couple of caps to blow out any cleaning oils from the nipples, or pick the touch holes of flintlocks. Then measure an equal volume of powder and shot, separated by the overpowder card or cushion wad, and finally, a thin overshot card.

When this load is rammed home, an audible hiss from the breech will alert you to the fact that the nipple or touch hole is clear and ready for priming. But always check the mark on your ramrod to be sure that the load is seated properly. Also, as a safety precaution, don't prime the shotgun until you have set up and are in a turkey hunting position. Smokepoles have only the half-

Smoothbore trade guns like the one used by Keith Bayha on Nebraska Merriams offer muzzleloaders new challenges and opportunities for satisfaction.

The thickness of plastic shot collar, fiber wads, and cardboard cards affects pattern destiny.

cock position for a safety, and by not capping or priming the gun before you walk to your setup, you are ensuring a safe day for everyone enjoying the sport.

Muzzleloading shotguns must be cylinder bore in order to get the wads and cards down the barrel. This is why many oldtime shotguns fell into disuse when breechloaders were invented. The muzzleloaders couldn't have chokes unless metal could be removed from their heavy steel barrels in a process known as jug choking. Today's muzzleloading shotguns are superior, in that they have screw-in chokes. This allows the constriction chokes to be removed for loading and then replaced, giving pattern performance equal to that of modern, effective chokes.

The type of choke is determined by its ability to throw 70 percent of the shot into a 30-inch circle at 40 yards. The following table lists expected patterns from various chokes:

System	Percent of Pellets at 40 Yards
Turkey extra full	≥ 80
Full choke	70–80
Modified	55–65
Improved cylinder	45–55
Cylinder	≤ 45

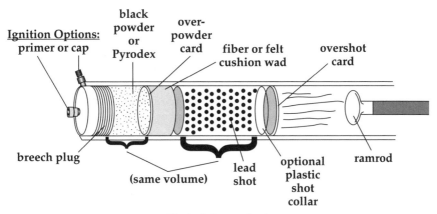

Typical shotgun load

Now that waterfowlers are required to use steel shot, modern muzzleloading shotguns are being outfitted with molychrome steel barrels and other alloys that allow the guns to weather the abrasion of the shot. Plastic shot collars really improve the performance of these modern pellets and reduce barrel wear as well. But although steel flies faster, it is still not the best choice for muzzleloading turkey.

Shotgun loads are heavy projectiles, ranging from 1 ounce (437.5 grains) to 2 ounces (875 grains) of lead or steel. With that

TURKEY HUNTING 101

- Clean the clean shotgun bore of grease and oil.
- Snap a cap to clear the nipple, and place the hammer at safe or half cock.
- Load 100 grains of FFg black powder.
- Load an overpowder card, followed by a cushion wad and plastic shot cup. Listen for the hiss from the nipple so that you know the channel is clear.
- Using the same powder measurer, load 100 grain-volume of #4 chilled lead shot.
- Load one thin overshot card.
- Cap the shotgun when you set up and hear the gobbler coming in.
- Smoke that under 30-yard gobbler when he flashes his red, white, and blue head by aiming just under the eye.
- Invite everyone you know to a backyard barbecue where "smoked gobbler" is on the menu.

much mass in front of your powder charge, be absolutely certain to use the right granule size of powder, FFg black powder or RS Pyrodex. Never load more than the manufacturer's safe maximum. Those thin shotgun barrels are not designed to be overloaded. Besides, hits of fewer than 6 pellets are usually lethal on any game bird, and you have 132 pellets of #4s in a light 1-ounce load. So shoot straight, and the shotgun will do the rest.

TURKEY-HUNTING GEAR

Powder. Regardless of whether you choose to shoot FFg black powder or shotgun replica powder, you need a way to carry it. Traditionalists like me prefer a black powder flask; modern shotgunners prefer plastic tubes.

Powder measurer. If you are not using premeasured loads, you need to carry a volumetric grain measurer or drams dipper to accurately measure the load. I like to carry a hollowed-out antler tip measurer; it never changes its volume during transit, unlike some plastic and brass expandable measurers.

Overpowder wads. Both cardboard and felt wads cushion the shot and seal the bore during the initial acceleration of the burning powder. This prevents the shot from distorting out of its round shape. It also improves your pattern density, because round shot flies a straighter trajectory than flattened shot does.

Plastic shot cups. These inexpensive shot collars prevent the shot from eroding against the steel barrel as it accelerates forward, improving patterns.

Shot. These tiny roundballs of lead, steel, bismuth, tungsten-iron, or other metal alloys are difficult to handle loose. They need to be stored in a shot flask, shot bag, or plastic loader.

Overshot cards. Slightly thinner than overpowder wads, overshot cards have only one job: to keep the shot from rolling down the barrel. Use the thinnest card of paper, cork, Styrofoam, toilet paper, or hornets' nest paper that will stop the shot from rolling around.

Primers. If you are using a flintlock, that means toting a priming horn filled with FFFFg black powder, as well as a spare flint. Percussion shooters need to carry a capping tool filled with the standard #11 cap, #2 musket cap, or 209 shotgun primer. Carried loosely, these metallic primers can get dirty, malfunction, and make a rattly noise.

Nipple pick, wrench, and cap remover. Even modern muzzleloaders may need a little preventive maintenance. You might even want to carry a breech plug wrench for an emergency takedown.

Turkey calls. Regardless of whether turkey calls are blown, vibrated, flipped, scraped, or rubbed, you need to call the bird into your lethal range.

Turkey-Hunting Basics

Shooting a muzzleloading shotgun is a far cry from shooting a rifle. Although an individual shotgun pellet doesn't have the power or accuracy of a longrifle's roundball, when the pellets are put together into an angry swarm of shot fired from a smoothbore, their knockdown power is immense.

Saplings kept getting in my way, and a platoon of lichen-covered boulders obscured a clear view of the bird. Aligning the shotgun's two brass beads on the bobbing and weaving head of this bronze-gilded ridge runner was testing every ounce of nerve I had. The gobbler was only 15 yards away, and I wouldn't have the opportunity to move into a better position.

TURKEY-HUNTING GEAR *continued*

Head net and gloves. The gleam of bare skin will not help you get a turkey close.

Fluorescent orange. As you walk in to your setup, and especially when you leave the field or forest with a turkey slung over your shoulder, it is vital that other hunters can identify your dark silhouette as a human—not something to shoot at.

Insect repellent. Mosquitoes and black flies can bring a world of hurt to exposed skin when the temperature gets above 50 degrees. Although turkeys cannot smell the DEET in repellent, the chemical can melt plastic. Better yet, carry a Therma-Cell to keep the flies 15 feet away.

Emergency and first-aid kits. We all get cut, scraped, and bumped as we sneak through dark woods. Don't forget tweezers for ticks that manage to get past your gaiters and insect repellent. Carrying an antihistamine can relieve nasty reactions to stinging insects. A whistle, flashlight, radio, and cell phone will bring help fast.

Binoculars. Without binoculars, you can't tell the difference between a dark object, a stump, or a hunter—let alone a hen or a jake—in the limited light of predawn. I like to carry compact binoculars, regardless of what I am hunting.

Laser range finder. Knowing the maximum distance for putting the hammer down on a gobbler is vital for muzzleloaders. Target and range different natural features before you start calling to answer any question about lethal distances.

Compass or GPS. Getting lost is not fun.

When using a muzzleloading shotgun at full choke, it is possible to get too close.

Flushed with exuberance for spring, this talking tom was letting it all hang out—his beard, his tail, and his booming gobble. Only an arm's length from permanent cover, he stopped, strutted, fanned, and flaunted his maleness. My love-struck plastic hen did not respond to his ardor, but a load of #4s driven by a century's worth of FFg black powder did. Before the white smoke cleared and the echo of the shot could return from the opposite ridge, this baron of the beech ridge was down for the count.

Knowing that a flock of turkeys roosts on a ridge and feeds in a valley field is not enough information for a muzzleloading turkey hunter to be successful. In most states, spring gobbler hunting is restricted to the morning hours. This means that the hunter should be putting the turkeys to bed the night before. Fortunately, the birds help us in this regard, as they love to cackle while flying up into their favorite roost trees, saying good night.

A load of #4s driven by FFg black powder downed this gobbler.

Roosting areas are usually used more than once, as evidenced by the incredible amount of turkey droppings found beneath certain favored trees. A typical roosting tree is large and open and provides a good escape tunnel through the canopy. If you find such an ideal roost, don't automatically count on the birds' being there every night, however. Weather has a definite effect on whether they roost high on a ridge or lower on a bench. Hunting pressure can also force the flock to change location.

Having located an often-used roosting site, the next detail to ponder is where you should set up to call. Wild turkeys can be mindful of details, especially when something in their environment is new or misplaced. If that clump of bush sprouting a major branch wasn't within sight last night when they roosted, the turkeys will certainly be upset by its appearance the next morning. In other words, don't invade their bedroom when you are setting up—you are too close. Even the less experienced jakes know every rock, shrub, and tree within 50 yards of their favorite roost tree.

When smoking a gobbler, you need to call the bird within 30 yards of your setup, but 20 would be even better. Put yourself in a spot with an open forest floor that provides good visibility and uncluttered shooting fields. This is especially important when using decoys. But be aware of barriers. One of the main reasons a gobbler won't come in past that magic 40-yard barrier may be because a creek, pond, road, or fence has stopped the strutting gobbler cold.

If you are not familiar with an area that may have unknown obstacles, opt for a flat ridgetop, because there are generally few natural disruptions. If your state allows the construction of a blind, particularly a natural one made from green vegetation, use one. A natural fence of branches or ferns allows you to make the necessary adjustments in your aiming posture without allowing the bird to key in on your movement. But be careful not to silhouette your blind along a ridgetop edge. Gobblers can pick up on this faster than a gunner can blink.

Once you have located your gobbler, either by putting him to roost the night before or by causing him to divulge his position in response to your attractor calls, it is time to get serious about calling. My advice to greenhorns is to start with the basics. A gobbler comes in to a hen for one reason: he's in pursuit of a willing mate. To get him started in the right direction, a soft cluck or series of soft yelps will bring him off the roost. If you don't score shortly after the fly-down, and the bird has left the area, you need to create a shock-gobble situation. Use of a loud crow, red-tailed hawk, or lost turkey call will most likely get a single nasty gobble from your phantom bird, allowing you to key into the bird's new location.

One of the earliest types of turkey calls, which was shown to our early muzzleloading ancestors by the woodland Indians, is made from the turkey wing bone. Many self-styled modern mountain men forsake all other calls as inauthentic, but I have noticed the widespread improvement attained with a cow-horn-tipped bellows. With a bit of practice, this call can be made to thunder across the valley or to softly "sing in" a shy tom. Perhaps the best all-around call for honest sound and versatility is the wooden box call. I have called in more gobblers with my faithful Lynch box call over the years than with all the slate, glass, diaphragm, and other calls

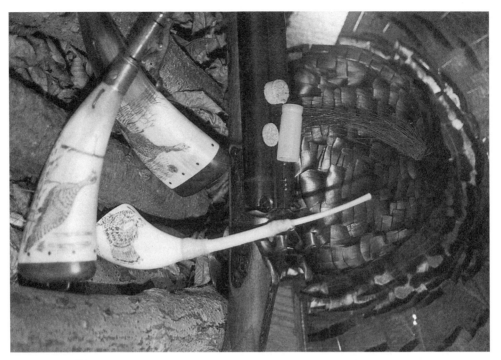

One of the earliest types of turkey calls, which was shown to early muzzleloaders by American Indians, was the turkey wingbone call.

put together. It just seems to be the easiest for me to control, and the birds respond to the sounds in spite of the less than perfect cadences. And when you are making a loud, rapid series of clucks and yelps (called "cutting"), the box call is the simplest to control.

The bottom line for getting a gobbler into black powder range is to tone down your calling. In other words, whisper your love yelps. Loud, aggressive calling is great when you are shouting across the room to get someone's attention, but when you want to get intimate, you need soft, sweet music.

Safety Considerations

Red, white, and blue—those colors are true, and they don't run, unless they are atop the bronze-edged black feathers of a wild turkey. Add a booming *gobble-gobble* to the still air of early dawn,

It is easy to tell a gobbler's head from a hen's. The hen's shades of blue and gray can't match the intensity of the mature gobbler's red, white, and blue.

and it is easy to see why hunters become so emotional about this sport. However, the thrill needs to be kept within a safe framework.

From a nonhunter's perspective, it might seem incredible that anyone could mistake a human for a turkey. Although hunting is a far safer sport than it was just a few decades ago, Pennsylvania continues to have nearly 100 shooting accidents each year. And turkey season continues to be one of the leading periods when those accidents occur.

According to the Pennsylvania chapter of the National Wild Turkey Federation (NWTF), hunters should be aware of the three S's of turkey hunting: scouting, sight, and safety. Scouting means knowing where the birds are before the season, where they roost, where they feed, and what travel routes they follow. The edges of wheat fields and unplowed corn stubble leave visible signs that turkeys are present. Glassing for turkey in grass fields is another popular spring pastime that reaps benefits. A hunter who knows where to set up for decoying and calling birds gains a real advantage. Sight reminds hunters to absolutely identify a target before pulling the trigger.

"Safety is the number-one issue when turkey hunting," states Don Heckman, executive officer of the Pennsylvania chapter of the NWTF. "No turkey is worth shooting someone or being shot at. It could cost you your life or someone else's. No turkey is worth being crippled and left to die because of a mistake in shooting judgment." Heckman offers the following defensive turkey hunting guidelines.

Be careful when choosing a type of turkey call for your spring hunt. While it might challenge a turkey to reveal his location, it may also attract other turkey hunters in your area. Stick with the love sounds of a calling hen.

- Never stalk a turkey. The chances of getting close enough for a shot are slim, but the chances of becoming involved in an accident are increased.
- Eliminate the colors red, white, and blue from your turkey hunting outfit. Red is the color most hunters count on to differentiate a gobbler's head from a hen's blue-colored head.
- Never move, wave, or make turkey sounds to alert another hunter of your presence. A quick movement may draw fire. Yell in a loud voice and remain motionless.
- Never attempt to approach closer than 100 yards to a roosting turkey. The wild turkey's eyesight and hearing are much too sharp to let you get any closer.
- Be particularly careful when using the gobbler call. The sound and motion may attract other hunters.
- When selecting your calling position, don't try to hide so well that you can't see what's happening. Remember, eliminating movement—not total concealment—is the key to success.

Select a calling position that provides a background as wide as your shoulders and one that completely protects you from the top of your head down. Position yourself so that you can see 180 degrees in front of you.

- Camouflage conceals you, but it does not make you invisible. When turkey hunting, think and act defensively. Avoid all unnecessary movement. Remember, you are visible to both turkeys and hunters when you move even slightly.
- Any time you use a turkey decoy, you are increasing the chance of an accident. If you use a decoy, place it so that you are not in danger of being shot.
- Finally, when hunting with companions, be certain of everyone's location, and know the area where they are going to hunt. Even if you are on land where you have sole permission to hunt, do not assume that there are no other hunters.

The joys of turkey hunting include the colors of dawn in the spring woods, the smell of earth and early wildflowers, and the sounds of birds awakening to the new day. Bagging a gobbler is only an exclamation point to a great morning. Make it a safe trip by hunting defensively.

Lessons Learned in the Field

The predawn stillness and the trees, silhouetted by stretched rays of sunlight battling against the night, were suddenly brought to life by the piercing scream of a coyote greeting yet another Nebraska day. This was fur trade country, the rolling Pine Ridge of the Sioux. Prairie grasses, invigorated with the nurturing water of melted snows, flushed green with life as white wildflowers dotted the rolling hills like errant snowballs. And answering the early-morning challenge of the coyote's wail was the booming thunder of a Merriam turkey gobble.

Spring gobbler season brings a sense of relief to hunters. The long period of cabin-crazy winter inactivity is finally over. The spring gobbler hunt also brings the anticipation of getting back to the woods with a renewed sense of purpose. Like many sportsmen,

Here's where we took the Nebraska Merriam.

I too felt the pull of camouflage and turkey calls and couldn't wait for the calendar to reveal the month of May. Sports show seminars and TV programs had armed me with everything I needed to know—or so I thought—when suddenly the phone rang.

"Dave," the enthusiastic voice questioned, "how would you like to go to Nebraska?" Pause. "We'll fly out of Newark and get a rental car in Denver, meet up with Keith Bayha, NMLRA field rep from Alaska, and head to Chadron. What do you think?" Pause. "Yeah, it will be a quick out and back, maybe four days, but we might get a crack at a bunch of Merriams!"

Merriams. Jim Fulmer, president of the National Muzzle Loading Rifle Association, had said the magic word. Having hunted Eastern, Osceola, and Rio Grande turkey species, I was anxious to experience the big bird of the western Sand Hills and Pine Ridge country.

"The NMLRA will be sponsoring one of the dioramas at the Museum of the Fur Trade in Chadron. Keith and I will present a

The Museum of the Fur Trade bears witness to another time, an age of smoothbore trade guns and Plains Indians.

check to the museum director, Gail DeBuse Potter, to help with the expansion program at the museum. One of the members, Jody Stumf, has a 2,500-acre ranch nearby that is crawling with Merriams and offered to take us hunting. We leave in a week. Okay?" Pause. "Hey. What do you think? Want to go?"

"Would Jeremiah Johnson pass up the opportunity to see something new in the high country?" I replied in the affirmative. "How about getting together and patterning what we're going to shoot?"

The Museum of the Fur Trade has the world's largest and most complete collection of Indian trade guns, Kentuckies, Henry of Boulton (Pennsylvania) trade guns, Hawken rifles, buffalo guns, and Winchesters. All are historic guns with a personal story to tell, and each had the potential of being used on Merriam turkeys. Usually about .58 caliber in smoothbore, they accurately shot a half-ounce ball of lead for big game or an ounce of shot for turkey. These 28-gauge smoothbores may seem a tad light by today's 10-gauge standard, but historically, they got the job done.

Motivated by the thought of being in the land visited by Lewis and Clark's Voyage of Discovery, Jim and Keith decided that they would also be carrying historic smoothbores. Jim chose a .69 Charlotteville flintlock smoothbore musket, while Keith went with a .62-caliber, custom-built, flintlock trade gun. Not possessing anything remotely historic, I picked a T/C 12-gauge New Englander percussion, modified with a Remington extra-full choke, from my cache of muzzleloading shotguns.

Patterning? Shot density? Apparently, the Shawnee, Sioux, Crow, and other Native American tribes didn't worry about such things. These original Americans just placed a patched ball over the powder, followed by a bunch of birdshot, and the buck and ball load was expected to take care of whatever got in front of it. Unfortunately, today's hunting regulations don't allow for buck and ball loads, so Jim and Keith needed to get serious about creating as tight as pattern as possible with their cylinder-bore trade guns.

Volume for volume refers to the volume of powder compared with the volume of shot. Jim fed his Charlotteville 85 grains of FFg, followed by a vegetable-oiled fiber wad over the powder; a Cabela's plastic shot cup, which he sliced twice to create petals; $1^3/8$ ounces of #6 chilled lead shot; and a paper overshot card.

CHILLED LEAD SHOT VOLUME (NUMBER OF PELLETS)

Size	1 oz.	$1^1/8$ oz.	$1^1/4$ oz.	$1^3/8$ oz.	$1^1/2$ oz.	$1^5/8$ oz.
$7^1/2$	345	388	431	474	518	561
6	223	251	279	307	335	362
5	172	194	215	237	258	280
4	136	153	170	187	204	221
2	88	99	110	121	132	143

Note: Always follow the safety recommendations for each manufacturer's shotgun. *Never* exceed the maximum safe load.

Without the shot cup, the shot density could be described, at best, as a pathetic cylinder-bore pattern at 25 yards. With the shot cup, the pattern tightened to a definite modified choke pattern. Although neither of the loads inspired confidence on a big gobbler beyond 25 yards, Jim felt that he could sweet-talk a bird in close enough so that the swarm of shot from the venerable .69 would have a lethal effect.

After shooting the T/C New Englander, it was immediately obvious that the extra-full Remington choke made a difference. Thirty-yard patterns were impressive, and even the 40-yarders were lethal. By reducing the diameter of the bore near the muzzle, the shot string was compressed and elongated, creating a large percentage of pellets on target. Even with the century load of FFg and #5 shot, and using a red Ballistic Products shot cup, the balanced volume of powder and shot seemed to produce the best pattern.

Nickel-plated, copper-plated, and chilled lead shot were all tested. In spite of their higher price, the nickel- and copper-plated shot didn't do better in patterning, and in some tests, they were worse than the chilled lead. Though the results were eye-popping, we weren't sure why that happened. We realized that the plating had been done for other reasons, such as preventing corrosion and perhaps better penetration. However, if the shot didn't produce tighter patterns, we weren't going to use it on this trip.

It isn't easy traveling by air with firearms, especially muzzleloading firearms, so I called Continental Airlines beforehand for instructions. The answer was unequivocal: "Do not carry black powder!" Otherwise, a lockable hard case containing the gun, shot, and necessary tools would have to be declared upon entering the airport. I would have to prove that the gun was unloaded and incapable of being fired, sign the firearms declaration, run the cased gun through the X-ray scanner, ask security personnel to lock and tape the case, and

Without the shot cup, the shot density could best be described as a pathetic cylinder-bore pattern.

then I could be on my way. The major stumbling point is that most security staff don't understand why they can't see into the breech area to inspect for a cartridge, and their eyes bulge when you pull out the long ramrod to prove the bore's emptiness.

Denver's baggage claim considers gun cases oversized, but with a little identification, a lot of patience, and a bit of politeness, guns and luggage present little problem. The road trip to Chadron happened to take us through Sidney, a mandatory stop. We had only a half hour to make some last-minute muzzleloading purchases, such as the percussion caps and shotgun shell speed loaders that I needed. I happened to meet up with Mark Nelsen, Cabela's Internet communications manager, who had just come back from a successful Merriam hunt near Chadron. Mark and I had shared an adventure in Manitoba last September, and we were looking forward to our upcoming caribou hunt in Quebec in June.

Nickel-plated, copper-plated, and chilled lead shot have all been tested in the full-choked 12-gauge Turkey Pro. In spite of the higher price, the nickel- and copper-plated shot didn't perform any better in the patterning tests.

But talk soon focused on turkey calling and hunting strategies. His enthusiasm was contagious, and our trio couldn't wait to get back on the road again.

Three miles east of Chadron, on Route 20, we found the Museum of the Fur Trade. Noted on the Nebraska historical marker as the Bordeaux Trading Post, the museum grounds include the site of the trading house and warehouse, built of sod and logs into the bank of the Bordeaux Creek about 1833. It was an American Fur Company post until 1849; then Frenchman James Bordeaux operated it independently for the Sioux trade until 1872. Francis Boucher, a successor, ran the post until August 1876, when calvarymen confiscated illegal ammunition being sold to warring Indians. The actual museum exhibits the entire range of trade goods, including munitions, cutlery, axes, firearms, textiles, costumes, paint, beads, and countless other collections of the era.

The large Merriam turkey looms black against the golden prairie grasses. The flocks are large, and the birds challenging. Around Chadron, they're everywhere. Even the museum has its own resident flock along the Bordeaux Creek. But you can't hunt there beside the bird feeders and wandering cattle. To take a Merriam in fair chase, you need to suffer.

All turkey hunters are masochists. They punish their bodies with lack of sleep (we awoke each morning at 3 A.M.), lack of food (bad coffee and sugary doughnuts at the all-night convenience store), and endless miles of punishing terrain. Throw in a prickly pear cactus that Keith mistakenly thought was a green whoopee cushion, and you begin to understand the mind-set necessary for having fun.

With only a day and a half to find birds for three nonresident hunters (licenses are $79), Jody Stumf had his work cut out for him. Jody, the great-great-grandson of Oregon Trail homesteaders, is a full-time rancher. Fixing fences and running steers, plowing for winter wheat, and managing the timber operations allowed him to keep daily tabs on local flocks. Having already successfully called in a big tom for his son, he knew where to find the birds.

Compared with Eastern wild turkey, the Merriams were not very vocal, either on the roost or on the ground. Even the Buckwing decoys set into a seductive spread were not enough to dis-

Jody Stumf, a descendent of those who rode and settled along the Oregon Trail, is able to work magic on Merriam gobblers with his primitive wingbone turkey call.

tract the gobblers from their many hens. Without trees and under-brush to mask our movement, getting close enough for a muzzle-loading shot was difficult.

On the first morning, Jody used a turkey wing-bone call to pull a jake away from the flock. But the bird raised its periscope head above the buffalo grass, spotted Keith and Jody, and quickly exited. Later in the morning, Jody's gunsmith friend Tom Owen got Jim close enough for a shot, but the big black bird with buff-colored edges to his feathers didn't show a beard. No beard, no shot—that's the law.

Later that day, while hunting alone, I called a Merriam gobbler to within 75 yards. As he sneaked along a barbed-wire fence, paus-ing long enough to scope out my position, he never gobbled but did a spot-and-stalk parallel to my position. I purred with my Lynch box call, made soft alluring yelps and clucks with my River Valley glass and slate, even poured insistent cuttings into the air

Keith Bayha stares a hole through the bead at the end of his trade gun. Unfortunately, the Merriam is too far away for an ethical shot.

with my Hally Game Calls diaphragm (a mouth call). Nothing. Holding the brass bead of my New Englander just below his eyeball, I fought back the eagerness of my trigger finger. Sixty yards was too chancy with a muzzleloading shotgun, so I had to shut down that day's hunt.

Meanwhile, about a half mile up the hill behind my position, Jody's soft yelping on the turkey wing-bone call got Keith close once again. Jody loves to challenge Merriams the way his ancestors did with wing bones and primitive friction calls. His ranch also sponsors an annual "Fur Trade Days" rendezvous each July, when his fields come alive with tepees and lean-tos filled with buckskinners and Native Americans. This is a historic celebration of the fur trade era in Chadron.

Hearing only one gobble isn't unusual for a Merriam tom in the company of hens, so they decided to set up a little closer. What they found only 100 yards away was a pile of feathers. Apparently, the coyotes were doing a little spring gobbler hunting of their own.

That night, the museum's board got together at Jim and Ann Hanson's historic log cabin for dinner. Jim's collection of antique arms and native prairie wildlife renewed our enthusiasm for the next day's hunt. We were sure that we had the Merriams figured out. Almost.

Instead of the previous morning's drizzle and gray skies, Saturday's blazing sun had the turkeys making music from the tops of the ponderosa pines. With spirits high, we set off in two different directions. The gobblers were talking and walking. Jody's wing bone was exactly what they wanted to hear, and it wasn't long until a big Merriam appeared—on the other side of the canyon.

Meanwhile, Jim and Tom started several different birds that were reluctant to come in. Desperate times call for desperate measures. They decided to pull a "sneak." Prairie grass doesn't give a hunter a whole lot of cover, but using the pines along the edge of one canyon, Tom was able to close the distance to 40 yards. A crushing *whomp* echoed down the canyon as the load of #4s flipped the gobbler onto its back. As Tom ran to claim his prize, the big bird rolled over, ruffled his feathers, and headed for the pine ridge in a pitched footrace. The gobbler won.

As I set up my Buckwing jake and hen decoys at the edge of a Pennsylvania wheat field two days later, I kept getting flashbacks of the wide open spaces of western Nebraska and the trappers and traders who lived among the Sioux near Chadron. The Museum of the Fur Trade is a great destination for those who want to understand the westward migration; the Native Americans; the thriving trade of furs, muzzleloading guns, iron ware, and textiles; and

It took only one morning back in Pennsylvania and a spread of Buckwing decoys to bring a successful conclusion to the 2004 spring gobbler season.

The old Thompson/Center New Englander 12-gauge works its magic once again. Updated with a screw-in choke and a new kind of black powder, Swiss Authentic, this rig proved lightweight and devastatingly effective on gobblers.

melding of two cultures. The museum is open every day from Memorial Day until September from 8 A.M. to 5 P.M. It is located in northwestern Nebraska, three miles east of Chadron, on U.S. Highway 20. The Black Hills are 60 miles north, and the museum is on the way to Yellowstone National Park.

Kaboom! A fine 19-pound Eastern wild turkey lay silent at the edge of the wheat field as two hens flew away. While smoke from the 100 grains of FFg flavored the morning mist with sulfur, I could see how effectively the equal volume of #5s did their job. Hefting the big bird to my shoulder, I couldn't help but wonder how that early trapper must have felt as he gave a sigh of relief at the promise of food. Trade guns were born of the fur trade, but they live on in the hearts and minds of those who love to re-create history, as well as the few who cherish the added challenge.

The wild turkey was not only Ben Franklin's first choice as a symbol for the United States, it is also the professor emeritus of Woods Wisdom University. All who have hunted this noble bird have walked away in awe and wonder at its toughness and sagacity. Such was the case for Karl and me.

Now that my friend has joined the ranks of the retired, he has the time to do something he never did before: hunt spring gobblers. Karl is an avid deer hunter, an adventurer; he has even challenged the elk of Colorado with success. But as a successful senior engineer for one of the major automobile makers, his constant travel and dedication to his work had never allowed for a spring vacation.

But Karl's rural home in Longswamp Township is right in the middle of Eastern turkey country. More than once, he has looked out the kitchen window and watched a parade of turkeys walk through his backyard. Thinking that this might be a relaxing way to spend some mornings in May, he asked me to help him get started.

Camouflage clothing, a head net and gloves, and a full-choked shotgun were tools already in his possession. What Karl wanted was a chance to use them. If you have ever hunted the Appalachians in spring, you already know what happened. Rain, rain, and more rain not only dampened our spirits; it also caused the trees to rapidly leaf out, the bushes to green, and wildflowers to cover what was left of the forest floor. Visibility was taken from 50 yards down to less than 10 much earlier than we'd hoped. Even worse, the gobblers stopped gobbling. But there were lessons to be learned from the professor.

Lesson 1. The setup location is far more important than the music from slate, box, or mouth calls. On several occasions, a gobbler would sound off from the roost as we softly called in the dawn's early light. After locating the bird, decoys would be set, masks raised, gloves pulled, and communication commenced. But the bird and his harem always flew down toward the field, in the opposite direction of our setup. *Lesson learned:* Know the travel routes from roost to food, and get there first.

Lesson 2. As they say, patience is a virtue. When a gobbler no longer wanted to talk, I would get up and start folding my decoys. And on more than one occasion, I was stunned by a *putt, putt, putt* alarm call of a startled turkey. Recovering from the shock of a disappearing gobbler is not easy for any hunter. It is like unfolding a test and seeing a failing grade. *Lesson learned:* Be patient, sit tight, and wait. Many times, jakes and less-than-dominant gobblers will sneak in to mate with a hen while the boss gobbler does battle with a rival.

Lesson 3. Think green, wet, and bugs. The first two weeks of the spring season normally mean open woods, soft brown leaves,

The setup location is far more important than the music from slate, box, and mouth calls.

and cool temperatures. But this year, brown camo patterns were too dark a silhouette in the yellow-greens of spicebush, blueberry, and mayapple; camo patterns designed for green foliage invisibility would have been a better choice. With two constant weeks of rain, finding a dry place to sit was difficult. Because bagging a turkey requires immobility, a good waterproof seat is vital. My Breedlove cushion seat softened the rocks and sticks and kept my "foundation" off the wet leaves. Bugs can be intimidating. Not only do they bite and make irritating humming noises inside your ear; they also distract your eyes from the turkey as they maneuver inside your head net. *Lesson learned:* Spray your hat, netting, and cushion seat with repellent before you enter the woods.

Lesson 4. Get away from people. A 1-mile hike out the ridge produced a spot that reeked with turkey sign. The telltale scratchings of a flock were easy to spot. Turkey droppings, particularly the question-mark shapes left by the gobblers, signaled that the spot had recently been used. I had found this spot back in the flint-

Extra-full choke is not always the best option.

lock season and couldn't wait to try it. But apparently, others had too. My first soft clucks of the day were challenged by the louder yelps of another caller. When I didn't respond, the yelps grew more insistent. But as expected, the form moving through the brush wasn't a turkey; it was another hunter. After bumping into two others, I went home. *Lesson learned:* Remote is better than close to the road.

Lesson 5. Extra-full choke is not always extra special. While talking with a coworker, she related that her husband, a turkey hunter, had finally got a bird. Yes, I was jealous, but when I heard the whole story, I knew that life wasn't fair. This fellow, Jeff, had missed two birds in as many days, only to have a jake take flight in front of him as he was walking back to the car. It seems that Jeff had called in a big boss gobbler on the first morning. It strutted up between the decoy and Jeff, only 10 yards away, and when it came out of strut, Jeff fired at the head. Jeff's bird ducked, pirouetted, and scrambled to safety before a second shot could be fired. A few days later, the same ballet was performed with a different bird. Apparently, after patterning the gun at 10 yards, Jeff learned that the shot pattern made a single 3-inch hole on the paper. *Lesson learned:* Extra tight chokes are at their best when the turkey is beyond 30 yards. Any closer, and a modified choke would be better.

Although Karl and I didn't get a turkey, we got an education and can't wait until next year to use it. If you would like to get closer to the sport, contact the National Wild Turkey Federation.

The Wild Turkey Grand Slam

Turkey hunters are fanatics. They carefully acquire the perfect turkey calls, match their camouflaged clothing to the targeted environment, and zero in their shotguns for perfect patterns. And for many, the spring season is over with one squeeze of the trigger. In time, they lament not having more of a challenge.

Well, there is one challenge left for the few and proud, including fanatical muzzleloaders. You might call it the ultimate muzzleloading shotgun challenge. It will require not only skill and well-tuned equipment but also money, travel, and time away. The challenge is the pursuit of the four U.S. wild turkey species—called the grand slam. Every state but Alaska has at least one species, represented by the following:

Eastern wild turkey (*Meleagris gallopavo silvestris*). This is the most widely distributed of the four U.S. turkey species. The Eastern can be found almost everywhere east of the Mississippi River.

Eastern wild turkey

It has also been successfully introduced into the Pacific coast states of California, Oregon, and Washington. It even exists along the southern portions of Canada's 10 provinces. Easterns are large birds, often exceeding 30 pounds. The heaviest bird recorded by the National Wild Turkey Federation is 35.81

pounds. This bird is thought to be the most difficult to harvest, in spite of the large population of hunters in its range.

Merriam's turkey (*Meleagris gallopovo merriami*). Originally located in Arizona, New Mexico, and Colorado, the Merriam has expanded its range into Nebraska, South Dakota, Oregon, and Wash-

Merriam's turkey

ington. Slightly smaller than the Eastern, it has distinctive white edging to its lower back and tail feathers. Hunters west of the Mississippi will find this bird along the hills and ridges above the grassy prairie. It is typical for this turkey to feed and roost in large flocks.

Rio Grande turkey (*Meleagris gallopavo intermedia*). Named for its range, which encompasses the Rio Grande River dividing Texas and Mexico, this turkey is a survivor of arid desert country. Noted for their long legs and their ability to use them, hens weigh about 10 pounds, and toms usually tip the scales at less than 20. Trees, when available, are favorite roost sites, but this nomadic bird is often found roosting atop power lines and windmill towers. The states hosting populations of Rios include Texas and other Central Plains states, as well as Mexico. They have been successfully introduced into Nevada, Utah, Wyoming, South Dakota, California, Oregon, and Washington.

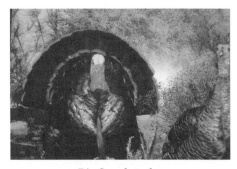

Rio Grande turkey

Osceola turkey (*Meleagris gallopavo osceola*). This is the rarest turkey species in the United States. Limited in range to the Florida peninsula, this turkey is similar in appearance to the Eastern, but it checks in at about half

Osceola turkey

Gould's wild turkey

Ocellated wild turkey

the weight. Hunting the Osceola in the palmetto swamps of Florida is a real challenge, and this bird may prove to be the most difficult of all four species to harvest.

I know of about a dozen muzzleloading hunters who have completed this lofty challenge. An additional achievement, a royal slam, requires the addition of a Gould's wild turkey. This species is a resident of Mexico, and hunters will find it an interesting challenge to get their gear and black powder into this country. The Gould is similar in appearance to the Merriam because of its white-tipped tail feathers, but it is smaller in body size.

The ultimate in turkey hunting success for a muzzleloader is the world slam, which requires the Eastern, Merriam, Rio Grande, Osceola, and one more—the Ocellated wild turkey. This species makes its home in the dense jungles of Central America and, like the Mexican Gould, it poses a daunting challenge for traveling muzzleloaders. This small, spotted turkey looks quite different from the more typical U.S. turkey species. Even its call is unlike the normal gobble that hunters expect. A secretive jungle bird, it must be ambushed, rather than calling it in.

Although it is not necessary to achieve the ultimate "slams" of turkey hunting to feel real achievement, you have to envy those who have the time and resources to make the quest.

MUZZLELOADING ORGANIZATIONS, COMPETITIONS, AND SHOWS

National Organizations

National Muzzleloading Rifle Association (PO Box 67, Friendship, IN 47021; 821-667-5131, 800-745-1493; www.nmlra@nmlra.org). Preserves, promotes, and supports shooting sports and hunting with muzzleloading guns.

Longhunter Society (PO Box 67, Friendship, IN 47021; 812-667-5131, ext. 221, or 800-745-1493, ext. 221; www.nmlra.org/long hunter.htm). Promotes the hunting of big game with muzzleloaders.

National Rifle Association (11250 Waples Hill Road, Fairfax, VA 22030; 703-267-1500; www.nra.org). Supports firearms ownership, gun safety, and hunter education.

Boone & Crockett Club (250 Station Drive, Missoula, MT 59801; 406-542-1888, www.boone-crockett.org). Nonprofit organization founded in 1887 by Theodore Roosevelt; this is the primary organization for compiling big-game records, and its system of measurement is the benchmark among organizations. See the next two pages for a sample entry sheet.

Hunt Fair Chase (www.huntfairchase.com) is a new organization that focuses on hunting ethics.

National Shooting Sports Foundation (Flintlock Ridge Office Center, 11 Mile Hill Road, Newtown, CT 06470-2359; 203-426-1320, 203-426-1087; www.nssf.org). Nonprofit trade organization that focuses on communication and marketing for all the shooting sports organizations.

Records of
North American
Big Game

250 Station Drive
Missoula, MT 59801
(406) 542-1888

BOONE AND CROCKETT CLUB®
OFFICIAL SCORING SYSTEM FOR NORTH AMERICAN BIG GAME TROPHIES

TYPICAL
WHITETAIL AND COUES' DEER

MINIMUM SCORES		
	AWARDS	ALL-TIME
whitetail	160	170
Coues'	100	110

KIND OF DEER (check one)
☐ whitetail
☐ Coues'

Detail of Point
Measurement

Abnormal Points	
Right Antler	Left Antler
SUBTOTALS	
TOTAL TO E	

SEE OTHER SIDE FOR INSTRUCTIONS			COLUMN 1	COLUMN 2	COLUMN 3	COLUMN 4
A. No. Points on Right Antler		No. Points on Left Antler	Spread Credit	Right Antler	Left Antler	Difference
B. Tip to Tip Spread		C. Greatest Spread				
D. Inside Spread of Main Beams		SPREAD CREDIT MAY EQUAL BUT NOT EXCEED LONGER MAIN BEAM				
E. Total of Lengths of Abnormal Points						
F. Length of Main Beam						
G-1. Length of First Point						
G-2. Length of Second Point						
G-3. Length of Third Point						
G-4. Length of Fourth Point, If Present						
G-5. Length of Fifth Point, If Present						
G-6. Length of Sixth Point, If Present						
G-7. Length of Seventh Point, If Present						
H-1. Circumference at Smallest Place Between Burr and First Point						
H-2. Circumference at Smallest Place Between First and Second Points						
H-3. Circumference at Smallest Place Between Second and Third Points						
H-4. Circumference at Smallest Place Between Third and Fourth Points						
		TOTALS				

ADD	Column 1		Exact Locality Where Killed:	
	Column 2		Date Killed:	Hunter:
	Column 3		Owner:	Telephone #:
	Subtotal		Owner's Address:	
SUBTRACT Column 4			Guide's Name and Address:	
FINAL SCORE			Remarks: (Mention Any Abnormalities or Unique Qualities)	

OM I.D.
Number

I, _____ , certify that I have measured this trophy on _____

PRINT NAME   MM/DD/YYYY

at _____

STREET ADDRESS   CITY   STATE/PROVINCE

and that these measurements and data are, to the best of my knowledge and belief, made in accordance with the instructions given.

Witness: _____   Signature: _____   I.D. Number

                                                B&C OFFICIAL MEASURER

INSTRUCTIONS FOR MEASURING TYPICAL WHITETAIL AND COUES' DEER

All measurements must be made with a 1/4-inch wide flexible steel tape to the nearest one-eighth of an inch. (Note: A flexible steel cable can be used to measure points and main beams only.) Enter fractional figures in eighths, without reduction. Official measurements cannot be taken until the antlers have air dried for at least 60 days after the animal was killed.

A. Number of Points on Each Antler: To be counted a point, the projection must be at least one inch long, with the length exceeding width at one inch or more of length. All points are measured from tip of point to nearest edge of beam as illustrated. Beam tip is counted as a point but not measured as a point.

B. Tip to Tip Spread is measured between tips of main beams.

C. Greatest Spread is measured between perpendiculars at a right angle to the center line of the skull at widest part, whether across main beams or points.

D. Inside Spread of Main Beams is measured at a right angle to the center line of the skull at widest point between main beams. Enter this measurement again as the Spread Credit if it is less than or equal to the length of the longer main beam; if greater, enter longer main beam length for Spread Credit.

E. Total of Lengths of all Abnormal Points: Abnormal Points are those non-typical in location (such as points originating from a point or from bottom or sides of main beam) or extra points beyond the normal pattern of points. Measure in usual manner and enter in appropriate blanks.

F. Length of Main Beam is measured from the center of the lowest outside edge of burr over the outer side to the most distant point of the main beam. The point of beginning is that point on the burr where the center line along the outer side of the beam intersects the burr, then following generally the line of the illustration.

G-1-2-3-4-5-6-7. Length of Normal Points: Normal points project from the top of the main beam. They are measured from nearest edge of main beam over outer curve to tip. Lay the tape along the outer curve of the beam so that the top edge of the tape coincides with the top edge of the beam on both sides of the point to determine the baseline for point measurements. Record point lengths in appropriate blanks.

H-1-2-3-4. Circumferences are taken as detailed in illustration for each measurement. If brow point is missing, take H-1 and H-2 at smallest place between burr and G-2. If G-4 is missing, take H-4 halfway between G-3 and tip of main beam.

ENTRY AFFIDAVIT FOR ALL HUNTER-TAKEN TROPHIES

For the purpose of entry into the Boone and Crockett Club's® records, North American big game harvested by the use of the following methods or under the following conditions are ineligible:

   I.   Spotting or herding game from the air, followed by landing in its vicinity for the purpose of pursuit and shooting;
   II.   Herding or chasing with the aid of any motorized equipment;
   III.   Use of electronic communication devices, artificial lighting, or electronic light intensifying devices;
   IV.   Confined by artificial barriers, including escape-proof fenced enclosures;
   V.   Transplanted for the purpose of commercial shooting;
   VI.   By the use of traps or pharmaceuticals;
   VII.   While swimming, helpless in deep snow, or helpless in any other natural or artificial medium;
   VIII.   On another hunter's license;
   IX.   Not in full compliance with the game laws or regulations of the federal government or of any state, province, territory, or tribal council on reservations or tribal lands;

I certify that the trophy scored on this chart was not taken in violation of the conditions listed above. In signing this statement, I understand that if the information provided on this entry is found to be misrepresented or fraudulent in any respect, it will not be accepted into the Awards Program and 1) all of my prior entries are subject to deletion from future editions of **Records of North American Big Game** 2) future entries may not be accepted.

FAIR CHASE, as defined by the Boone and Crockett Club®, is the ethical, sportsmanlike and lawful pursuit and taking of any free-ranging wild, native North American big game animal in a manner that does not give the hunter an improper advantage over such game animals.

The Boone and Crockett Club® may exclude the entry of any animal that it deems to have been taken in an unethical manner or under conditions deemed inappropriate by the Club.

Date: _____ Signature of Hunter: _____

                                          (SIGNATURE MUST BE WITNESSED BY AN OFFICIAL MEASURER OR A NOTARY PUBLIC.)

Date: _____ Signature of Notary or Official Measurer: _____

National 4-H Shooting Sports Program (National Shooting Sports Committee, Clemson University, 232 Poole Agricultural Center, Clemson, SC 29634-0753; fyd.clemson.edu/ssports.htm). This program teaches life skills through the shooting sports. Muzzleloading is one of the six disciplines taught by its national and state certified instructors.

Safari Club International (4800 West Gates Pass Road, Tucson, AZ 85745; 520-620-1220; www.safariclub.org). Involved in the protection of hunters' rights at the local, state, and national levels.

International Hunter Education Association (PO Box 490, Wellington, CO 80549; 970-568-7954; ihea.com). Continues the hunting heritage worldwide by encouraging safe, responsible, and knowledgeable hunters.

Kentucky Rifle Association (3539 Oak Ridge Drive, Slatington, PA 18080; www.kentuckyrifleassociation.org). Nonprofit corporation organized to promote its members' interest in the collection and preservation of the Kentucky rifle, Kentucky pistol, and related accoutrements.

American Single Shot Rifle Association (ASSRA, 15770 Rd. 1037, Oakwood, OH 45873; www.assra.com). Dedicated since 1948 to the use, study, and preservation of old cartridge target and buffalo rifles.

National Wild Turkey Federation (PO Box 530, Edgefield, SC 29824; 803-637-3106; www.nwtf.org). Dedicated to the conservation of the wild turkey, as well as the hunting tradition.

Quality Deer Management Association (Box 227, Watkinsville, GA 30677; 800-209-3337; www.qdma.com). Advocates a management philosophy that unites landowners, hunters, and managers in the common goal of producing biologically and socially balanced deer herds within existing environmental, social, and legal constraints.

International Black Powder Hunting Association (PO Box 1180, Glenrock, WY; 307-436-9817; www.blackpowderhunting.org). Publishes a magazine devoted entirely to black powder hunting.

American Longrifle Association (www.liming.org/alra/). Designed to promote historical accuracy in clothing, rifle items, safety, and marksmanship during the flintlock rifle era (1750–1815).

Contemporary Longrifle Association (PO Box 2097, Staunton, VA 24402; 540-886-6189; www.longrifle.ws). Promotes the interest in traditional muzzleloading rifles, their accoutrements, and related objects handmade after the mid-twentieth century.

Coalition of Historical Trekkers (106 Yearling Court, Fountain, CO 80817; www.coht.org). Dedicated to the preservation and study of the pre-1840 frontier people in America by means of literary research and experimental archaeology.

Museum of the Fur Trade (6321 Highway 20, Chadron, NE 69337; 308-432-3843; www.furtrade.org). Three unique galleries exhibit items from the fur trade, from early colonial days to the present century.

American Mountain Men (2893 West 10460 South, South Jordan, UT 84095; www.xmission.com/%7edrudy/amm/assoc.html). An association of individuals dedicated to the preservation of the traditions and ways of our nation's greatest, most daring explorers and pioneers.

State Organizations

Alabama State Muzzleloading Association (3445 Self Creek Road, Warrior, AL 35180; www.angelfire.com/al3/asmla). Dedicated to the promotion of safe and responsible use of muzzleloading firearms for hunting and target shooting and to the preservation of the history of early American firearms.

Kentucky Corps of Longriflemen (www.homestead.com/ CORPSofLongriflemen/Corpspage~ie4.html). Promotes longrifle history, the Kentucky Long Rifle Corps of Longriflemen shooting competition, and interstate shoots.

New York State Muzzle-Loaders Association, Inc. (200 Clifford Drive, Vestal, NY 13850; 607-965-8849; www.ascent.net//dmyers/index.htm). The Web site provides information on shooting, primitive camping, and affiliated clubs.

Pennsylvania Federation of Black Powder Shooters, Inc., has a long history of welcoming new shooters and hunters to its fold. There are more than 38 different clubs. For more information, contact in Pennsylvania: John Pensyl, 122 Pensyl Lane, Bedford, PA 15522; 814-839-2939; in New Jersey: Richard Dagenais, 75 Broughton Avenue, Bloomfield, NJ 07003; in New York: Donald Palinkas, 3851 Erwin Hollow, Painted Post, NY 14870, 607-962-6768.

Pennsylvania Deer Association, Inc. (3004 Smoketown Road, Spring Grove, PA 17362-9503; www.padeer.net). Promotes quality deer management, particularly in supporting youth hunters.

United Nebraska Muzzleloaders Association (3851 I Road, Palmyra, NE 68112; 402-780-6754; www.nebraskamuzzleloaders. com). Promotes the sport of muzzleloading, buckskinning, history of the fur trade, and the safe use of black powder in Nebraska.

Wyoming State Muzzleloading Association (1824 Sage Lane, Worland, WY 82501; http://asuwlink.uwyo.edu/%7edwwilson/wsmla.htm). Dedicated to the sport of black powder shooting and the promotion of muzzleloading events and activities.

Rendezvous and Muzzleloading Shoots

Rendezvous sites and dates change from year to year. The National Muzzle Loading Rifle Association serves as the sponsoring organization and clearinghouse for contacts. Contact the NMLRA early in the calendar year for rendezvous in your area.

To locate a shoot near you, contact your state's black powder association. Many of them publish booklets or have Web sites. There are 42 states listing charter club shoot dates and locations in the NMLRA magazine *Muzzle Blasts.* For more information on charter clubs, contact your state's muzzleloading association, or contact the NMLRA.

Blue Ridge Rifles, Inc., (Henry Rohleder, 717-854-7251; BRRifles@msn.com) sponsored a unique Women's Primitive Rendezvous in 2004, as well as its annual Memorial Day and Labor Day rendezvous. Period dress is encouraged.

Whispering Pines Cap and Flint Club, Inc., (Jim Holleran, RD 7, Box 85-A, Wellsboro, PA 16901; 570-724-7285), sponsors annual rendezvous in northern Pennsylvania.

First Pennsylvania Regiment of the Continental Line (Rod Farmer, 610-527-1044; or Ralph DeStefano, 610-323-7108) has its home range at the Daniel Boone Homestead, Birdsboro, Pennsylvania. Only traditional-style flintlock rifles and muskets with round-balls are shot. Colonial and Revolutionary War period attire is required.

Land of the Seneca Living History Rendezvous and Rifle Frolic (jad11@cornell.edu, or www.landoftheseneca.org) requires pre-1840 period dress and equipment, but new pilgrims and tenderfeet are cordially welcomed. Shooting is done with black powder, patched roundballs, and fixed iron sights.

Single Action Shooting Society (23255 La Palma Avenue, Yorba Linda, CA 92887; 717-694-1800 or 877-411-SASS; www.SASSnet.com) sponsors cowboy action shoots.

Gun Shows

Gunmakers Fair (Dixon Muzzleloader Shop, RD 1, Kempton, PA 19529; 610-756-6271; www.dixonmuzzleloading.com), scheduled for the last weekend in July for 23 consecutive years, offers hunters every aspect of the muzzleloaders' craft. Custom-made flintlocks, percussions, accoutrements, powder horns, hunting pouches, knives, hawks, and other forms of craft and art are on display. Judging takes place in various categories.

Muzzleloading Arms and Pioneer Craft Show (25825 104th Avenue SE, Suite 301, Kent, WA 98031; www.cascademountain-men.org). Advertised as a "pre-1850 shopping experience," this event is held the second weekend in March at the Evergreen State Fairgrounds. Sponsored by the Cascade Mountain Men, the show includes live demonstrations along with the exposition of muzzleloading arms and accoutrements.

Eighteenth-Century Colonial Fair (Historic Mansker's Station Frontier Life Center, 705 Caldwell Drive, Goodlettsville, TN 37072; 615-859-3678). Visitors take a step back in history at this fair, held during the first weekend in May for the last 15 years at the Moss-Wright Park in Goodlettsville, Tennessee.

Prairie Frontiersman Historic Arms & Craft Show (Teutopolis, IL; 217-728-7369). This exposition of pre-1898 guns, knives, and accoutrements has been presented for the last 15 years during the last weekend in March in the Teutopolis Knights of Columbus Hall.

Batavia Gun & Sportsman Show (14 Wilson Parkway, Lockport, NY 14094; 716-434-6535). Held the third weekend in April.

NMLRA's Gunmaker's Hall displays the handiwork of all comers on a first come, first served basis. Many of the fine craftspeople who make their living at gun building and related crafts conduct seminars on the back porch and under the seminar roof. The NMLRA's Living Arts Demonstrations are conducted daily in the demonstration areas on both sides of the creek. The hall and seminars are open during all NMLRA official functions. For more information, contact www.nmlra.org.

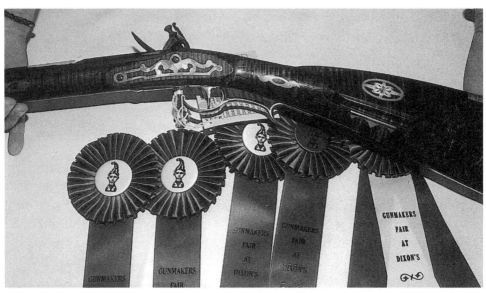

George Seisler of Fleetwood, Pennsylvania, has been building custom longrifles since 1946. He has the distinction of winning in every competition in which he has entered his guns. This flintlock of his garnered five blue ribbons at the 2004 Dixon Gunmaker Fair in Kempton, Pennsylvania.

MUZZLELOADER MANUFACTURERS, GEAR SUPPLIERS, AND OTHER RESOURCES

Muzzleloader Manufacturers and Importers

America Remembers (10226 Timber Ridge Drive, Ashland, VA 23005; 804-550-9616; www.americaremembers.com) has a complete line of historic and notable American firearms.

American Historical Foundation (www.ahrichmond.com) privately commissions historical commemoratives.

American Western Arms, Inc. (www.awaguns.com), manufactures Colts SAA models and Richards-Mason-type cartridge conversions of the Colt 1851 Navy, 1860 Army, 1861 Navy, and 1872 Open Top.

Arm Sport LLC (www.armsportllc.com) specializes in authentic, hand-built conversions of Colt and Remington black powder pistols to metallic cartridge.

Austin & Halleck Gun Crafters (1099 Welt, Weston, MO 64098; 816-386-2176; www.austinhalleck.com) has an owner's manual at the bottom of its home page, as well as other useful links.

Beretta, Pietro (www.berettausa.com) manufactures Beretta black powder shotguns.

Browning (www.browning.com) manufactures the Jonathan Browning mountain rifle.

C. Sharp Arms, Inc. (100 Centennial Drive, PO Box 885B, Big Timber, MT 59011; 406-932-4353), has reproduction Sharp rifles.

Cabela's (1 Cabela Drive, Sidney NE 69160; 800-237-4444; www.cabelas.com) distributes muzzleloaders, as well as a complete line of muzzleloading, casting, reloading, and gunsmithing supplies.

Caywood Gunmakers (www.caywoodguns.com).

Cherry's (www.cherrys.com) is a secondary market for Colt black powder collectibles.

Cimarron, F.A. Co., Inc. (105 Winding Oak Rd., Fredericksburg, TX 78624; www.cimarron-firearms.com), has authentic western reproductions of Colt and Remington black powder pistols.

Colt's Manufacturing Co., Inc. (PO Box 1868, Hartford, CT 06144; 800-962-COLT; www.colt.com), manufactures second-generation Colt percussion revolvers.

Connecticut Valley Arms (CVA) (5988 Peachtree Corners East, Norcross, GA 30071; 770-449-4687; www.cva.com) manufactures muzzleloading flintlocks, percussion rifles, in-lines, pistols, and shotguns.

Dixie Gun Works (Box 130, Gunpowder Lane, Union City, TN 38281; 901-885-0700; www.dixiegun.com) has the largest variety of muzzleloading guns.

E.M.F. Company (www.emf-company.com) is an importer of an extensive line of Civil War–period pistols and rifles.

Euroarms Italia S.r.l. (www.euroarms.net) manufactures muzzleloading pistols, revolvers, flintlock and percussion rifles, and shotguns.

Getz Barrel Company (www.getzbarrels.com) manufactures muzzleloading rifle barrels.

Gonic Arms (www.gonicarms.com) designs magnum muzzleloading pistols and in-line rifles.

Gun Works (www.thegunworks.com) custom-builds flintlock pistols, longrifles, American fowlers, and English sporting rifles.

Hartford Armory (100B Main Street, Collinsville, CT 06022; 860-693-8932; www.hartfordarmory.com) markets classic Remingtons and Colts.

Hawken Shop (www.thehawkenshop.com) manufactures original Hawken rifles.

Hornady Manufacturing Co. (Box 1848, Grand Island, NE 68802; 800-338-3220; www.hornady.com) is a full-range manufacturer, including reloading equipment, bullets, and cartridges.

Jim Chambers Flintlocks (www.flintlocks.com) is a custom maker and manufacturer of Pennsylvania longrifles and kits.

Knight Rifles (PO Box 130, 21852 Highway J46, Centerville, IA 52544; 515-856-2626; www.knightrifles.com) manufactures in-line pistols, rifles, and shotguns.

Lyman Products Corporation (475 Smith Street, Middletown, CT 06457; 860-632-2020; www.lymanproducts.com) manufactures a complete line of black powder bullets, accessories, pistols, and flintlock, percussion, and in-line rifles.

Markesbery Muzzle Loaders' (7785 Foundation Drive, Suite 6, Florence, KY 41042; 606-342-2380; www.markesbery.com) Web site has an interesting discussion on muzzleloading projectiles.

Mid-Western Outdoor Specialties, Inc. (902 East 4th Street, Joplin, MO 64801; 800-693-7455; www.mw-os.com), manufactures in-line rifles.

Millennium Designed Muzzleloaders Ltd. (RR1 Box 405, Maidstone, VT 05905; 802-676-3311; www.MDM-muzzleloaders.com) manufactures in-line pistols, rifles, and shotguns.

Mowry Gun Works, Inc. (PO Box 246, Waldren, IN; 765-525-6181), specializes in muzzleloaders designed by Ethan Allen.

Navy Arms Company (219 Lawn Street, Martinsburg, WV; 304-262-9870; www.navyarms.com) manufactures, imports, and distributes flintlock and percussion pistols, percussion revolvers, in-lines, and flintlock and percussion rifles and shotguns.

New England Firearms (www.newenglandfirearms.com) manufactures in-line rifles.

New Ultra Light Arms LLC (www.newultralightarms.com) manufactures the Model 209 in-line.

North American Arms, Inc. (www.naaminis.com), manufactures percussion revolvers.

North Star West, Inc. (202 Smokey Road, Frenchtown, MT 59834; 406-626-4081; www.northstarwest.com), manufactures flintlock pistols, rifles, and shotguns.

October Country Muzzleloading, Inc. (www.oct-country.com), manufactures and distributes large-bore percussion rifles, custom bullet molds, patches, and wads.

Palmetto Arms Company (Via Oberdan 48, I-25125, Brescia, Italy; 860-349, 1772; www.palmetto.it) produces the Walker revolver.

Pedersoli, Davide & C. S.n.c. (Via Artigiani 57, I-25063 Gardone V.T. (BS), Italy; www.davide-pedersoli.com) manufactures a huge variety of flintlock, percussion, and in-line pistols, rifles, shotguns, and revolvers, as well as a large array of muzzleloading accessories.

Pietta, F.lli S.n.c. (www.pietta.it) manufactures high-quality black powder revolvers, as well as percussion rifles and shotguns.

Remington Arms Co., Inc. (870 Remington Drive, PO Box 700, Madison, NC 27025; 800-243-9700; www.remington.com), manufactures in-line rifles and accessories.

Rightnour Manufacturing Co. (www.rmcspors.com) manufactures muzzleloaders and supplies.

Rossi (www.rossiusa.com) manufactures in-line rifles.

Savage Arms, Inc. (100 Springfield Road, Westfield, MA 01085; 413-568-7001; www.savagearms.com), manufactures smokeless powder in-lines.

Shiloh Rifle Mfg. Co. (www.shilorifle.com) manufactures percussion rifles.

Stoeger Industries (17603 Indian Head Highway, Suite 200, Accokeek, MD 20607; 301-283-6300; www.StoegerIndustries.com) imports Uberti firearms.

Sturm, Ruger & Co., Inc. (1 Lacey Place, Southport, CT 06490; 203-259-7843; www.ruger.com), manufactures percussion revolvers and in-line rifles.

Taylor's & Co., Inc. (304 Lenoir Drive, Winchester, VA 22603; 504-722-2017; www.taylorsfirearms.com), imports and distributes percussion pistols, revolvers, and flintlock and percussion rifles.

Tennessee Valley Muzzleloading, Inc. (14 CR521, Corinth, MS 38834; 662-287-6021; tvm@avisa.com), offers muzzleloading kits.

Thompson/Center Arms (PO Box 5002, Rochester, NH 03866; 603-332-2333; www.tcarms.com) manufactures in-line pistols, rifles, and shotguns, as well as flintlock and percussion rifles. T/C also has a wide variety of bullets and accessories.

Traditions Performance Firearms (1375 Boston Post Road, PO Box 776, Old Saybrook, CT 06475; 860-388-4656; www.traditions-firearms.com) has a complete line of miniature cannons; in-line pistols, rifles, shotguns, and revolvers; and flintlock and percussion rifles. Traditions also has a wide line of accessories.

Uberti, A. & C., S.r.l. (Via G. Carducci 41, I-25068 Porte Zanano (BS), Italy; www.ubertireplicas.com) manufactures black powder revolvers, cartridge conversion revolvers, and flintlock and percussion rifles and accessories.

White Rifles LLC (PO Box 1044, Orem, UT 84059; 801-932-7950; www.whiterifles.com) manufactures in-line rifles and shotguns, as well as accessories.

Winchester Muzzleloading (5988 Peachtree Corners East, Norcross, GA 30071; 877-892-7544; www.winchestermuzzleloading.com) manufactures in-line rifles and accessories.

Gear and Accessory Manufacturers

Accurate Bullet Co. (159 Creek Road, Glen Mills, PA 19342; 610-399-6584) manufactures cast bullets, molds, brass, casting alloys, lubes, and reloading supplies.

Ammodirect (877-266-6377; www.ammodirect.com) has black powder shotshells and reloading supplies.

ASAT Camouflage (www.asatcamo.com) manufactures camouflage clothing and accessories.

Ballistic Products, Inc. (20015 75th Avenue North, Corcoran, MN 55340; 612-494-9237; ballistpro@aol.com), has a full line of reloading supplies for black powder shotshells.

Barnes Bullets, Inc. (PO Box 215, American Fork, UT 84003; 801-756-4222; www.barnesbullets.com), has an interesting section on its Web site called "Bullet Talk."

Biowerk USA (jackcurlee@comcast.net) makes the Deer & Bear Glide. Birchwood Laboratories, Inc. (7900 Fuller Road, Eden Prairie, MN 55344; 800-328-6156; www.birchwoodcasey.com), is a supplier of solvents.

Black Hills Ammunition (PO Box 3090, Rapid City, SD 57709; 605-348-5150) has black powder for breechloaders.

Brownells, Inc. (200 South Front Street, Montezuma, IA 50171; 515-623-5401; www.brownells.com), is a major supplier of gun and gunsmithing accessories and gear.

Brunton (620 East Monroe, Riverton, WY 82501; 307-856-6559; www.brunton.com) supplies optics.

BSA Optics, Inc. (3911 SW 47th Avenue, Suite 914, Fort Lauderdale, FL 33314; 954-581-2144; www.bsaoptics.com), supplies optics.

Buckwing Products, Inc. (www.buckwing.com), manufactures turkey decoys and accessories.

Burris (PO Box 1747, Greely, CO 80632; 303-356-1670; www.burriscompany.com) supplies optics.

Bushnell Performance Optics (9200 Cody, Overland Park, KS 66214; 800-423-3537; www.bushnell.com) manufactures sports optics, scopes, range finders, and accessories.

Butler Creek Muzzle Loading Products (290 Arden Drive, Belgrade, MT 59714; 406-388-7204; www.info@butler-creek.com) manufactures loading, sling, and numerous muzzleloading accessories.

Carl Zeiss Optical, Inc. (1015 Commerce Street, Petersburg, VA 23803; 800-338-2984; www.zeiss.de), supplies optics.

Cash Manufacturing (201 South Klein Drive, PO Box 130, Waunakee, WI 53597; 608-849-5664; www.tdcmfg.com), manufactures brass cappers.

CCI/Speer (2299 Snake River Avenue, PO Box 856, Lewiston, ID 83501; 866-286-7436; www.cciammunition.com) manufactures percussion cap primers, 209 primers, muzzleloading bullets, and ammunition.

Circle Fly Wads (717-862-3600; www.circlefly.com) manufactures black powder shotgun cards, wads, and other components.

Colt Blackpowder (110 8th Street, Brooklyn, NY 11215; 718-499-4678; www.coltblackpowder.com) manufactures black powder.

DeLorme Mapping Company (PO Box 298, Freeport, ME 04032; 207-865-4171; www.delorme.com) has topographic and highway maps.

Dynamit Nobel-RWS, Inc. (89 Ruckman Road, Closter, NJ 07624; www.dnrws.com), manufactures percussion priming caps and primers.

Garmin International, Inc. (www.garmin.com), manufactures electronic devices, including GPS products.

GOEX, Inc. (PO Box 659, Doyline, LA 71023; 318-382-9300; www.goexpowder.com), manufactures black powder.

Haas Outdoors (www.mossyoak.com) manufactures camo clothing and accessories.

Hi-Viz Sight Systems (1375 Ken Pratt Boulevard, Suite A, Longmont, CO 80501) offers add-on fiber-optic sights.

Hodgdon Powder Company (6231 Robinson, PO Box 2932, Shawnee Mission, KS; 913-362-9455; www.hodgdon.com) manufactures Pyrodex and Triple Seven muzzleloading gunpowders.

Hunter's Specialties (www.hunterspec.com) manufactures turkey calls and accessories.

Kahles USA (1 Wholesale Way, Cranston, RI 02920; www.kahlesoptik.com) supplies optics.

Knight & Hale (www.knight-hale.com) manufactures turkey calls and accessories.

Kwik-Site (735-326-1500; www.kwiksitecorp.com) supplies optics.

Kyper Rifle Flints (700 Petersburg Pike Road, Huntingdon, PA, 16652; 814-643-4275; www.rifle-flints.com) manufactures flints.

Lee Precision, Inc. (427 Highway U, Hartford, WI 53027; 414-673-9273; www.leeprecision.com), manufactures casting equipment, molds, lubes, and reloading equipment.

Leupold & Stevens (PO Box 688, Beaverton, OR 97075; www.leupold.com) manufactures scopes and optics.

Lohman Manufacturing (www.outland-sports.com) manufactures turkey calls and accessories.

Lyman Products Corporation (475 Smith Street, Middletown, CT 06457; 800-225-9626 or 203-349-3421; www.lymanproducts.com) manufactures casting equipment, bullet molds, lubes, rifles, and reloading equipment.

Magma Engineering Co. (PO Box 161, Queen Creek, AZ 85242; 602-987-9008) manufactures bullet casting machines, molds, lubing machines, and associated supplies.

Midway USA (3875 West Van Horn Tavern Road, Columbia, MO 65203; 800-992-8312; www.midwayusa.com) supplies casting, reloading, and shooting accessories.

Muzzleload Magnum Products (www.mmpsabots.com) manufactures plastic sabots for in-line muzzleloader bullets.

NEI Handtools, Inc. (51583 Columbia River Highway, Scappoose, OR 97056; 503-543-6676; www.neihandtools.com), manufactures aluminum and meehanite (cast iron) single-, double-, and four-cavity molds.

Nikon Sports Optics (1300 Walt Whitman Road, Melville, NY 11747; 800-NIKON US; www.nikonusa.com) manufactures scopes and optics.

Nomadic Tipi Makers (www.tipi.com) manufactures Indian tepees.

Nosler (PO Box 671, Bend, OR 97709; 800-285-3701; www.nosler.com) manufactures muzzleloading bullets.

Ox-Yoke Originals (34 West Main Street, Milo, ME 04463; 800-231-8313; www.oxyoke.com) manufactures muzzleloading patches, lubricants, and accessories.

Pentax (PO Box 6509, Englewood, CO 80155; 303-799-8000; www.pentaxusa.com) supplies optics.

Petro-Explo, Inc. (7650 U.S. Highway 287, #100, Arlington, TX 76017; 800-588-8282; www.petro@fastlane.net), markets Swiss and Schuetzen brands of black powder.

Quaker Boy (www.quakerboygamecalls.com) manufactures game calls.

R. E. Davis Company (www.redaviscompany.com) manufactures flintlock locks for eighteenth-century longrifles.

Rapine Bullet Molds (9503 Landis Lane, East Greenville, PA 18041; 215-679-5413; www.bulletmoulds.com) manufactures bullet molds and supplies.

RCBS (a division of Blount, Inc., 605 Oro Dam Boulevard, Oroville, CA 95965; 800-533-5000; www.rcbs.com) manufactures molds, lubes, casting equipment, and reloading equipment.

Realtree (www.realtree.com) manufactures camouflage clothing and gear.

Redding/SAECO (1089 Starr Road, Cortland, NY 13045; 607-753-3331; www.redding_reloading.com) manufactures casting equipment, lubes, and reloading equipment, and sells a hardness tester based on a relative hardness scale (not the Brinnell hardness number).

Redfield (5800 East Jewell Avenue, Denver, CO 80224; 303-757-6411; www.redfieldoptics.com) supplies optics.

Rice Barrel Company, Inc. (www.ricebarrels.com), manufactures muzzleloading rifle barrels.

RMC Sports (Box 168, 259 Hecla Road, Mingoville, PA 16856; 814-383-4079; www.rmcsports.com) supplies optics.

Robinson Outdoors, Inc. (www.robinsonoutdoors.com), manufactures ScentBlocker clothing and Scent Shield accessories.

Schuetzen Powder, LLC (7650 US Highway 287, Arlington, TX 76001; 866-809-9704; www.elephantblackpowder.com) manufactures imported Schuetzen, Swiss, and Elephant black powder.

Shooter's Choice (Ventco, Inc., 15050 Berkshire Industrial Parkway, Middlefield, OH 44062; 440-834-8888; www.shooterchoice.com) manufactures cleaning supplies.

Shooting Chrony (www.shootingchrony.com) manufactures chronographs.

Simmons Outdoor Corp. (201 Plantation Oak Drive, Thomasville, GA 31792; 904-878-5100; www.simmonsoutdoor.com) supplies optics.

Starline (1300 West Henry Street, Sedalia, MO 65301; 800-280-6660; www.starlinebrass.com) is a supplier of black powder cartridge brass.

Steiner/Pioneer (216 Haddon Avenue, Suite 522, Camden, NJ 08108; 800-257-7742; www.steiner.com) supplies optics.

Swarovski Optik N.A. (1 Wholesale Way, Cranston, RI 02920; 800-426-3089; www.swarovski.com) supplies optics.

Tasco (PO Box 520080, Miami, FL 33152; 305-591-3670; www.bushnell.com) supplies optics.

Ten-X Ammunition (4035 Guasti Road, Suite 308, Ontario, CA 91761; 909-605-1617) carries black powder cartridges.

Tentsmiths (www.tentsmiths.com) manufactures primitive camping tents.

Track of the Wolf (18308 Joplin Street NW, Elk River, MN 55330; 763-633-2500; www.trackofthewolf.com) is a supplier of English, French, and German flints.

Tru-Glo (PO Box 1612, McKinney, TX 75070; 972-774-0300; www.truglosights.com) manufactures fiber-optic sights.

Walker's Game Ear (800-424-1069; www.walkersgameear.com) manufactures sportsmen's assisted-hearing devices.

Weaver (Box 856, Lewiston, ID 83501; 208-746-2351; www.weaveroptics.com) manufactures scopes, mounts, and optics.

Williams Gun Sight Co. (7389 Lapeer Road, Box 329, Davison, MI 48423; 800-530-9028; www.williamsgunsight.com) manufactures various types of gun sights, including iron and fiber-optic, open and aperture.

Woodswise Products (PO Box 681552(W), Franklin, TN 37068; 800-735-8182; www.woodswise.com) manufactures scents, lures, and wildlife calls, as well as turkey hunting accessories.

Artisans

Ronald F. Cradle (villagerestoration@yahoo.com) is a horn maker.

Arthur J. DeCamp (ajdecamp@penn.com) is a horn maker.

Gary Fatherree the "Leatherman" (2216 Ritner Highway, Carlisle, PA 17013; 717-249-5977; www.blackpowderbagsl.com) makes leather possibles bags and accessories.

Paul "Skip" Hamaker (1309 North 10th Street, Reading, PA 19604; 610-373-4419; www.skipshorns.com) manufactures historically correct Pennsylvania- and early American-style powder horns, engravings, and knives.

Lee A. Larkin (PO Box 275, Bedford PA 15522) is a horn maker.

Steve Lodding (patentbreech1@earthlink.net) is a horn maker.

Harry McGonigal "Reverend Harry" (531 Chester Street, Perkasie, PA 18944; 215-257-1006; www.flaminharry.com/revharry.html) manufactures leather hunting pouches.

Orville "Spark" Mumma (108 Hemlock Hill Lane, Jonestown, PA 17038; 717-865-5721) is a scrimshander specializing in priming horns.

John C. Proud (686 Sterling Park, Cortland, NY 13045; 607-756-2207; jcproud@usadatanet.net.) manufactures French and Indian War–style powder horns.

Ken Scott (317-261-0751; www.kenscottpouches.com) makes leather hunting pouches.

Mike Small (wbgv@yahoo.com) is a horn maker.

Mark Thomas (mtgraver@juno.com) is a horn maker.

H. David Wright (hdwright007@comcast.net) is a horn maker.

SAFETY TIPS AND TROUBLESHOOTING FOR PROBLEMATIC MUZZLELOADERS

Muzzleloading guns are far more complex than modern centerfire firearms. This is a direct result of the larger number of parts in the triggers, locks, sights, and barrels, not to mention the many variables involved in loading powders, patches, sabots, roundballs, lead slugs, and jacketed bullets. But regardless of the complexities, we all have a responsibility to practice gun safety every time we use a firearm.

The Ten Commandments of Gun Safety

1. Keep the gun's muzzle pointed in a safe direction.
2. Be sure of your target and what lays beyond.
3. Never rely on a gun's "safety."
4. Keep the gun unloaded until you are ready to use it.
5. Wear ear and eye protection.
6. Ensure that the barrel is clear of any obstructions before you shoot it.
7. Handle every gun as if it is loaded.
8. Keep guns and ammo separate and in a locked storage area.
9. Avoid alcoholic beverages and drugs before and while using a firearm.
10. Do not alter or modify your firearm, and have it checked regularly by a competent gunsmith to ensure that all parts work properly.

For muzzleloaders, there are another 10:

11. Never use more black or replica powder than the manufacturer recommends.
12. Never use duplex (half black powder and half smokeless) in a muzzleloader that was designed for black or replica powder.
13. Never use smokeless powder in a muzzleloader that was not designed to shoot it.
14. Never smoke while loading or operating a muzzleloader.
15. Never load powder directly from any container, powder horn, or flask into the barrel. Always load from a powder measurer or premeasured quick load.
16. Never carry a primed or capped firearm in a vehicle, or hand it to another person.
17. Never pull a bullet, or debreech a capped or primed muzzleloader.
18. Never lift or carry a primed muzzleloader up into a tree stand.
19. Never store a loaded muzzleloader in a cabinet or safe.
20. Never shoot a muzzleloader around powder horns, cans, or flasks of black or replica powders.

Troubleshooting Tips

Regardless of whether you are a greenhorn "pilgrim" or a grizzled old mountain man, there will be times when your muzzleloader will drive you crazy. This section addresses some common problems in the context of the type of ignition: flintlock, external percussion lock, or in-line percussion lock.

FLINTLOCK

PROBLEM

LOCK

SOLUTION

PROBLEM	SOLUTION
The lock won't spark.	Knap the flint's edge. Replace the flint. Tighten the top jaw screw of the cock. Tighten the bolt at the base of the cock. Align the flint edge to strike the frizzen squarely in the center. Lubricate the cam or frizzen spring. Reharden the frizzen. Replace the mainspring to increase speed. Replace the frizzen.
Flints keep breaking.	Loosen the frizzen bolt and lubricate. Lubricate the cam or frizzen spring. Replace the leather around the flint in the jaws. Tighten the top jaw screw. Try an English flint. Use smaller flints. Check the alignment so the flint doesn't strike the barrel or pan.
Priming powder disappears.	Check the pan alignment to the barrel flat. Tighten the lock-plate bolts. File the edge of the pan so that it's flush with the barrel flat (or pay a gunsmith to do it). Clean the base of the frizzen so its sits flush on the pan. Grind the base of the frizzen to sit flush to the pan.
The rotating cock won't stop at half-cock.	Dismantle the lock, and lubricate the little L-shaped detent inside the tumbler. Check the half-cock notch on the tumbler to be sure it isn't broken off. Check the sear spring for proper tension.

FLINTLOCK *continued*

PROBLEM	SOLUTION
LOCK	
The rotating cock won't stop at half-cock.	Check the cam at the end of the sear to make sure that it engages the tumbler. Replace the lock.
The lock fires too slowly.	Clean and degrease the interior lock parts. Use a light machine oil for lubrication. Check the lock mortise for rubbing. Remove wood or synthetic high spots. Replace the mainspring. Reduce the amount of priming powder (use only half a pan). Keep the primer away from the touch hole. Buy a new lock.

When the flinter's lock fires too slowly, try using half a pan of powder. Keep the powder away from the barrel so that the flash of fire has clear access to the touch hole—you don't want the primer burning like a fuse into the barrel.

FLINTLOCK continued

PROBLEM

LOCK

SOLUTION

PROBLEM	SOLUTION
I often get a flash in the pan.	Use a wire pick to open the touch hole. Use less priming powder. Keep priming powder away from the touch hole. Clean the bore of oils and grease before you load that first shot. Put a new, coned liner in the touch hole. Check and repair touch-hole alignment. It must be forward of the face of the breech plug.
When fired, the cock stops at the half-cock position.	Check the L-shaped detent and lubricate with a light machine oil or replace it if broken.

You will get a flash in the pan if you don't pick open the touch hole every time you load the flintlock.

FLINTLOCK continued

PROBLEM	SOLUTION
STOCK	
The ramrod is loose and falls out when I aim down from a tree stand.	Replace the leaf-spring keeper (if originally equipped). Insert a folded cloth patch between the ramrod and the barrel or ramrod channel. Buy a larger-diameter ramrod. Compress the ramrod pipe slightly.
The keys or pins are loose and fall out.	Lightly bend them so they are snug into the mortise. Make slightly larger diameter pins from finishing nails. Use a small ball peen hammer to upset the brass or iron flat key to increase its diameter.
I have a dent in the wood.	Use a steam iron and wet cloth to swell the wood back to the original surface. Stain and finish.
I have scratches.	Stain and refinish. Oil finishes are easier to touch up than hard synthetic finishes. Use a dark oil such as Old English to darken or cover up the scratches. Ignore them. They add character.
There is a stress crack in the stock.	If the gun is under warranty, send it back for replacement. Use a pin to sneak a combination of epoxy and sawdust (which you can stain) into the crack. Stain and refinish. Visit a gunsmith if the gun's integrity is in question.
The stock is too big.	Measure your trigger pull. Remove the butt plate or recoil pad, and cut the wood or synthetic stock. Replace the plate or pad and refinish. Pay a gunsmith to fix it.

FLINTLOCK *continued*

PROBLEM	SOLUTION
STOCK	
The stock is too small.	Add a thicker recoil pad.
BARREL	
I can't sight it in.	If under warranty, send it back. Drift the front sight left or right. File down the front sight, or file the rear. Replace the rear sight. Bend the barrel; if timid, visit a gunsmith.
My cloth patches are cutting at the crown.	Recrown the bore with a coned or round grinder. Visit a gunsmith.
The bore is very rough.	Wrap some OOOO steel wool on your cleaning jag and ramrod it up and down to eliminate rust or burrs in the bore. Make a lead bore-sized jag and use grinding compound to lap the bore.
BARREL	
Grease and oil squeeze out of the breech-plug joint each time I shoot.	This is dangerous. It means that the breech plug is not sealing the bore. Visit a competent gunsmith and have the barrel rebreeched, or send it back.
The barrel can't be easily removed from the stock.	Insert a ramrod to add leverage to front of the barrel. Use a scraper or sandpaper to slightly increase width or depth of the stock's barrel channel. Don't use oil on a wood channel; it causes the fibers to swell, making the channel tighter. Use furniture wax.

FLINTLOCK continued

PROBLEM	**SOLUTION**
BARREL	
No matter how many different combinations of powder, patch, and ball or bullets I use, the barrel won't shoot accurately.	Use a tighter- or looser-fitting patch-ball or sabot-bullet combination. Replace the barrel.
I can't see the sights clearly.	Move the rear sight forward until your farsighted eyes can focus. Paint the sights. Switch to fiber-optics. Where legal, switch to a peep (aperture) sight such as the ghost ring. Where legal, use an optical sight. Get prescription eyeglasses.

PERCUSSION

PROBLEM	**SOLUTION**
LOCK	
It won't fire.	The cap is not seated tightly on the nipple. There is a spent cap up inside the cup of the hammer. Remove it. The hammer bolt is not tight to the tumbler. Use a screwdriver. Replace the mainspring. If under warranty, send it back.
The cap fires, but the rifle won't.	Use a nipple pick to open the flash channel. Switch from pellets to loose powder. Use black powder; the ignition temperature is lower. Use a magnum-type primer. Remove caked fouling from the coned breech. Replace the nipple (often).

PERCUSSION continued

PROBLEM	SOLUTION
LOCK	
The hammer flies back to half or full cock after firing.	This is dangerous because blowback gases are coming up through the nipple. Replace the nipple. Check the nipple base threads. You may need the services of a gunsmith to recut the base threads.
The lock time is too slow.	Replace the mainspring. Reset the hammer so that it is closer to the lock when at full cock. Clean the grease out of the internal lock parts. Use a light machine oil, not grease.
The hammer "hangs up."	Check the lock mortise for rubbing. You may need to remove some wood or synthetic to provide space for free movement of sear spring, tumbler, and mainspring.

If your percussion rifle won't fire, the first step is to check the hammer.

PERCUSSION *continued*

PROBLEM	**SOLUTION**
LOCK	
The hammer "hangs up." *(continued)*	Check the L-shaped detent in the tumbler. If it is broken or lost, replace it. Replace the lock.
STOCK *(see flintlock)*	
BARREL	
My gun won't shoot sabots accurately.	Reproduction percussion rifles, such as Plains styles and Hawkens, may have slow rifling rates (1:66, 1:56, or 1:48). These rates of twist are too slow to adequately stabilize the elongated bullets sheathed in the plastic sabot.
My percussion won't fire pellets.	Switch from a standard #11 cap to a #11 magnum percussion cap. Retrofit rifle to use a #2 musket cap. Stick with loose powder. Black powder has a significantly lower ignition temperature.
Three 50-grain pellets give my rifle terrible accuracy.	Most manufacturers don't recommend a load this heavy. Besides the punishing recoil on the rifle and your shoulder, the barrel probably isn't long enough to provide the time necessary to burn all the propellant.

IN-LINE PERCUSSION

PROBLEM	**SOLUTION**
LOCK	
The striker locks up.	Fouling gases blow back through the nipple. The receiver must be cleaned after each session. Use a light oil for lubricant.

IN-LINE PERCUSSION continued

PROBLEM	SOLUTION
LOCK	
The rifle won't fire.	If you have a knurled safety or the lever type, make sure that they are both set at "fire."
	After cleaning, did you reassemble the spring, striker, and bolt correctly? Reassemble and lubricate with light oil.
	Run a wire nipple pick through the nipple flash channel.
	Replace the nipple.
	Check the breech plug or flash channel.
	Replace the mainspring.
Pellets fire inconsistently.	Switch from a standard #11 cap to a #11 magnum cap.
	Retrofit to a 209 shotgun primer ignition system, which is available for earlier models of in-lines.
Three pellets don't shoot well.	The load may be too heavy for your rifle. Check the manufacturer's manual.
I can't get patched roundballs to shoot accurately.	Cut back on the powder volume. The fast rifling rate (>1:48) is keeping the ball from stabilizing. Load a volume of powder that equals the caliber size, and you should see an improvement.
The bottom of my scope gets all fouled up.	This is a result of blowback gases. Commercial scope protectors are available, or a low-cost option is to cover the base with easily removed electrical tape.

If pellets fire inconsistently in your in-line, you may want to retrofit that #11 cap with a 209 primer system.

IN-LINE PERCUSSION *continued*

PROBLEM	SOLUTION
STOCK	
My gun seems to go out of alignment every time I shoot.	If you have a wood stock, rising and falling humidity can swell or shrink the barrel channel. Because many barrels are anchored by a bolt under the barrel, this can be responsible for small changes in zeroing. Store your gun in a dehumidified cabinet or gun safe. Retrofit a synthetic stock.
My synthetic stock has fingerprints and smudges.	Don't use DEET and other insect repellents on your hands. The chemicals can melt plastic. Look on the bright side: if someone steals your gun, the fingerprints will prove that it's yours!

In-line actions can gum up with thick grease, dirt, and assorted other gremlins. Clean the action and lubricate with a light oil before resuming the hunt.

IN-LINE PERCUSSION *continued*

PROBLEM	SOLUTION
BARREL	
My rifle fires inconsistently.	If you use a #11 percussion cap, try a #11 magnum percussion cap. Retrofit to a 209 shotgun primer system. Stick with bulk powder, especially black, with its lower ignition temperature.
When the gun was new, it shot very accurately, but not two years later.	If you have been using plastic sabots, you need to remove the buildup of plastic on the lands of the rifling. This makes loading more difficult and changes the zero of your sights. Scrub the bore with a bronze brush and plastic solvent (the type used for shotguns) or hydrogen peroxide. Replace the nipple or vent liner of the 209 primer, because the worn and enlarged hole in the flash channel changes velocities and causes blowback gases and inconsistent ignition. If the barrel heats up, the plastic in the sabot gets soft. This could allow blow-by of gases and inaccuracy. Check the sight and scope bases. If the mounting screws are loose from recoil, reinstall them with Lock-Tite.
I want to use smokeless powder in my in-line.	Unless you have a Savage 10ML, your rifle is not equipped with a vent liner that keeps the very high pressures from blasting back into your face. Many muzzleloading barrels are built with mild steel barrels that won't withstand the pressures generated by smokeless powder.

The reason you can't use smokeless powder in most muzzleloaders is safety. Most barrels and breech plugs are not built to withstand the high breech pressures cause by igniting smokeless propellants.

IN-LINE PERCUSSION *continued*

PROBLEM

SOLUTION

BARREL

My gun shoots fine when I'm practicing, but when I go hunting, it misfires.

You need to remove the oil or grease you applied after cleaning.

Snap a cap or 209 primer to clear the flash channel, but do it into a clean patch on the end of the ramrod. Sometimes the exploding primer jams fouling or grease into the flash channel or breech chamber.

A loose-fitting pellet or sabot load leaves too much space in front of the cap or primer.

Very cold weather can constrict the nipple or flash channel. Use magnum primers.

IN-LINE PERCUSSION *continued*

PROBLEM	SOLUTION
BARREL	
The 209 primer gets stuck.	This primer generates a lot of gas, which expands the brass shell. Some of the gas condenses in the primer chamber, and some of the primer compound may also be left as fouling. These three things demand cleaning and lubrication of that chamber if you do repetitive shooting. If you don't have an extractor, make or buy one.
The stainless steel barrel is rusted.	Stainless steel is not impervious to the chemical effects of fouling. Even stainless compounds are made with iron, and iron rusts. Fine steel wool or Naval Jelly should remove the rust. Clean your gun after you shoot it.

STATE-BY-STATE MUZZLELOADING REGULATIONS

United States

Alabama Division of Wildlife and Freshwater Fisheries
64 North Union Street, Montgomery, AL 36130; 334-242-3467;
www.dcnr.state.al.us/agfd
> Minimum caliber: .40 caliber (.40-caliber pistols legal)
> Ignition types: flintlock, percussion, in-line
> Powders: only black powder and replica powder or pellets; no
> smokeless propellant
> Projectiles: any
> Sights: any, including fiber-optics; no scopes
> Minimum barrel length: none
> Seasons: three days in November; three weeks in January
> (dates vary)

Alaska Department of Game and Fish
PO Box 25526, Juneau, AK 99802; 907-465-4100;
www.state.ak.us/adfg
> Minimum caliber: .54 caliber for elk, musk ox, mountain goat,
> bear, moose, and bison; .45 caliber for other big game; no
> minimum for pistol
> Ignition types: flintlock, percussion, in-line
> Powders: any
> Projectiles: at least 250 grains for .45 calibers
> Sights: any, including fiber-optics; no scopes
> Minimum barrel length: none
> Seasons: August 1 to December 31; no special muzzleloader
> season

Muzzleloader certification or equivalent NMLRA course required

Arizona Game and Fish Department

2221 West Greenway Road, Phoenix, AZ 85023; 602-942-3000; www.azgfd.com

Minimum caliber: none for rifle or pistol
Ignition types: matchlock, flintlock, percussion, in-line
Powders: any
Projectiles: any
Sights: any, including scopes
Minimum barrel length: 16 inches
Seasons: October, November, December (dates vary)

Arkansas Game and Fish Commission

#2 Natural Resources Drive, Little Rock, AR 72205; 501-223-6300; www.agfc.state.ar.us

Minimum caliber: .40 caliber; .45-caliber pistol with minimum 9-inch barrel
Ignition types: flintlock, percussion, in-line
Powders: any
Projectiles: single only
Sights: any, including scopes
Minimum barrel length: 18 inches
Seasons: 20 zones, with most occurring mid-October or late December (dates vary)

California Department of Game and Fish

1416 Ninth Street, Sacramento, CA 95814; 916-445-0411; www.dfg.ca.gov

Minimum caliber: .40 caliber for rifles; pistols prohibited
Ignition types: flintlock, percussion, in-line
Powders: any
Projectiles: any; no sabots
Sights: open; no fiber-optics or scopes
Minimum barrel length: none
Seasons: a variety of special muzzleloader hunts in various zones, from October to December (dates vary)

Colorado Wildlife Division

6060 Broadway, Denver, CO 80216; 303-297-1192; www.wildlife.state.co.us

Minimum caliber: .40 caliber for deer, antelope, and bear; .50 caliber for elk and moose; pistols prohibited

Ignition types: flintlock, percussion, in-line

Powders: black powder or replica powders; pellets, smokeless powder, and shotgun primers illegal

Projectiles: minimum of 170 grains for under .50 caliber, 210 grains for over .50 caliber; weapons must fire a single roundball or conical projectile; no sabots

Sights: open and fiber-optics; no scopes

Minimum barrel length: none

Seasons: September (dates vary)

Connecticut Department of Environmental Protection

Wildlife Division, 79 Elm Street, Hartford, CT 06106; 860-424-3011; www.dep.state.ct.us

Minimum caliber: .45 caliber for deer; .36 caliber for small game

Ignition types: flintlock, percussion, in-line

Powders: any

Projectiles: single only

Sights: any, including scopes

Minimum barrel length: none

Seasons: December (dates vary)

Delaware Division of Fish and Wildlife

89 Kings Highway, Dover, DE 19901; 302-739-3440; www.dnrec.state.de.us/dnrec2000/wildlife.asp

Minimum caliber: .42 caliber for rifles; pistols prohibited

Ignition types: flintlock, percussion, in-line

Powders: any black powder or replica powder; no smokeless propellants

Projectiles: lead only; no jacketed bullets

Sights: any, including scopes

Minimum barrel length: none

Seasons: October and January (dates vary)

Florida Department of Game and Freshwater Fish

620 South Meridian Street, Tallahassee, FL 32399; www.state.fl.us/fwc

Minimum caliber: .40 caliber

Ignition types: flintlock, percussion, in-line

Powders: any black powder or replica powder or pellets; no smokeless propellant

Projectiles: any

Sights: any, including scopes

Minimum barrel length: none

Seasons: Northwest zone, November and February (dates vary); Central Zone, October–November (dates vary); Southern Zone, October (dates vary)

Georgia Department of Natural Resources

Wildlife Division, 2111 Highway 278, Social Circle, GA 30025; 770-918-6416; www.dnr.state.ga.us

Minimum caliber: .44 caliber

Ignition types: flintlock, percussion, in-line

Powders: any

Projectiles: any

Sights: open and fiber-optics; scopes illegal in primitive weapons season

Minimum barrel length: none

Seasons: October (dates vary)

Hawaii Division of Forestry and Wildlife

1151 Punchbowl Street, Honolulu, HI 96813; 808-587-0166; www.dofaw.net

Minimum caliber: .44 caliber for rifle and pistol

Ignition types: flintlock, percussion, in-line

Powders: any

Projectiles: any

Sights: any, except in restricted areas

Minimum barrel length: 16^1/$_2$ inches

Seasons: first and second Saturday of March, Island of Lanai for axis deer (by lottery)

Idaho Department of Fish and Game

PO Box 25, Boise, ID 83707; 208-334-3700; www.state.id.us/fishgame

Minimum caliber: .45-caliber rifle for deer, antelope, and mountain lion; .50 caliber for moose, bighorn sheep, goat, and black bear; .45 caliber for pistol

Ignition types: flintlock, percussion; no in-line

Powders: any black powder or replica powder or pellets; no smokeless powder or 209 primers

Projectiles: sabots, conicals, roundballs of at least 0.428 inch; no jacketed bullets

Sights: open, including fiber-optics; no scopes

Minimum barrel length: none

Seasons: units 4 and 7, November (dates vary for all units); Unit 8A, December; Unit 10A, November–December; Unit 16, November–December

In traditional, muzzleloader-only season, hunters must use a muzzleloader with an exposed hammer that pivots and is loaded with loose black powder, Pyrodex, or a patched roundball projectile.

Illinois Department of Natural Resources

1 Natural Resources Way, Springfield, IL 62702; 217-782-6431; www.dnr.state.il.us

Minimum caliber: .45 caliber for rifle; pistols prohibited

Ignition types: wheel lock, matchlock, flintlock, percussion, in-line

Powders: any black powder or replica powder or pellets; no smokeless propellants

Projectiles: minimum diameter of 0.44 inch

Sights: any

Minimum barrel length: 16 inches

Seasons: December (dates vary)

Indiana Department of Natural Resources

402 West Washington Street, Indianapolis, IN 46204; 317-232-4080; www.wildlife.in.gov

Minimum caliber: .44 caliber, .50-caliber pistol

Ignition types: flintlock, percussion, in-line

Powders: any

Projectiles: must be ball-shaped or elongated, minimum of .44 caliber

Sights: any

Minimum barrel length: 12 inches

Seasons: December (dates vary)

Iowa Department of Natural Resources
Wallace State Office Building, Des Moines, IA 50319;
515-281-5918; www.iowadnr.com
> Minimum caliber: .44 caliber, not to exceed .775 for rifle; .44-caliber pistol
> Ignition types: flintlock, percussion, in-line
> Powders: any
> Projectiles: any; single only
> Sights: any
> Minimum barrel length: 16 inches
> Seasons: residents only, October (dates vary); nonresidents, December–January

Kansas Parks and Wildlife
512 Southeast 25th Avenue, Pratt, KS 66612; 785-296-2281;
www.kdwp.state.ks.us
> Minimum caliber: 0.39-inch in diameter, loaded through the front of the chamber; .45 caliber for pistol loaded through the front of the chamber
> Ignition types: flintlock, percussion, in-line
> Powders: any
> Projectiles: any; single only
> Sights: open; no scopes
> Minimum barrel length: 10 inches for pistols
> Seasons: September, December (dates vary)

Kentucky Department of Wildlife Resources
#1 Game Farm Road, Frankfort, KY 40601; 502-564-4336;
www.kdfwr.state.ky.us
> Minimum caliber: none for rifles or pistols
> Ignition types: flintlock, percussion, in-line
> Powders: any
> Projectiles: any, except full metal jacket
> Sights: any
> Minimum barrel length: none
> Seasons: October, December (dates vary)

Louisiana Department of Wildlife and Fisheries
PO Box 9800, Baton Rouge, LA 70898; 225-765-2800;
www.wlf.state.la.us
> Minimum caliber: .44 caliber for rifle and pistol

Ignition types: flintlock, percussion, in-line
Powders: any black powder or replica powder or pellets;
   no smokeless propellants
Projectiles: any
Sights: any
Minimum barrel length: none
Seasons: October through January, specific dates are controlled
   by Areas 1 to 7 (dates vary)

Maine Department of Inland Fisheries and Wildlife
284 State Street, 41 State House Station, Augusta, ME 04333;
207-287-8000; www.state.me.us/ifw
   Minimum caliber: .40 caliber for rifles and pistols
   Ignition types: wheel lock, flintlock, percussion, in-line;
      no 209 primers
   Powders: black powder and replica powders; no pellets
   Projectiles: roundballs and bullets; buckshot legal
   Sights: any
   Minimum barrel length: none
   Seasons: December (dates vary for management units
      and statewide seasons)

Maryland Department of Natural Resources
Wildlife Division, 580 Taylor Ave., E-1, Annapolis, MD 21401; 410-
260-8540; www.dnr.state.md.us
   Minimum caliber: .40 caliber for rifles and pistols
   Ignition types: flintlock, percussion, in-line
   Powders: any
   Projectiles: 60-grain minimum propellant charge, lead or
      lead-alloy, sabot, copper soft-nosed or expanding bullet or
      ball; 40-grain minimum for pistols
   Sights: any
   Minimum barrel length: 7 inches for pistols
   Seasons: Region A, antlered only, October and December–
      January (dates vary) for public and private lands; Region B,
      antlered or antlerless hunts, October and December–
      January; Region C, antlered or antlerless, October and
      December–January, and antlerless only, October; Region D,
      antlered or antlerless, October and December–January

Massachusetts Department of Fisheries and Wildlife
One Rabbit Hill Road, Westboro, MA 01581; 508-792-7270;
www.masswildlife.com
>   Minimum caliber: .44 caliber for rifles; pistols prohibited
>   Ignition types: flintlock, percussion, in-line; break-open breech
>   designs are not permitted during muzzleloading season
>   Powders: any black powder or replica powder or pellets;
>   no smokeless propellants
>   Projectiles: any, single only; no jacketed bullets
>   Minimum barrel length: 18 inches
>   Seasons: December (dates vary)

Michigan Department of Natural Resources
PO Box 30031, Lansing, MI 48909; 517-373-1263;
www.michigandnr.com
>   Minimum caliber: .40 caliber for rifles; pistols prohibited
>   Ignition types: flintlock, percussion, in-line
>   Powders: any black powder or replica powder or pellets;
>   no smokeless propellants
>   Projectiles: any
>   Sights: any
>   Minimum barrel length: none
>   Seasons: December (dates vary)

Minnesota Department of Natural Resources
Box 7, 500 Lafayette Road, St. Paul, MN 55155; 651-296-6157;
www.dnr.state.mn.us
>   Minimum caliber: .40 caliber for rifle and pistol
>   Ignition types: flintlock, percussion, in-line
>   Powders: any
>   Projectiles: any
>   Sights: open; no fiber-optics, or scopes
>   Minimum barrel length: none
>   Seasons: November–December (dates vary)

Mississippi Department of Wildlife
1505 Eastover Drive, Jackson, MS 39211; 601-432-2400;
www.mdwfp.com
>   Minimum caliber: .36 caliber; pistols prohibited
>   Ignition type: flintlock, percussion, in-line
>   Powders: any black powder or replica powder or pellets;
>   no smokeless

Projectiles: any

Sights: any

Minimum barrel length: none

Seasons: December (dates vary)

Missouri Department of Conservation

PO Box 180, Jefferson City, MO 65102; 573-751-4115; www.conservation.state.mo.us

Minimum caliber: .40 caliber for rifles and pistols

Ignition types: flintlock, percussion, in-line

Powders: any

Projectiles: any; single only

Sights: any

Minimum barrel length: none

Seasons: November–December (dates vary)

Montana Department of Fish, Wildlife, and Parks

1420 East 6th Avenue, Helena, MT 59620; 406-444-3186; www.fwp.state.mt.us

Minimum caliber: .45 caliber

Ignition types: matchlock, wheel lock, flintlock, percussion, in-line

Powders: any black powder or replica powder or pellets; no smokeless propellants

Projectiles: lead only; no sabots or jacketed bullets

Sights: any

Minimum barrel length: none

Seasons: October–November (dates vary); no special muzzleloader season, but specific areas set aside for muzzle-loaders during the regular deer season

Nebraska Game and Parks

2200 North 33rd Street, Lincoln, NE 68503; 402-471-5003; www.ngpc.state.ne.us

Minimum caliber: .44 caliber, .62-caliber smoothbores; pistols prohibited

Ignition types: flintlock, percussion, in-line

Powders: any

Projectiles: roundballs, conicals, sabots; single only

Sights: any open; scopes limited to 1× or red dot

Minimum barrel length: none

Seasons: December 1–31

Nevada Division of Wildlife
1100 Valley Road, Reno, NV 89520; 775-688-1500; www.ndow.org
Minimum caliber: .45 caliber for rifles and pistols
Ignition types: wheel lock, matchlock, flintlock, percussion, in-line; hunters must use a cap that fits on a nipple; no 209 primers
Powders: any
Projectiles: any lead, semijacketed, or metal-alloyed expandable bullet, including sabots
Sights: open; no fiber-optics or scopes
Minimum barrel length: none
Seasons: September (dates vary); late hunts in various areas

New Hampshire Fish and Game Department
2 Hazen Drive, Concord, NH 03301; 603-271-3211; www.wildlife.state.nh.us
Minimum caliber: .40 caliber for rifles and pistols
Ignition types: flintlock, percussion, in-line
Powders: any
Projectiles: any; full metal jackets prohibited
Sights: any
Minimum barrel length: none
Seasons: November (dates vary)

New Jersey Division of Fish and Wildlife
PO Box 400, Trenton, NJ 08625; 609-259-2120; www.state.nj.us/dep/fgw
Minimum caliber: .44 caliber for rifle; 20 to 10 gauge for smoothbores; double barrels prohibited during muzzle-loader season; pistols prohibited
Ignition types: flintlock, percussion, in-line
Powders: any black powder or replica powder or pellets; no smokeless propellants
Projectiles: single projectiles for rifles; #4 to triple L buckshot
Sights: any
Minimum barrel length: none
Seasons: dates vary by zones

New Mexico Department of Game and Fish
PO Box 25112, Sante Fe, NM 87504; 505-476-8066;
www.gmfsh.state.nm.us
> Minimum caliber: none for deer, antelope, bear, cougar,
> Barbary sheep, ibex, or javelina; .45 caliber for elk, bighorn
> sheep, bison, and oryx; pistols prohibited
> Ignition types: flintlock, percussion, in-line
> Powders: any black powder or replica powder or pellets;
> no smokeless propellants
> Projectiles: any
> Sights: any
> Minimum barrel length: none
> Seasons: September–October (dates vary by unit)

New York Department of Environmental Conservation
50 Wolf Road, Albany, NY 12233-4750; 518-402-8843;
www.dec.state.ny.us
> Minimum caliber: .44 caliber for rifles and pistols
> Ignition types: flintlock, percussion, in-line
> Powders: any
> Projectiles: any; single only
> Sights: any
> Minimum barrel length: none
> Seasons: Northern Zone, October (dates vary);
> Southern Zone, December

North Carolina Wildlife Resources Commission
Division of Wildlife Management, 512 North Salisbury Street,
Raleigh, NC 27640; 919-662-4381; www.ncwildlife.org
> Minimum caliber: none; pistols prohibited
> Ignition types: flintlock, percussion, in-line
> Powders: any
> Projectiles: any
> Sights: any open and fiber-optic; no scopes
> Minimum barrel length: 18 inches
> Seasons: Eastern Region, October (dates vary);
> Western Region, October; Southern Region, November;
> Northwestern Region, November

North Dakota Game and Fish Department
100 North Bismarck Espressway, Bismarck, ND 58501;
701-328-6300; www.state.nd.us/gnf
    Minimum caliber: .45 caliber for rifles, .50 caliber for pistols
    Ignition types: flintlock, percussion, in-line
    Powders: any
    Projectiles: any, except for altered projectiles
    Sights: any; scopes can only be 1×, nontelescopic
    Minimum barrel length: 16 inches
    Seasons: November–December (dates vary)
Ohio Division of Wildlife
1840 Belcher Drive, Columbus, OH 43224; 614-265-6300;
www.dnr.state.oh.us/wildlife
    Minimum caliber: .38 caliber for rifles; pistols prohibited
    Ignition types: flintlock, percussion, in-line
    Powders: any
    Projectiles: .357 or larger for pistols; one ball per barrel during
        primitive season
    Sights: any
    Minimum barrel length: none
    Seasons: antlered deer only, October (dates vary);
        primitive weapons, December
Oklahoma Division of Wildlife
1801 North Lincoln Boulevard, Oklahoma City, OK 73152;
405-521-3853; www.wildlifedepartment.com
    Minimum caliber: .40 caliber for rifles and pistols
    Ignition types: flintlock, percussion, in-line
    Powders: any
    Projectiles: any
    Sights: any; laser sights illegal
    Minimum barrel length: none
    Seasons: October–November (dates vary)
Oregon Department of Fish and Wildlife
PO Box 59, Portland, OR 97207; 503-872-5260; www.dfw.state.or.us
    Minimum caliber: .40 caliber for deer, pronghorn, antelope,
        black bear, and cougar; .50 caliber for bighorn sheep,
        Rocky Mountain goat, and elk; pistols prohibited
    Ignition types: any, but must be open

Powders: black powder and replica powders, but no pellets; no centerfire primers or smokeless propellants

Projectiles: any

Sights: open; no fiber-optics or scopes

Minimum barrel length: 18 inches

Seasons: October–November (dates vary); deadline for applications, May 15

Pennsylvania Game Commission

2001 Elmerton Avenue, Harrisburg, PA 17110; 717-787-4250; www.pgc.state.pa.us

Minimum caliber: .45 caliber for rifles; pistols prohibited

Ignition types: flintlock, percussion, in-line during early season and in special regulations counties; flintlock only statewide in late season

Powders: any

Projectiles: any expanding

Sights: any during early season; scopes prohibited in late flintlock season

Minimum barrel length: none

Seasons: early season, October (dates vary); late flintlock season, December–January

Rhode Island Fish and Wildlife

Oliver Steadman Government Center,
480 Tower Hill Road, Wake Field, RI 02879; 401-789-3094; www.state.ri.us/dem

Minimum caliber: .45 caliber for rifles; pistols prohibited

Ignition types: flintlock, percussion, in-line

Powders: any

Projectiles: any

Sights: any

Minimum barrel length: none

Seasons: statewide, November; bonus permits, October, November, December (dates vary)

South Carolina Department of Natural Resources

Wildlife Division, PO Box 167, Columbia, SC 29202; 803-734-3886; www.dnr.state.sc.us

Minimum caliber: .44 caliber; pistols prohibited

Ignition types: flintlock, percussion, in-line

Powders: any black powder or replica powder or pellets;
  no smokeless propellants
Projectiles: any
Sights: open; no scopes or fiber-optics
Minimum barrel length: none
Seasons: Zones 1, 2, and 4, October (dates vary)

South Dakota Department of Game, Fish and Parks
  523 East Capitol, Pierre, SD 57501; 605-773-3485;
  www.state.sd.us
  Minimum caliber: .44 caliber for rifles; pistols prohibited
  Ignition types: flintlock, percussion, in-line
  Powders: any black powder or replica powder;
    no smokeless powders
  Projectiles: any
  Sights: any; scopes legal; no fiber-optics
  Minimum barrel length: none
  Seasons: December–January (dates vary)

Tennessee Wildlife Resource Agency
PO Box 470747, Nashville, TN 37204; 615-781-6500;
www.state.tn.us/twra
  Minimum caliber: .40 caliber for rifles and pistols
  Ignition types: flintlock, percussion, in-line
  Powders: any
  Projectiles: any
  Sights: any
  Minimum barrel length: none
  Seasons: Unit A, November, December, January (dates vary);
    Unit B, November, December, January (seasons overlap)

Texas Parks and Wildlife
4200 Smith School Road, Austin, TX 78744; 800-792-1112;
www.tpwd.state.tx.us/hunt
  Minimum caliber: None for rifles and pistols
  Ignition types: flintlock, percussion, in-line
  Powders: any
  Projectiles: any
  Sights: any
  Minimum barrel length: none
  Seasons: January (dates vary)

Utah Wildlife Resources
1594 West, North Temple, Suite 2110, Salt Lake City, UT 84114;
801-538-4700; www.wildlife.utah.gov
> Minimum caliber: .40 caliber; pistols prohibited
> Ignition types: flintlock, percussion, in-line
> Powders: any black powder or replica powder or pellets;
> no smokeless propellants
> Projectiles: lead or expanding bullet, 170+ grains (including
> sabots) for deer or pronghorn; 210+ grains for elk, moose,
> bison, bighorn sheep, and Rocky Mountain goat
> Sights: any, including fiber-optics; scopes may only be 1×
> Minimum barrel length: 18 inches
> Seasons: September–October (dates vary)

Vermont Department of Fish and Wildlife
103 South Main Street, 10 South Building, Waterbury, VT 05671;
802-241-3727; www.vtfishandwildlife.com
> Minimum caliber: .45 caliber for rifles; pistols prohibited
> Ignition types: flintlock, percussion, in-line
> Powders: any black powder or replica powder;
> no smokeless propellants
> Projectiles: single ball or bullet
> Sights: any
> Minimum barrel length: 20 inches
> Seasons: December (dates vary)

Virginia Department of Game and Inland Fisheries
4010 West Broad Street, Richmond, VA 23230; 804-367-1000;
www.dgif.state.va.us
> Minimum caliber: .45 caliber for rifles; pistols prohibited
> Ignition types: flintlock, percussion, in-line
> Powders: any black powder or replica powder or pellets;
> no smokeless propellants or 209 primers
> Projectiles: single only, .38 or larger propelled by 50+ grains of
> black powder or replica powder; no jacketed bullets; county
> ordinances must be obeyed (contact department)
> Sights: any
> Minimum barrel length: none
> Seasons: east of Blue Ridge, November (dates vary);
> west of Blue Ridge, November; late special season, west of
> Blue Ridge, December–January

Washington Department of Fish and Wildlife
600 Capital Way North, Olympia, WA 98501; 360-902-2515;
www.wa.gov/wdfw
> Minimum caliber: .38 caliber for rifles; pistols prohibited
> Ignition types: wheel lock, matchlock, flintlock, percussion,
> in-line; must use original-style percussion caps that fit on
> the nipple and are exposed to the elements
> Powders: any black powder or replica powder; no pellets or
> smokeless propellants
> Projectiles: lead only
> Sights: open, peep, and fiber-optic; no scopes
> Minimum barrel length: 20 inches
> Seasons: high buck, September (dates vary); early deer,
> October; late deer, November–December

West Virginia Department of Natural Resources
1900 Kanawha Boulevard East, Capital Complex, Building 3,
Charleston, WV 25305; 304-558-3380; www.dnr.state.wv.us
> Minimum caliber: .38 caliber for rifle and pistol
> Ignition types: flintlock, percussion, in-line; no 209 primers
> Powders: any black powder or replica powder or pellets;
> no smokeless propellants
> Projectiles: any
> Sights: any open; scopes legal; no fiber-optics
> Minimum barrel length: none
> Seasons: December (dates vary)

Wisconsin Department of Natural Resources
PO Box 7921, Madison, WI 53707; 608-266-2621;
www.dnr.state.wi.us
> Minimum caliber: .45-caliber smoothbore or .40-caliber rifle;
> pistols prohibited
> Ignition types: flintlock, percussion, in-line
> Powders: any
> Projectiles: any lead bullets; no jacketed bullets
> Sights: any open or fiber-optic; no scopes
> Minimum barrel length: none
> Seasons: December (dates vary)

Wyoming Game and Fish Department
5400 Bishop Boulevard, Cheyenne, WY 82006; 307-777-4600;
http://gf.state.wy.us
  Minimum caliber: .40 caliber for rifles; .45 caliber for pistols
  Ignition types: flintlock, percussion, in-line
  Powders: any black powder or replica powder or pellets;
    no smokeless propellants
  Projectiles: any
  Sights: any, including scopes; no fiber-optics
  Minimum barrel length: none for rifles; 10 inches for pistols
  Seasons: no special season, but muzzleloaders may be used
    during the regular deer season; dates vary by area, ranging
    from October 1 to the end of November

Canada

Contact the following provincial authorities for muzzleloading
  regulations in Canada:

Alberta Department of Environmental Protection
  Main Floor, Information Center, Bramalea Building, 9920
  108 Street, Edmonton, AB T5K 2G6; 403-944-0313;
  www.gov.ab.ca/dept/env.html
British Columbia Wildlife Branch
  780 Blanshard Street, Victoria, BC V8V 1X5; 250-387-9717;
  www.gov.bc.ca/wld/hunting.htm
Manitoba Wildlife Branch
  Box 24-200 Saulteaux Crescent, Winnipeg, MB R3J 3W3;
  204-945-0135; 800-214-6497; www.gov.mb. ca/laws/regs
New Brunswick Department of Natural Resources and Energy,
  Fish and Wildlife Branch
  PO Box 6000, Fredericton, NB E3B 5H1; 506-453-2440;
  www.gov.nb.ca/dnre/index.htm
Newfoundland Department of Tourism, Culture, and Recreation
  4th Floor West Block Confederate Building, PO Box 8700,
  St. John's, NF A1B 4J6; 800-563-6353;
  www.gov.nl.ca/env/wildlife/publications/2004huntguide.pdf

Northwest Territories Department of Resources, Wildlife, and Economic Development
600-5102-50 Avenue, Yellowknife, NT X1A 3S8; 403-873-0293; www.nwtwildlife.rwed.gov.nt.ca

Nova Scotia Department of Natural Resources
Wildlife Division, 136 Exhibition Street, Kentville, NS B4N 4E5; 902-679-6091; www.gov.ns.ca/natr/hunt/

Ontario Natural Resources Information Center
Room M, 1-73, Macdonald Block, 900 Bay Street, Toronto, ON M7A 2C1; 416-314-2000; www.mnr.gov.on.ca/MNR/pubs/pubmenu.html

Prince Edward Island Department of Environment and Fisheries
PO Box 2000, 11 Kent Street, Charlettetown, PE C1A 7N8; 902-368-4683; www.gov.pe.ca/visitorsguide/explore/hunting.php3

Quebec Service d'Accueil et de Renseignements
67, boul. Rene-Levesque Est, Rez-de-chausse, PQ, G1R 5V7; 800-561-1616; 418-643-3127; www.fapaq.gouv.qc.ca/en/publications/chasse/html

Saskatchewan Department of Environment and Resource Management, Wildlife Branch
3211 Albert Street, Regina, SK S4S 5W6; 306-787-2700; www.se.gov.sk.ca/fishwild/huntingguide/

Yukon Renewable Resources, Field Service Branch
PO Box 2703, Whitehorse, YK Y1A 2C6; 403-667-5221; www.environmentyukon.gov.yk.ca/hunting/index.shtml

GLOSSARY

Accessory. Any tool useful to the carrying, loading or unloading, priming, cleaning, or maintenance of a muzzleloader

Action. Ignition part of a muzzleloading gun where the trigger, lock, and barrel come together

Aperture sight. Rear sight consisting of a flat disk with a small pinhole at its center; also referred to as peep or receiver sights

Backstrap. Grip support used to attach and support the grips and frame

Ball. Any projectile fired from a gun; in muzzleloading, a lead roundball

Ballistic coefficient. Measure of the ability of a bullet to fly to a target with minimal distortion from air resistance

Ballistics. Science of the motion of projectiles; loosely used to describe velocity, energy, trajectory, powder burning characteristics, chamber pressure, and penetration of bullets

Barleycorn sight. Early-eighteenth-century front sight, shaped like a barley seed, inletted so that the top of the front sight was low and very close to the top barrel flat of an octagonal barrel

Barrel. Steel tube, either smoothbore or rifled, that contains the powder train and bullet or birdshot

Barrel wedge. Flattened metal wedge that runs through the forestock or pistol frame to attach the bottom of the barrel to the stock or pistol frame

Battery. Eighteenth-century term for the frizzen; also the cock or hammer and frizzen or cap as a unit

Bay. Second point of an antler, after the brow tine and before the tray

Bead. Rounded top of a front sight

Bench rest. A solid rest used for sighting in a gun

Big-bore. Any muzzleloader larger than .50 caliber

Birdshot. Tiny lead pellets used in shotguns for the hunting of small game and turkey

Black powder. Granulated mixture of potassium nitrate, charcoal, and sulfur; designated a class A explosive

Blowback. Escape of propellant gases past the breech plug, nipple, or touch hole

Blueing. Chemical process of artificial oxidation applied to metal to attain a dark blue or nearly black appearance

Bore. Interior diameter of a barrel

Box lock. In shotguns, a type of lock recognized by its squared appearance

Breech. Threaded steel plug at the rear end of the bore; also the back of the muzzleloader's barrel or action

Browning. Chemical process of artificial oxidation applied to metal to attain a plum brown or dark brown appearance to the barrel, lock, and iron furniture

Browse. Small saplings and branches consumed by browsing deer

Buckhorn sight. Rear sight with left and right extensions sweeping upward like the tines of a whitetail buck

Buckshot. Large lead shot used in smoothbore trade guns and shotguns for deer hunting

Buffalo Bullet. Commercial lead slug similar in appearance to a minié ball

Bullet. Projectile of metal, usually lead, or one jacketed in brass or copper, with an elongated and pointed nose shape

Bullet board. Board drilled to the bore size of a particular muzzleloader, into which a greased, patched roundball is inserted

Bullet mold. Iron, brass, aluminum, or even stone block with cavities into which molten metal (usually lead) is poured to form bullets

Butt. Rearmost end of a gun stock

Butt pad. Soft material, such as rubber added to the back of the stock to reduce felt recoil on the shoulder

Butt plate. Metal plate attached to the back of the stock to protect it

Butt stock. Part of the stock that contacts the shooter's shoulder

Caliber. Diameter of a bore in hundredths of an inch (e.g., .50 caliber is .50 inch)

Camo (camouflage). Patterned design representing leaves, limbs, tree trunks, tall grasses, prairie vegetation, snow, and other designs that reduce the hunter's silhouette so that game animals are not aware of his or her presence

Cap. Percussion cap placed on the nipple of an external hammered or in-line breech plug

Capper. Tool that contains and then applies percussion caps to a barrel or cylinder's nipple

Carbine. Shorter-barreled rifle that is usually lighter in weight than the standard 26- to 42-inch barrels on muzzleloading rifles

Case hardening. Gunsmithing technique for heat-treating metal and then plunging it into water to harden its outer shell

Casting. Act of pouring molten lead into a mold

Centerfire. Refers to the ignition of gunpowder in the center of its base; another name for an in-line percussion system

Chamber. Opening in the breech of a barrel into which a cartridge or shotshell is inserted

Charge. Another name for load; usually refers to the powder, patch, and ball or pellets, sabot, and bullet loaded in a muzzleloader or to the cartridge and shotshell in a breechloader

Chilled shot. Birdshot containing a greater percentage of antimony alloy than soft lead

Choke. Constriction of a shotgun's muzzle area to increase the pattern density at distances; the least choked shotguns are described as "cylinder," while the most choked shotguns as described as variations of "full"

Cock. Eighteenth-century term for a flintlock's hammer, based on its resemblance to a cock rooster's head or neck with a stone in its beak; cocking a gun refers to drawing the hammer back to the firing position

Color case hardening. Unusual mottled light and dark coloration, generated by a mixture of bone, charcoal, and leather, applied to the metal during case hardening

Comb. Raised portion of the gun stock on which the face is rested when aiming the rifle

Combination tool. Tool that includes a screwdriver and nipple wrench, among others

Conical. Describes cone-shaped points on cylindrical bullets

Conoidal. Describes the ogive or pointed nose of a bullet

Crimp. Top portion of a brass shell, case, or paper or plastic shot-shell that is rolled inward to grip the bullet or hold the overshot card in place

Crosshairs. Crossing lines of a scope's reticule

Cylinder. On black powder pistols, the rotating barrel that contains the powder train, bullet, and percussion cap

Cylindrical bullet. Another name for a slug, or any bullet with an elongated shape

Deer drive. Deer hunting strategy in which "drivers" walk through cover to move whitetails forward to waiting "standers"

Disc. Patented plastic device on knight rifles that holds the percussion cap and assists in sealing the breech

Double action. Ability of a black powder revolver to cock and fire with a single pull of the trigger

Double. Any shotgun with two barrels, regardless of whether they are side by side or over-under

Dram. Unit of weight equivalent to 27.34 grains

Dram equivalent. Measure to bridge the transition from black powder to modern nitrocellulose "smokeless" gunpowder; a 3-dram equivalent load of nitro is far less in volume but equal in velocity to a 3-dram load of black powder

Drift. Movement to the left or right—in shooting, it refers to movement caused by a crossing wind; in gunsmithing, it refers to the movement of the fixed front or rear sight to sight in the muzzleloader

Drop. Distance from the plane of the barrel's bore

Dross. Layer of solid particles (impurities), sometimes alloys of tin, antimony, or zinc, that floats atop molten lead

Ejector. Mechanism that extracts a spent primer, cartridge, or shot-shell

Elevation. Angle at which the rear sight is raised or lowered to sight in a muzzleloader

Entry thimble. First ramrod tube by the muzzle

Extractor. Another name for an ejector

Field dressing. Thre act of removing an animal's entrails and preserving the meat for transportation or final preparation for storage

Firing pin. Pointed nose of a hammer, striker, or bolt that strikes a primer, igniting a powder charge or cartridge or shotshell

Flash in the pan. Misfire of flintlocks that occurs when the primer powder in the pan ignites, but the clogged touch hole doesn't allow ignition inside the bore

Flask. Flattened horn, molded leather, or metallic container used to store powder or birdshot

Flint. Hard, silica-based stone that can be chipped into sharp, angular edges; the knife-sharp edge of the flint is slammed into a steel frizzen by the rotating cock, cutting loose molecules of iron at high temperature (sparks) to ignite the priming powder

Flint knapping tool. Small, hammer-like tool used to knap or chip away pieces of the flint to create a new sharp edge

Flintlock. Rifle with a primitive spring-powered lock that drives a sharpened, angular flint into a steel priming pan cover (frizzen) to generate sparks that ignite the priming powder

Fluting. Concave depression in a cylinder or barrel that increases rigidity while reducing weight

Forearm. Part of the stock located forward of the lock or action toward the muzzle

Forend. Forward part of a one-piece rifle or shotgun stock

Fouling. Corrosive chemical salts left in the bore and pan or nipple after black powder or replica powder has been ignited

Fowler. Lighter-barreled smoothbore, but having a longer barrel similar to a longrifle, that is capable of shooting a patched ball, buck and ball, or birdshot; often .62 to .72 caliber

Frame. Part of a black powder pistol that contains the hammer, trigger mechanism, cylinder, and barrel

Frizzen. Flintlock steel mechanism that provides a battering surface for the flint to cut spark; it hinges forward over the priming pan so that priming powder can be ignited by the spark, allowing the resulting fire to flash through the touch hole and ignite the main powder charge; also known as the steel, battery, or pan cover

Frizzen spring. V-shaped leaf spring that provides snap and resistance to the travel of the frizzen when it is struck by the flint

Front sight. Sight at the muzzle end of a gun

Fusil. Light musket often carried by trappers, explorers, and military officers in the eighteenth century; very similar to a fowler in appearance

Gauge. The diameter of a shotgun barrel; the smaller the number, the larger the bore

Grain. Measurement of weight—there are 7,000 grains (453 grams) in 1 pound, therefore 1 ounce contains 437.44 grains; in wood, the grain indicates the direction of the fibers

Gram. Metric equivalent of 15.43 grains

Grip. Part of a gun that is grasped with the hand when firing the weapon

Grooves. Deep spiral cuts made in the bore of a rifle after the process of cutting the rifling

Hair trigger. In double-set triggers, the more sensitive trigger (which is usually "set" or made more sensitive by the pull of the rear trigger)

Hammer. Mechanism used to cock a percussion rifle, shotgun, or pistol

Hang-fire. Delayed ignition due to damp black powder or a dirty flash channel between the primer and the main powder train

Hawken. Type of Plains rifle attributed to the Hawken brothers, Sam and Jake

Henry repeaters. Guns popular among ranchers and cowboys; forerunners of the early Winchester repeating black powder rifles

Henry trade guns. Made by the Henry gun makers of Boulton, Pennsylvania, these were the largest group of trade guns supplied to jacob astor and his rocky mountain trapper-traders; also very popular with the Plains Indians

Hinged loading lever. Lever that presses the plunger into each cylinder chamber to seat the powder charge and lead ball

Horn. Another name for a powder horn

Hunting bag. Large leather-covered pocket to carry all the tools necessary for the care of a muzzleloader; also known as a pouch or possibles bag

Ignition. The act of setting fire to black powder, Pyrodex, or other replica powders with a priming system (flintlock or percussion)

In-line ignition. Ignition system that allows a percussion cap or 209 primer to be placed in-line with the powder and projectile in the barrel

Iron sights. Simple open, fixed sights (generally made of iron)

Kentucky rifle. Type of Pennsylvania longrifle that was carried into the Kentucky frontier during the eighteenth century

Kentucky windage. Aiming left or right to compensate for wind drift

Lamination. Process of gluing together layers of wood for use in a gun stock

Lands. Uncut parts of the bore that are left higher than the grooves after a barrel has been rifled

Lever action. Action that requires the lowering of a lever to cock the hammer and load the next brass cartridge into the receiver

Loading lever latch. Release pin used to connect the loading lever to the barrel when not in use

Loading plunger. Part of the loading lever that seats a lead ball into a cylinder or barrel

Lock. Mechanism that fires the rifle

Lock plate. Large, flat plate that anchors the interior and exterior moving parts

Lock time. Speed at which a bullet is fired after the trigger is pulled

Longrifle. Flintlock or percussion full-stocked muzzleloader, generally with a barrel length more than 36 inches

Mainspring. Flattened V-shaped or coiled spring used to impart forward movement to the hammer of a percussion gun, striker of an in-line, or cock of a flintlock

Measurer. Volumetric device that allows accurate transfer of powder from the horn to the muzzle for safe, accurate shooting

Minié ball. Named after its inventor, this pointed, hollow-based conical lead slug became the preferred long-range bullet for Civil War muskets

Minute of angle. Unit of adjustment on adjustable open and telescopic sights

Misfire. Failure of the main charge to ignite, due to dampness, inadequate spark, or other reasons

Mounts. Metal bases used to mount a scope to the top of a barrel

Musket. Type of smoothbore military musket used in the seventeenth and eighteenth centuries; later, rifled muskets were used in the Civil War

Muzzle. End area and opening of the bore from which shot, ball, and bullets exit

Muzzle brake. Holes and porting in the muzzle to vent gases and reduce recoil

Muzzle energy. Initial energy imparted to a bullet by a powder charge that is measured at the muzzle

Muzzle velocity. Highest velocity imparted to a bullet, measured by a chronograph as it exits the muzzle

Nipple. Tube extension from a cylinder or barrel on which a percussion cap is placed for ignition of the percussion system of a muzzleloader

Nosecap. Protective cup of brass at the muzzle end of a full stock

Off-hand. Shooting from a standing position with no use of sling or fixed rest

Ogive. Pointed arch; the rounded nose of a bullet

Pan. Another name for the priming pan

Pan brush. Small brush used to clean fouled priming powder from the pan

Partridge sight. Long arching front sight similar to the shape of a partridge's feather

Patch. Cotton or linen cloth of specific size (0.010 to 0.025 inch) that carries lubricant and is wrapped around a roundball to make the undersized ball feel the effects of the rifling

Patchbox. Shallow to deep excavation in the butt of the stock, away from the shooter's face, that is covered with a sliding wood or hinged brass cover

Patch knife. Small knife kept in or on the hunting patch, used to cut excess patch from around the roundball once the patched ball is inserted and seated in the muzzle

Pattern. Distribution of birdshot fired from a smoothbore; a tight pattern created by a full-choked barrel will keep 70 percent of the shot inside a 30-inch circle at 40 yards

Peep sight. Another name for an aperture sight

Pellet. Very small round shot, ranging in size from 9 (smallest) to BB (largest); larger sizes are called buckshot

Pellets. Compressed Pyrodex and Triple Seven muzzleloader propellant

Pennsylvania longrifle. Flintlock longrifle developed by Pennsylvania German gunsmiths in the valley between the Delaware and Susquehanna rivers during the early eighteenth century

Percussion. Type of ignition system in which a pressure-sensitive chemical is struck to create fire to set off the main powder charge

Plains rifle. Shorter, later version of the Pennsylvania or Kentucky longrifle

Powder. Another name for black powder, a simple mixture of charcoal, sulfur, and saltpeter; modern "smokeless" powder is a chemical compound made of nitroglycerin or nitrocellulose, or a combination known as double-base powder

Powder horn. Storage container for black powder made from a cow horn and plugged with wood

Primer. FFFFg-sized black powder; also used to refer to the priming horn

Priming horn. Small powder horn that carries fine-grained black powder for a flintlock rifle's ignition

Pump gun. Common name for a slide-action rifle or shotgun

Pyrodex. Muzzleloading replica powder produced by Hodgdon Powder Company for use in black powder cartridges and percussion ignition guns

Ramrod. Long rod (originally wooden) used for loading and cleaning muzzleloaders; most ramrods have a threaded tip for the attachment of screws, worms, brushes, and clean jags; also known as a rammer in the eighteenth century

Rate of rifling. Number of turns that the rifling imparts to the bullet in a specific distance; slower rates of rifling (1:72, or one turn in 72 inches) are favored for stabilizing roundball flight, and faster rates of rifling (1:24, or one turn in 24 inches) are favored for stabilizing sabotted bullets

Receiver. Frame of a gun that includes the breech, lock, and loading mechanism

Recoil. Backward "kick" force generated by the explosion of gunpowder

Recoil pad. Soft rubber or fiber pad that absorbs and softens the felt recoil against the shooter's shoulder

Recoil shield. Upper rounded half of the frame that supports the cylinder pin and encloses the hammer and the hand; it prevents powder flashback and secures the percussion caps

Reticule. Crossed hair, wire, picket, post, or other division system installed in a telescopic sight

Revolver. Handgun or revolving drum rifle that has a cylindrical magazine for repeated shots

Rib. Raised bar of metal that forms a sighting plane for shotguns, particularly double-barrels

Rifle. Gun featuring a long barrel that contains spiral grooves cut into its inner surface

Rifling. Spiral grooves cut or engraved on the inside of a barrel's bore; these impart rotation to the bullet to stabilize its flight

Rimfire. Cartridge in which the priming compound is contained in the rim around its base

Roundball. Sphere-shaped bullet developed for flintlock and percussion longrifles

Sabot. Plastic sleeve or cup that surrounds a bullet; upon firing, it drops away from the bullet

Safety. Mechanism to prevent the ignition of propellant in a muzzleloader

Scope. Another name for a telescopic sight

Sear. Mechanism that holds the lock at the half-cock and full-cock position; the sear is tripped by the trigger, allowing the cock, hammer, or striker to move forward into the primer

Sear spring. Small spring that acts against the sear, engaging it into the tumbler, which prevents the gun from firing until the trigger is depressed; the sear spring causes the audible click when cocking the firearm

Sectional density. Proportion of the bullet's mass to its caliber; longer bullets have higher sectional densities

Set trigger. Mechanism that allows a trigger, or a second trigger, to become more sensitive to firing

Shell. Common name for a shotgun shell; also refers to the spent hull or empty cartridge after it has been fired

Shot. Another name for birdshot or lead pellets used in a smoothbore gun

Side-by-side. A shotgun in which the barrels are soldered to each other's sides

Sight radius. Distance between the rear and front sights; usually, the longer the distance between the sights, the greater degree of aiming accuracy

Sights. Aiming devices on guns

Single action. On a revolver, this action requires the hammer to be cocked before it can be fired by a single pull of the trigger

Slug. Cylindrical lead bullet

Smoothbore. Trade gun, fowler, or shotgun that has an unrifled barrel

Spitzer. Sharply pointed bullet nose

Sprue. Top opening of a bullet mold

Sprue cutter. Scissors-like cutter that shears off excess sprue lead from the top of a bullet mold

Stock. Part of the gun, made of wood or synthetics, on which the barrel and action are mounted

Swamped barrel. Narrowed barrel, generally referring to the long octagonal barrels found on Pennsylvania longrifles; swamping reduces the weight of the barrel, enhances the overall feel of balance, and increases the aesthetics of longrifles

Toe. Lower part of the butt on a muzzleloader's stock

Touch hole. Tiny entry hole that is aligned with the center of a flintlock's pan; ignition of the main powder train is dependent on a flash of priming powder coming through the touch hole

Touch-hole pick. Thin wire inserted through the touch hole after the bore is loaded with powder and ball, ensuring free pass of the priming powder's hot flash

Trade gun. Type of inexpensive smoothbore gun, prized by trappers who traded with the American Indians in the Great Plains and Rocky Mountains

Trajectory. Flight of a bullet from the muzzle to the target

Trigger. Release lever that frees the cock, hammer, or striker to slam forward, creating spark or percussion fire

Trigger guard. Wrap of metal around the trigger to prevent accidental discharge of the weapon

Trigger pull. Distance from the face of the trigger to the edge of the butt plate

Triple Seven. Improved version of Pyrodex replica powder for muzzleloaders

Tumbler. Part of the lock mechanism that changes mainspring energy into rotation; this causes the cock or hammer to rotate forward

Twist. Another name for rifling; this is what gives rotational stability to a speeding bullet

Underhammer. Type of percussion rifle with a hammer under the barrel

Velocity. Speed of a bullet expressed in feet per second

Vernier sight. Rear aperture sight that is elevated by a knurled knob; a vernier scale on the frame indicates the elevation in hundredths of an inch

Wedge screw. Screw used to retain the barrel wedge on a black powder revolver

Worm. Eighteenth-century term for the steel corkscrew-shaped wire used to hold a ball of tow (flax fibers); the tow and worm were then used for cleaning the bore; today, the worm is more commonly used to retrieve patches that have slipped off a cleaning jag

Zero. When sighting in a rifle, term used to indicate that the bullet is striking exactly where aimed

Zouave. An 1863 type of rifled military gun (.58 caliber) used during the Civil War and made by Remington Arms

INDEX